NEIL SUTHERLAND is a member of the Faculty of Education at the University of British Columbia.

In the late nineteenth century a new generation of reformers, believing that it was possible to free Canadian society from many of the problems of humanity, committed itself to a program of social improvement based on the more effective upbringing of all children. This commitment involved changing people's definition of children: they were no longer inherently sinful, yet malleable into little adults by discipline and hard work, but rather like innocent plants, requiring a great deal of careful and therefore professional nurture.

Children in English-Canadian Society examines the growth of the public health movement and its various efforts at improving the health of children. It treats the new juvenile courts, with their use of family care as the preferred means of rehabilitation. And in the schools, the main hothouse for this new society, such activities as manual and vocational training, school gardening, physical education, and conscious Canadianization of immigrants were introduced. The revolution in attitudes and institutions was complete by the 1920s and for some fifty years its reforms have been an established part of Canada's social life – some would say too established.

Professor Sutherland has a keen eye, both for the illuminating and for the typical, and has assembled this history from English-language sources across the country. It is a readable and important work that will interest social historians and all involved, in whatever capacity, with the care and development of children.

NEIL SUTHERLAND

Children in English-Canadian Society: Framing the Twentieth-Century Consensus

UNIVERSITY OF TORONTO PRESS

TORONTO AND BUFFALO

Library of Congress Cataloging in Publication Data

Sutherland, Neil, 1931-
Children in English-Canadian society.

Bibliography: p.
Includes index.
1. Children in Canada. 2. Child welfare—Canada.
3. Education of children. 4. Education—Canada.
I. Title.
HQ792.C3S9   301.43'14'0971   76-44228
ISBN 0-8020-5340-8

Contents

Acknowledgments

Each stage in the preparation of this study has been immeasurably lightened by the help of others. A Canada Council fellowship gave me the necessary period of uninterrupted time to shape the original draft of the manuscript. The Committee on Research, Faculty of Graduate Studies, University of British Columbia, assisted me with research expenses. I am deeply indebted to the staffs of the Public Archives of Canada, the federal Division of Immigration, the Ontario Department of Public Records and Archives, the Provincial Archives of Manitoba, the Saskatchewan Archives Board, the Provincial Archives of British Columbia, the Archives of the Canadian Woman's Christian Temperance Union, the Library of the University of Guelph, and, especially, the Library of the University of British Columbia. The English author John Stroud generously shared with me products of his extensive research on the Church of England Waifs and Strays Society. Charles Burgess, John Calam, Frank C. Hardwick, Jorgen Dahlie, F. Henry Johnson, and Marvin Lazerson carefully read and commented on various drafts of the manuscript. Lillian Thirkell, Shirley Black, and Nina Thurston typed its many versions.

It is a particular pleasure to acknowledge three very special debts. Over many hours of discussion, through considerable correspondence and painstaking reviews of the manuscript, Timothy L. Smith helped me to understand what I wanted to say and to write it as clearly as I could. By searching through the library, by reading microfilm, by supervising the preparation of the manuscript, and by listening patiently, my wife, Janet Catherine Sutherland, took on the most burdensome tasks of the whole project. Emily, Duff, Frank, and Jessie Sutherland kept reminding me that the subjects of my study had not merely existed in records but had once been young and very much alive.

This book has been published with the help of a grant from the Social Science Research Council of Canada, using funds provided by the Canada Council, and a grant from the Andrew W. Mellon Foundation to University of Toronto Press.

Young girls leaving a candy factory in Toronto. Even after provincial governments enacted legislation providing for compulsory schooling and preventing
youngsters from working before a certain age, parents, employers, and the children themselves often broke the law (*courtesy of the United Church Archives*).

A group of Toronto girls off for a cycle (*courtesy of the City of Toronto*).

Newsboys waiting to pick up their copies of the Vancouver *Daily Province*. Many newsboys worked full-time (*courtesy of the Vancouver Public Library*).

Three Toronto lads rolling hoops.

A Toronto school nurse conducts a medical inspection
(*courtesy of the City of Toronto Archives*).

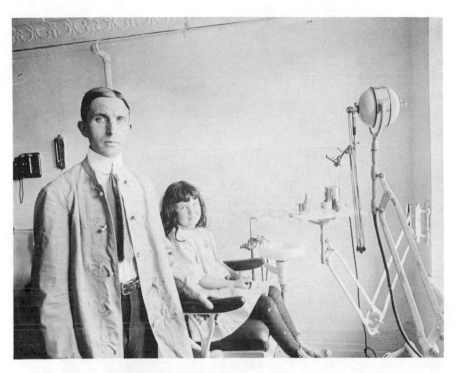

One of Toronto's school dentists and a patient
(*courtesy of the City of Toronto Archives*).

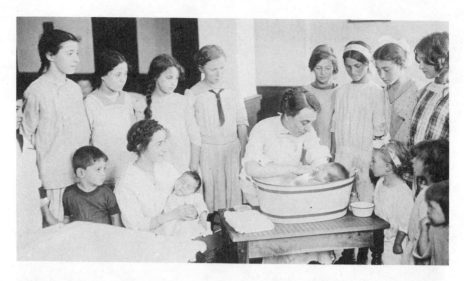

A 'Little Mothers' class in a Toronto school. These girls are learning skills that they will use to help their mothers take care of their younger brothers and sisters, some of whom are in the photograph (*courtesy of the City of Toronto Archives*).

Nose-blowing drill supervised by a Toronto school nurse (*courtesy of the City of Toronto Archives*).

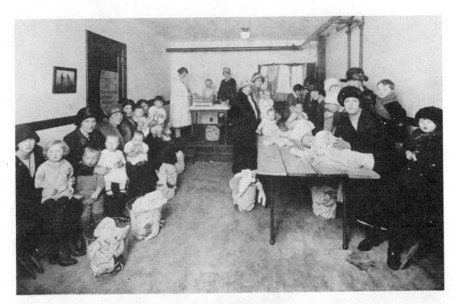

A 'well-baby' clinic about 1920 (*courtesy of the United Church Archives*).

School gardening at the Macdonald Consolidated School, Hillsborough, PEI
(*courtesy of the University of British Columbia Library*).

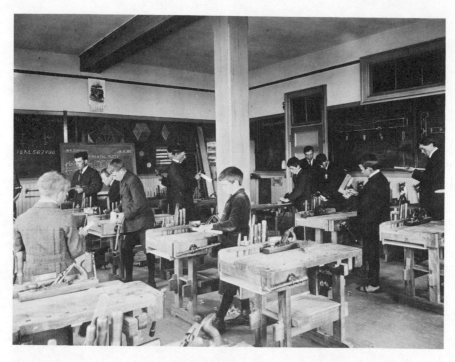

Manual training at the Macdonald Consolidated School, Hillsborough, PEI (*courtesy of the University of British Columbia Library*).

School vans in front of the Macdonald Consolidated School, Hillsborough, PEI (*courtesy of the University of British Columbia Library*).

The 'Jam Pots Chorus' at the Macdonald Consolidated School, Hillsborough, PEI (*courtesy of the University of British Columbia Library*).

Moncton children lined up for sacks of coal at the coal office
(*courtesy of the United Church Archives*).

British emigrant boys at a home in Ontario
(*courtesy of the Public Archives of Canada*).

A Winnipeg tenement (*courtesy of the United Church Archives*).

PART I

'Elevate the Home':
Changing Attitudes to Children
in English-Speaking Canada, 1870-1900

1

'A Good Home and Kind Treatment': Late-Nineteenth-Century English-Canadian Attitudes to Children and Child-Rearing

In July 1886, six-year-old Alice Maud Johnson said goodbye to her mother in England and left for Canada in the care of Miss Charlotte Alexander.[2] Alice's mother had deserted her husband, a Camberwell shopkeeper, because, although 'he was so peculiar [she] could not live with him' the lunacy commissioners would not declare him insane. Since she was 'very poor and often without food,' Mrs Johnson proved unable to maintain herself and her girls. When Alice left for Canada, Mrs Johnson told Miss Alexander that she was thankful to have the child provided for. In Canada, Miss Alexander left Alice at Miss Annie Macpherson's 'Marchmount' Home in Belleville, Ontario. Later the same year, a Mr and Mrs Featherstone of Arnprior took the youngster as a companion for their only child and promised to treat Alice 'as their own.' When Miss Alexander visited Arnprior, she found Alice 'well and happy.' A few months later Miss Alexander learned that the girl was 'enjoying the most perfect health,' and the Featherstones were so 'warmly attached to her' that they would feel 'most terribly if they lost her.' Later in 1887, however, Mrs Featherstone returned Alice 'because of her temper.' Miss Alexander then placed her with Mr and Mrs Isaac Coyne of Ingersoll. In December 1887, Mrs Coyne wrote to Miss Alexander that since one of her own boys was very ill she had 'to give ... back little Maudie.' In June 1888, Mrs Coyne explained that Alice had been living for about two months with Dr and Mrs D.W. Carroll, also of Ingersoll, who had taken 'a great fancy to her,' and were 'anxious to adopt her.' By August 1890, however, Mrs Carroll declined to keep the girl any longer because she was 'disobedient, untruthful and rude.'

After leaving the Carrolls, Alice lived for seven months in the farm home of the Thomas Hamblys. On the death of Mr Hambly, Miss Alexander offered Alice to Mrs W. Hayward, of Kenilworth, to whom she wrote that she was anxious to get Alice settled and 'not have too many more experiments.' She wanted to place the child where she would 'get a certain amount of schooling' and be 'well cared for till she marries' or could 'earn her own living.' At the end of a two-week trial period, however, Mrs Hayward explained to Miss Alexander that neither she nor her husband thought that the youngster's 'disposition' was suitable to them; they did not 'like her manner at all.'

Early in August 1891, Alice went to Mrs Richard Rivers of Springhill Farm, near Walkerton. A week later, Mrs Rivers reported that Alice seemed to be 'a very nice child' who appeared to be 'contented and happy so far.' Although she was 'small,' her tasks were 'light.' The work, wrote Mrs Rivers, was not 'heavy as much as continuous, dish-washing, setting table, peeling potatoes, dusting, feeding chickens and being feet for my stepdaughter' who had 'lately lost a limb.' When Mrs Rivers died early in 1892, her stepdaughter reported to Miss Alexander that Alice had 'been very well except for an occasional bilious attack.' At this point in her life, five-and-a-half years and six homes after she had arrived in Canada, this twelve-year-old girl disappeared from view. Probably she remained with the Rivers family until, in accordance with Miss Alexander's wishes, she either married or was able to earn her own living.

Alice Maud Johnson was but one of 73,000 children 'unaccompanied by parents and guardians' who came from the United Kingdom to Canada between 1869 and 1919.[3] These boys and girls, in turn, were the late-nineteenth-century beneficiaries of a practice of transporting dependent children to the colonies that English officials had intermittently followed since the seventeenth century. While their story remains a chapter still only partly recounted in the history of English emigration and Canadian settlement, it will not be examined here.[4] Instead, the story of their experiences in their new homeland will be used to help answer certain questions about Canadian childhood.

Towards the end of the nineteenth century, reformers began to urge English Canadians to change their methods of bringing up their youngsters. What, however, was the situation that these people wanted to alter? How did English-speaking Canadians in the generation preceding that of the 1890s look upon children? How did they rear them? Answers to these questions are harder to arrive at than may first appear to be the case. In contrast to the characteristic unease that many of their successors displayed, Canadians of the 1870s and 1880s rarely discussed these subjects. This is not to say that they did not have strongly felt opinions on what was the proper way to bring up children, only that Canadians of the time were so generally agreed upon what that way was that they had no need to talk about it. The problem thus posed by inferring what people thought and did from what they did not discuss is also complicated by what others later said about what came to be called the 'traditional' child and family relationship. In their eagerness to stress the virtues of the changes they advocated, reformers tended to etch a bleak picture of the place of the child in the society that they wanted to reconstruct. Later, as new fashions failed to bring about the millennial state promised by the most extreme proponents of change, critics began to look fondly back on the childhood that reformers had tried so hard to make over.

However, in their treatment of little Alice Maud Johnson and her thousands of compatriots, in their response to a sharply worded English criticism of their care of these youngsters, in their very occasional discussions of some aspects of childhood, and in the books which they provided to school pupils, English Canadians of the 1870s and 1880s did reveal something of what they thought about child-rearing and how they put their beliefs into effect. These values and customs, in turn, accurately reflected the harsh needs of their basically rural and agricultural society.

Fifty little girls from the Kirkdale Workhouse in Liverpool formed the first party of British children to arrive in Canada.[5] Under the supervision of Miss Maria S. Rye, the group landed in Quebec in November 1869 and proceeded by train to her receiving home at Niagara-on-the-Lake, Ontario.[6] Because people 'were a little afraid to take them' they remained there for some time. Ultimately, however, Miss Rye succeeded in placing all of the girls in what she regarded as 'good homes.' In entering this work, Miss Rye reflected her earlier experience in placing young women in Canada, Lord Shaftsbury's suggestion that she try to find homes there for impoverished children, and her observations of the work of Charles Loring Brace.[7] Since 1854, Brace, the founder of the New York Children's Aid Society, had been sending parties of homeless boys from New York city to the western states for adoption.[8] The member of Parliament for Liverpool and the board of guardians of the Kirkdale Workhouse each put up one-half of the costs of bringing out her first group.[9] In 1870, after the Poor Law Board authorized the scheme, other workhouses joined Kirkdale in sending children with Miss Rye.[10] By March 1875, she had brought 202 boys and 1102 girls to Canada, the latter ranging in age from six months to fourteen years.[11]

Favourable publicity given Miss Rye's efforts suggested to other English child-rescue organizations that they should also enter the emigration business.[12] In 1870, Miss Annie Macpherson, of the Revival Refuge and Home of Industry of Spitalsfield, in London, proceeded to Canada with her first party.[13] By the spring of 1875 she had brought nearly 2000 boys across the Atlantic. By 1874, over a dozen British organizations were sending a total of over 1000 children a year to Canada.[14] Miss Rye, Miss Macpherson, and the other agencies recruited two sorts of youngsters: 'paupers,' that is, legal wards of the Poor Law Union Workhouses, and what were variously described as 'children rescued from the streets, "waifs and strays," "arabs," and "gutter children." ' Many of these latter boys and girls came from 'distressed and orphaned families' – such as the Johnsons of Camberwell – while the rest were 'waifs gathered from the streets of London and other large cities.'[15] William Quarrier described how he found the Glasgow boys he sent to Canada with Miss Macpherson. 'We go out on the streets and invite those who are needy to come to the Home,' he said. 'We are known to most of the street children. Some come asking to get in, and others are brought by Bible women and missionaries.' Most of the boys previously made their homes, Quarrier continued, in 'the night asylum, the police office, cold stairs, haylofts, and barrels and boxes along the harbour.'[16] After they left Britain, however, the distinction between the two types of children disappeared because agencies distributed them without regard to their origins.[17]

Since pauper children remained state responsibilities, in 1874 England's Local Government Board sent Inspector Andrew Doyle to investigate all aspects of the care and placement of its young dependents in Canada.[18]

At the end of an extensive visit to Canada, Doyle prepared a report highly critical of what he had discovered. He found fault with the travel arrangements, the indiscriminate mixing of 'pauper' and 'arab' children – which he felt was a grave injustice to the former – the facilities in the distributing homes, the way that Miss Rye and Miss Macpherson kept financial records, the casual manner in which the children were placed, and, most serious of all, the lack of frequent and systematic inspection of the children in their new homes. 'No class of Canadians,' Doyle generously concluded, 'would consent to accept such terms of service for their own children.'[19]

Doyle's report roused considerable public controversy on both sides of the Atlantic.[20] Although English defenders of Miss Rye and Miss Macpherson were quick to point out the many errors and faults they found in the report, the administrators of the Poor Law decided to withdraw workhouse children from the plan. The British government also forcefully requested that the Canadian government inspect, at British expense, the placement of the children whom private agencies continued to send to Canada. After trying without success to persuade the provinces to conduct these visits, the federal government reluctantly agreed to have its immigration agents inspect each child once, usually during the first winter he or she spent in Canada.[21]

On the basis of the Doyle report, of Canadian discussion of it, and of other supporting evidence, one can draw some conclusions about the condition not only of the immigrant but of all children in English-Canadian society at this time: first, English Canadians showed little awareness of children as individual persons; second, they saw nothing of the inner, emotional life of youngsters; third, young people played an important and often central role in rural and in family economies; finally, contemporary English-Canadian child-rearing theory was intimately related to these perceptions and practices. One must be careful, of course, not to over-generalize on the basis of a single situation.

Most of the Canadian discussions of the Doyle report took place in extensive hearings conducted by the House of Commons Select Committee on Immigration and Colonization. These generally humane people, many of them imbued with a deep sense of Christian charity, saw the whole enterprise as one in which a benign Providence worked for the extremely fortunate beneficiaries through the good efforts of Miss Rye, Miss Macpherson, and the welcoming Canadian farm families. The committee heard many witnesses, including Miss Macpherson and Miss Rye, and received many letters from people familiar with various aspects of the work. Without exception, witnesses and writers in Canada sharply criticized Doyle's report and unanimously praised the work of the people involved. However, only a very small group of primarily well-to-do Canadians, many of whom had special interests in various phases of the movement, contributed to the hearings. More important, perhaps, they obviously were not talking about their own children. On the other hand, their statements clearly demonstrate that, in making their judgments, these participants were not evaluating the experience of immigrant children by any other standard than the one which they applied to the poorer classes of Canadian children and often, indeed, to their own as well. In the 1870s no one seems to have viewed the newcomers as different in any important way from the children amongst whom they were placed. Of particular significance is the fact that no Canadians complained, as many did in the 1890s, that the immigrants, as England's refuse, posed a threat to morals of other youngsters in their new homes or to the well-being of Canadian society generally. Indeed, accounts of the youthful newcomers indicate that they lived mostly in small farmers' homes, in necessarily intimate if not always loving association with the families with whom they were placed. They customarily attended the common school and the Sunday school, church, and neighbourhood picnics, and participated in the other activities which bound communities together. For these reasons, then, it is fair to conclude that many other Canadians shared the opinions and assumptions of those who did take part in the public discussion.

The organization of the immigration scheme provided no opportunity for anyone to look upon or treat any child individually. In the day or two before sailing, parties of one hundred to two hundred children from all over England assembled in Liverpool. To help them supervise the youngsters on board ship, both Miss Rye and Miss Macpherson employed a matron and six to ten adult women recruited from amongst the passengers. In Canada, the boys and girls first went to 'distributing' homes or local orphanages. From these establishments, the women promptly gave the children to Canadian families willing to take them.[22]

By modern standards, both women followed very informal placement procedures – Alice Maud Johnson's were typical.[23] Both Miss Macpherson and Miss Rye tried to select suitable homes for the children. The former 'always required a recommendation from a minister or other responsible person, as to the respectability of those applying for the children.' Miss Rye required applicants to give two references to whom she wrote 'for *confidential* information.' When, 'through incompatibility of temper, insubordination or wrong-doing,' a child proved to be unsatisfactory, he or she was returned to the distributing home. In 1875, Miss Rye reported that, of the 1304 youngsters she had placed, she 'had had in all 290 children sent back, for whom she had had to find over 700 places.'[24] While Andrew Doyle was extremely critical of 'this want of sufficient care in selecting homes for the children,' he felt it was 'far less injurious in its results than ... the want of proper supervision of them afterwards.'[25] Miss E.G. Barber, who was in charge of Miss Macpherson's Knowlton Home, explained that she tried 'to watch over every child as thoroughly as possible, by visiting, writing to, sending love gifts &c.' She noted, however, that the children were 'scattered over a very large tract of country,' and to visit them was 'one of the great difficulties' of her work. Although Miss Macpherson also sent a schoolmaster to Canada to supervise children already placed, she and Miss Rye relied on friends or acquaintances in different districts to oversee their charges.[26]

Neither in commenting on these arrangements nor anywhere else in the discussion did any Canadian indicate that he or she was aware of the inner, emotional life of the youthful immigrants. To one observer, they were 'healthy and intelligent, prompt in their replies to questions, and modest and respectful in demeanor.'[27] Another saw 'between 200 and 300 happy, healthy, well-dressed girls ... with every token and evidence of home care and comfort.' No witness or writer commented that at least some of the children might be heartbroken by their separation from family and friends or mentioned the possibility that youngsters who had lived all their lives in large cities and were now placed on remote Canadian farms might be lonely and homesick. Although one person reported that Miss Rye invariably strove 'to place sisters in close proximity to each other,' in fact youngsters from the same family were often sent to widely separated foster homes. When one presses beyond the economic ties between foster parent and immigrant child – well expressed in the remark that the placement work was beneficial not only 'for the poor children of England, but also for the poor housewives' of Canada – he sees that observers viewed the developing relationship between them from one side only, that of the 'incalculable benefit to the children themselves.'[28] No one said, for example, that young people could add joy to a home; in the words of one witness, the main job of the foster parent was to take the children 'and drill them into usefulness.'[29]

Why, then, did ten times as many Canadian families as could be provided with a British boy or girl volunteer to take someone else's child into their homes? The answer to this question is a simple one: in their preindustrial, mostly rural society, Canadians needed children for the work that they could do. In a period when over three-quarters of the population lived in rural areas, life imposed very heavy burdens of work on all members of farm families.[30] In his comparison of the efforts of two British immigrant families in an agricultural colony in Mooso-min, Assiniboia, the Reverend Hugh Huleatt indicated just how important children were to making a success of farming in Canada. The first farmer, who had done the best for himself of all the colony in the four years it had been established, not only had cattle, pigs, and 'fowls innumerable' but also had 'estimated his crops at over sixty acres.' Although in Britain he had found that his children were 'like a rope around his neck,' in Canada they were 'the source of his wealth.' He had hired out his eldest boy, a sixteen year old, over the working season 'for a hundred dollars, with his keep.' The second boy, a fourteen year old, had been offered 'nearly the same wages' but was needed instead to work on the homestead. The second farmer, who although initially regarded by Huleatt 'as one of the most certain to succeed,' had in fact 'the least success of any of our families.' While he was a 'total abstainer,' a 'first-class carpenter, with a tidy, good wife,' had excellent land, and good oxen, 'yet he had only twelve acres under crop instead of sixty.' The real 'secret of this great difference,' explained Huleatt, was that this man was childless and his progress had been barred by 'the want of children to help on the farm.'[31]

From its very beginnings, therefore, many Canadians had looked upon the immigration scheme with real enthusiasm. In 1871, the federal minister of agriculture – who had jurisdiction over immigration – praised the work. In the autumn of 1871, Saint John, New Brunswick, paid the expenses for a party of Miss Rye's children to travel there from Halifax. Citizens warmly welcomed the children when they arrived.[32] It must be emphasized, however, that Canadian good will towards the children was more than a matter of humanitarianism or Christian charity, although both were often present. From Confederation on, a constant refrain in the reports of the officials responsible for immigration was that Canada had a desperate need for farm labourers and domestic servants. In 1870, the Halifax immigration agent explained that he could provide homes for a 'large number of young girls from eight to ten years of age' in which 'they would be instructed and trained in the domestic customs and habits of the best families in our land.' The next year, the Toronto agent reported that 'any number' of 'farm labourers, mechanics, domestic servants, and boys from fourteen to eighteen years of age' could find 'ready employment at good wages.'[33]

The legal ties between foster parent and English child underlined the economic nature of their relationship. 'People applied to her for children,' explained Miss Rye, 'sometimes for the purpose of adopting them, and sometimes as servants.' It was usually only the younger children who were 'adopted'; she 'did not allow them to be adopted after they were nine years of age.' Children between nine and eighteen she put out under a contract of indenture until they were eighteen. In return for their general work, girls up to fifteen were 'clothed and taught,' those from fifteen to seventeen – now no longer at school – were paid three dollars a month, and those seventeen and eighteen, four dollars a month. Boys were paid by the year on a 'scale commencing at thirty dollars, and rising ten dollars every year till it rose to seventy or eighty dollars.'[34] In practice, the distinction between adopting a child and taking him under contract was less sharp than Miss Rye's explanation of her arrangements suggests. Although English common law did not recognize the relationship, in the nineteenth century many people began to use 'adoption' to refer to placement schemes for homeless children.[35] While two Ontario statutes of the 1860s used the term as an alternative to the more common and traditional form of apprenticeship for orphaned and neglected children, this legislation neither defined what it meant by adoption nor described what rights and responsibilities it entailed.[36] In response to a query on the matter, Miss Barber of Miss Macpherson's Knowlton Home replied that it was 'somewhat difficult to definitely answer your question as to the number *adopted* by contract, as every person taking children has them on trial for the first year, with the right of returning them if not satisfied.' Despite these legal uncertainties, however, Miss Rye accurately argued that she followed contemporary Canadian routines; her testimony shows that she used the same procedures as the Infants' Homes of Toronto and similar Canadian institutions of the time.[37] Andrew Doyle harshly assessed the whole practice: he estimated that in approximately 90 per cent of the cases foster homes made their choice 'with a view to the future service of the child.' There was, indeed, probably much truth in the remark made by a young girl to Doyle that ''doption, sir, is when folks gets a girl to work without wages.'[38]

Making a virtue out of a necessity, English Canadians viewed work as the central characteristic of a good upbringing and proper education. Through hard work over long hours children not only discovered the positive and life-long benefits contained within work itself but were also kept from the temptations which immediately crowded in on the indolent and the idle. Andrew Doyle noticed that Canadians put their 'children to work at a very early age.'[39] To school children, the sad story of the frog, impaled by the shrike on a thorn until he was eaten, was but one of many repetitions they heard of the same lesson. It was of no use 'to be able to hop well, or to be a fine swimmer,' reported the sparrow to her little ones, 'if one sat all day on a bank.' Food, she went on, 'didn't drop into people's mouths' and the sooner they managed 'to fetch their own worms the better she should be pleased.'[40]

This emphasis on work was, in turn, built on the bedrock of unarticulated but nonetheless widely held and unquestioned assumptions about the nature of children and the function of childhood. Since by their implicit definition a *person* as such was an adult, English Canadians of the time saw a child merely as a partially formed and potential adult. They judged the quality of a particular upbringing – a term they so often used – by observing the conduct of the person which it produced. In their eyes, children were a resistive, refractory (from the 'Old Adam' they carried in their bones), but nonetheless basically plastic raw material. Out of this tough matter, parents and other adults could, if they were persistent enough, fashion moral, hard-working, productive adults. With the help of the church and the school, the family was the main instrument for this essential but not necessarily pleasant social task. In the context of these basic assumptions, most people evaluated the events which went into the years between infancy and adulthood almost solely as to how they thought that each would serve as a means towards the achievement of their clearly defined end. While they hoped that parents would provide children with a satisfactory though preferably Spartan physical environment – wholesome food, sufficient but often uncomfortable clothing, and basic shelter – they did not consider these nearly as important as other elements of a good upbringing. Most of all, they expected parents to inculcate morals and good work habits. Both of these virtues were achieved, they believed, by precept repeated at home, at school, in Sunday school, in books and in papers, and by the example of their parents and other adults.[41] Christ's youth suggested a number of practical lessons to Canadian young people: 'submission to parents,' the 'dignity of labour,' the need for 'personal improvement,' and, finally, 'submission to the Divine will.'[42]

Most English Canadians of the 1870s and 1880s were clearly content with the way in which they raised their own youngsters and the other children who joined their households. They would have been baffled by twentieth-century concerns for the emotional life of their own or of the immigrant children. The writer of the time who argued that people did not generally treat boys 'wisely and justly' preached sentiments which were not widely shared in these years.[43] To say this, however, does not imply that Canadians were uninterested in the health, education, and welfare of their young, only that people expressed their concern within the framework of what they believed. Many Canadians showed their interest in children not only in unrecorded private family ways but also in providing for unfortunate youngsters who lived in their midst. Over the years 1874 to 1893, Ontarions, mostly through voluntary means and with an eye to the protection of society as well as the welfare of their inmates, doubled the number of institutions caring for neglected and dependent children in their province and more than doubled the number of children whom they cared for in them.[44] This trend was not confined to Ontario. In 1871, there were twenty-three orphanages in Canada. By 1881, the number had increased to forty-six with 2770 inmates. By 1891, while the number of institutions had declined to forty-one, they held 3827 children. Moreover, in Ontario anyway, each of these institutions was carefully and thoroughly inspected by the provincial government to ensure that it maintained a high minimum level of care for its inmates. However, the institutions characteristically showed little interest in individual youngsters, and in their management they emphasized hard work and firm discipline. Soon after it was established, the Protestant Orphan's Home in Ottawa decided to stop sending its inmates to the common school and teach them within its grounds. Discipline, its report explained, would be easier to maintain 'if the children were not sent out for instruction.'[45]

As English Canadians of the 1870s and 1880s went about their daily rounds, rearing their youngsters in traditional ways, changes were already afoot in their society which would put into question many of their assumptions and practices. In a new era, characterized by the rapid growth of industry and of cities and a rising standard of living, some Canadians began to use new ideas about children and childhood within their own homes and to apply them in the wider society as well.

2

'Multitudes Better Equipped ... than Their Fathers': A New Childhood for a New Society

'There have always been beautiful homes and lives,' explained Dr Emily Stowe in 1894; the real task then at hand was to increase their number. Dr Stowe contributed this remark to a discussion held by the first meeting of the National Council of Women on the need for Canadian schools to teach girls the art of home-making. The discussion reflected the quickening interest of English-speaking Canadians in children and families. In her opening address to the meeting, its president, Lady Aberdeen, explained that one of the principal missions of the newly formed organization was to support and improve the home. In the late 1880s and 1890s an increasing number of English Canadians made a self-conscious effort to describe the 'good' family and to explain how it should raise its children. While greatly concerned about the nurture of their own youngsters, those taking part also appraised what they saw as the 'problem' of the family in their society as a whole. Although some of their talk and writing to modern ears sounds flowery and sentimental, nonetheless what they said accurately reflected one of their most serious concerns. By examining this discourse one can discover much of what they thought would form an ideal childhood, not only within the walls of an ideal household but in the world outside it as well. 'Can anything be more patriotic,' asked Henrietta Day Smith of her fellow members of the council, 'than to give to the on-coming generations the glorious inheritance of pure blood in their veins, pure homes in which to grow, pure streets in which to walk, pure schools in which to be educated, pure legislative halls where the laws of a free and capable people are enacted, and the gospel of truth and purity that leads to and prepares for the true homeland in the soul?'[2] In the context of such ideas a generation of reformers laboured to transform infant and child care in their society.

Before I begin to examine what these Canadians of a new era had to say about raising children, I should like to emphasize three points. First, there were probably important differences between what people thought was happening to children and families and what actually was happening, and the reformers were acting according to their own perceptions. Second, those doing most of the talking spoke from and for the middle class. And, third, in what follows I have selected from the discussions about families only those elements dealing with children.

Two census monographs have outlined some of the real changes taking place in Canadian families in these years.[3] However it is still not known which of the changes they described, or others not yet investigated, made any real difference to the internal dynamics of family living and particularly to child-rearing. These studies showed, for example, that from Confederation on the average size of both rural and urban families in Canada dropped steadily, that urban families were smaller than rural ones, that as late as 1931 Canadian rural families generally retained their traditional function of being working as well as child-rearing units of society, and that between 1898 and 1921 the fertility of Canadian women dropped 13 per cent. The authors of these monographs worked within the framework of the now classical explanation that these changes were the generally undesirable effects on the family of urbanization and industrialization.[4] Historians and sociologists, however, have come to doubt that the family is an institution in decline in modern society.[5] The American sociologist William J. Goode, for example, theorizes that industrialization and changing family patterns were really independent variables which interacted with each other in a very complex way.[6] The English sociologist Frank Musgrove argues that in modern society family influence over the development, prospects, and life chances of the young has greatly increased.[7] Given the present state of historical and sociological knowledge about the family, and the scarcity of historical research on the Canadian family, it is necessary to be wary of making definite statements about what was actually happening to Canadian families in these years.[8] Nonetheless, whatever *was* happening, it is possible to say that from the 1890s onward many Canadians talked about, analysed, and reacted strongly to changes they thought were taking place in the family.

Middle-class men and women led the reform movement. While late-nineteenth-century Canadians did not follow English and European custom in drawing sharp lines between the classes in their society, they were nonetheless keenly aware that 'the members of a community,' as a book of the time put it, 'inevitably' fell into 'certain more or less well-defined groups.'[9] Families whose breadwinners ranged in calling from prosperous farmers, skilled artisans and craftsmen, through public employees, the commercial and business occupations, to professions such as preaching, law, medicine, dentistry, and high school teaching formed the Canadian middle class of the time.[10] Except for the well-to-do farmers, these families lived mostly in towns and cities, and their numbers were increasing at least as fast as the urban population of the nation. From 1891 to 1921, the number of physicians in Canada grew from 4448, or one for every 1065 persons in the country, to 8706, one for every 1008. Over the same years, the number of dentists rose from 753, one for every 6290 people, to 3158, one for every 2779. Between 1901 and 1921, the number of nurses in Canada increased from 280 to 21,385. In 1920, the population of Ontario was one and a half times as large as it had been in 1880; the number of teachers in the province with matriculation and four or more years of further education was four times as large.[11] In 1905, of the 383,000 persons working in manufacturing, 35,000 were supervisory and office employees; in 1920 the comparable numbers were 576,000 and 77,000. As the rapid increase in vocational and commercial forms of education which began in the late 1880s testified, many ambitious young men took advantage of the opportunity to better themselves made possible by business and commercial growth.[12] Others entered the growing public service. During the decade between 1912 and 1921, the federal civil service alone increased from 20,000 to 42,000 employees.[13] Of particular significance to the subject of this study, members of the middle class dominated the new professions – especially teaching, social work, public health medicine, and nursing – that actually looked after children and families. Further, middle-class Canadians established the standards for membership in these professions and directed the work of the public and private agencies that employed those who met the qualifications. Finally, many middle-class people worked hard to impose their new notions on all their fellow citizens.

Wherever middle-class Canadians lived or settled, they displayed much of the townsman's outlook on life and society. By 1897, women's organizations in Toronto, Montreal, Halifax, Winnipeg, and Vancouver had come together into local units of that distinctly urban-oriented organization, the National Council of Women. Their counterparts, however, in Yarmouth (1901 population 6430), Regina (population 2249), Vernon (population less than 1000), Calgary (population 4392), Brandon (population 5380), and Rat Portage (population 5202) had also organized Local Councils of Women.[14] Further, as an integral part of their urban focus, many middle-class people living in the smaller centres shared the practical expressions of concern, which had begun in the cities, to improve the health, education, and welfare of children. The fact that between July 1893 and December 1895 Ontario's superintendent of neglected and dependent children helped no less than twenty-nine Children's Aid societies to organize, ten of them in towns with a population between 5000 and 10,000 and seven in centres with less than 5000 inhabitants, is one of the most striking examples of this interest.[15]

Nevertheless, such evidence must not obscure the fact that small-town people and organizations customarily echoed what their counterparts in the cities were already saying and doing. As this and later chapters will reveal, a host of middle-class city-dwellers, with Torontonians generally in the lead, first expressed the new ideas on childhood and family life and organized the many associations, campaigns, and the like, which tried to put new theory into practice.

The middle classes, however, had no monopoly on changing attitudes to children and families. The working class shared some of the new beliefs and played a varying role in implementing new standards derived from them. Unionized workmen in the early 1880s, for example, gave the welfare of their families as the main reason they wanted the sixty-hour week and the half-day on Saturday. 'When a hard working man had himself washed and dressed, and walked out in the afternoon with his wife and family,' argued the Trades' Council, 'he was not likely afterwards to go and get drunk.'[16] Many workers both within and outside the growing labour movement expressed dismay over the length of the day, the pay, and other working conditions of children in factories. Some of the 'darkest pages' in the testimony it heard, reported the Federal Royal Commission on the Relations of Labor and Capital, were those recording 'the beating and imprisonment of children employed in factories.'[17] Unions lobbied for control of child immigration, for limitations on the ages and hours of work for children, for the elimination of 'sweating' – which bore down with particular harshness on women and their child-helpers – and for changes in the educational system.[18]

In addition to the constraints posed by gaps in the information available and by the dominance of the discussion by the middle class, this investigation of children and families is limited in two ways. First, the family has traditionally performed social functions other than child-rearing. As they had in earlier generations, Canadian families of the 1890s generally cared for the dependent old, the sick, and life's temporary or permanent casualties. The family remained the prime institution through which one generation passed on property to the next, and the families of farmers and of operators of small-scale commercial or artisan enterprises continued to function as economic units, as producers of goods and services. When one examines the emotional dimensions of family life, wives and husbands were bound together in a relationship which was also becoming the subject of increasing interest. Second, children were not merely appendages of their parents; in some ways society treated them without reference to their membership in families. The public health movement made its initial efforts to improve child health not through the home but the school. Further, while educational reform was partly a product of public interest in the well-being of the family, it also reflected such other issues as the need to provide trained workers for new industries and to transform agriculture in eastern Canada. In short, since this study is focused not on the family but on the child, it will examine only those aspects of family life concerned with the relationship between parents and children.

I

How did concerned English Canadians in the 1890s look upon that 'gravest of individual ties and obligations' – the relationship between child and parents?[19] Although their views were articulated mostly in bits and pieces rather than in a general program, many would have agreed with the following propositions. They believed, as the core idea around which they built everything else, that the welfare of their society as a whole, both then and in the future, was intimately bound together with the health of the family. 'Take care of the children,' explained the Reverend J. Edward Starr, 'and the nation will take care of itself.'[20] Many looked not merely to maintain the nation but to improve it. Children who were properly looked after, explained the Reverend Albert D. Carman, a general superintendent of the Methodist Church, would 'come forth holy, earnest well-informed Christian men and women; multitudes better equipped for the great struggle than their fathers; better furnished in a godly understanding and instructed mind.'[21] The changing nature of society, however, made social improvement a difficult task. The advance of civilization, J.J. Kelso explained, had also brought with it a rising tide of criminality, much of it due 'to the neglect of child-training in the homes of vice and drunkenness.' To remedy this baneful condition Canadians must insist on raising the standards of home life to a level that would 'ensure for every child a fair chance to attain self-reliant and self-respecting citizenship.'[22]

Parents were expected to tackle their duties carefully and systematically. Mothers were advised to search out methods of child-rearing that practice had shown to be successful so that their own efforts would be 'consistent, instead of arbitrary or capricious – the result of impulse.' Instead of blaming their child, or fate, for any failure, parents were expected to shoulder the responsibility for surrounding their youngster 'with conditions contrary to its nature.'[23] To ensure that mothers-to-be learned their job properly, some men and women began to argue that 'motherhood' should become a subject in the school curriculum. Society, the argument went, provided training for any profession that a woman might choose except that of motherhood.[24]

In contrast to the general opinion of the 1870s parents now learned that a child was not 'plastic clay ... to mold and shape after a human pattern but a seed of divine life' for them 'to nurture and tend.'[25] In this rhetoric one can see the growing influence that a popular and simplistic form of the ideas of Friedrich

Froebel were beginning to have in English Canada. By following his suggestions, a mother could 'advance from instinctive action with her children, to conscious insight concerning her child's wants and how to meet them.' Froebel had shown that the child already contained 'the germs' of whatever he was to be; that as he developed he was to be judged at each stage according to the standards of that stage; and that he developed 'only through the exercise of self activity.' Although this activity was at first an involuntary product of instinct, it rose 'through imitation to free creativeness.' Parents must ensure that the three-fold nature – mental, moral, and physical – of their child developed harmoniously. Moreover, since the child existed, in turn, in a three-fold relationship to nature, to his fellow man, and to God, parents were obliged to develop him as a rational being who displayed awareness to these relationships.[26] By 1895 his followers had established Froebelian societies in Toronto, Ottawa, London, and Winnipeg.[27] Toronto school inspector James L. Hughes and his wife, Ada Marean, were influential spokesmen for Froebelian ideas from the 1880s on into the new century.[28]

Discussion of Froebelian sentiments exemplified English Canada's strongly developing belief in the influence of environment on children. Since a child was a 'plant' rather than a 'marble being' to be 'pounded into shape,' both parents and teachers had to be sure that his physical, spiritual, and educational setting were well suited to growth.[29] Again and again, parents were told that how they treated their youngsters at home governed what sorts of adults the latter would become. If parents were 'cross, petulant and unreasonable' their children would turn out the same; on the other hand, if they displayed 'patience, gentleness, forebearance, genuineness,' their children would also 'exhibit these qualities.'[30] In a true home, parents provided love and taught obedience and service. Since neither excessive indulgence or severity were conducive to the nurture of these qualities, parents were urged to avoid both extremes.[31] In this context, while some questioned the merits of using corporal punishment both in the home and at school, most seemed to favour its use where absolutely necessary and as a last resort.[32] So important did they look upon a 'right' family environment that the new Children's Aid societies felt they were justified in coercing all parents to conform to their notions. When a family situation became so unsatisfactory that it could not be rehabilitated, they argued, the state was entirely justified in taking the children and placing them with another family.[33]

Parents were also expected to concern themselves with what happened to their children outside the home. Believing that children by their very nature were morally fragile, and thus always on the verge of yielding to temptation, reformers expressed great concern about such matters as 'unhealthful surroundings, improper sanitation, improper postures' and an 'unwise curriculum with perhaps too many school hours or too severe lessons for the untried growing brain.'[34] In this framework, parents also worried about the possible ill effects of concerts, music halls, and other entertainments on children, were generally agreed upon the evil effects of smoking and alcohol, and debated the merits of giving sex education to their children.[35]

Middle-class reformers also feared that badly brought up or poorly cared for children would menace the well-being of their own more carefully reared offspring. In their efforts to help neglected, dependent, and delinquent youngsters, they displayed their belief that the children of the poor and of the working classes were in particular need of attention.[36] Looked at 'from a selfish point of view,' explained Toronto dental reformer J.G. Adams, people could not 'afford to neglect the children of the poor' and still let their own youngsters 'sit in the same room, side by side, with these neglected children and inhale the vile gases, constantly emanating from them, caused by their rotten teeth' or 'drink out of the same cup these children have fouled with the poisonous pus' which exuded 'from the gums around their abscessed teeth and roots.'[37]

As they discussed what reading matter was suitable for their children, these proponents of a new sort of childhood displayed with particular clarity the tremendous intensity of their concern about the pernicious effects of environment on their boys and girls. 'I ... witnessed in real life the striking and tragic contrast between two families,' explained Lady Schultz in a paper that may have put some strain on the credulity of her fellow members of the National Council of Women. In one household, which had no reading matter that was unsuitable for children, the youngsters grew up around their mother 'in honor, beauty and virtue.' Her sons were 'strong and stalwart,' her daughters 'gentle, retiring, modest and womanly to a degree.' The other family believed that it was better to satisfy youths' 'craving for excitement and knowledge' early in life so that when the children were older 'they might turn their attention to more serious matters.' When the latter parents therefore gave ten cents a week for 'yellow-covered dime novels,' this indulgence 'bore its inevitable fruit.' The daughter 'married, was divorced and married again,' the elder son 'lived a dissipated and disgraceful life,' and the younger met with 'an early and tragic death.'[38] A few years later, a jury considered dime novels to have been one of the major causes leading to the killing of Toronto businessman Peter McIntyre by his thirteen-year-old son.[39]

Parents were enlisted in the battle to prevent poisonous literature from being distributed on railway cars or by newsboys, and from being imported from the United States. They were also asked to encourage the reading and writing of good books and magazines for young people, to buy such literature for their own youngsters, and to ensure that it was in school libraries. In one demonstration of the effectiveness of this campaign, the National Council of Women's Sub-Committee on Literature listed fifty-two publications – the titles of which ranged from *The Police Gazette* and *The Hornet* to such innocuous-sounding periodicals as *House and Home, The American Farmer*, and *The Household Guest* – whose 'transmission by mail' Canada prohibited. The report also noted another eighteen periodicals which had been removed from the list when the publishers promised 'to omit the objectionable matter in future.'[40]

A child's need for firm but loving family care, the central importance of his mother in ensuring he received it, and her concern that his tender, plant-like nature not be menaced in an inappropriate environment – these were the important dimensions of the relationship between parents and children as urban, middle-class English Canadians saw them towards the end of the nineteenth century. In their discussions at least, these people displayed a greater and perhaps more humane concern for the conditions under which their own and other youngsters spent their early years than had their predecessors of a generation before. They used their new ideas not only as a guide to their own performance as parents but also to evaluate and to change the care received by other children in their society. What was at stake, they believed, was not only the future of their own children but also the future of society as a whole. To ensure that their offspring would live their adult lives in a satisfactory social environment, they had to interest themselves in how all the young in their society were brought up. Thus these concerned Canadians did not view the family as a sentimental end in itself, but as a means; it was the social agency that had the prime responsibility for ensuring that the whole of the next generation represented the best that Canadian society could produce. It is important for us to note that there was no late-nineteenth-century 'discovery' of the child *per se*, no sudden coming upon him in a new and more enlightened way. Prodded by the need to solve newly emerged, perceived, or discovered practical problems, Canadians gradually sorted out various groups of children who needed particular kinds of care. As they did so, they set more and more precise and increasingly high standards for various phases of a 'proper' childhood and proposed remedies for those who did not meet them. It was a very *ad hoc* process with few precedents for anyone to follow.

Those English Canadians who wanted to change childhood in their society therefore went to work with a varied group of allies on a wide range of projects in what they slowly came to see could be clustered around four closely related spheres of interest: improving conditions for good family life, establishing systems of child and family welfare, transforming the educational system, and organizing a pattern of child and family health care. In their effort to protect and improve the quality of childhood and the nature of family life, they pursued such matters as infant care and child-rearing practices, child psychology, temperance education and prohibition of the liquor traffic, workmen's compensation, control of immigration, elimination of pernicious books, censorship of music hall and movie performances, improved housing, day nurseries for working mothers, supervised playgrounds, neighbourhood houses, and sex and family life education in home and school. In the area of child and family welfare, they worked for factory legislation for women and children, mothers' pensions, the proper care and placement of neglected and dependent children, separate detention homes, industrial schools, and juvenile courts for delinquent youngsters, changes in legislation affecting the age of consent, desertion, divorce, support and the custody of children, and the suppression of the activities of prostitution rings that forcibly abducted and transported young girls, a practice they called 'the white slave traffic.' Out of their concern for child and family health they campaigned for the reduction of infant and childhood mortality, for maternity and children's hospitals, pure water and pure milk supplies, compulsory immunization, medical and dental inspection in the schools, special care and education for defective children, and 'fresh air' camps for slum families. In their efforts to establish a 'new' education to fit their children into the new society, they strove for the extension and enforcement of compulsory attendance laws, the introduction of kindergartens, libraries, physical education, manual training, domestic science, agricultural and other vocational training, and technical education into the school system, the consolidation of rural schools, and special efforts to acculturate through the schools the rising tide of non-English-speaking immigrants.

II

What prompted the increasing interest of English-speaking Canadians in the ways in which children were reared and families were organized? Was this an autonomous development or was it related to other aspects of Canadian society? While one cannot lay bare a linear, cause-and-effect relationship between economic change and patterns of child-rearing and family organization, there were some important links between the two. Several characteristics of the era were closely interconnected: the Canadian economy went through many changes, including a rapid growth in industrial towns and cities, the standard of living rose for both middle and working classes, and the different nature of work increased the mother's responsibilities in many Canadian families. In a context of social optimism, and in a cooperative enterprise with other parts of the industrialized and industrializing world, urban Canadians began to make over many components of child life in their society.

Growth in agriculture, in primary and secondary manufacturing, in transportation facilities, and in mining brought new wealth to the Canadian economy. In the classic view of the nation's economic history, since Canada was severely affected for two decades by the world-wide depression after 1873, the real period of modern growth did not begin until the 'change in circumstances' in the mid-1890s.[41] More recent research, however, indicates that the effects of the depression have been exaggerated and that the country experienced steady growth and increasing prosperity from 1870 onward.[42] Towards the end of the century the 'wheat boom,' which caused that product to emerge as a major staple in the Canadian economy, greatly augmented an already healthy economic situation. This boom, in turn, settled the Canadian West and led to the last great phase of railway-building. Not only did railway companies construct the second and third transcontinental lines, but in a frenzied effort to capture markets they also made heavy investments in branch lines. Immigration, wheat culture, and railway-building in turn further stimulated Canadian manufacturing. In constant (1935–9) dollars, Canada's gross national product rose from $764 million in 1870 to $1366 million in 1890, $1877 million in 1900, $3225 million in 1910, and $3834 million in 1920.[43]

Economic growth affected Canadian families in four important ways. First, in addition to creating many new jobs, it produced a real increase in wages and salaries, which in turn promoted the rapid rise in the size of the urban middle class and laid the basis for its prosperity. O.J. Firestone described the 'startling progress' made by this first generation of the Canadian industrial revolution 'in terms of the level of real incomes and standard of living ...' He showed that, in constant dollars, Canada's national income per capita grew from $184 in 1870 to $252 in 1890, $298 in 1900, $371 in 1910, and $388 in 1920. A closely related increase in consumer expenditures per capita displays the fact that individual Canadians received and disposed of much of the increased national income. In constant dollars, per-capita consumer expenditures rose from $163 in 1870 to $231 in 1890, $276 in 1900, and $320 in 1910, declining slightly to $318 in 1920. Perhaps even more suggestive of improving family welfare was the sharply rising share of their income which Canadians devoted to life insurance. Again in constant dollars, life insurance in force per capita climbed from $17 in 1870 to $83 in 1890, $139 in 1900, $163 in 1910, and $213 in 1920.[44] Although Firestone did not break down any of his data by class, the earlier discussion of the middle class suggests that its members benefitted substantially from such changes. Rising living standards were not, however, confined to this one class; many labouring people also felt that the quality of their lives was improving. In 1889, the Royal Commission on the Relations of Labor and Capital in Canada reported that the testimony it had received indicated that wages 'were generally higher than at any previous time,' hours of work had been somewhat reduced, and the 'necessary and ordinary comforts of life' were of lower price, so that 'the material condition of the working people' had 'been greatly bettered, especially during the past ten years.'[45] This trend continued: a quarter of a century later, the British Columbia Royal Commission on Labour stated that 'the conditions of life of the working-man' were improving; that 'on every hand' there was evidence of a higher standard of living, and that 'what were the luxuries of former days' were 'now becoming to be considered as the ordinary necessities of a well-regulated household.'[46]

Second, the addition of industrial pursuits – and the related development of urban transit systems – to the already present agricultural and commercial occupations of English Canadians forced many mothers to assume a greater share of the family's responsibility for rearing its youngsters. Traditionally, in the home-workshop, in the small family business, and on the family farm, children grew up under the eyes of both their parents. Artisan and commercial fathers were customarily at hand all day, every day throughout the year. Even the farmer-fathers who laboured away from their families in the woods in the winter were at home for much of the year. As their youngsters became old enough to join in the work of the household, such fathers gradually assumed an increasing share of the responsibility for rearing and educating them. As one observer explained: the life of the country people gave 'them opportunities for constant superintendence over their children.' The farmer lived his life upon the farm, and the children had 'their work and play under the direction and observation of their parents.'[47] As late as 1931, and after sixty years of what the census monograph on the family described as the urbanizing of the 'social outlook and economic life of the rural population,' the farm family retained many attributes traditionally associated with it. Most Canadian farms, the census revealed, were still owned and operated by families. These families were generally self-sufficient so far as farm labour was concerned and, if the presence of milch cows, poultry, and swine were an accurate measure, still produced much of their own food.[48] Change came much more rapidly in the cities where, increasingly, the father was likely to work away from home, having to 'attend to his breadwinning at all hazards.'[49] In mapping the 'journey to work' for a sampling of occupations in Toronto in 1860 and in 1890, Peter G. Goheen illustrated the physical dimension of what was taking place. In 1860, with but one exception in the case of bakers and confectioners and two in that of physicians and surgeons, the workplace and the residence of all Torontonians in these callings were the same establishment. In contrast, employees of three small manufacturing enterprises, clerks employed by two banks, and directors of three banks all travelled some distance from their homes to their jobs. By 1890, the growth of the city and the spread of streetcar lines had separated even further the job and the home in such varied examples as the employees of a brewery, a publishing company, a newspaper, a life insurance company, two banks, and a large department store.[50] Furthermore, the working day and working week was a long one for both the middle and working classes: in addition to their travelling time, most employees put in a five-and-a-half- or six-day, sixty-hour week.[51] A father, explained Mrs Adelaide Hoodless, 'must go out at 8 o'clock in the morning and engage in a struggle, almost always an exhausting one, to provide bread for his family.'[52]

In these new circumstances, mothers came to wield 'an influence so potent with their children' that it became 'almost omnipotent.' This increased responsibility, which came at a time when the new perceptions of childhood were laying greater burdens on parents, made many middle-class women into rather self-conscious artisans in a new and highly specialized occupation called 'Motherhood.' Its practitioners were eager to learn and pass on to others the knowledge and skills which made up their craft. 'The influence of a truly good woman,' proclaimed a member of the Vancouver Council of Women, could not be overestimated, 'and in the Teaching and Training of her children it must be very great.'

In the 1890s both men and women indicated, directly and indirectly, that they sensed this expanded role for women in child-rearing. In their rhetoric, both sexes commented more than ever on a theme that had developed in the nineteenth century – the moral purity and superiority of women and how important this was to the well-being of the family. The 'most exalted sphere of women' was the home, preached the Reverend W.T. Herridge, and 'from this centre' radiated 'all her best influence.' She was 'the invisible figure that in quiet prayer and toil' weaved 'the web of human destiny.'[53] More practically, many women turned in these years to an effort to bring their legal position more in line with their real and growing responsibilities. Because affairs decided by school boards touched 'the very foundation of the homes of our land,' the National Council of Women argued that 'Motherhood' could claim representation on the boards.[54] On a broader scale, many women wanted to change the situation in which, as one of the campaigners explained, the father as 'sole guardian' could 'bind out his infant children, apprentice them, give them in adoption, educate them how and when' he pleased, and in what religion he chose. To her children a mother then stood 'legally in exactly the same position as a stranger.'[55] As early as its second meeting, in 1895, the National Council of Women appointed a Committee on Laws 'for the protection of women and children.'[56] Over the next two decades, the council, the Woman's Christian Temperance Union, and other women's organizations worked with great persistence and growing success to improve the legal situation of Canadian women.[57]

Third, the fact that so much of the economic change took place in towns and cities was of central importance in transforming childhood and family life in the nation. Despite the great growth in Canadian agriculture and other rural activities, the percentage of the population that lived in urban areas more than doubled over forty years, going from 23.3 per cent in 1881 to 29.8 in 1891, 34.9 in 1901, 41.8 in 1911, and 47.4 in 1921.[58] From 1890 to 1920 the proportion of the Canadian population working in manufacturing remained constant.[59] The latter growth underlines the fact that, in addition to retaining their traditional commercial functions, Canadian cities were rapidly becoming manufacturing centres as well. While they grew with remarkable speed, however, in one major respect Canadian urban centres did not change. As they had risen to commercial maturity earlier in the century, Toronto and other towns had initiated such changes in caring for boys and girls as establishing permanent institutions to look after the neglected and the dependent and setting up provincial systems of free public schools.[60] In the new industrial era, urban Canadians continued to lead their fellow citizens in reform.[61] The cities introduced most of the new notions designed to improve the health, education, and welfare of Canadian children; only very gradually did these practices extend into the countryside. Indeed, not only were even those ideas, such as the use of the school to teach farming skills, that were mostly rural in orientation promoted by city people or by the most urbanized of rural residents but the changes themselves had an urban form and cast.

The reasons for this continued urban leadership are perhaps more complex than may initially appear to be the case. At the simplest level one can argue that, as the case of the changing role of the mother suggested, the new urban environment itself created most of the newly perceived needs and social problems relating to the young. It was, therefore, entirely natural that urban Canadians should be the first to press for necessary reforms. While probably true, such an opinion does not take into account the answers to a number of important questions. How many of the children who posed problems to agencies in cities and towns had fled or were forced to leave the countryside? Did the city actually produce more problem children than did the old rural environment or were they just more visible in the city? Did these youngsters become more visible because their proportions were actually increasing, or because urban Canadians had sharpened their perceptions from learning about what was going on elsewhere? Did urban Canadians come to notice problem families because they had raised their standards of civic order, or because they had instituted a more thorough kind of law enforcement? How important to change was the growing interest and involvement of women in civic affairs? Although later chapters will deal with some of these questions, at this point I should initiate an examination of two key aspects of urban leadership – the central part that Toronto played in the whole process and the closely related matter of foreign influence in framing Canadian practice.

While not Canada's largest city, Toronto in the late nineteenth and early twentieth centuries led the nation in most forms of social experimentation. Between 1870 and 1900, explains Goheen, the Ontario capital changed from a nineteenth-century commercial city into a twentieth-century industrial metropolis.[62] As they made over their city, Torontonians introduced many new ideas in public health, social welfare, and education. Our later examination of some of their pioneering efforts raises the question as to the role that work already under way in other countries played in stimulating that in Toronto and other Canadian cities and, in turn, the latters' influence in encouraging smaller centres to undertake new ventures in caring for children and families. To measure the exact effect of foreign influences, however, is a particularly difficult problem. Did Canadians perceive an unsatisfactory situation in their society and then look elsewhere for models of how other places had coped or were coping with it? Alternatively, did they see what was being done in other countries in child welfare and did this discovery prompt them to examine their own society to see if it too contained similar problems? While one may often answer 'yes' to both queries, evidence presented throughout this study strongly suggests that the answers to these particular questions do not show what was really taking place. On the one hand, for example, for two decades Canadians really did not see the significance of the new form of caring for dependent children which the English child emigration societies so prominently displayed in their midst. On the other, the American Public Health Association met in Toronto in 1886, the National Prison Association in 1887, the American Humane Society in 1888, the American Society for the Advancement of Women in 1890, the National Educational Association in 1891, the National Conference of Charities and Correction in 1897, and the National Household Economics Association in 1900. This series of meetings by American societies certainly served not only to make many Canadians aware for the first time of new ways of looking at social conditions but also stimulated the morale of the nation's small corps of professionals in each field. In his opening address to the National Conference of Charities and Correction in the Toronto Pavilion in July 1897, its president, Alexander Johnson, underlined the 'missionary effect' of the Conference, noting its 'stimulating and tonic influence upon the whole work of charities and correction' in the areas visited by it.[63] Equally important, however, these meetings emphasized that Toronto was rapidly becoming one of the principal 'model' cities in North America for new approaches to all sorts of problems and that some Canadians, including James L. and Ada M. Hughes, J.J. Kelso, Adelaide Hoodless, and Peter H. Bryce, were innovators in their fields.[64] Indeed, an examination of their careers shows that many Canadians were integral parts of a series of developing international professional communities in public health, in education, and in social welfare. As such, they both contributed to and drew from the expanding pools of knowledge and practice characteristic of each field.

Finally, Canadian economic growth of the late nineteenth and early twentieth century affected Canadian families because it was accompanied by a state of mind which encouraged social experimentation. In the context of the Victorian 'sense of safety,' Canadians shared with the rest of the English-speaking world in a sense of great vitality, of movement, of positive change, and of the inevitability of progress.[65] Those calling for new methods of child-rearing, and for new approaches to child health, child welfare, and education were not trying to restructure a static social order along different lines but to shift the general flow of events in a society changing at a rate faster than any earlier era of the Canadian experience. Many Canadians were very deeply stirred by the lively quality of what was going on around them. Some were frightened and called for a restoration of an old-fashioned childhood which they saw fast disappearing. Others, however, identified with what was new and were confident that they could forge out of the new environment something better for themselves and especially for their children. 'Life in these last days of the nineteenth century,' explained Mrs Charles Archibald of Halifax in 1896, was a 'wonderfully complex thing.' Even the home itself, she continued, was not 'free from the reflex influence of these surging tides of restless energy.'[66] Those in the reform movement doubted neither the rightness nor the inevitability of what they wanted. When the Prince Edward Island WCTU failed to secure child protection legislation in that province, its president was 'not yet discouraged'; it was, she concluded, 'the keeping at it that wins success.'[67] In 1907, at the closing exercises of the McGill Normal School, Professor Abner W. Kneeland urged the graduates, in a phrase which could have served as the motto for all the reformers, to 'be earnest, be vigilant, be progressive; fulfil your mission to the 20th century.'[68]

Towards the end of the nineteenth century and under the leadership of the urban middle classes, Canadians began to look in new ways upon child-rearing. A rising standard of living permitted those Canadian parents who chose to do so to devote an increasing amount and even a greater share of their personal income to the improvement of the lives of their youngsters. It also permitted Canadian society as a whole, if it chose to do so, to invest an increasing amount and an even greater proportion of the national wealth to this end. At the same time, the most important function of many families, *qua* families, changed from economic production to the nurture of children. In turn, mothers came to assume most of the responsibility for this latter task. In the context of these intimately inter-related developments, a generation of generally optimistic English Canadians moved children towards the forefront of its consciousness. The nation embarked upon a major era of change which, before it was over, had most Canadian children growing up in ways which were fundamentally different from those which had characterized the youth of their parents and grandparents.

III

By helping to found the Toronto Humane Society in 1887, Toronto *World* reporter J.J. Kelso set out on what was to be a lifetime of work in child-saving. In taking this step, Kelso joined a growing band of English Canadians who began, over the late 1880s and 1890s, to give practical expression to the new attitudes to children.

In Ontario in 1890, that province's Royal Commission on the Prison and Reformatory System gave an enormous amount of attention to child welfare generally and particularly to how youthful delinquency might be prevented and cured. In cities and towns all across Canada, men and women founded new institutions. In Saint John, New Brunswick, Mrs Turnbull established the Little Girls' Home to give temporary care and to arrange permanent placement for neglected and deserted children who until then, for want of a better place, had sometimes been lodged by the province in its local gaols.[69] Its 'great purpose,' explained the WCTU, was 'the protection of the home by individual pledges of total abstinence, by educating the young, by creating and fostering temperance sentiment, and by securing the total Prohibition of the Liquor Traffic ...'[70] For a second time, too, Canadians scrutinized the place of immigrant children in their society. The crisis of the 1870s laid bare the general satisfaction with which Canadians of those years had looked upon most aspects of child-rearing in their society; they were content to work within a consensus on childhood which an earlier generation had framed for them. The second debate over exactly the same sort of youngster not only confirmed that Canadians were changing their opinions on bringing up children but also that they were eager to put their new ideas into practice. Events of this second quarrel showed, too, some of the weaknesses of activities based not on what was actually taking place but on what some people thought was going on.

After the controversy of the 1870s died down, immigration statistics began to show growth in both the number of children coming to Canada and in the organizations bringing them out. In 1883, the Local Government Board again permitted the emigration of pauper children 'on a small scale, under properly organized conditions.'[71] Indeed, the English historian Kathleen Heasman explains that the publicity which the Doyle Report aroused actually increased interest in child immigration.[72] By the mid-1880s, a bewildering array of English organizations had become involved in child emigration. Between 1883 and 1888, at least fifty different agencies sent children to Canada, with totals ranging from the one child sent by the Protestant Orphan Asylum of Dublin to the 1961 children sponsored by Dr Thomas J. Barnardo. Of the 10,883 children sent over these years, however, 8621 were sent by thirteen individuals or societies.[73] Dr Barnardo was the most important addition to the list of workers in the field. Like Miss Rye, Miss Macpherson, and most of the others, Barnardo's efforts grew out of a deeply felt religious commitment. From very small beginnings in 1867, Barnardo developed his child-rescue work in the London slums, and by the 1880s his was the largest English organization in the field. After sending a number of children to Canada through Miss Macpherson's organization, in 1882 he organized his own emigration scheme.[74] Between 1883 and 1888 he sent out nearly one-fifth of all the children arriving in Canada; by 1900 his proportion of the annual total had climbed to nearly half. In a retrospective account of the work from 1868 to 1923, the Department of Immigration reported that over 25,000 of the 77,000 children brought to Canada by child emigration societies over these years had come from the Dr Barnardo Homes.[75] In addition to being the largest agency in this field, Dr Barnardo's was also amongst the best managed. In selecting children to be sent to Canada, Barnardo set high standards of physical health and personal character, and his organization efficiently supervised those it placed out in foster homes.[76]

Throughout the 1880s, federal inspectors, provincial immigration agents, and representatives of the emigration societies reported favourably on the children, on the receiving homes for them in Canada, and on the foster homes into which they had been placed. In 1886, an Ottawa immigration agent, W.J. Wills, explained that he 'found all of them in comfortable homes with only two exceptions.' This generally positive tone also characterized the reports for that year by the Kingston, Hamilton, London, and Halifax agents, and by visitors from England who came to inspect the work.[77] Towards the end of the 1880s, as well, some Canadian inspectors began to make some long-term, if subjective, evaluations of the work. In his report for 1888, Hamilton immigration agent John Smith noted that 'a large number of the boys' were 'yearly growing up to manhood, capable of earning their own livelihood' and a number of them had 'accumulated sufficient capital to take up homesteads in Manitoba, the North-West Territories, and British Columbia.' Of the girls, he wrote that 'the great majority' had 'done well, a large number of them being married and comfortably settled, and not a few of them having been married amongst the farmers' sons into whose family they were adopted.'[78]

In the same year that Smith uttered his praises new opponents of the immigration scheme began to attack it. In contrast to the earlier occasion, however, this time Canada was the principal centre of the dispute. Further, Canadians showed more awareness and understanding of the problems faced by boys and girls who were taken so casually from Britain to Canada and distributed with so little attention to the nature of the homes into which they were placed. Nevertheless, those English Canadians taking part made it very clear that their main worry was not the fate of the English youngsters. They saw their task as one of protecting Canadian homes, families, and children from a peril whose real nature they had just discovered. The second discussion opened in the House of Commons Standing Committee on Agriculture and Colonization. After its investigations of 1875 and 1876, the committee ignored the immigrant children for over a decade.[79] In 1888, however, the member for Welland, Ontario, Dr C. Ferguson, attacked the newcomers, describing them as 'the offal of the most depraved characters in the cities of the old country.' After spirited debate, the committee recommended that 'a strict medical inspection and certificate of healthiness be exacted' before the children were permitted to enter the country.[80] After the committee discussed the matter again in 1889, parliamentary interest in it died down until 1894.

Parliament's silence, however, did not indicate that concerned Canadians had forsaken the issue; on the contrary, a growing number of them expressed strong opinions on the matter.[81] In particular, the public hearings and subsequent report of Ontario's Royal Commission on the Prison and Reformatory System acutely aroused public feeling about immigrant children. Echoing what had been said in the House of Commons committee in 1888 and 1889, witnesses before the commission expressed three principal complaints against the youngsters; they flooded the Canadian labour market and drove down wages; 'very many of them' went 'wrong through hereditary taints'; and they corrupted others with whom they associated, putting them up 'to all sorts of evil habits.' Despite a vigorous personal defence of his own work and, implicitly, that of some of the other organizations, Dr Barnardo himself was completely unable to overcome these unfavourable sentiments. 'The importation of children taken from the reformatories, refuges and workhouses of the old world' the commissioners concluded, was 'fraught with much danger and ... calculated, unless conducted with care and prudence, to swell the ranks of the criminal classes in this country.' They strongly recommended that if the practice were to continue 'such precautions be taken' as would 'effectually prevent the bringing into this country of children of parents known to be criminal,' or of children who had 'spent their whole lives in an atmosphere of vice and crime,' and were 'so saturated with evil' and knew 'so little of good.'[82] In 1892 the federal inspector of penitentiaries argued that 'these street Arabs' speedily returned 'to their old habits, on arriving in Canada, and, as a consequence, became a burden and an expense upon the taxpayers of the Dominion in our reformatories, gaols, and penitentiaries.' Similar charges were made by the Brandon, Manitoba, Assizes in the autumn of 1893.[83]

The federal government responded promptly to these reports and the public outcry that accompanied them.[84] While officers of the Department of the Interior believed that the feeling against the children was 'not justified,' they tightened supervision of the medical inspection which they had made compulsory in 1887.[85] In particular, senior officials recognized the dangers to the whole scheme posed by 'irresponsible adventurers' such as the Reverend W.J. Pady, who, all on his own, gathered up, brought out, and distributed children with no institutions in support of his work on either side of the Atlantic. Despite their efforts and exhortations, however, as late as 1897 departmental officers were still having difficulties with smaller organizations and individuals bringing out young people who had not had a proper medical inspection.[86] Federal officials also made a retrospective examination of the reports made between 1887 and 1892 by its own inspectors. Of the 2494 boys and girls inspected over that period, reported the survey, 'only 19 were described as having dishonest tendencies and these were of such trivial character [that] in not a single instance' was 'it recorded that a child was prosecuted before the Courts.'[87] In an independent study he made in 1891, the chief of the detective staff of the Toronto police force, William Stark, gave strong support to this conclusion.[88] In an additional effort to dampen criticism, the Department of the Interior stopped employing temporary inspectors and directed its regular officers to do the visiting. The report of J.M. McGovern, whose regular job was that of a travelling immigration agent, was representative of those made by permanent officials. While he 'ascertained that there was a very considerable feeling against this class of immigrant' he found it difficult 'to get anyone who was willing to make a direct charge or complaint.' McGovern concluded that the distributing homes 'had been careful in selecting good places for the children, who, in a large majority of cases, were well contented and gave good satisfaction.' He went on to recommend more frequent inspections of the children on the part of the agencies responsible for them.[89] Nevertheless, despite the fact that in the official view 'all the evidence available' indicated 'the good moral standing of the immigrant children,' the campaign against them continued throughout the 1890s.[90]

Typical of the individuals and organizations implacably opposed to the importation of children was the Toronto Trades and Labor Council. As early as 1888, organized labour had complained about the youngsters, but their most effective spokesman was D.J. O'Donoghue of the Toronto council. Not only did he appear before the Ontario Royal Commission, but continued his campaign in the years following its report. As a delegate to the First Ontario Conference on Child-Saving, held in Toronto in October, 1894, for example, O'Donoghue argued that Canadians had enough dependent children of their own to care for without importing more from abroad, that too many of the boys and girls became criminals, and that they not only took 'the place of a native of this country' but took it 'at a less wage than the native would get.'[91] Proponents of the immigration schemes also carried their message to Parliament and various other suitable forums. While the foster parents, the vast majority of whom were farm families, did not enter the debate other than by continuing to request far more children than the organizations could supply, the agencies and their Canadian friends expressed strong and continued public support for the youngsters.[92] At the Ontario Conference on Child-Saving, at least eight delegates, representing seven agencies, were present. Their message was that their children turned out 'as well, if not better than the average Canadian-born child.'[93]

The National Council of Women showed how an organization with a strong interest in children but which initially had no special brief either for or against immigrant youngsters came to use the new ideas to evaluate these young people. In May 1896, the London Local Council of Women presented an elaborate brief in support of its resolution that the National Council 'investigate the effect of the importation of pauper children on the social condition of Canada.' The London document repeated three familiar arguments: first, that some of the immigrants were 'morally unfit to become companions of other children'; second, that because of their 'bad heredity,' they 'must have a bad effect on the race as a whole'; and, third, that those who were permitted to come to Canada should be placed in foster homes not by the agency bringing them from Britain but by the newly formed Children's Aid societies. A seemingly impressive array of evidence bolstered the London council's brief. This material included copies of a petition against the children by the Stratford Grand Jury and another by the council of the County of Grey, Ontario, and letters denouncing the youngsters, supposedly based on professional experience and judgment, from the superintendent of the London Insane Asylum, the medical superintendent of the Rockwood Hospital in Kingston, the superintendent of the Hamilton Asylum for the Insane, the medical superintendent of the Toronto Asylum for the Insane, and the superintendent of the Mercer Reformatory for Females. In anticipation of the debate, the president of the National Council, Lady Aberdeen, asked for precise data on the matter from A.M. Burgess, deputy minister of the interior. In hopes of persuading the delegates that the immigration of juveniles was 'not the unmitigated evil which some of the opponents of the system' had so positively asserted, Burgess prepared a detailed answer to all charges. Despite his efforts, and the persuasive arguments of some delegates, however, the content of the debate indicated that a majority of those present agreed with the London council.

Since the resolution called only for an 'investigation,' even those who spoke warmly in favour of the children were reluctantly able to support it and it eventually passed unanimously.[94] Lady Aberdeen then suggested that local councils collect information on immigrant children and send details of complaints regarding them to Burgess. While the councils in London, Hamilton, Toronto, and Montreal established investigating committees, the others ignored this suggestion.[95] Continuing its crusade, the London council presented a resolution to the next meeting of the national body which called for increased controls and inspection of the children. In comparison to the previous year, however, the discussion in 1897 was both shorter and less heated. Speakers generally agreed that the provisions of Ontario legislation on the matter provided a satisfactory answer to the problem and, with the exception of the negative vote of the Dominion Women's Enfranchisement Association, the resolution passed unanimously.[96]

The debate of the late 1880s and 1890s produced three substantial results. First, both Ontario and Manitoba passed bills which regulated the immigration of children into their provinces.[97] Second, the federal government completely reorganized its administration of the scheme. In addition to the public pressures in Canada and the suggestions of its own agents that inspection procedures be tightened, the department was notified by the Local Government Board in England that both the board and the Poor Law Schools Committee strongly favoured an annual inspection of each child until he or she was sixteen. This suggestion, in turn, grew out of an elaborate investigation which the Poor Law Schools Committee had conducted earlier in the decade.[98] After objecting that such extra inspections were both unnecessary and too expensive, the federal government reluctantly agreed to undertake annual visits at the expense of the Board of Guardians. In order to do the extra work which public opinion, the Ontario and Manitoba legislation, and the agreement made with the British government had forced upon it, the department took the inspections out of the hands of regular immigration officers and in 1900 set up a special division to supervise juvenile immigration.[99] Finally, the number of children coming to Canada again declined temporarily. From a total of 3015 in 1896, the number dropped to only 977 in 1900.[1] It was not until mid decade that immigration levelled off to the pattern, which persisted until the beginning of the First World War, of about 2500 youngsters a year. While English societies objected, as one of them put it, to the necessity of taking seriously enactments of a legislature which not only displayed an 'entire absence of knowledge as to the conditions of English children' but also represented scarcely as many inhabitants as covered by 'any one board of guardians in London,' they complied with them nonetheless.[100]

These changes took the life out of the campaign against importing children into Canada for another two decades. Ontario repealed its legislation. The Commons committee showed no interest in the matter. While the National Council of Women continued to grow and to extend its interest in all matters affecting youngsters between 1900 and 1914, it gave only perfunctory attention to immigrant children.[101] Canadians did not make a major issue of juvenile immigration again until the early 1920s, when J.S. Woodsworth raised it in Parliament, the Trades and Labor Congress thoroughly discussed it, and the Canadian Conference on Child Welfare began a systematic study of the matter.[102]

IV

Were the immigrant children a fair target for those in the child-saving movement and the others who turned their attention on them? In trying to answer this question one can also evaluate one of the early efforts of Canadians to apply their new standards on child care. Certainly, no quick and easy judgment is possible. On the one hand, it is hard to quarrel with the major agencies involved: they believed that the settings from which they took most of the children were so deplorable that almost *any* change was for the better. In addition, their extensive use of foster homes instead of institutions to care for their wards, based on the evangelicals' belief that each child needed individual and personal attention, was in advance of Canadian practice of the time.[103] Indeed, as Kelso himself acknowledged, the Barnardo and other placement programs eventually served as one of the models for Ontario's system of care for neglected and dependent children.[104] Nevertheless, there is little doubt that many of the Canadian homes that took the children looked upon them mostly as a source of inexpensive labour. If we can believe the extensive reports of investigators, most homes treated the children kindly and sometimes with real affection; but it was unrealistic for some of the agencies to argue that love was the primary motive of foster parents. Given these circumstances, critics in both Britain and Canada were surely correct in insisting that the foster homes needed to be much more rigorously selected and more regularly supervised. In terms of effectiveness and efficiency, however, Dr Barnardo's arrangements of the 1890s – which became the model for other societies – were undoubtedly the equal of the newly formed Canadian Children's Aid societies. Over the first two decades of the new century, however, these new societies improved and professionalized their procedures, while the immigration agencies did not. By the time the whole matter became an issue again in the early 1920s the practices of the English agencies had an archaic air about them. 'We differ now with the emigrating agencies,' explained a spokesman for the Ontario Red Cross in 1925, not because they were 'worse or more lax than previously, but because we have learned more about the science of child welfare.'[105] There was some merit in the argument that the agencies were naive in their basic assumption that a change of environment was sufficient in itself in remedying the ills of many of their charges.[106] Their claim that over 95 per cent or more of the children eventually became good Canadian citizens may well have been excessive. '*Not two per cent of his emigrant boys and girls turns out unsatisfactorily*' was the customary claim of Dr Barnardo and his supporters.[107]

How well, then, did the youngsters actually do? Since most of the children involved were undoubtedly reticent about their backgrounds once their indentures had run out and they moved to other parts of the country, evidence on this point is hard to come by, and, because of the high emotional content of the situation, that which is available must be carefully evaluated. A study on immigration commissioned by the Canadian National Committee on Mental Hygiene, published in 1920, made a neutral report on the long-term effects of the immigration of the children.[108] In the mid-1920s, in a document prepared under the guidance of Dr C.K. Clarke, director of the National Committee on Mental Hygiene, the Social Service Department of the Toronto General Hospital reported that between 1917 and 1924 it had dealt with 125 girls who were wards of the Barnardo organization. In preparing what was in effect a brief against admitting immigrant children to Canada, the Executive Committee of the Canadian Council on Child Welfare used some of the data collected by the hospital. According to the report, 77 of the girls worked as domestics and 11 in factories. As to their mental condition, the Social Service Department had not diagnosed 37 of the girls, but of the rest it evaluated only 5 as normal, 77 as mentally defective, and 5 as suffering from dementia praecox. In addition, the department explained, 18 of the girls had had two or more illegitimate children, 36 were prostitutes, 12 had gonorrhoea, 16 had syphilis, 3 had both venereal diseases, and 4 had served terms in custody.[109] In responding to these charges, a Barnardo official noted that of the 740 Barnardo girls emigrating to Canada after the First World War, one had venereal disease, one suffered from tuberculosis, and eleven had 'fallen,' nine of whom were 'back making good.' Since, as the critics immediately pointed out, these figures did not necessarily refer to the same population of youngsters as those in the Toronto General Hospital report, the data did not answer the charges.[110] Some of the findings of the Social Service Department, particularly those dealing with the facts of physical disease, may have been reasonably accurate. Others, and especially those dealing with the mental condition of the girls, must, for reasons which are outlined later, be viewed with a great deal of scepticism.

As a result of this tempest, the Canadian Council on Child Welfare commissioned a study of a sampling of the emigrants. Its investigator examined the records of ninety-eight children who had emigrated to Canada in 1910. Of this total she found that over twenty subsequently got into difficulties of one kind or another. The council's sample, however, was a small one and, because some of the major societies refused to cooperate in the investigation (in part because many of those involved were 'now married ... settled in life and in communities' and would 'resent the interference'), it may not have been representative of the 2500 children who had entered Canada in 1910.[111] Nevertheless, even if it is assumed that the sample was a fair cross-section, one can fairly conclude that the vast majority of the children made satisfactory additions to the Canadian population. Given their origins, early influences, and the minimal standards of child care involved, the record is a good one. Later chapters will indicate whether, in their work with Canadian youngsters, Canadian reformers were any more successful than the English emigration societies.

PART II

'To Create a Strong and Healthy Race': Children in the Public Health Movement, 1880-1920

3

'Our Whole Aim Is Prevention':
Public Health in the Schools,
1880-1914

Of all the reform efforts for children that grew and flourished between the 1880s and the 1920s, the public health movement had the most immediate, the least ambiguous, and the most precisely measurable positive effects on the lives of Canadian children. Over these years an increasing number of private, semi-public, and public organizations tried to improve many facets of public health. They generated their own knowledge and put to use that which was discovered elsewhere. As their numbers and their support increased, Canadian public health workers sharpened the focus of their work. To their initial preoccupation with sanitation as a means of protecting and improving the health of Canadians as a whole, they added the task of identifying particular groups for which they could expect more specialized public health measures to yield worthwhile results. As part of this process they gradually centred their attention upon three aspects of child health: protecting and improving the health of school pupils; reducing mortality amongst infants and young children; and trying to come to grips with what they described as 'feeble-mindedness.' By the end of this era, the public health movement had brought about an undoubted improvement in the health of school-aged children – especially those in urban areas – and was beginning to make large gains against the more stubborn problem of infant mortality. It had also come to regard youngsters as its most important clients. As Hamilton's medical health officer told his fellow members of the Canadian Public Health Association in 1911, their central concern was the 'rising generation' through whom they must 'aim first of all to create a strong and healthy race.'[3]

Canadians moved to improve the public health at a particularly auspicious time. The first secretary of the Ontario Board of Health, Peter H. Bryce, later recalled that 'three wholly remarkable events' took place in 1882: Louis Pasteur proved the effectiveness of immunization for anthrax in sheep, Robert Koch discovered the tuberculosis germ, and Ontario established a board of health.[4] The Ontario Provincial Board of Health was the first permanent public health organization in Canada. Prior to this time, provinces had set up such agencies only on a temporary basis in response to the threat of emergency situations. In 1884, the provincial legislature passed a new measure, based on the English Consolidated Public Health Act of 1875, which greatly strengthened the powers of the Board.[5] Between 1887 and 1909, all other provinces passed legislation similar to that of Ontario. On the basis of this legislation, Canadians began to build a public health movement around a professional core of public health physicians, sanitary inspectors, and, later, public health nurses. These trained workers came to be employed by municipal and provincial boards of health and, to a lesser extent, school boards and provincial departments of education.[6]

Initially this new movement was able to build upon the achievements of nineteenth-century improvements in sanitation. Moreover, because provincial and municipal boards of health were new institutions, not tied by tradition to any past procedures, they could nurture the characteristic enthusiasm of the first generation of reform enterprises. This freedom and enthusiasm enabled them to incorporate easily into their practices many of the dramatic bacteriological discoveries of the last two decades of the nineteenth century. In Canada, children and infants thus became the principal, although by no means the only, beneficiaries of many of the medical discoveries made in the battle against communicable diseases.

When Canadians began to understand, as the Ontario minister of education explained in 1880, that prevention of disease could be made 'more certain than the curing of the disease itself,' those interested in public health naturally focused their attention on the school. Here was an institution not only under public control but one that the state was gradually compelling one whole age group to attend. Because school-aged children were conveniently grouped together, they were much easier to get at for examination, treatment, and propagandizing than their preschool counterparts. Health workers also discovered that youngsters were more likely to catch diphtheria and other infectious diseases at school than anywhere else. In this regard, as the state gradually enforced compulsory schooling it was obliged, the Ontario Board of Health argued, to aid rather than hinder 'the physical and mental growth of our children.'[7]

In the first phase of their effort, from the 1880s to the early years of the twentieth century, health officers made sanitation the school's first line of defence against disease. In 1883, the Ontario Board of Health noted that many schoolrooms in the province were 'in a very unsanitary condition' and that 'neglect of precautions to prevent the spread of contagious and infectious diseases, overcrowding and many other causes of diseases' were common. The board therefore directed school and health officials to enforce minimum standards pertaining to site, ventilation, heating, water supply, sewage system, furniture, cleanliness, and age of buildings. To prevent the spread of tuberculosis, its Committee on School Hygiene set a minimum standard of 500 cubic feet of air space per pupil.[8] It was, however, one thing for a board of health to set minimum sanitary standards and quite another to persuade local school boards to apply them. In 1891, the secretary recorded in the minutes of a rural school meeting in the London area that a vote was taken 'of those present how they feel on ventilating the schoolhouse. Twenty-eight against it and one for it.'[9] In rural areas the battle against filth continued to be an unremitting one. As late as 1920, a rural medical health officer in Nova Scotia explained that of thirty schoolhouses he had recently visited, only one had satisfactory toilets, and in no less than twenty-eight of them 'urine and feces were over the seats and floors.'[10] Even urban school systems were slow to implement the new sanitary standards. In 1897, teachers, parents, and pupils directed many complaints to the local trustees about sanitary conditions in Victoria schools. The state of Toronto schools at the turn of the century provoked sharp debate in that city.[11]

If disease breached these modest and ineffectively enforced sanitary barriers, then regulations which excluded infected children from school formed the next line of defence for both pupils and the wider community. After suffering through a particularly widespread diphtheria epidemic in 1886, Ontario decided to compel parents, teachers, and health officials to report cases of 'smallpox, cholera, scarlatina, diphtheria, whooping cough, measles, mumps, glanders or other contagious diseases'; it forbade children with these diseases or their families to associate with other children and excluded them from school.[12] When they faced substantial outbreaks of infectious diseases, local school and health officials characteristically responded by closing schools entirely until the contagion declined. Public health workers initially faced both apathy and outright opposition in their efforts to control such diseases.

In the century since Jenner's work of 1796–1800, medical workers had demonstrated time and again the efficacy of vaccination against smallpox. As recently as the epidemic of 1885, Canadians saw how, by means of a well-organized and vigorously pursued campaign of vaccination and quarantine, Ontario kept its deaths from smallpox to 84 while in Montreal alone 3175 people died of the disease.[13] In most provinces school trustees had the power to exclude unvaccinated children from school. Except when faced by an actual outbreak of smallpox, however, such as the one in British Columbia in 1892, trustees were extremely reluctant to enforce vaccination regulations.[14] In 1911 the Toronto

School Board refused to enforce compulsory vaccination laws and the Ottawa Board of Health took the same stand in 1912.[15] In 1920, Saskatchewan health officials found that very few school-aged children had been vaccinated.[16]

Public health officials also worked for changes in curriculum which would support their objectives. They tried to interest teachers in public health and to ensure that recruits to the profession had proper grounding in physiology, hygiene, and public health.[17] They argued that hygiene, physiology, and, later, physical culture should be compulsory subjects.[18] The nature of such instruction when it was given was well characterized by the health textbook that explained that to 'eat or drink what we know is unhealthful, because it tastes good' was 'not only foolish but wicked.'[19]

In the two decades after the turn of the century, an astonishing growth in medical science, especially in bacteriology, wrought radical changes in preventive health work for Canadian school children. From the early 1880s onward, rapidly expanding and worldwide research efforts fed into the public health movement substantial quantities of new knowledge and clinical procedures based on this knowledge, and began to change public expectations regarding disease. For a variety of reasons, too, this 'golden age' of bacteriology placed children amongst its principal beneficiaries.[20]

In this new context, Canadians established two specialized health services for children: one for infants and the other for those attending school. Since diphtheria found its main victims amongst school-aged children, a summary of the highlights of the battle to overcome it provides an excellent example of the intimate and extremely complex connection between bacteriology and the health of the young. As the Ontario Board of Health reported in 1892, not only was diphtheria 'peculiarly liable to attack with malignity children under ten years,' but also 'no single cause' contributed 'so largely to the dissemination and continuance of this pest as the introduction of its contagion in the schoolroom.'[21]

The fight against diphtheria proceeded almost simultaneously on a number of different fronts. While scientists and physicians developed practical applications of a series of laboratory discoveries, public health officers were hard at work explaining to colleagues, to physicians in private practice, and to the general public precisely what they had learned and persuading, cajoling, and occasionally coercing them to use this new knowledge. Between 1884 and 1894, French, German, and American bacteriologists – particularly Friedrich Loeffler, Emile Roux, Alexandre Yersin, Karl Fraenke, Emil von Behring, and W.H. Park – made the discoveries which gradually led to the control of diphtheria. They proved, first, that a powerful, soluble toxin produced by the Klebs-Loeffler bacillus caused the general symptoms of diphtheria, and that convalescents and even well persons could infect others with the disease. Second, they demonstrated that laboratories could use the blood of animals (especially horses) to produce an antitoxin that was an effective agent against cases of diphtheria. Finally, they showed that the antitoxin also prevented diphtheria from developing in persons who had been exposed to the disease.[22] Three practical results flowed from these discoveries. First, with proof that diphtheria was what scientists then defined as a 'zymotic' disease – that is, a contagious disease caused by a morbid agent through a process akin to fermentation – public health officials took responsibility for controlling it. Second, physicians began to use laboratory tests both to diagnose accurately cases of diphtheria and to govern the quarantine period for those with the disease and their relatives who had been incarcerated with them. Third, doctors began to use antitoxin to treat both diagnosed cases of diphtheria and those who had been exposed to the disease. Since the Ontario Board of Health had established a laboratory in 1890, it was able to conduct tests for diphtheria and to produce antitoxin almost as quickly as those undertaken by the pioneer of this effort in North America, the New York City Public Health Department.[23] By 1899, Ontario's use of antitoxin had produced a notable decline in diphtheria deaths in that province.[24] By 1905, the decline was clearly worldwide.[25]

As health workers embarked on a crusade against diphtheria, they encountered problems with physicians and parents. Hamilton's medical health officer, Dr W.F. Langrill, demonstrated that his fellow physicians could be a major difficulty. 'Just recently,' he reported in 1901, 'a child died from what the attending physician called laryngitis ...' Suspicious of this diagnosis, Langrill interviewed the doctor, who claimed the disease was not diphtheria, but admitted that two children in the same family had exhibited symptoms that were consistent with a diagnosis of diphtheria. Meanwhile the child's family conducted a public funeral for their son, using 'small boys acting as pallbearers.' As a result of this negligence, Langrill concluded, five neighbouring children came down with severe cases of diphtheria.[26] In contrast to Langrill's cautionary tale, the medical superintendent of the Vancouver Children's Aid Society, Dr A.P. Procter, showed how effective the new treatment could be. In the spring of 1910, five cases of diphtheria – two very serious – appeared amongst the more than eighty children in the society's home. Procter immediately immunized children and staff with antitoxin, which, he concluded, 'completely and immediately controlled the outbreak.'[27] Families of infected children also stood in the way of effective control of the disease; although children placed in isolation hospitals stood a better chance of surviving than those cared for at home, parents were often very reluctant and had to be forced to take this step by the health officers.

Recalcitrant parents and physicians, however, were not the only problem; through long experience Canadian public health workers came to believe that only if they distributed free antitoxin would physicians and families use it as early, as frequently, and as widely as was necessary to exploit its full potentiality as a means for controlling the disease. In 1907, the Ontario Board of Health decided to make antitoxin available 'free of charge for use in the case of indigent or poor patients.'[28] In 1914, the province began to distribute diphtheria antitoxin as well as other biological products from its own laboratories at prices much below commercial ones. Two years later, the Ontario government made these products free to everyone.[29] In 1917, the Saskatchewan Bureau of Public Health began to distribute free antitoxin in that province. According to the bureau this practice had a dramatic impact on the incidence of diphtheria: the number of cases in the province dropped from 1005 in 1917 to 776 in 1918 and 278 in 1919. Further, during the first full year 'of free distribution of antitoxin ... the percentage of mortality from diphtheria was reduced from 16 per cent to 9.2 per cent ...' Even so, the death rate from the disease remained at about 8 per cent of cases because, as the bureau lamented, people failed to recognize the symptoms 'in the early stage when if anti-toxin were freely used the death rate would be negligible.'[30]

While the public health movement gradually implemented the results of early bacteriological discoveries, medical researchers continued to investigate the disease. By using the Schick test, devised in 1913, physicians could sort out in older children those susceptible to diphtheria from those who had developed an immunity to it. To the former, they could then give toxin-antitoxin to build up their immunity to the disease.[31] By the early 1920s Canadian public health authorities and physicians were beginning to use both procedures fairly regularly. The campaign against diphtheria had positive, measurable effects on the disease. In Ontario, the death rate for the disease fell from 31 of every 100,000 of population in 1903 to 12 in 1918.[32] A worldwide decline in the morbidity and mortality of the disease – a long-term product of improving sanitation – accounted for part of this drop.[33] Increasingly widespread use of antitoxin and vigorous searching out of cases by school and other medical inspectors did the rest. As toxin-antitoxin gradually provided children with permanent immunity from the disease, the incidence of diphtheria in the Canadian population fell from 76.7 per 100,000 of population in 1926 to 57.1 in 1931, 18.6 in 1936, 24.9 in 1941, to 20.7 in 1946, 1.8 in 1851, 0.8 in 1956, and 0.3 in 1972.[34]

Since it contrasted so sharply with the plodding progression characteristic of improvements in sanitation, the very momentum with which one bacteriological discovery followed upon another, and the speedy and dramatic way in which many of them displayed their effects, helped to improve child health. The rapid series of discoveries seem, indeed, to have been at the root of the missionary zeal and the sometimes almost millennial expectations of many health workers. Their enthusiasm quickly spread to the general public as well, raising the level of popular expectation. 'One cannot read the daily papers,' reported the Public Health Committee of the National Council of Women in 1911, 'without being struck by the amount of knowledge and interest of the community in matters of public health and in the enforcement of by-laws governing same.'[35] Not all Canadians, of course, were caught up in the enthusiasm. In dealing with a diphtheria epidemic in Oshawa in 1920, the district medical health officer had great difficulty in persuading the local board of health and the school board to agree that 'all school children should have an immunizing dose of Antitoxin.'[36]

School pupils were the first group of children to reap benefits from bacteriological discoveries. As their knowledge increased, public health workers sorted out two very obvious weaknesses in the school health arrangements that they had set up over the last two decades of the nineteenth century. First, while a physician or a sanitary inspector decided whether or not a particular school met minimum sanitary standards, the teacher had the far more difficult task of deciding that one of the pupils had an infectious disease. Especially when the school itself was an important centre for the spread of controllable diseases, it was obviously no longer sufficient to rely on teachers or private physicians to locate and quarantine infected children. In the summer and early autumn of 1903, the local public health officer traced an outbreak of diphtheria in Ingersoll, Ontario, to the local public school. Although the town had but one case of the disease in July, and none in August, the opening of schools brought twelve cases in September and sixteen in October. Second, even when teacher or family physician accurately diagnosed infectious disease and kept the child out of school, the community had very little assurance that his family would provide him with the necessary treatment, that they would protect themselves from the infection, or that the child would not, outside of school hours, pass the disease on to his friends and acquaintances. 'Many parents,' wrote the London, Ontario, medical health officer, showed 'an utter disregard of the golden rule.'[37]

To solve these problems, public health officers concluded that they should inspect and visit pupils as well as schools. In 1901, the Windsor, Ontario, School Board required that children who had been away for over a week be examined by their family physicians or the medical health officer before they could return to school. But this step, worthwhile as it probably was (it did bring a dramatic improvement in school attendance), focused on the wrong end of the problem; doctors examined children only after a disease had run, or almost run, its course. By the turn of the century, the Ontario Board of Health concluded that the next stage in the control of infectious diseases in children was, at least during emergencies, to have 'physicians visit the schools to examine for suspects ... and to follow up the absentees to their homes ...'[38]

Once Canadians decided to take this step, contemporary efforts in Europe, Britain, and the United States provided them with plenty of models to follow. While the French had discussed medical inspection of school children as early as the end of the eighteenth century, it was not until the last three decades of the nineteenth that any nation tried to implement such ideas. Regular medical inspection had begun in Brussels' schools as early as 1874; it was required throughout Sweden in 1878 and in Paris in 1879. Early efforts made in Britain and particularly in the United States, however, were the major influences on what happened in Canada.[39] In the sanitary phase of the public health movement, provincial, state, or national agencies generally took the initiative. In contrast, and probably because the problems were more clearly seen in the cities than in the countryside, municipal authorities in urban centres led the way in introducing school medical inspection in Canada as well as England and the United States. In 1890, the London School Board appointed the first school medical officer in Britain and other boards gradually followed suit. Their pioneering work eventually led to national legislation that encouraged local school authorities to undertake regular medical inspection of school children.[40]

In the face of an epidemic of diphtheria in 1894, Boston established North America's first school medical inspection system. The next year Philadelphia and Chicago took the same step.[41] The New York City Department of Public Health, however, created the scheme which became the most influential model for Canadian practice. In 1897, the department appointed 150 physicians as part-time school medical inspectors. Dr Hermann Biggs explained to a meeting of the British Medical Association in Montreal later the same year that he directed the doctors to inspect, each day, the children that teachers excluded from class and to send home every pupil suffering from any form of contagious disease.[42] In 1902, Biggs added two new steps to the procedures. First, he required school physicians to make a routine examination, every seven to ten days, of all pupils for contagious disease and minor infections of eyes or skin. Second, yielding to the persuasion of Lillian D. Wald of the Henry Street Settlement, he appointed a corps of school nurses. A year later, the department claimed that school nursing was so successful in dealing with pediculosis, minor communicable diseases, and eye infections that it had reduced pupil exclusions on account of illness by 98 per cent. In 1905, Biggs further broadened the scope of the school medical system in New York by instructing the doctors to examine children for non-contagious physical defects, and to notify parents of any they found. The department soon discovered, however, that parents went on to correct only a very small proportion – about 6 per cent – of the defects reported to them. To deal with this situation and other problems of child health, the New York Board of Health established a separate Division of Child Hygiene. In September 1908, nurses began to call on the homes of all children discovered to be suffering from physical defects in order to persuade the parents to provide the necessary treatment. One year later, the department claimed that already the nurses' visits had raised the level of treatment from 6 to 83 per cent.[43]

To learn at first hand about European and British activities, Canadians attended both the second and third medical congresses on school hygiene, where delegates from all over the world reported on, discussed, and evaluated the latest developments in the field.[44] Canadian organizations also brought out English officials to explain what they did.[45] More often, Canadians measured their early efforts against American systems. Dr Peter Bryce argued that in operating school medical inspection, Canadians should copy the example of New York.[46] In outlining the aims for medical inspection in public schools in Canada, an editorial in the *Public Health Journal* used only American experience as its evidence.[47]

In 1906, under the aegis of the municipal Board of Health, Montreal began the first regular and systematic medical inspection of school pupils in Canada.[48] The following year the Sydney, Nova Scotia, medical health officer began to inspect school pupils on an annual basis. In the same year, the Vancouver School Board appointed a physician as full-time medical inspector of school children and the Hamilton board appointed Canada's first school nurse. That year, also, Ontario passed legislation that permitted school boards, if they wanted to, to undertake school medical inspections.[49] By the end of 1910, Halifax, Lachine, Toronto, Brantford, Winnipeg, Edmonton, and Nelson, British Columbia, in addition to the four communities already noted, made some form of medical inspection of their pupils.

Though beginning late, the Toronto School Board rapidly surpassed the others and erected one of the most comprehensive and widely reported school medical systems in the world. As such, it quickly became the model for many other Canadian communities. Starting about 1906, the Toronto Local Council of Women and other groups tried to persuade local health and school officials to introduce the practice into the city's schools.[50] In this endeavour they met the very firm opposition of Dr Charles Sheard, Toronto's chief medical officer, who believed that school medical inspection was 'a pure fad, instituted principally by women,' who were 'apt to give way to sentiment' and listened 'to the talk of agitators' who wanted 'easy billets for their friends, with good pay and little work.'[51] In 1910, John Ross Robertson, publisher of the Toronto *Telegram* and life-long worker for child health, entered the affair. Robertson investigated how New York and other places managed school nursing and medical inspection, then wrote a series of reports on the subject for his newspaper and offered $2500 to the Toronto School Board to pay the costs of a nursing experiment for a year. In deciding early the same year to conduct a medical survey to discover the number of mentally defective children in the schools of Toronto, the school board had already demonstrated its own growing interest in health matters.[52] Robertson's intervention apparently convinced the board that it would have to begin medical inspections. It turned down Robertson's offer, but on 25 February 1910, by-passing the municipal Board of Health, it put $2500 in the year's estimates for medical inspection. Very soon thereafter it hired Lina Rogers as its first school nurse and soon-to-be director of school nursing.[53] Miss Rogers, a graduate of the Hospital for Sick Children in Toronto and later of the Royal Victoria Hospital in Montreal, had been New York's first school nurse and was superintendent of school nurses from 1902 to 1908; in 1909, she organized a school nursing system in Pueblo, Colorado.[54] Once the health inspections were under way, the Toronto School Board rapidly expanded its school medical system. By 1914, the School Health Department cared for 45,000 Toronto pupils with a staff of one chief medical officer, twenty-one physicians who worked as part-time medical inspectors, one dental inspector and four dental surgeons who worked part time, one superintendent of nurses, and thirty-seven full-time school nurses.

In 1914, the *Public Health Journal* surveyed the extent and nature of school medical work in Canada.[55] In the three Maritime provinces, only four Nova Scotia communities – Amherst, Halifax, Truro, and Sydney – reported that they conducted any form of school medical inspection. In Quebec, the cities of Montreal, Westmount, and Lachine inspected their pupils. In Ontario, fourteen communities – Toronto, Ottawa, Kingston, London, Brantford, Niagara Falls, Brockville, Saulte Ste Marie, Steelton, North Middlesex, Hamilton, Peterborough, Stratford, and Fort William – had instituted the practice.[56] In the prairie provinces, the cities of Winnipeg, Regina, Saskatoon, Prince Albert, Calgary, and Edmonton inspected their youngsters. Under the terms of British Columbia's legislation, passed in 1910, which called for an annual inspection of all school pupils, teachers, and janitors in the province, medical inspectors worked in Victoria, Vancouver, Nelson, New Westminster, and South Vancouver.[57] Other communities across Canada reported that they were seriously considering instituting school medical inspection.

School and public health authorities could put their responses to the *Journal* into the context of twenty years of North American and about eight years of Canadian experience in this matter. Partly because they had been able to build effectively on American efforts, Canadian workers had accumulated a surprisingly wide range of practical experience over a short time. Such urban centres as Toronto, Regina, Montreal, and Vancouver operated inspection systems which were as comprehensive and thorough as the very best described by the Russell Sage Foundation survey of American efforts in the field.[58] One may, therefore, appropriately ask of the 1914 reports and other contemporary Canadian material three important questions: what were school and health workers actually trying to do through school medical inspection; what means did they use to accomplish their task; and how effective were they in reaching their goals?

In common with their British and American counterparts, Canadian school medical workers and their supporters found that the very nature of what they did shifted them away from their initial goal of controlling disease to a more positive one of ensuring that the children were all in rude good health. The function of school medical systems, explained Lina Rogers, was 'not simply to cure the ills we have already acquired, but our whole aim is "prevention." We want to build up a nation whose men and women will be physically and mentally sound.'[59] To bring about this condition, most school health workers would have agreed that a proper school medical program detected contagious disease, discovered physical defects in pupils, made the school 'the most sanitary place in the community,' inculcated hygienic habits in young people, provided for their physical training, and improved the methods and materials of health instruction.[60] Physicians and nurses viewed this task as an uphill one for not only were children naturally dirty in their habits but also in the years when they were most susceptible to contagious disease they mingled with each other most intimately without 'any degrees of nicety in their personal habits.'[61]

By 1914, many urban centres had shifted the focus of their public health work in schools from premises to pupils. To control communicable disease, health professionals regularly inspected school buildings and examined pupils, teachers, and janitors. Instead of the teachers having to do so, physicians or nurses now excluded sick pupils and readmitted those who had recovered. In Ottawa, the school physician checked the children for scarlet fever, diphtheria, tonsilitis, measles, German measles, mumps, smallpox, chicken pox, whooping cough, ring worms, contagious skin diseases, and pediculosis. In Vancouver, Edmonton, Calgary, Winnipeg, Toronto, Montreal, and Halifax, physicians inspected the pupils. In Regina, Prince Albert, Kingston, and Niagara Falls, school nurses made the initial inspections.[62] In some places, physicians conducted their examination *en masse*. The South Vancouver medical inspector reported that pupils were 'brought into the teacher's room apart from the class-rooms in groups of ten, boys and girls separate.'[63] Although medical inspectors in British Columbia were supposed to examine teachers and janitors for infectious diseases annually, there and elsewhere they seem to have made such inspections only on initial appointment. Since these were the years in which the great crusade against tuberculosis was growing rapidly inspectors showed particular interest in this disease.[64] Toronto placed one assistant medical officer in charge of tuberculosis inspection and in 1913 the city opened up a 'forest' school for pretubercular and other sickly children.[65] Other centres, such as Hamilton and Vancouver, instituted 'open air' classrooms for the same group.[66] In all areas, school nurses gave particular attention to locating tubercular children and those who were 'contacts.'[67]

Most inspectors also looked for chronic defects. As the examiner in North Middlesex put it, 'the body of the school child was considered a machine in order to answer the question, "is it in good running order?"'[68] In Regina, the school nurse examined 'particularly for defective eyesight, defective hearing, enlarged tonsils and adenoids, carious teeth, pediculosis, for symptoms of tuberculosis, lateral curvature, goitre, and chorea.'[69] Generally, as the Nelson, British Columbia, medical inspector explained, her duty in such cases began and ended 'with recommendation for treatment' and she customarily notified parents 'requesting them to take the child to the family physician.'[70]

The incidence of inspection varied greatly from place to place. Probably the most thoroughly examined pupils were those of Toronto: there each child was inspected by a school nurse every two weeks and by a school physician four times every year. In other centres, such as Regina and Edmonton, a physician or school nurse inspected all the pupils twice every year. In many centres, such as most of those places having inspections in British Columbia, in Winnipeg, Lachine, and Sydney, an inspector examined each child only once each year. Often the main task of the doctor was to deal with those pupils referred to him by the school nurse or teacher. In Montreal, physicians visited large schools every day and small schools at least twice a week to examine such referrals. In Kingston, a school nurse visited each school twice each week and inspected all the pupils in their classrooms every two weeks.

Such a bewildering array of practices, only sampled here, obviously reflected local differences in what the school or health board knew or believed about child health and preventive medicine, how much interest they had in the matter, and how much they felt the local taxpayer would pay for. It also clearly demonstrated that the public health movement had not yet developed an optimum pattern of inspection and referral, or divided the task between physician and nurse in such a way that the skills and time of both were used effectively and efficiently. Nevertheless, by 1914 the school nurse was clearly moving into the central position in school medical programs. It was she more than anyone else who actually enlarged the scope of public health work for school children. As she moved between school and home she found of necessity that she had to add preventive medicine, teaching, and even social welfare to her primary task of controlling the spread of communicable disease. In the school, she did some or all of the routine inspections, examinations, re-admissions, and often minor first aid work as well. She kept up the medical records of the pupils, taught health to teachers and pupils through lectures, demonstrations, nose-blowing and tooth-brushing drills, and ran school health clubs like the Little Nurses League in Winnipeg, or Little Mothers classes in Regina, Vancouver, Victoria, and Stratford. In most places, however, her main task was to visit the home of the sick pupil who had been excluded from school and of the child who had an untreated chronic condition. Often, these early home visits opened the school nurse's eyes as to just how much there was to do.[71] In Regina, Jean Browne found during her home visits that some mothers did not even 'know how to make a simple mustard plaster.'[72] Particularly on visits to poor homes, nurses found children who were in urgent need of medical attention. They kept a sharp eye out for all cases of infectious diseases, especially those that parents were trying to conceal. In Lachine, the medical inspector discovered contagious diseases in 17 per cent of the 751 homes he visited over one school year.[73]

When they saw how fruitful such work could be, school and health boards directed nurses to exploit to the full the wider opportunities opened up by home visits. While the school nurse was in the home, explained Lina Rogers, she became 'a friendly adviser of the parents' who was often able to reform their health habits. Nurses reported unsanitary conditions to the health department, and gave advice on diet and ventilation to the parents of incipient cases of tuberculosis. They gathered data to pass on to those who provided food, clothing, eye glasses, and such other free services which were available to the needy.[74]

When their powers of persuasion proved to be insufficient, school nurses in Toronto and other cities used the juvenile courts to coerce the parents. When the Toronto court fined some parents for refusing to carry out school medical officers' orders for operations 'on children suffering from adenoids and enlarged tonsils,' the editor of the *Public Health Journal* argued that 'parents must not be allowed to stand in the way of their children's complete recovery ...'[75]

As physicians and nurses sorted out their separate roles in school health services, Canadian dentists began to argue that they too had an important place in any comprehensive program. In coming to this decision they were following in the footsteps of their pioneering colleague, Dr John G. Adams of Toronto. In the late nineteenth century, Adams had established a 'dental hospital' for the children of the poor.[76] In 1896, he reported that his own extensive surveys and similar work in Britain and Germany pointed to the fact that children's teeth decayed 'at a much earlier period than they did formerly' and that the teeth and mouths of 'a large percentage' of children were 'in a very unhealthy and often disgusting condition.' To correct this situation, Adams called for regular dental inspection in the schools. Although a committee of the Ontario Board of Health recommended that local boards of health and school trustees appoint dental inspectors to examine the teeth of pupils, nothing came of the matter until nearly fifteen years later.[77] Then, in November 1910, at the last of a series of public meetings in Ontario, Dr John W. Dowd, formerly of Toronto and more recently inspector of schools in Toledo, Ohio, addressed a dinner held in his honour by the Toronto Dental Society. This impressive public occasion culminated a campaign by the society 'to have a dental inspector appointed ... to instruct teachers and pupils how to take care of their teeth and mouths to the end that length of life and happiness may be increased.'[78] In his address Dowd ingeniously argued that if one assumed that 'the dental surface in the ordinary mouth is from 22 to 24 square inches' and only 8 per cent of this area was properly cared for, then there was left '5 square feet of uncleaned surface in every schoolroom.' If this area were visible to the naked eye, Dowd went on, 'there would be a panic,' but because it was not pupils continued to spread disease by 'breathing everywhere, coughing everywhere, expectorating nearly everywhere.'[79] In 1911, an editorial in the *Public Health Journal* claimed that 'fully 99 per cent' of children were 'in need of dental treatment.'[80]

The activities of the Toronto society were the most active Canadian manifestation of what its promoters called the 'oral hygiene crusade.'[81] This campaign, which began in Germany in the closing decades of the nineteenth century, had a variety of roots in contemporary dentistry. A new generation of better-trained professional practitioners displayed a growing concern for preventive work. Some of the excitement and sense of imminent accomplishment which the bacteriological discoveries gave to medicine in these years spilled over into dentistry as well. Finally, dentists were anxious to demonstrate that their craft was rising to become one of the important professions of the modern community.[82]

These factors alone, however, could not account for the successes achieved by the dental movement. On one hand, behind all the exaggeration and the somewhat self-seeking quality of the campaign, there was a serious situation. The pioneers of medical inspection were appalled at the dreadful state of the teeth of the children they examined. In his annual report for 1911, the Montreal health officer explained that 19,843 of the 59,685 children his department had examined over the year suffered from decayed teeth.[83] On the other hand, the public support for the school to inspect and even to treat children's teeth which revealed itself in the Toronto dinner was but another example of the sharp rise in the standards which Canadians were applying to the care of children. Dentists in the crusade offered little evidence that the teeth of Canadian children were then any worse than they had ever been. In contrast, however, to their response to Adams' alarms in 1896, by 1910 some Canadians were clearly willing to do something about the situation. Despite the enthusiasm of the dental profession for a separate school dental service, and the model for one which Toronto and later Vancouver provided, however, it was the school nurse who eventually undertook most preventive dentistry in the school. She examined teeth, persuaded parents to have caries treated, demonstrated the proper use of the tooth brush, conducted tooth-brushing drills, sometimes provided children with free tooth brushes, and often arranged for free treatment for poor and indigent children.[84]

Although after the turn of the century school health campaigners gave their main effort to developing inspection systems, they continued in this era of rapid population growth to try to improve school design, lighting, sanitation, and ventilation and to have 'health' taught as a school subject.[85] Particularly in the cities, but also in areas erecting buildings larger than one or two classrooms, new standards devised by engineers and architects had considerable influence on school design.[86] In 1906, the Vancouver School Board boasted that as a result of its new fan system its pupils breathed 'purer and fresher air' than they could obtain 'in their own homes.'[87] In many rural areas, on the other hand, the problems remained the same as those faced by the public health pioneers of the 1880s. In 1916, Thomas J. McNally, a medical health officer in Ontario, reported that 'perhaps the most delicate problem confronting the local medical officer' in rural areas was school sanitation. It dovetailed, he said, 'into the duties of school trustees, the public school inspector, and the teacher,' while at the same time it touched 'that most sensitive organ, the ratepayer's pocket book.'[88]

Health reformers had more luck with the school curriculum. In an action typical of such occasions, the 1910 annual meeting of the Manitoba Medical Association called for compulsory hygiene teaching both in the schools and in teacher training programs.[89] The next year, a prominent Winnipeg doctor collaborated in the writing of a new health text for Manitoba schools.[90] Concentrating on 'the life of the body' and the means 'by which it can be preserved in a state of high efficiency,' the authors suggested a number of health experiments which children could perform. The book was very much better than nineteenth century examples of the genre; in the opinion of one reviewer, it presented 'life facts, beautifully, simply and most interestingly told.' Eventually, British Columbia, Alberta, Saskatchewan, Manitoba, Quebec, Nova Scotia, and Prince Edward Island authorized its use in their schools.

Public health workers, school officials, and school and health board members often expressed their pleasure with the early results of the medical inspection of Canadian school children. While one may fairly ask whether the effects of what they did supported these generally subjective feelings on the matter, two difficulties stand in the way of a precise and accurate answer to this question. First, as the example of diphtheria showed, the vigorous pursuit of this disease by medical inspectors was perhaps only the most important of a number of factors which initiated its decline. Second, Canadian school medical systems neither subjected their early work to rigorous scientific analysis nor did they keep the kinds of records which would permit others to do so. In their speeches, articles, and official reports on the topic, Canadians generally took as given the fact that foreign and Canadian centres already inspecting their pupils had fully proved the value of the practice. Such statements of worth as they did offer were general ones explaining, as did the British Columbia Board of Health, that there could be 'no doubt of the progress ... being made' by means of medical inspection.[91] Health statistics recorded without analysis such items as the number of classrooms and pupils that they had inspected over the year, and the number and types of defects they had discovered. In 1918, the Calgary School Board reported, its medical inspector conducted 950 physical examinations, and its school nurses made 3862 inspections and visited 969 classes and 219 homes. In addition, the board's eye, ear, nose, and throat clinic tested 4981 pupils and treated 392 eye cases, 72 ear cases, and 52 nose and throat cases; its dental clinic treated 522 children, performing 1041 dental operations on them.[92] Such reports showed that the public health movement felt no strong need to scientifically justify what it did but instead saw its main tasks as extending inspection to areas where it did not yet exist and expanding the scope of the service where it did.

Nevertheless, the movement offered a great deal of not very precise though definite evidence that medical inspection was an effective device for the improvement of public health generally and the health of children in particular. Montreal, with the longest experience in the work, made consistent though low-keyed claims as to the worth of what it did. Three years after the city began the practice, Mrs J.N. Smillie reported that medical inspection had sharply decreased the incidence of contagious diseases in the city's schools and particularly that 'no serious epidemic of measles, scarlet fever or diphtheria' had occurred 'since the installation of regular inspection ...'[93] In 1914, the Montreal Board of Health concluded that school medical inspection had almost eliminated pediculosis and scabies from the schools and had sharply reduced the incidence of infectious diseases in the city. The board was so pleased with these and other results of its work that in 1918 it organized a separate division of child hygiene for Montreal schools.[94]

Elsewhere, medical inspectors also reported many positive results of their work. In an entirely typical statement, the school medical inspector for Saint John, New Brunswick, reported, four years after beginning the work in that city, that there had been 'a great lessening of the number of more serious conditions found in the school.' The effect of this change, he went on, was to make his work increasingly 'preventive as well as curative.' Of the physical defects calling for reports to parents he found that, in 70 per cent of cases, they were 'promptly attended to' and even in poorer districts he obtained this percentage of treatment 'eventually by following up and rectifying the cases.'[95] By the early 1920s most health officials would have concurred with the conclusion on school medical inspection reached by the chief medical officer for New Brunswick, Dr George G. Melvin. Although no public health activity in his province presented such difficulties and involved 'so great a direct expenditure,' he wrote, yet in view of what was 'possible to accomplish, and the outstanding importance of that accomplishment,' the province just had to overcome the difficulties.[96]

By the time the nation went to war in 1914, public health workers and their supporters had persuaded urban Canadians of the undoubted merits of maintaining sanitary schools and of medically inspecting school children. While reformers had taken a long time to implement sanitary standards, in only fifteen years they had popularized the idea of inspection to the extent that most urban school systems in Canada either inspected their pupils or were about to begin. In their school medical services members of the public health movement firmly believed that they had developed and demonstrated the worth of a practical and effective way of making Canada a healthier and happier nation. By this time, too, many workers were eager to take what they saw as the next obvious step in their efforts, that of extending their service to all the children in small towns and country districts. When pediatrician Alan Brown observed, however, that Canadian child care materials gave him 'the impression that they were not intended for use outside the city limits' he put his finger on a major flaw in the whole public health apparatus.[97]

As they began to tackle rural work systematically, public health officers first discovered that they had to shift their principal sphere of activity from the municipal to the provincial level of government. Next, and far more important, they found that they had to subsume the school medical inspection campaign under what had been a distinctly separate crusade to protect and improve the health of infants and young children. At this point, the effort to improve the health of school children ceased to be a separate entity in the public health movement and became but one part of a much wider campaign to improve the health of all Canadian children.

4

'Education ... Carried on Principally in the Home': The Campaign to Reduce Infant Mortality, 1895-1920

Within a few paces of the main gate to the cemetery in New Westminster, British Columbia, a representative headstone, that of the Ladner family, records: 'Lena Aged 21 Days / Freddy Aged 1 year 1 month / Edith Aged 3 Years 11 Mos / Ella Aged 3 Years 10 Mos.' Nearby stones record similar family tragedies. Thomas and Martha Bradshaw Allen, both natives of Madoc, Ontario, had three children. The first born, George, lived to middle age, but his sister, Martha, born 25 December 1881, and his brother, Thomas, born 30 July 1883, died two days apart in March 1885. Charles, the son of Robert and Maggie Anderson died on 29 June 1878 'Aged 3 mos. 13 days.' After expressing New Westminster's sympathies to the Andersons, the local newspaper continued its report of the event in verse:

> Gather pale flowers, a spirit has fled,
> Twine Cypress garlands, the baby is dead.
> Fold the white fingers, close its blue eyes,
> Angels have carried the gem to the skies.[2]

The single issue of the New Westminster *British Columbian* for Wednesday, 28 March 1883 – when the city had a population of about 1500 – listed the deaths of Charles Digby, 'aged 3 years and 7 months,' Bertha Shiles, 'aged 3 years,' and Alexander Coutis, 'aged 3 months.'

What headstones and newspaper obituaries did not report, however, was how Canadians looked upon a rate of deaths which, from the vantage point of three generations later when infant mortality has sunk to less than 20 per 1000, was exceedingly high. At the turn of the century, indeed, probably one out of every five to seven Canadian babies died in the first year or two of life. That public records of the time provide figures no more precise than these for the nation as a whole or even any of its towns, cities, or provinces indicates the lack of public anxiety about the matter. That a lot of babies died in the hot summer months from what was usually called 'summer complaint' caused intense family grief but it was not a matter for public concern. What actually prevailed was a vague and generally unstated sense of inevitability and resignation.[3] Thus in 1886, a Winnipeg immigration agent casually reported that mortality had 'been very light, and that only among children.'[4] In 1887, the Ottawa medical health officer noted without comment that of the 175 children who had that year come under the care of a local foundling home, no less than 109 had died.[5] As late as the turn of the century, even those most actively and personally concerned about public health, the medical health officers, clearly demonstrated in their reports that they had not yet defined infant mortality as a major challenge. F.W. Langrill, Hamilton's vigorous pursuer of diphtheria cases, was content in his reports for 1901, 1902, and 1903 merely to record the number of infant deaths in his jurisdiction and to speculate on what he thought were the causes. Not one other Ontario medical health officer reporting in these years went beyond this step and many did not comment on infant deaths at all.[6]

There were other dimensions to the matter. Canada's apparently high birth rate and the onset of a great wave of new settlers made it a rapidly growing nation. Only later would a combination of large-scale immigration from southern Europe and the casualties of the First World War stimulate widespread alarm over birth and mortality rates. Nor did Canada have a system of compulsory military service, which in other countries readily signalled a declining birth rate. In the 1890s, a drop in the rolls of potential inductees compelled France to define infant and childhood mortality as a national problem. Canadian opinion was probably well reflected by the Galt, Ontario, medical health officer who reported in 1910 that the town birth rate of 21 per 1000 showed that 'race suicide' had 'no hold on the people of Galt.'[7]

However, as soon as the public health movement showed that a high level of infant mortality was not necessary, Canadians made it a matter of private initiative and public concern to lower the rate. As early as 1885, Peter H. Bryce concurred with the opinion of the board of the Toronto Infants Home that there was a particularly high rate of mortality amongst illegitimate infants, especially those cared for by 'baby farms.' As a result, the Ontario legislature passed an act calling for the licensing of such boarding places, but apparently the province did not actively enforce its provisions.[8]

In the 1890s several organizations became interested in infant health. The annual meeting of the National Council of Women heard a paper on 'Infant Mortality' in 1895 and, three years later, the Ontario synod of the Church of England discreetly discussed the low birth rate, contraception, and infant mortality.[9] Early meetings of the newly established Women's Institutes gave careful attention to the health of infants and young children.[10] Most of these early efforts emphasized household practices, such as home pasteurization of milk, that mothers could follow. The Montreal Local Council of Women, however, went beyond helping its own members and began to promote public interest in infant health. Beginning in 1895, the council directed a series of 'Health Talks' and 'Health Cards' at the families of the very poor.[11]

In 1901, the council joined the Foundling Hospital and some concerned physicians in a small-scale effort to establish a pure-milk dispensary for infants in Montreal. During its first summer of operation, the 'Milk Depot' claimed that its efforts saved at least five babies. Out of this beginning grew the Pure Milk League of Montreal, which for a year or two provided milk for two to three hundred babies, and which conducted a campaign to reduce infant mortality in the city.[12] In neither effort, however, did the league meet with much success and, except for the talks to mothers, it dropped the work 'for want of effective assistance from the City and from the charitable public of Montreal.'[13]

In 1906, Miss Eliza Ritchie of Halifax, convener of the National Council of Women's Committee on Public Health, made what was probably the first national survey on the state of infant mortality in the country. While her principal conclusions were that 'in many places' rates were said to be decreasing and the general rate did 'not seem to be high in comparison with other countries,' she cautioned that it was in most cases 'impossible ... to obtain accurate information.'[14] She did not discover any special campaign anywhere in the country to reduce infant mortality. Over the next two or three years, however, this situation changed greatly.

These scattered early efforts were closely related to what was going on elsewhere in the world.[15] In the early 1890s, French physicians began to take some effective action against infant mortality. In 1892, Pierre Budin developed a system of infant consultation centres and Gaston Variot established the first of a series of depots where mothers who could not nurse their babies could get clean cow's milk at reasonable prices. In 1893, the American philanthropist Nathan Straus copied the idea in the city of New York. In 1897, under the direction of Dr George W. Goler, Rochester, New York, set up the first municipal milk station in North America. At about the same time, physicians and scientists assembled some evidence to support other aspects of the work against cholera infantum. In England, a statistical comparison of infant mortality over twenty years in Leicester and Nottingham demonstrated that one effect of replacing pail closets with water closets was to reduce infant mortality by half.[16] In New York, in 1901 and 1902, W.H. Park and L.E. Holt proved that infant illness and mortality during hot weather were related to the kind of milk they were fed. This conclusion, published in December 1903, stimulated a great public effort in New York city to improve milk supplies.[17]

These and other developments aroused a worldwide interest in infant mortality. One consequence was that France called the first Congrès des Gouttes de Lait in Paris in 1905. There, delegates shared the results of their experiences and stimulated each other's enthusiasm for saving babies. The Paris meeting, in turn, inspired British campaigners to call their National Conference on Infantile Mortality in London the following year. A larger band assembled in 1907 in Brussels for the second Congrès des Gouttes de Lait and in 1911 in Berlin for the third Congress on Infantile Mortality.[18] This change in the name of the world gathering reflected exactly the way in which the early interest in pure milk quickly expanded into other areas of prevention.

In Canada and elsewhere the first successful steps in the campaign were those taken to diminish the very high rates of infant deaths during the summer months. As some of its various names imply – summer fever, summer complaint, summer dysentry, summer diarrhoea, and infantile diarrhoea – cholera infantum was a disease which struck with particular severity in warm weather.[19] In 1910, the Saskatchewan Bureau of Health reported that the disease had caused 313 deaths that year. Of these, 9 occurred in June, 43 in July, 130 in August, 63 in September, and 20 in October.[20] The Fort William, Ontario, medical health officer explained in the same year that no less than 82 of the 121 infant deaths – 63 in July and August – reported to him were caused by intestinal disease.[21]

In theory, the health problem posed by cholera infantum was a reasonably simple one to solve. Although medical research never isolated a particular germ as its cause, Park and Holt demonstrated that controlling the purity of the milk fed to infants was the key to conquering the cluster of diseases subsumed under the general term. Breast-feeding was obviously the most effective preventive. The Fort William medical health officer investigated each of the infant deaths in his area in 1910 and reported that 'not one breast-fed baby had died from intestinal trouble.'[22] Nursing mothers soon learned not to wean their babies in July, August, or September. For those infants who had been weaned or who for one reason or another could not be breast fed, public health and family physicians recommended a rigid regimen. They directed the mother to maintain a very high level of sanitation in her home and especially to exclude all flies. They recommended that she buy only pure milk, store it in a clean place, and pasteurize or boil it before feeding it to the child in scalded feeding bottles. They forbad giving any sort of soother to infants.[23]

As Canadians became aware of these simple facts, they followed the Montreal pioneers in efforts to improve the quality of milk used in artificial feeding.[24]

While a growing number of people had tried to tighten controls over milk supplies before this date, the 'pure milk' campaign began in earnest in June 1908, when the Canadian Medical Association appointed its Milk Commission.[25] The CMA Commission explained that milk carried typhoid, scarlet fever, diphtheria, infantile diarrhoea, and tuberculosis, particularly the bovine kind which accounted for a large proportion of this disease amongst children.[26] While youngsters were undoubtedly the principal victims of bad milk, the commission noted that milk-borne diseases could also infect adults. Its report laid out a set of standards for cows, for farm workers, for farms, for milk, and for storage and delivery systems. The document had an immediate effect. Ontario passed legislation to carry out the commission's recommendations and other provinces followed suit.[27] Many municipalities began to set and enforce standards. Even before the Ontario legislature passed its bill, the cities of Guelph, Niagara Falls, Port Arthur, Stratford, Owen Sound, Toronto, and London began to control the quality of the milk sold in their jurisdictions. London made a particularly vigorous effort not only to get certified milk on the market for children, but also to improve the quality of all milk marketed in the city.[28]

In their efforts to establish milk stations, the pure-milk and infant mortality campaigns overlapped and even occasionally merged their forces. Sometimes, as in Montreal in 1910 and in the work of the Toronto Settlement houses, those primarily concerned with infant health established and operated milk stations. In other places, such as London and Hamilton, municipal milk commissions set up the depots. Important as they undoubtedly were in both campaigns, however, these dispensaries were essentially temporary expedients organized to get pure milk to those who needed it most over the duration of whatever period was necessary to establish and enforce high municipal milk standards. Once communities had reached these goals then the function of the milk commissions became mostly supervisory, while infant health crusaders went on to work on other dimensions of their complex problem.[29]

In 1909, the city of Hamilton began what became a model campaign to reduce infant mortality. It provides a well-documented example of how such work usually began, its early and close relationship with pure-milk efforts and, most important, the way that hard-won and sometimes discouraging experience changed the focus and expanded the scope of what was done.[30] In the spring of 1909, the Hamilton medical health officer, Dr James Roberts, and a number of concerned physicians began what they described as a 'clean milk' campaign in the city. Their first step was to send a delegation to Rochester, New York, to observe Dr George W. Goler's system of milk-control. They then tried to persuade the local medical association to cooperate and to raise the necessary funds. Eventually, the Board of Health and the Medical Association jointly formed a

Milk Commission which, with the aid of private subscriptions and a small civic grant, opened two widely publicized depots in the city where the Victorian Order of Nurses provided 'clean, fresh milk for bottle-fed infants during the summer months.' The first year's results discouraged the Hamilton campaigners. Instead of the 50 per cent reduction in mortality they had hoped for, the city achieved only a modest one-sixth drop, from 152 deaths in July, August, and September 1908 to 125 in the same months of 1909.[31] Although the commission made a similar though more extensive effort the next year, this also proved to be, as one of the participants put it, a 'costly experiment' which 'showed little in the way of results.'[32]

The Milk Commission and its supporters therefore organized a separate, provincially chartered charity, the Babies' Dispensary Guild of Hamilton, which began operating in June 1911. The guild had wider concerns than those of the Milk Commission. First, it operated over the whole of the year. Second, it asked mothers to bring their babies with them to its milk dispensaries so a physician could examine them and prescribe individual feeding formulas. Nurses mixed the formulas for mothers to pick up at regular intervals. The guild soon found this an awkward and unsatisfactory practice. As its nursing superintendent explained, they were coming to understand that the real need was education 'in hygiene, in sanitation and in ventilation, as well as in the care of milk, and that education must be carried on principally in the home.'[33]

Accordingly, the guild transformed its dispensaries into infant health clinics, held weekly in the city hospital and a number of school basements. The staff attempted to reach all new-born infants in the city. They encouraged pregnant women to make prenatal visits to one of its clinics. At a time when most babies were born at home and birth registration was neither immediate nor universal, they asked physicians and charity, church, and other organizations in the city to recommend their services to anyone needing them.

The guild tried to persuade mothers to attend the clinic with their infants as soon as possible after birth. There a physician examined each child, recommended breast-feeding when that was possible, and prescribed certified milk when it was not. He did not treat ailing infants but sent them to family physicians or the outpatient department of the city hospital. Next, a nurse showed the mother how to prepare the food prescribed by the doctor. The nurse immediately followed up this instruction with a visit to the home, returning 'daily, weekly or monthly, according to the necessity of the case.'[34]

Home visits quickly became the real core of the work. The nurses' visits, reported the nursing superintendent, were remarkably effective: the mother was no longer 'blindly giving her child prepared milk from a bottle, made up in some peculiar way' but had herself become 'an intelligent factor in her child's recovery or well-being.' Her knowledge led her to 'independence.'[35] The guild also encouraged its nurses to show mothers how to improve the health of the whole family.[36] While its services were available to everyone in Hamilton, the guild drew most of its clientele from the industrial working class. When the physician prescribed certified milk, the guild arranged for it to be 'delivered direct to the home at a reduced rate.' In some cases, the women's board assisted particularly needy mothers by providing the milk and other food supplies 'practically free of cost.' Its members distributed blankets and clothing where necessary, organized sewing classes, and gave talks to mothers. After four years of operation, the guild claimed most of the credit for reducing the proportion of deaths from gastrointestinal disease amongst children under three in the city from 57 per cent in 1908 to 19 per cent in 1914.[37]

In response to these successes as well as to the growing interest in child welfare in Canada, a group of citizens in May 1915 established the Baby Welfare Association of Greater Hamilton. The organization began a campaign to acquaint families not using the guild's service with the 'simple methods' which would protect their children and to arouse wider community interest in reducing infant mortality. Under the slogan, 'Come, Let's Save the Kiddies,' the association held a 'Baby Week' in June 1915. It proclaimed its message through newspaper articles, sermons, talks to all school children, and open houses at clinics, hospitals, playgrounds, and children's homes. It distributed 40,000 folders and 12,000 booklets and, at the end of the week, held a picnic which attracted between 12,000 and 15,000 mothers and children to Dundern Park. Thereafter 'Baby Week' was an annual affair in Hamilton, and other Canadian cities copied the practice.[38]

By broadening its efforts from an attack on one specific cause of infant deaths to an assault on infant mortality as a whole, Hamilton followed a pattern that became typical during these years in other Canadian cities and elsewhere in the world. Indeed, the public health movement was beginning to frame worldwide experience into a coherent body of knowledge. Ontario physician Helen MacMurchy played an important part in this crystallizing process. In three eloquent and widely distributed reports which she wrote for the provincial government, Dr MacMurchy defined the real enemy as infant mortality, rather than cholera infantum; she explained that a wide range of causes was involved; and she outlined steps being taken in various parts of the world to deal with them.[39] In their long list of agents of high rates of infant deaths, Dr MacMurchy and others in the movement included poverty, ignorance, poor housing, overcrowded slums, low wages and other social conditions that forced mothers of young children to work outside their homes, impure water and milk, loose controls over the spread of communicable diseases, poor prenatal care, inadequate medical attendance at birth, tardy registration of births, and the lack of clinics and nursing services devoted to helping mothers care for their babies properly.

Over these years, and particularly after 1910, Canadian social reformers worked on all of these problems. Through the Commission of Conservation and other organizations they tried to improve the quality of Canadian housing.[40] They encouraged schools to teach 'mothercraft' both to older girls who cared for their younger brothers and sisters and to all girls as potential mothers. They demanded provincial pensions for widows with dependent children. They agitated for pure water and pure milk. For many years, however, those most concerned with reducing infant mortality gave most of their attention to the child and his family. More than anything else, education was the thread which unified the great variety of their efforts. Teaching went on at two levels. On the first, the movement had to convince each of the groups directly involved in the care of infants – mothers, baby sitters, physicians, and public health nurses – that they must follow certain procedures. On the second, as in the Hamilton 'Baby Weeks,' it made an extensive effort to demonstrate to the general public the efficacy of the means it proposed for reducing infant mortality and to gain support for them. In sharp contrast to the parallel efforts of their colleagues in the school medical movement, who needed publicity campaigns only to initiate their program, those trying to reduce infant mortality had to integrate the public into their work. They soon discovered that only a cooperative, on-going community effort by both professionals and volunteers could make significant changes in mortality figures. As in other aspects of this public health work, urban municipal and volunteer agencies took the lead. Only when such work was well under way in cities did it begin to spread to small towns and rural areas of the country.

In the decade after 1910, reformers concentrated their efforts on improving the care of babies after they were born, particularly on getting them through their first year. The reason for this concern was simple enough: pediatrician Alan Brown explained that a new-born baby had 'less chance of living a week than a man of ninety, and of living a year than a man of eighty.'[41] To improve on these odds, health professionals and volunteers tried to ensure that the rapidly increasing number of well-baby clinics gave their full range of services to every infant. If they could achieve this desirable state, they argued, they could cut infant mortality by 30 to 50 per cent. Since most babies were born at home, however, clinics first had to find their clients.[42] If the infant death rate was to be cut to the minimum, argued the Toronto Department of Public Health in 1915, 'all births must be reported immediately.' A delay of even two days often meant 'death through neglect or ignorance.'[43] In addition to telling clinics where the babies were so that they could, as one worker put it, bring welfare work 'to bear upon the individual problems of babyhood,' universal birth and death statistics also enabled workers to 'measure the task presented and the results obtained.'[44]

At first, Canadian birth and death registration agencies could not meet these new and urgent demands on them.[45] When Toronto's vital statistician, Robert E. Mills, explained that, for the years before 1910, 'the error in the infant death rate ... based on registered births, was so great as to render that figure useless as a measure of our infant mortality' he described the situation not merely in Toronto but for the nation as a whole. Mills estimated, for example, that about 28 per cent of live births in Toronto in 1908 were not registered.[46] All three levels of government began to improve this situation. In urban areas, public health departments used their visiting nurses and well-baby clinics to search out the newborn. Despite such efforts, improvements were painfully slow in coming. As late as 1915, the statistical division of the Toronto Public Health Department, then the best in Canada, did not publish its birth rate and infant death rate statistics because they were 'the least dependable.'[47] By the end of 1917, Mills explained, the department had reduced incomplete registration in Toronto to the point where it did not, he believed, 'greatly exceed 15 per cent.'[48] In this context and the growing general need for birth data which the First World War produced, the provincial and federal governments agreed to collect vital statistics on a national basis. In 1918, the federal government set up the Dominion Bureau of Statistics, which made agreements with the provinces regarding standard collecting and reporting procedures. One important feature of these arrangements was that each province had to ensure that its birth and death registration covered at least 90 per cent of actual cases. In 1921 the bureau published the first national figures – with the exception of the province of Quebec which did not join the arrangement until 1926.[49]

As they subjected this increasingly accurate data to intensive analysis, statisticians and health officials learned more about their task. These studies underlined again and again the need to concentrate on the child's early hours and days when its hold on life was most precarious. The Saskatchewan Bureau of Public Health explained that the 1456 deaths of infants and young children (exclusive of stillbirths) reported in 1914 occurred at these ages: under one week, 371; one to four weeks, 186; one to three months, 204; three to six months, 176; six to nine months, 102; nine to twelve months, 72; one year, 166; two years, 80; three years, 57; four years, 42.[50] Statistics also precisely identified the causes of death and sorted out particular groups in the population – usually the 'poor and ignorant' but sometimes also the immigrant – who apparently had contributed more than their share of infant deaths.[51]

While over these years those working to reduce infant mortality gave most of their attention to the new-born, they also recognized the importance of prenatal care not only as 'a means of reducing infant loss' but also as a 'significant means of saving a great many mothers.'[52] Under the leadership of its commissioner of public health, Maurice M. Seymour, an enthusiastic advocate of prenatal care, Saskatchewan initially went further in this work than did any other province.[53] In his first report on infant mortality in 1914, Seymour explained that to encourage prenatal care and the 'securing of competent medical attendants at birth' the Saskatchewan government had begun to assist 'needy expectant mothers to the extent of twenty-five dollars,' fifteen of which went to the doctor and ten to the mother.[54] Provincial records do not show just how widely the bureau distributed such subsidies during the first few years of the scheme, but in 1921–2 '206 such ... grants were paid, amounting in all to $5,245.'[55] In 1915, Regina introduced prenatal care through its baby clinics and others across the country began the practice at about the same time.[56]

In the postwar years, public health researchers marshalled more evidence on the matter. One study conducted on the records of Toronto's Burnside Lying-In Hospital showed that for the semiprivate (that is, reasonably well-to-do) maternity cases, the mortality rate of mothers was 8 per 1000 births, 'the public ward unsupervised cases 35 per 1,000, while in the supervised public ward cases the rate was only 4 per 1,000 ...'[57] As pure-milk campaigns began to reduce cholera infantum, other causes of infant death, including those connected with the mother's health, increased in relative importance. After a careful investigation of the cause of each infant fatality in Edmonton in 1921, the city's medical health officer reported that gastrointestinal diseases did not appear among the three most important causes, and that 92 out of the 165 deaths were 'due to or connected with the condition of the mother's health.'[58] Such discoveries prompted public health nurses and physicians to give much more attention to prenatal work.[59]

As it had already done for school medical and dental inspection, Toronto soon organized the most elaborate and systematic infant health system in Canada. Two Settlement Houses, Evangelia and University, began baby welfare work in the city when they each established a milk station. Duplicating the experience elsewhere, these depots gradually expanded their work so that by 1912 they had become baby health clinics. Meanwhile, to help control tuberculosis, the city hired its first public health nurse in 1908. Responding to growing civic interest in the matter, it appointed its first child welfare nurse in 1912.[60] By 1914, Toronto had nine tuberculosis nurses and eight child welfare nurses spending, as one report on the matter put it, 'much time and money on the streetcars, visiting frequently the same homes, and co-operating with the same social agencies.' That year, the Health Department reorganized itself 'to specialize in homes rather than in diseases,' set up its Child Welfare Division, and took over the privately run health stations in the city.[61] By the end of the year, it operated ten municipal well-baby clinics. In 1916, 'owing to the safeguarding of our milk supply ... and the continual education of the mothers in the preparation of infant feedings,' the department closed the milk depots which had been a part of each clinic up to this time.[62]

By 1918, Toronto was operating twenty-two child welfare stations. The department used a pin map showing 'infant deaths throughout the city' to select the site of new clinics. As the main task became educational, public health nurses took over most of the work. As soon as the Child Welfare Division learned of a birth from its registration, from the hospital, from social welfare workers, from priests and ministers, or from others asked to make such reports, the division mailed out a booklet on infant care and feeding and sent a nurse to visit the mother and infant. This was the trickiest part of the work, for the nurse had to employ considerable tact 'to win the mother and to do nothing to antagonize the visiting physician.'[63] The nurse frequently felt 'required to bathe the baby and dress it in the presence of the mother,' since a surprising number of mothers did not know how to do so properly.[64] Nurses also made great efforts to persuade mothers to bring their infants regularly to the nearest clinic. There, under the direction of a physician, nurses weighed and examined the infants, and if they or the physician felt a child needed treatment they referred the mother to her family physician or to the out-patient department of a hospital. In addition, some of the stations sponsored 'mothercraft' classes at which nurses gave talks and demonstrations. In one typical clinic in Toronto, held one day a week over the month of March 1918, the physician attended for five hours and the nurse for nineteen hours and thirty-five minutes. The nurse saw seventy-seven cases (of which ten were new) and referred forty-seven of these to the doctor. Together they gave an average of seven and a half minutes to each case.[65]

Partly to reach mothers who were not attending and partly to garner general public support for its activities, the Toronto Health Department also gave careful attention to publicity. It organized a panel of nurses to speak and demonstrate at meetings of church and other women's groups. It made effective use of newspaper publicity; it was, for example, able to convince the editor of the *Toronto Star Weekly* to provide space for articles on infant and child care and to advertise the time and place of its clinics. Since infant welfare work in Toronto was much more centrally organized and professionally controlled than was typical of Canadian cities, it involved proportionally far fewer volunteers than took part in the work elsewhere.

In contrast, Montreal became the site of an enormous amount of voluntary child welfare work. In October 1912, a host of civic organizations sponsored an enormously successful child welfare exhibition. Although the displays, which were 'to present evidence of all the various activities – educational, religious, charitable, philanthropic and medical – working for the improvement of conditions of child life,' undoubtedly taught much to the thousands of adults and pupils who attended the exhibition, probably the real educational enterprise went on in the various study groups which worked for about a year in planning the exhibition.[66] Here leaders of voluntary organizations discovered many dimensions of child welfare work and lessons other cities had learned about reducing infant mortality. After the exhibition was over, these leaders helped to organize broad support for follow-up activities that the exhibition demonstrated Montreal needed. While not nearly as elaborate as the Montreal effort, in 1913 the Vancouver local Council of Women sponsored a child welfare exhibit as part of the local fair.[67] Beginning in 1912, the Ontario Board of Health did the same thing annually at the Canadian National Exhibition. The idea gradually spread from these larger exhibitions to become regular features at smaller local fairs across the nation.

Montreal also showed how limited voluntary efforts were if they were not part of a sustained municipal drive to improve the milk supply and conduct infant welfare stations. Despite the child welfare exhibition, parish milk depots, pamphlets distributed by priests and ministers at baptisms, lectures to mothers, and all the other volunteer activity in the city, Dr J.A. Baudouin, secretary of the Annual Convention of Quebec Sanitary Services, reported that in 1913 infant mortality in Montreal was 'as high as in the previous year.' If infant mortality in the city and the whole province was to be reduced, Baudouin argued, then it was 'most urgent' that the province improve its milk supply.[68] In August 1918, Montreal therefore set up a Division of Child Hygiene in its Public Health Department. In conjunction with the Child Welfare Association (an outgrowth of the 1912 exhibition) and the *Gouttes de laits paroissiales*, the city slowly began to reduce its infant mortality rate.[69]

The experiences of Hamilton, Toronto, and Montreal offer three examples of ways in which urban Canadians tackled the problem of infant mortality. Most cities began by establishing privately or publicly sponsored milk depots. In varying combinations of public and private support, these depots gradually added well-baby clinics and home visits by public health nurses to their services. Eventually, as local commissions improved the quality of the milk supply, these depots ceased supplying milk for infant-feeding. Soon the volunteers and professionals began to divide the work between them in such a way that the municipal health authorities operated the clinics and employed the visiting nurses. Successful baby welfare clinics, however, relied extensively on volunteers to help in their operation, to persuade mothers to use them, and to maintain a climate of public opinion that valued and supported 'better babies' work in the community.

By the early 1920s most Canadian cities and the larger towns had some system of clinics and visits in operation.[70]

The influence of the infant-health campaign spread far beyond the rising number of mothers and infants who attended clinics. While their role has not yet been investigated, private companies played a part in the improvement of infant, child, and family health. The Metropolitan Life Insurance Company printed and distributed copies of its child care pamphlets in Canada.[71] Between 1921 and 1923 alone, the federal Health Department distributed 220,000 copies of Helen MacMurchy's *Canadian Mother's Book* and tens of thousands of copies of her fourteen pamphlets on home and family life that Canadian mothers affectionately called the 'Little Blue Books.'[72] All infants benefitted from pure milk and water supplies. Also, there were undoubtedly thousands of mothers who had not studied domestic science at school, who had never visited a pure-milk depot or baby welfare station, who had never received a visit by a public health nurse, who had not read a copy of the *Canadian Mother's Book* or a Metropolitan Life pamphlet, but whose infant and child care practices were nonetheless very much influenced by the climate of opinion generated to improve the life chances of the newly born.[73]

How successful was the campaign against infant mortality? By the early 1920s, urban areas could point to statistics which appeared to prove that some places had reached and even surpassed the original goal of reducing the rate by half. In 1921, Winnipeg's Bureau of Child Hygiene claimed that the infant mortality rate in that city had dropped from 207 per 1000 live births in 1912 to 106 in 1915, 92 in 1918, and 78 in 1921.[74] London, Brantford, and Vancouver reported proportionate decreases.[75]

These figures and their counterparts from other cities and towns across the country, however, told a deceptively simple tale. To arrive at a less precise but undoubtedly more accurate evaluation of what the campaign actually achieved, one must judge such bold announcements in terms of three important qualifications. First, even if there was a real reduction in infant mortality, to what extent could those specifically working in child health claim the credit for it? As already noted, improved milk supplies was one cause of the decline in gastrointestinal diseases. Sanitary reform and a rising standard of living had cumulative effects. Second, mortality statistics were not a valid basis for evaluating a city's progress or comparing it to another. Despite the gradual improvements leading to the establishment of the Dominion Bureau of Statistics, Dr David James Evans' national survey in 1920 noted the persisting differences amongst provincial enactments and the tremendous variety in their enforcement from place to place across the country.[76] Until all provinces and municipalities began to apply the standard DBS procedures, commentators could make comparisons only very tentatively and with extreme caution. Third, and most important, the figures demonstrated a downward trend rather than measured its precise extent. One effect of substantial under-registration of births had been to exaggerate initially the rate of infant deaths. Ontario, Robert Mills explained in 1918, had 'long suffered from the publication of slanderously high infant death rates.'[77] Dr Evans' 1920 survey and the original DBS agreement calling for an initial registration rate of 90 per cent clearly indicated that this observation applied to the whole of Canada. Even after the national system had been in effect for a decade, Enid Charles estimated that for the years 1930–2, under-registration ranged from 1 per cent in Quebec and Alberta to 5 per cent in British Columbia and that the national figure for these years was about 3 per cent.[78] Thus, while it is impossible to state accurately the exact proportion, increasingly accurate birth registration accounted for some of the decline in infant mortality which the published figures displayed. On the other hand, because there was less incentive for parents to report such cases, infant deaths and the births of infants who died shortly after birth were not recorded at a pace equal to the registration of those who survived. Therefore, as the registration of births of survivors approached completeness, this particular factor tended to reverse the initial situation: where recorded rates of infant mortality had once been higher than actual rates, they eventually became lower.

At this point one is bound to ask whether infant health had changed at all between 1895 and 1920: did increasingly thorough birth registration not entirely account for the declining rate of infant mortality? Three sorts of evidence suggest that this was not the case. First, there was the already noted gradual but definite decrease in the proportion of infant deaths attributed to cholera infantum. Second, although the data is subject to all of the limitations of pre-1921 vital statistics, the gradual reduction of the proportion of younger age groups amongst all recorded deaths very probably indicated the direction if not the rate of change.[79] Both infant and school health workers shared, for example, in changing the proportion of those under ten in the distribution of recorded deaths in British Columbia from 34 per cent in 1889 to 33 per cent in 1894, 26 per cent in 1899, 27 per cent in 1904, 28 per cent in 1909, 23 per cent in 1914, and 16 per cent in 1918–19.[80] Probably the most important indicator, however, that there was a real as well as an apparent decline in infant mortality was that the downward trend has continued in an unbroken fashion ever since.[81] And, since birth registration became more and more universal, improved health care must have been responsible for a larger and larger proportion of the decline.[82]

As in the school medical campaign, urban youngsters were the prime beneficiaries of the first quarter century of the work against infant mortality. Even had they wanted to, only a minority of Canadian mothers could have taken their infants to a child welfare clinic. The 1921 census showed that 5,295,000, or about 60 per cent, of Canada's population of 8,788,000 lived either on farms or in centres of less than 5000 people.[83] To carry infant welfare work and reduced rates of infant mortality to the small towns, the villages, and the rural population of Canada was an important next challenge for the public health movement.

5

'Invariably the Race Levels Down': Mental Hygiene and Canadian Children

From the earliest years of the movement to improve the health of children, Canadians expressed concern over the effects of what some of them called 'the inexorable law of heredity.'[2] In the 1880s, Dr Daniel Clark, medical superintendent of the Asylum for the Insane in Toronto, explained to Canadian Methodists that people inherited their 'moral, intellectual, emotional, affectional qualities and instincts' in the same way and 'even through collateral lives of ancestry' as they did their physical characteristics. One generation handed down to the next good qualities as well as evil ones, and, unfortunately, the latter predominated. Clark therefore warned Canadians that they should be perturbed about 'ill-adjudged marriages, with all their dread heritage of misery.'[3] In the 1890s, the National Council of Women began to discuss what it saw as a 'preventable' increase in insanity.[4] In 1901, the fourth Canadian Conference on Charities and Correction devoted one of its sessions to the care of the feeble-minded.[5] Shortly after it took office in 1905, Ontario's new Conservative government appointed Dr Helen MacMurchy as inspector for the feeble-minded in Ontario. Over the next few years, she prepared a series of widely read reports of her investigations.

As with her concurrent efforts on infant mortality, the prime function of Dr MacMurchy's reports and speeches on the feeble-minded was obviously educational. In them, she drew attention to the dangers of racial decline if Canadian society did not put curbs on the procreation of this unfortunate class of citizens. She explained to the minister, to the legislature, to significant people in health, education, and welfare, and to those of the general public who would listen, what problems these people posed to society and tried to persuade the community to do something about them. She surveyed the situation in Ontario and in other parts of Canada and reported carefully on how the feeble-minded were dealt with elsewhere.[6]

Dr MacMurchy's reports also made abundant use of the florid rhetoric that was the most distinguishing characteristic of mental hygienists. Like most of her colleagues, she knew what Mrs M.K. Stead, convenor of the National Council of Women's Committee on the Care of the Mentally Deficient, explained in her report for 1918: an 'expert investigation of one case' made 'a stronger appeal to the authorities than general statistics and many citations of average cases.'[7] In sharp contrast to the factual argumentation typical of the rest of the public health movement, the mental hygienists' essays and speeches were often alarmist and sometimes hysterical in tone.[8] In addition to using the famous Jukes and Kallikak families as horrible examples, Canadian crusaders also looked for local cases. In the 'wreakage of our boasted civilization,' one found the 'centre of infection' in a particular community to have been 'a family of feeble-minds – father, mother, one son and three daughters – *also two grandchildren.*'[9]

By their use of evidence, the leaders demonstrated their governing assumption that the causes of feeble-mindedness and mental illness were primarily hereditary rather than environmental. Mrs Willoughby Cummings told the National Council of Women that she knew a recently married young clergyman whose 'two uncles and grandfather were insane' and whose wife's mother and sister were in the Toronto Lunatic Asylum. Although their children probably would be insane, yet the couple 'had not the slightest idea that there was any reason why they should not marry.'[10] J.P. Downey, superintendent of the Hospital for Feeble-Minded in Orillia, Ontario, argued that while it was 'useless to talk of breeding men like farm stock to a type' all the forces of society 'should be directed against the procreation of those doomed to be diseased and defective.'[11] In 1914, Mrs Adam Shortt told the National Council of Women that biology taught the 'we cannot level up, and that invariably the race levels down.'[12]

Out of an amalgam of humanitarianism, patriotism, science, and pseudo-science, Canadians sharing these interests gradually patched together after 1900 a mental hygiene and eugenics movement. While the history of this enterprise lies outside the scope of this study, one of its major concerns was the mental health of children.[13] In particular, efforts directed at what were called 'mentally defective' or 'feeble-minded' youngsters impinged not only on general health work for the young but also on related activities in child welfare and education. Noticeably 'slow' children have probably always formed roughly the same proportion of the total population. In rural society, those relatively few who stood out clearly as major 'problems' were looked upon as family burdens rather than social responsibilities. Further, most such boys and girls had in former days gradually but naturally learned the routine of farm, family workshop, and housekeeping. They were, however, less able to fit successfully into the quicker pace of school, commerce, and factory.

From 1910 onward people interested in mental hygiene, eugenics, and the care of the feeble-minded came together into local and provincial organizations.[14] In 1918, Dr C.K. Clarke, dean of medicine at the University of Toronto and perhaps Canada's most distinguished psychiatrist, gathered many of these groups into the Canadian National Committee for Mental Hygiene. Because of their extreme emphasis on hereditary factors, these organizations initially directed their activities towards excluding and eliminating feeble-mindedness and insanity by genetic controls. Only in the 1920s did some of them turn their attention to treating and curing mental illness.

These new organizations concentrated upon four ways of improving the mental health of Canadian children. First, they wanted the Canadian government to make a much more intensive effort to exclude mentally defective children and adults from the ranks of immigrants entering Canada. They were sceptical, Dr J.G. Adami explained, of the 'widely proclaimed' opinion that 'children of the slums and of degraded parentage,' would 'develop into citizens of good quality, citizens every whit as good as those of good parentage' provided they were 'brought to Canada and given a healthy life upon the farm.'[15] In 1916, C.K. Clarke reported that research conducted since 1911 at the psychiatric 'Social Service' Clinic at Toronto General Hospital showed that the federal government's inspection of immigrants at the ports of entry had not been successful. 'Children whose defects should have been apparent to the veriest tyro in feeble-mindedness or psychiatry,' he declared, had passed 'the so-called test with success.'[16] Hygienists often confused the intelligence of immigrants with their willingness to assimilate. Describing Mennonite children from 'progressive' stock, the Saskatchewan Mental Hygiene Survey concluded that many of them 'rated far above the average'; they 'would make Canadians of the best kind'; they had no more defectives than could be found 'in any good community in Canada'; and 'their physique was notably good.' On the other hand, the children of 'Old Colony' Mennonites 'proved much inferior in intelligence' and evidently had not 'profited by their association with other groups.' The surveyors concluded, not altogether logically, that the 'Old Colony' communities demonstrated that compulsory education was 'after all the chief factor in bringing about the assimilation of the numerous foreign element' and, further, made it clear that these Mennonites were 'not of as good mental calibre as the progressive types.'[17]

Second, leaders of the mental hygiene movement wanted feeble-minded youngsters excluded from public schools and taught elsewhere. Since they were 'not able to take advantage of the instruction given,' this step seemed necessary for the sake of the afflicted children themselves. More important than this consideration, however, was the fact that people came to believe that the presence of the feeble-minded impeded the academic progress of normal pupils and often posed a 'moral menace' to them as well.[18] Undoubtedly some children needed a form of special education. As school systems gradually enforced compulsory attendance legislation, they brought under their care many retarded children who otherwise would have stayed at home. Better trained teachers with smaller classes saw each pupil more clearly and could distinguish more accurately those who could not learn from those who could. They therefore picked out the mentally retarded for special concern. Teachers and mental hygienists gave particular attention to those children who were over-age for their grade. Discussing the problem of 'retardation' – by which he meant those pupils who were below the appropriate grade level for their chronological age – M.C. MacLean of the Educational Division of the Dominion Bureau of Statistics cautioned that mental deficiency was only one minor cause of this situation. After allowing for retardation caused by 'irregular attendance, differences between the sexes, the attendance of under-age children, lateness in beginning school,' and other adverse conditions, MacLean concluded it was clear that 'the proportions suffering from extreme degrees of retardation on account of mental deficiency' were 'very small.'[19]

As their rhetoric made apparent, in the early stages of the movement, mental hygienists displayed little rigour in defining mental deficiency. After 1910, however, Alfred Binet's influence on intelligence testing in Europe and the United States sharpened the discrimination of at least the academic and professional members of the movement. In this context, Professor Peter Sandiford of the University of Toronto explained that the term 'intelligence' referred to 'a child's degree of mental development or mental maturity' which was 'an absolute not a relative thing.'[20] While some argued that an adult's particular location on the scale of mental age – twelve or thirteen were the usual figures – divided the deficient from the rest of the population, others preferred to look at what Clarence M. Hincks of the Psychiatric Clinic of Toronto General Hospital called the child's potential for 'social efficiency,' by which he meant his ability to function at least minimally in the world of work.[21] William D. Tait, a psychologist at McGill University, divided subnormal children into two categories:

A *retarded children*
1 weak body
2 normal body

B *defective children*
1 borderline
2 morons
3 imbeciles
4 idiots.[22]

Surveys based on such formulations brought a very sharp increase in estimates of the numbers of feeble-minded children in Canadian schools. In 1911, Dr MacMurchy estimated that only 0.03 per cent of the school population was feeble-minded.[23] In its various surveys, however, the Canadian National Committee for Mental Hygiene found that between 2 and 3 per cent of the pupils were 'so far below the average mentally' that they could not 'acquire the academic training' ordinarily offered in public schools.[24] In the postwar years, the National Committee as well as certain psychiatrists and psychologists undertook a number of these mental hygiene surveys of school children.[25] At the request of the Guelph, Ontario, Public School Board, C.K. Clarke and C.M. Hincks conducted such a survey in October 1919. They reported that 'no less than' 3.34 per cent of the board's 2245 pupils had an 'Intelligence Quotient of 75% or less,' and recommended that the board establish two industrial classes for these children.[26]

Third, mental hygienists drew a relationship between feeble-mindedness and delinquency. By 1920 they argued, as Judge Helen Gregory MacGill put it, that because he lacked 'the mentality to do right' and 'had no power of inhibition,' the 'abnormal' juvenile delinquent was 'the real menace to society.'[27] The movement's mental hygiene surveys claimed that nearly 60 per cent of the boys in detention homes and similar institutions were mentally abnormal. In its study of juvenile delinquents in British Columbia, the National Committee found that 58.7 per cent of them were 'mentally abnormal.' Its data showed, the committee explained, that 'mental deficiency' lay 'at the root of such conditions as crime, juvenile delinquency, prostitution, and pauperism,' and posed a significant problem to schools as well.[28]

Finally, and most strongly and consistently over the whole period, mental hygienists were determined to ensure that the feeble-minded not be 'allowed to reproduce their kind.'[29] Their reason for proposing legislation and institutional segregation which would accomplish this restriction was, as Professor Tait explained, that the results of 'scientific investigation' showed that the feeble-minded reproduced 'much more rapidly than normal persons' and 'the offspring of feeble-minded parents' were 'always feeble-minded.'[30] In her second report, in 1907, Dr MacMurchy pointed out that 'the only satisfactory and thorough method of dealing with the problem' was to select the feeble-minded out during childhood, train them separately from other children, and 'protect them from the crimes and evils which threaten them in the outside world.'[31] The National Council of Women was particularly active in demanding that feeble-minded women be kept away from temptation.[32] The National Committee's Saskatchewan mental health survey stated that four groups needed institutional care: 'low grade defectives' (idiots and imbeciles); 'certain high grade cases with depressing home conditions'; defectives who were wards of the provincial Department of Neglected and Dependent Children; and 'defective delinquents, including feeble-minded girls with immoral tendencies.'[33] Although some considered sterilization as an alternative to custody, others rejected the practice. Tait, for example, argued that society should avoid taking such an 'extreme step' until it gave up 'the hope of cure' and also because 'as ordinarily meant' sterilization operations were given only to males. The feeble-minded female, he believed, posed 'much more danger' than her male counterpart.[34] Eventually, however, both Alberta and British Columbia passed legislation permitting sterilization.[35]

By 1920, those in the mental hygiene movement could point to what they described as a number of substantial achievements. Under the leadership of its medical director, Dr C.K. Clarke, the Canadian National Committee for Mental Hygiene had developed into an effective organization with a well-articulated program set forth in its *Canadian Journal of Mental Hygiene*.[36] In the psychiatric clinic which Clarke established in 1914 at the Toronto General Hospital, the movement had a research institution which provided evidence to substantiate its rhetoric.[37] The federal government had meanwhile tightened up Canadian immigration legislation and procedures, although the new standards were still not rigorous enough to satisfy mental hygienists.[38] Leaders of the movement also claimed responsibility for the fact that, with the support of provincial legislation, many urban school boards had established separate classes for feeble-minded and slow children.[39] From 1911 to 1917, for example, Vancouver maintained two special classes for 'low grade defectives, most of whom were imbeciles.' When the British Columbia government began to provide custodial care for those who were most defective, the school board closed these classes and turned its attention to what it called 'the higher forms of mental defect, the Moron problem.' The board established a psychological clinic under a well-trained professional to sort out the retarded from the rest of the pupils. In April 1921, the Vancouver supervisor of special classes reported that in two and a half years the clinic had studied 393 cases. Of these, 307 were recommended for special classes and 30 sent to the provincial institution. At the end of 1920, the city had 15 classes 'caring for 205 sub-normal pupils' under fifteen trained teachers and two full-time manual training instructors.[40] By 1923, the National Committee estimated that there were then 161 such classes in operation throughout the country.[41]

What was more important than any of these individual achievements, however, was that by the early 1920s the mental hygienists had placed themselves and their ideas in a very central place in the whole child welfare movement. This new importance of mental hygiene was displayed in many ways. While the organizers of Montreal's first child welfare exhibit in 1912 would not permit the Local Council of Women to mount a eugenics display, their booths on the matter were an important part of the exhibits of 1918, 1919, and 1920.[42] In 1920, Helen MacMurchy was appointed the first chief of the federal Department of

Health's Child Welfare Division, in recognition of her work in both mental hygiene and infant health. Mental hygiene was an important item on the agenda of the first two meetings of the newly formed Child Welfare Association of British Columbia, held in 1918 and 1919.[43] By its second annual meeting in Vancouver in June 1920, the Canadian National Committee for Mental Hygiene had attracted public acceptance and support to the extent that its patron was the governor-general and its vice-presidents included Sir Arthur Currie, Sir Robert Falconer, Sir Lomer Gouin, and Lord Shaughnessy.[44]

In an address on mental hygiene given in September 1925, Professor E.D. MacPhee of the Department of Psychology of the University of Toronto observed that there were four stages in the development of a body of scientific principles. First, humanitarians promoted an enquiry into certain conditions. Next, these persons gave 'wide and often exaggerated publicity to their findings' with the result that they recruited to their cause 'individuals or public bodies usually less well informed and more enthusiastic.' Third, people gave the problem 'more critical study,' eliminated much which was 'untrue or unessential,' and defined 'the real issues involved and the real problems to be attacked.' Finally, people recognized that to solve the problem they had to prepare a program to prevent or eliminate the causes of the conditions which concerned them.[45] By the early 1920s, the mental hygiene movement in Canada had clearly moved through the first two of these four stages. From their position in the child welfare movement, leading mental hygienists moved on to MacPhee's third stage, that of a more critical examination of the premises under which they had been operating.

From their obsession with sorting out and locking up the feeble-minded, the National Committee turned to a search 'for more fundamental knowledge and for methodology in applying mental hygiene principles.'[46] This research was accompanied by a decline in an extreme emphasis on the effects of heredity. In the late 1920s, in a careful study of mental patients in British Columbia that she prepared for the province's Royal Commission on Mental Hygiene, Helen P. Davidson concluded that by putting 'the worst complexion on our figures' they showed that '30 per cent' was the 'largest amount of insanity due to hereditary taint of varying degrees.' Syphilis, alcoholism, and preventable psychoses accounted for most of the other patients.[47] It was probable, argued a monograph on the 1931 census, that 'in studies of differential fertility too much attention' had been paid 'to the fertility of extreme classes.' While a 'high rate of increase among imbeciles and idiots' might create a problem for asylums, it did 'not necessarily result in racial degeneration of serious consequences.'[48]

Proponents of mental hygiene became more cautious in their opinions on the rapid spread of mental illness and feeble-mindedness. Dr. A.T. Mathers, provincial psychiatrist for Manitoba, told the British Columbia Royal Commission that after careful study he had concluded that while the number of mental patients in Manitoba had gone up in recent years, the 'actual number of cases of mental disease' had probably 'increased little, if any.' The commission itself agreed that Mathers' explanation of the situation also applied to British Columbia: while it found that there had been a disproportionate increase in the number of mental patients in the province, the cause of this situation was 'a growing tendency of the public to seek hospital accommodation' when faced with problems of feeble-mindedness or insanity.[49]

For some Canadians the new moderation in mental hygiene probably came too late. Some nervous, hesitant, shy, or perhaps undernourished children, from families lacking the interest or perhaps the skill to overturn such hasty judgments were labelled 'mentally deficient' or 'feeble-minded' through crude application of intelligence testing. Many such people undoubtedly carried through the whole of their lives the brand that hygienists had put on them. Others, from a family where a person or other relative suffered from mental illness brought on by syphilis or acute alcoholism were either afraid to marry at all, or continually searched their children or grandchildren for appearances of the hereditary 'taint.'[50] If rural infants and children had to wait an extra generation to receive the benefits of infant and school health care, they were at least spared the ministrations of early mental hygiene crusaders.

6

'How Can We Reach Them?':
Making Child Health
a Nation-Wide Enterprise

By 1914, a physician or school nurse regularly examined most Canadian children who attended school in the large cities of the nation. Sanitary inspectors made routine visits to school premises. The pupils themselves studied personal health care from interesting and up-to-date textbooks and learned of the wonders wrought by modern bacteriology. In their new domestic science laboratories, older girls discovered and practised a wide range of practical health and nutritional habits and skills which many would later put to use in their own homes. Infants and young children in those cities were finding their health protectors as well. Municipal health departments gradually made the nurture and protection of this class of children their most important activity. Especially in Toronto, Canadians could see public health ideals regarding infant and child health almost wholly realized. The city had established and maintained high standards for water and milk supplies and for sanitary services. For families who would make use of them, Toronto readily and freely provided preventive health services for the prospective mother and for her child from his birth until he left school.

As urban public health and school systems shifted from establishing health services for children to persuading parents and teachers to use them, some school and health officials turned to the needs of infants and children living in rural areas. There they found conditions that were not very different from those which they had already learned to overcome in the city. In 1918, Harold Foght explained to the Saskatchewan government that 'rural people ... presumed too much of the natural healthfulness of their environment'; they paid a 'startling toll in easily preventable diseases' because they ignored 'simple hygienic laws of drainage, water supply, pure air, etc.' To support this conclusion Foght cited data gathered in two separate surveys. In the first, the provincial director of school hygiene sent out questionnaires to 3741 rural schools in the province and received 2100 replies. Teachers in 229 schools reported that their schools had impure water supplies, and fully 75 per cent described their school privies as 'dirty.' In the second, the Saskatchewan minister of education proclaimed a school medical inspection day on which local practitioners examined pupils attending a wide range of rural schools. Physicians found that 74.8 per cent of the 2273 children had not been vaccinated, 46.2 per cent had carious teeth, 6.9 per cent had defective sight, and 0.7 per cent had pediculosis. Although they discovered that conditions were 'notoriously bad in the open country, they were little, if any, better in the town and village schools.'[2] Competent observers such as Mary Power, director of maternal and child welfare and public health nursing for Ontario, and the authors of the Putman-Weir Survey in British Columbia confirmed Foght's conclusions.[3]

In their initial efforts to come to grips with the health problems of rural children, Canadians tried to extend their urban organizations into the countryside. As they had already done in the city, school rather than health officials took the first steps. Although Ontario made it legally possible in 1907 for school boards to introduce medical inspection in schools, only urban areas took advantage of this opportunity. After cities and towns had demonstrated how effective inspection could be, and in response to pressure by Women's Institutes, the provincial Department of Education tried again in 1914 to establish comprehensive medical inspection, especially in rural areas.[4] So that the service could be organized on a large enough scale to make it efficient and inexpensive, the department encouraged neighbouring school boards to operate joint systems. Four years later, however, it noted that, except for some examples in the counties of Peel and Lincoln, boards had taken no advantage of the opportunity.[5] As they pressed the Ontario government to establish a province-wide inspection scheme, some Women's Institutes tried to fill the gap by operating their own school clinics. In 1919, the Department of Education took over full responsibility for these activities from the Women's Institutes and by 1921 it was making a concerted effort to provide 'some practical form of school health inspection in strictly rural districts ...' While in the short run the department was prepared to conduct some rural inspections with its own medical staff, it was more interested in persuading local school boards to establish their own medical and nursing services. Although a system of provincial grants prodded some districts to establish inspection systems, the department found that it had to expand continually its own corps of health workers to meet the demand for rural services and by 1922 employed seven physicians and twelve nurses.[6]

Just before the First World War, the provincial Board of Health also turned its attention to infant and child health in rural Ontario. Although it decided to set up a separate division to carry out the task, the war reduced available funds and Mary Power did not become head of the board's Child Welfare Bureau until 1918. Assisted by its consultant in pediatrics, Dr Alan Brown, and following the model that New Zealand had developed for such a scheme, in 1920 the board re-organized the bureau into a Division of Maternal and Child Hygiene and Public Health Nursing with Miss Power as its director. At the same time the board established a Division of Public Health Education to promote public health in Ontario, including child health and welfare. With the help of the Red Cross (which paid eight of the salaries) the board then appointed sixteen public health nurses. Unlike its sister agency, however, the Board of Health did not offer financial inducements to encourage municipalities to employ their own professional staffs. Nevertheless, in 1921 Miss Power reported the example provided by her division had already stimulated local areas to hire nineteen public health nurses.[7]

Saskatchewan also put together two provincially financed child health services. With an eye on the electorate, and especially the newly enfranchised women, the Saskatchewan government adopted a direct method to introduce medical inspection in rural schools.[8] In 1917, Premier W.M. Martin appointed Jean Browne to the recently created position of provincial director of school hygiene.[9] An honours graduate of both the Toronto Normal School and of the Toronto General Hospital Training School for Nurses, Miss Browne had organized the medical inspection services in the Regina schools in 1911 and supervised them since that time.[10] By 1922, the Saskatchewan Department of Education had fourteen school nurses travelling all over the province. During the winter, they visited schools in small towns on railway lines. In the summer, they travelled with the school inspector to teach and inspect in rural schools. When they were able to enlist teachers to the follow-up work, nurses reported that parents then gave 'serious consideration' to remedying defects. While Miss Browne still lamented that she did not have enough nurses to 'completely cover the province' even in this limited way, she also boasted that the school hygiene staff had done some work in every inspectorate in Saskatchewan.[11]

At about the same time that rural school inspection was getting under way, the province's Bureau of Public Health also extended its campaign against infant mortality to small towns and rural areas. In 1916, it began a series of child care exhibits and infant welfare conferences at community fairs. On other occasions the bureau assisted local organizations which were willing to sponsor such affairs.[12] Its example encouraged other organizations to follow suit. In 1917, the

Citizenship and Public Health Committee of the Moose Jaw Local Council of Women staged a 'Baby Welfare Campaign.' The city council granted fifty dollars towards the expenses and 'doctors, nurses and citizens appreciated its high educational and conservative value and enthusiastically offered their effort and time.' As a result of this campaign, the Council of Women reported, the Moose Jaw municipal council appointed a baby welfare nurse and agreed that the community needed a milk depot.[13] In 1918, the bureau reported that interest in such ventures was 'increasing rapidly' elsewhere, and, as in Moose Jaw, the effort was being taken up largely by women's organization.'[14] In 1919, the bureau appointed two child welfare nurses to its staff to do demonstration work, mostly in the rural areas of the province. In 1921, it organized a separate Division of Child Welfare and Hospital Management.[15]

From such pioneering ventures, Canadians learned what had to be done to make modern health care available to all their youngsters. First, they discovered how to organize it effectively. They learned that provincial governments and provincial agencies had to take on the major responsiblity for extending health services outside of the large cities. As part of this task, they had to select one provincial agency and assign it all child health care duties. Second, Canadians made child health into a national cause. Nation-wide organizations took the lead in prodding the public and all three levels of government to put into practice what the public health movement had painfully discovered.

Experiments in Ontario, Saskatchewan, and elsewhere showed that extending child health care meant that provincial governments and provincial agencies had to work in a dynamic partnership with local voluntary organizations and municipal authorities. Despite the prompting of church groups, Women's Institutes, and farmers organizations and their auxiliaries, rural school boards and municipal councils took little interest in health matters. Further, they lacked the population and tax bases to operate their own health agencies and needed more than rhetoric to stimulate them to cooperate with their neighbours. On the other hand, centralized agencies could not do the job on their own: the movement needed, Mary Power argued, 'strong backing and co-operation from all organized women in Canada.'[16] In such a cooperative arrangement, child health workers gradually learned, provincial agencies had two prime functions. First, they had to provide a satisfactory context in which local efforts might begin and, once under way, be supported effectively. At best, this meant that provincial authorities provided a legislative basis for municipal health work, practical demonstrations as to how effective it could be, and financial incentives to encourage local authorities to introduce it to their schools and communities. Second, they had to provide the professional health staff. Fulfiling this latter task usually meant that provincial governments or agencies trained a corps of public health nurses, furnished some to local areas, and, in the countryside, provided the administrative structure in which they worked. Successful prenatal and infant care, however, demanded that these services receive constant publicity through newspapers, magazines, and the efforts of local organizations. They also required the competent help of a large cast of local volunteers. School medical inspection required the active cooperation of the school board and the teachers.

Before Canadians could make a national effort to improve child health, they also had to resolve the conflict between school and public health organizations as to who should extend these services. The fact that a nurse who taught good health practices to mothers and children became the principal professional in both school and infant health work accentuated organizational conflicts. Initially, the Toronto and some other school boards had only reluctantly moved into health work after they had been unable to persuade health boards to do the job. As milk stations turned into well-baby clinics and medical inspection of pupils for infectious diseases into a device to maintain the general health of children, most of the real differences between the two services vanished. Nevertheless, once they had entered the field, school boards and their officials became unwilling to give it up to health boards who had at last either wakened to the need or saw a threat to themselves in a rival municipal body. In part, schoolmen hesitated because they had developed efficient health establishments with their own directors, staffs, and procedures. In addition, as Lina Rogers explained, school health professionals had broadened their conception of a proper school medical service to include in its duties everything that affected 'the child's physical, mental and moral development,' and to insist that health education was the 'first duty of the School Board.'[17] They believed that if their public health colleagues prevailed the latter's supposedly narrower focus on sanitation and the control of communicable diseases would downgrade the educational dimension of school health. Further, there was enough to do in the cities that physicians and nurses could specialize in school health or in infant care. Even New York's single public health organization usually assigned nurses to one duty or the other. On the other hand, public health departments insisted that they could 'more efficiently and economically' manage all child health activities including school medical inspection.[18] Despite the fact that even in the cities the debate often became very warm indeed, of Canadian centres with two services only Toronto, for local political reasons, at that time took the step of merging them into one health organization.[19]

Nevertheless, even if urban Canadians could provide effective health care for their youngsters through either one or two services, the experience of Ontario and Saskatchewan showed that such a dual effort was impractical in the Canadian countryside. When they introduced each specialty separately, districts lost the practical advantages of a nurse doing both jobs in one area. Indeed the intricate effort required to establish two systems may have inhibited some places from introducing any child health nursing at all.[20] Moreover, as district nurses extended and made more effective their preschool health services, school nurses found that they had less of a dramatic and exciting nature to discover and deal with; they merely followed through on what someone else had already begun.[21] In the end, then, the infant and child health campaign absorbed that for school inspection and outside of the big cities public health systems eventually took over both sides of the work. In 1925, Ontario placed its two bands of physicians and nurses under the health authorities and Saskatchewan followed suit in 1928.

The First World War made the health of Canadian children into a truly national issue. Canadians shared in the worldwide rise in interest in public health that the conflict stirred. People in small towns and rural districts, reported a member of the Manitoba Council of Women, were 'most earnestly' taking up matters of child health and welfare which before the war had been confined to the larger cities.[22] Public health supporters explained that there were 'lessons' for Canada in campaigns elsewhere, and particularly in the nationwide work of the New Zealand Society for the Health of Women and Children.[23] Community organizations began to tie their local health efforts into national and international campaigns such as 'Empire Baby Week.'[24] More important, a number of national bodies greatly expanded their activities in child health matters.

From the 1890s onward, Canadians had used national organizations to prod, support, extend, and supplement official efforts to improve the health of their children. Such prewar activities, however, as the public health committees of the National Council of Women and the Commission of Conservation were primarily designed to collect and distribute information on what was being done in Canada and elsewhere for local agencies to use. In addition to increasing the general support of such organizations as the National Council of Women, the Imperial Order of the Daughters of the Empire, and the Social Service Council, the war prompted three agencies – the Victorian Order of Nurses (VON), the Canadian Public Health Association, and the Canadian Red Cross – to take a more active part in initiating and extending child health measures. The VON changed itself the least. From its establishment at the 1897 meeting of the National Council of Women, the VON had helped to improve infant and child health as part of its main task of providing district nursing services and cottage hospitals in rural areas. In making home visits to mothers with infants the order encouraged breast-feeding, and its nurses sometimes conducted well-baby clinics. In 1920, when the British Columbia Division of the Canadian Red Cross entered public health nursing, it turned to the VON as the organization with the best practical field experience to train its first nurses.[25] From its inception in 1910, the Canadian Public Health Association displayed a continuing interest in child health, both in the programs of its annual meetings and in the *Public Health Journal*. Towards the end of the war, the association organized a separate section on child welfare. In turn, this group undertook a national survey of the state of child health work in Canada, made a substantial effort to publicize what was being done, and campaigned for what ought to be attempted.[26]

After 1918, the Canadian Red Cross Society, which had grown into a very substantial organization during the war, turned to public health.[27] In the early postwar years it arranged for the professional training of public health nurses and demonstrated the effectiveness of such nursing in rural areas.[28] The British Columbia Red Cross decided, for example, that its most useful immediate contribution to the province would be 'to train and maintain ten nurses for public health work.' To teach its own and other nurses it therefore helped establish and maintain a Chair of Public Health at the University of British Columbia.[29] The Red Cross hoped that when one of its nurses had demonstrated the effectiveness of district nursing, the local community would assume responsibility for it, and the society could move its 'demonstrator' on to another location.

The Canadian Red Cross also initiated two other services which benefitted children. In the early 1920s, it began giving short-term home nursing courses which included much practical material for mothers.[30] Second, the society enthusiastically expanded its efforts with Junior Red Cross societies. Originating in Canada in the early years of the war, the Junior Red Cross idea rapidly caught the imagination of organizers of children's groups both in and out of schools. After the war, the society decided to make the Junior Red Cross an organization for pupils based in their own classrooms. To direct the work the society recruited Jean Browne, director of school hygiene for Saskatchewan. Under her guidance the number of Junior Red Cross clubs grew rapidly, enrolling 75,000 Canadian children by 1923.[31]

Although it had limited constitutional responsibilities in the field, the federal government also contributed to the national effort for child health. In her new position as chief of child welfare in the federal Department of Health, Dr MacMurchy helped organize the National Council of Child Welfare which made health as one of its central concerns.[32] In 1922, she compiled a *Handbook of Child Welfare in Canada* which provided Canadians with the first reasonably clear picture of what they were doing in child health and welfare across the nation. Although their involvement in the matter was less direct than that of the Child Welfare Division, the federal Department of Agriculture, through its work to improve milk supplies, and the Dominion Bureau of Statistics, in its efforts to chart what was happening to Canadian vital patterns, also formed part of the federal government's work in child health. In 1919, to promote intergovernmental coordination and cooperation in all health matters the federal government set up the Dominion Council of Health, an organization made up mostly of senior federal and provincial civil servants. At its May 1920, meeting this council gave more than half of its time to child health and welfare matters.[33]

If by the end of the war Canadians had learned that child health was a unified enterprise requiring nationwide attention, they had only begun the process of putting this theory into practice. In the summer of 1918, and as part of the 'Empire Baby' campaign, some local Councils of Women in smaller centres sponsored baby welfare crusades modelled on those held earlier in the larger cities.[34] Over the next year or two their example was followed all across Canada by many other local councils, Women's Institutes, and farm women's organizations.[35] By themselves, however, these local campaigns, single occasion clinics, and 'baby saving' weeks served primarily to arouse public interest in the work rather than to effect any significant change in infant mortality figures.[36] Provincial public health or Red Cross nurses therefore began to help local organizations to turn their displays into permanent services. Under the sponsorship of a local organization or a special committee set up for the occasion, nurses put up child health displays, conducted, or assisted local physicians to conduct well-baby clinics, gave practical demonstrations of infant and child health care to mothers, Girl Guides, high school students, and to teachers, and gave talks to any organization willing to listen to them. In 1919, the local Women's Institutes invited Miss Beryl Knox of the Ontario Child Welfare Bureau to spend three weeks in the Haliburton area. There she made ninety-six bedside nursing visits to babies and adults, conducted six well-baby conferences, set up and demonstrated a small exhibit for mothers, helped the local doctor perform four operations in the patients' homes, and held a mothers' meeting in a rural school. As a result of these strenuous efforts, the local Women's Institutes decided to demand a permanent service in their community and offered to pay a proportion of the cost 'incident to the employment and maintenance of a nurse.'[37] Such demonstrations, however, were not always as successful as that conducted by the indefatigable Miss Knox. In 1921, Dr H.W. Johnston, district officer of health for the Sudbury area of Ontario, reported that while he and the provincial public health nurses in the region had cooperated in demonstrations in twenty municipalities only one appointed a nurse 'as a result of these demonstrations.'[38] In 1920, in a particularly imaginative example of demonstration work, the Nova Scotia provincial branch of the Red Cross sent out two caravans on six-week tours of the coastal towns and fishing villages. Each caravan was equipped with films and lantern slides and was accompanied by six doctors, a dentist, and a corps of nurses. As one measure of the effectiveness of this scheme, the provincial branch reported that, by 1923, counties themselves had assumed some or all of the cost.[39]

Dr MacMurchy's *Handbook* lays out in great detail Canadian infant and child health work as it actually was in the 1920s.[40] Three central characteristics come through all the detail. First, provincial efforts to provide medical inspection of school children were further advanced than those to reduce infant mortality. Second, the work in Ontario and western Canada was much ahead of that in Quebec and the Maritime provinces.[41] Third, and most important, the role of the nurse had become as central in rural public health as it was in the cities. Here, we need to elaborate only on this final characteristic.

During the second and third decades of the twentieth century, two lines of practice gradually came together to make public health nursing into a new health profession.[42] On the one hand, there was the visiting nurse, which in Canada was best exemplified in the members of the VON. Although visiting nurses saw their main purpose as giving bedside care in the home, they also did a great deal of incidental health teaching and demonstrating.[43] On the other hand, workers in various branches of public health saw with increasing clarity that preliminary inspections of infants and school children did not need a physician to perform them, that someone had to follow up cases to ensure that parents had their children's defects properly treated and, most important, that teaching and demonstrating were the key to solving a great many child health problems. The term 'public health nurse,' explained Dr Macgillivrary S. Fraser, Manitoba's medical health officer, was 'a misnomer, because she ... [was] a teacher.'[44] At first public health agencies established a number of *ad hoc* specialties such as tuberculosis nursing, school nursing, and infant welfare nursing. When health departments and civic officials began to see that there was enough in common amongst these jobs that one person could be trained to do them all, and that it was much more efficient to organize the work in this way, they began to merge the separate services. In Toronto, the city health department put its tuberculosis and baby welfare nurses into one organization in 1914 and, three years later, added the school nursing staff to it. Rather than having a variety of nurses in Manitoba's rurally focused service, Dr Fraser explained, 'we combined and had one nurse who knew all branches of the work.'[45] By the 1920s, as Canadians were extending public health care across the whole country, most of those involved saw not only the essential unity of community nursing but also that its function was education and preventive medicine.[46] Increasingly, then, a public health nurse organized and conducted well-baby clinics, weighing stations, and the like, visited the home to encourage breast-feeding and to teach basic infant care, made the preliminary and sometimes only inspection of school children, reported defects to the parents and urged that their children be treated, taught health and hygiene to women's organizations and school children, and often sponsored Little Mothers Leagues and Junior Red Cross branches. By the end of the 1920s, over 1500 registered public health nurses were at work in Canada.[47]

In 1921, Dr Peter H. Bryce retired from the federal civil service. Bryce's career and interests had been an important part of the whole history of child health work in Canada from its beginnings in concern over school sanitation through the medical inspection of school children to the infant mortality campaign and even the mental hygiene movement. Over four decades Bryce and thousands of other Canadians had wrought enormous improvements in the health of Canadian children. Pioneering health workers in Hamilton, Toronto, Montreal, Vancouver, and other cities had persuaded many of their fellow citizens that protecting and improving the health of Canadian children was not merely a worthwhile or a charitable duty but an urgent national necessity. They had thoroughly discussed, invented, and tried out many practical techniques to implement their policy. They had sorted out means which would work from those which would not and, in so doing, had created new associations and new specialities within the health professions. Although the whole framework was still quite shaky and tentative in many places, out of a few separate and at first largely amateur efforts in individual municipalities, they had built a set of organizations which quite effectively united public-spirited citizens and professional health teams made up of physicians, nurses, and sanitary inspectors into an effort to tackle the health problems of children across the nation. They had discovered that education was central to the success of the whole effort. 'To get the knowledge we possess,' said Dr J.A. Amyot, federal deputy minister of health, 'into minds and hearts of the people, that is our problem.'[48] With increasing clarity Canadian public health professionals also saw that their crusade to improve the health of children was intimately bound in with the efforts of others to improve family life, schooling, and social welfare. Consequently, when such opportunities arose, they were eager to coordinate their activities with those of other reformers into a wider movement to improve the conditions of Canadian childhood.

PART III

'Remove the Young
from Schools of Crime':
Transforming the Treatment of
Juvenile Delinquents, 1885-1925

7

From Reformatory to Family Home: Late-Nineteenth-Century Young Offenders in the Context of Changing Theory and Prevailing Practice

On a cool Saturday evening in September 1887, over two thousand Torontonians and delegates assembled in the Horticultural Pavilion for the first public session of the annual meeting of the National Prison Association of the United States. Many of them had undoubtedly come to hear the address of the association's president, who for this year was the former president of the United States, Rutherford B. Hayes. The Toronto *Globe* reporter thought the audience was 'keenly in sympathy' with the objectives of the association, one of which was the need to reduce the number of Canadian and American children who were growing up to be criminals. 'Do not crowd anybody ... hastily, needlessly, recklessly, into the ranks of our criminal classes,' one Canadian delegate proclaimed to the conference. Another argued that the 'monstrous and flagrant evil' of committing girls and boys to the common gaols was doing precisely this. These institutions, explained a third, were 'schools of crime, with compulsory attendance and compulsory education.'[2]

The conference exemplified the beginning of an important change in the means which English Canadians would employ to achieve the objectives articulated at the prison congress. Although from one generation to another the intent behind child welfare work may vary little, new conditions and theories sometimes produce substantial changes in methods. Nineteenth- and early twentieth-century child welfare had the defence of society as its first goal; throughout this period Canadians were determined to ensure that youngsters would not grow up to join the burdensome ranks of paupers, drunkards, and criminals. As well, many Canadians hoped that through their efforts with the young they would also make better the society in which they lived and which their offspring would inherit. There was, wrote Ontario's provincial secretary, J.M. Gibson, 'no surer and more effective mode of improving society' than 'rescuing ... children from dangerous environments, wisely caring and providing for them during their early years, and giving them a good chance for a fair start in life.'[3]

In redefining the role of the family, in defending public health, and in transforming the educational system, the generation of middle-class English-Canadians which grew to maturity towards the end of the nineteenth century displayed a heightened sense both of childhood itself and of the importance of the family in rearing children. How far outside the confines of their own relatively comfortable households did they try to put their ideas into effect? What success did they have? To answer these questions this section will examine the changes English Canadians made in their treatment of those youngsters whom most observers saw as already well on the way towards a life of crime. As a prelude to that task, however, one must briefly survey the wider context in which changes in child welfare took place, consider the ideas Canadians held about the causes of and cures for delinquency, and discover what actually happened at this time to those children who ran afoul of the law.

I

Throughout the nineteenth century, English-speaking Canada promoted the welfare of its children at three different levels. First, custom and law together provided families with strong, positive support. To ensure the stability and continuity of families, provincial governments gave parents complete authority over their minor children and provided schools to help them fulfil their educational duties. Second, the state gave special assistance to families with blind, deaf, or feeble-minded children, including preventive care for those youngsters likely to develop habits which disturbed the social order. Finally, governments tried to rehabilitate as well as punish minors guilty of criminal behaviour.

As many English Canadians of the 1890s began to see their time as a period of both crisis and opportunity for social betterment, they began first to question and then to change many of the traditional ways of caring for children. A few argued that the only way to stop victimizing many children would be to completely reorder the social structure through socialism, anarchy, or the single tax. Others who were reasonably content with the basic framework of their society insisted that it must adopt measures to ensure that all Canadian children were brought up properly and must eliminate institutions and practices which tended to create problem children. This latter group believed not only that the quality of family life was the critical variable in determining whether a child turned out satisfactorily but, further, that good families could cure boys and girls who had already fallen into evil ways.

These Canadians therefore tried first of all to bolster families who were already doing a reasonable job of rearing their youngsters. In their public health work, they tried to increase the life chances of all children. They strove for an educational system which, in addition to teaching the traditional three R s, would also prepare girls to be better housekeepers and mothers, and boys to be sober, honest, well-trained, and industrious breadwinners and fathers. They made strenuous efforts to improve the physical and social environment of homes and schools by eliminating the neighbourhood saloon and poolhall, strictly regulating music hall and, later, motion picture performances, and censoring books and magazines. They campaigned against cigarette smoking and for a 'closed' Sunday. They put children's sections in their public libraries and children's 'corners' in their newspapers and magazines. They set aside and began to supervise playing fields and parks. They supported many new organizations for boys, girls, and young people.

Some Canadians also tried to help children and families whom they saw as special problems. So that reluctant families and young people would take advantage of the school system, they pressed for regulation of child labour, compulsory school attendance, and appointment of truant officers. To prevent families breaking up on the death or serious illness or injury of the father, they campaigned for workmen's compensation and mothers' pensions. Through Factory Acts and anti-sweating legislation they tried to protect the health of working-class mothers. They established a few day nurseries for the children of single-parent families and those in which both parents had to work. At some schools they began to provide milk or hot lunches. They established 'fresh air' funds to take poor children and their parents out of their environment once a year. They attempted to improve the housing of the poor. To give greater protection to the children of divorced or separated parents, they tried to change the principle governing the custody of minors to one based on the welfare of the child. They tried to sort out and confine in institutions those children whose congenital weaknesses, if passed on, threatened to 'level down' the race.

English-Canadian society also changed the ways in which it tried to salvage youngsters whose families would not or could not rear them. Canadians gradually ended the grim practice of 'baby-farming.' They began adoption services to place illegitimate babies in family homes rather than in foundling institutions and legitimized children whose parents subsequently married. They shifted the care of vagrant, orphaned, neglected, dependent, 'incorrigible,' and delinquent children from institutions to families.

The process of improving the general condition of Canadian children – and particularly those of the poor and the unfortunate – over the years from the 1880s to the 1920s could be analysed by examining briefly the history of each of the many efforts across the whole range of changes in child and family welfare. Alternatively, a more thorough investigation of a single effort may lay bare more clearly how the new generation put together a set of ideas and organizations in child and family welfare which tried to come to grips in new ways with the problems they faced. While each reform campaign has certain exemplary merits, the most useful is the work of those who tried to rescue children who got into trouble with the law. To get and keep youngsters out of lock-ups, common gaols, reformatories, prisons, and penitentiaries, these men and women created new trial procedures, extended the number and range of separate institutions for children and young people, and began probation and other services to care for the delinquent in his own or in a foster home.

Three reasons dictated this choice. First, those in the 'child-saving' movement – as it was called for a time – saw an intimate connection amongst child, family, and crime. 'Child-savers' therefore tried to break into the family pattern through which they saw criminal behaviour being transmitted from one generation to the next. In contrast to public health and education reforms that were designed to benefit all children, their work shows how reformers developed organizations and practices to apply their notions to the most difficult cases. Second, the effort to cure delinquency clearly displays the immense problems advocates of change faced in trying to persuade staffs and community supporters of existing institutions to understand and to use new and supposedly better methods of solving old problems. Finally, these labours showed the limits of late Victorian and early modern social theory, at least as English-Canadian reformers, professionals, and institutional workers then put it into practice. They discovered – or, perhaps more accurately, re-discovered – that certain patterns of human behaviour reproduced themselves with marvellous persistency from one generation to the next. Clear-eyed, practical, and patient men and women often found, as one of them lamented, that some 'mentally defective, morally dense, proudly wayward or defiantly lawless' youngsters – perhaps a smaller proportion than before they began their efforts – fell, or drifted, or were lured into, or determinedly entered upon a pattern of behaving which appeared to lead, almost inevitably, to a life of pauperism, drunkenness, and crime.[4]

II

A combination of beliefs and precedents governed the way late-nineteenth-century English Canadians treated their problem youngsters. There have always been some children – usually the dependent, neglected, or delinquent – for whom society as a whole has had to assume some responsibility. From at least the seventeenth century onward, English, American, and Canadian history shows that the state has generally used some combination of families and institutions to care for these youngsters. Thus some dependent children were auctioned off to the lowest bidder or apprenticed to families while others were cared for in orphanages or workhouses.[5] The relationship between family and institutional care, however, has been a varying one. In some periods and places, as in pioneer Upper Canada, family arrangements were of necessity by far the more important device. At other times, as in Ontario between 1860 and 1890, the province made most of its increments in child welfare by extending and improving institutions. While these changes in emphasis were partly related to a lack of institutions or of available foster homes, the large-scale immigration of children to Canada after 1870, described in earlier chapters, showed that this explanation did not apply to Ontario in the late nineteenth century. Current opinion and institutional momentum are more important factors in explaining changes in practice. When, as in England in the eighteenth century, flagrant abuses in the disposition of poor law apprentices became a serious and well-understood problem, those managing well-run workhouses probably looked after the health, education, and welfare of their charges far better than most of the factory owners to whom such youngsters had previously been apprenticed.[6] On the other hand, once the zeal which lead to their founding and enlivened their early years faded away, children's institutions displayed both a grim determination to persist and, at best, a cautious drabness in their management. 'Homes' and 'schools' often introduced prison-like procedures that the second generation of custodians, who lacked the dedication of their predecessors, designed for their own convenience but justified with a pious cant about maintaining order and training children in self-discipline. From 1859 to 1879, the Boy's Reformatory at Penetanguishene, Ontario, went through this process.[7] Between the 1880s and the 1920s, English Canada continued both historical precedents. While many people shifted their faith from institutions to families as the best means of caring for neglected, dependent, and delinquent boys and girls, institutions made a determined effort to survive and even flourish in the new intellectual context.

Towards the end of the nineteenth century, English Canada intensified a century-long effort to impose higher standards of order on itself.[8] Municipal councils, provincial legislatures, and Parliament enacted by-laws and statutes which circumscribed the freedom of Canadians to do things which legislators and their constituents felt were bad or immoral – drinking in certain communities, spitting on the streets, and putting young children to work in factories – and for not doing things which the same group believed to be good or moral – sending all children to school regularly, having them vaccinated, and insisting that urban dwellers obey sanitary regulations regarding the keeping of pigs, cows, and chickens in the city.[9] One effect of these developments was that some Canadians regarded an apparent growth of crime and delinquency, particularly in the cities, as signalling the imminence of social disaster. In fact, at the beginning of this era anyway, a federal government monograph argued that, except in the case of juvenile males, crime in Canada was actually decreasing.[10] As time passed, the more perceptive observers saw that the legal system was evolving in such a way as to create more offenders. Arguing in the Senate debate on the juvenile delinquency bill in 1907 that crime was increasing in Canada Senator J.A. Lougheed pointed out that in 1901 there were 147 convicts under twenty years of age, while in 1905 the number was 169, 'an increase of 16 per cent in that period.' In retort Senator J.V. Ellis explained that in passing 'wholesale Acts to bring persons within the scope and operation of the law' – such as Sunday observance ordinances and those regarding the sale of intoxicating beverages – legislators had made it 'more difficult for the ordinary kind of character to get along without, sometimes, coming within the purview of the courts.'[11]

Most middle-class Canadians probably approved of this greater ordering of their society. They saw some circumscription of behaviour as an inevitable part of the tendency, as Ellis put it, of the world 'to improve'; they believed that more of the 'ordinary' characters in their society should come under the scrutiny of the law. In the past, noted Thomas Parker, president of the London Children's Aid Society, the law provided that men arrested for drunkenness were let off with a fine or a brief gaol sentence. Under the Ontario legislation of 1893, however, these drunkards – who, Parker explained, loved their children, 'though ... in a queer way' – would have to mend their behaviour or else lose their youngsters to the society and then to foster homes.[12]

Not all Canadians, however, favoured what C.S. Clark described as 'the absurdity of making children, or anyone else for that matter, good or virtuous by Act of Parliament.' It ought to be possible for Toronto to avoid the dangers posed by adults playing hard ball in the streets without passing a by-law which permitted 'police to exclude children from the streets and terrify them with threats of Police Court prosecution for the heinous offense of playing with a soft ball.'[13]

Whether most or even many neglected children of the time actually did go on to lead lives on the edge of or beyond the law would be very difficult to prove. One can, however, say with assurance that police, prison officers, and charitable workers were environmentalists; they believed that most of those who became paupers, drunkards, or criminals came from the ranks of children who were neglected, delinquent, or dependent on the state.[14] As the Hon. T.W. Anglin, a member of the 1890 Ontario Royal Commission, accurately summarized their evidence, 'a large number of witnesses' who appeared before the commissioners stated that of those who ultimately became the worst kind of criminals, many first fell into bad habits because their education was neglected, because they were 'allowed to run at large in the streets,' and had 'not been subject to proper parental control or training.'[15] These citizens saw, in turn, a close relationship between poverty and neglect. Many young people, wrote Roman Catholic Archbishop John Joseph Lynch of Toronto, were condemned to such 'nurseries of crime' as 'filthy lanes and miserable houses' where bad parents and bad companions brought about their ruin.[16] But the children of the poor were not the only youngsters to get into trouble; middle-class children also transgressed the law. Kelso noted, however, that for the latter there was 'always sufficient influence at hand to save them from the error of their way.'[17] In 1894, the chief of Toronto's detective staff, William Stark, provided some rough statistical proof that, indeed, criminals were made during their youth. Stark took from the city's criminal records 'the names of 100 persons, selected in order of entry,' who had 'four or more convictions each for felony.' Of the 100, 74 had been convicted before the age of 21 and nearly half of this latter group 'were convicted before the age of 15.'[18] Remove the young from 'schools of crime, and place them under virtuous and benign influences,' summarized J.M. Gibson, and 'almost in the same proportion' did society cut off what later on would 'form a part of our criminal population.'[19]

While English Canadians sometimes grouped together those youngsters who were a source of difficulty to society, there were, in fact, three different sorts of 'problem' children. First, there were those generally described as the 'neglected' – waifs, 'arabs,' strays, newsboys, hawkers, beggars, habitual truants, and other children of the streets, and children whose parents instructed them in intemperance, vice, and crime. Although earlier legislation gave broad definition of this class, Ontario's Act for the Prevention of Cruelty to, and Better Protection of Children, passed in 1893, provided for this period the most wide-ranging and widely used description of what, in law, was a neglected child.[20] The act empowered various officers to apprehend without warrant and bring before a judge as 'neglected' any child 'apparently under the age of fourteen' who fitted into one of five general groups. A neglected child, the act stated, was any child (1) who was found 'begging or receiving alms or thieving ... or sleeping at night in the open air'; (2) who was found 'wandering about at late hours and not having any home or settled place of abode, or proper guardianship'; (3) who was found 'associating or dwelling with a thief, drunkard or vagrant,' or who 'by reason of the neglect or drunkenness or other vices of the parents' was 'growing up without salutary parental control and education' or in circumstances which were exposing him 'to an idle or dissolute life'; (4) who was found 'in any house of ill-fame, or in company of a reputed prostitute'; and, finally, (5) who was found 'destitute, being an orphan or having a surviving parent' who was 'undergoing imprisonment for crime.'[21]

Next, there existed a group of children imprecisely defined as 'dependent.' While in a general sense all infants and most children depended on one or more adults, English Canadians customarily applied the terms to three groups of youngsters. First, the dependent were those children, such as illegitimate infants in foundling homes, who never had a family. Second, they were orphans and other youngsters who, on the death or desertion of their parents, were not absorbed into the households of aunts, uncles, grandparents, or other branches of their extended families.[22] Third, they were children – such as Alice Maud Johnson and her English and Canadian compatriots – who were housed in or bound out and supervised from orphanages, children's shelters, houses of industry, and other institutions. Obviously, if some 'dependent' children were not intercepted by their extended families or by an institution, they could easily join the ranks of the neglected as well. 'My office,' Kelso told the Child-Saving Conference in Toronto in 1894, was 'that of Superintendent of Neglected and Dependent Children, because the two classes' of youngsters were 'so closely related.'[23]

Finally, there were the delinquent. Under the simplest definition, these were boys or girls between the ages of seven and fourteen who appeared in court and were found guilty of breaking a municipal, provincial, or federal statute. Under English common law, which of course applied in Canada as well, children under the age of seven were presumed to be unable to distinguish between right and wrong. Between the ages of seven and fourteen, Blackstone wrote, 'though an infant shall be *prima facie* adjudged to be *doli imcapax*, yet if it appear to the court and jury that he was *doli capax*, and could discern between good and evil, he may be convicted and suffer death.' As cases presented later in this chapter clearly indicate, Canadian courts decided that many youngsters, especially towards the upper limits of Blackstone's age range, were indeed *doli capax*. Those over fourteen, of course, were *doli capax* and thus subject to the full weight of the law.[24] While nineteenth-century Canadian judicial practice generally circumscribed minors in the traditional Blackstonian limits, mid-Victorian reformers had embedded two key attitudes towards young offenders into the Canadian consciousness. By the 1880s, most workers in child welfare and prison reform, and those with an interest in these fields, while generally accepting the traditional view that in order to deter others from committing crimes all criminals must be punished, agreed that, so far as youthful offenders were concerned, rehabilitation was more important than deterrence. They also believed that if juvenile offenders were to be turned from their ways they must be cared for separately from the common run of adult criminals.

Of early concern to Canadians, therefore, were young and especially first offenders. In their report on the penitentiaries, the royal commissioners of 1848–9 recommended the establishment of an institution for juvenile law-breakers. In response to this advice and other pressures, the government established two reformatories, one in Canada East and the other in Canada West.[25] In 1875, the federal government amended the Criminal Procedures Act to make it possible for courts to substitute sentences to provincial reformatories in place of penitentiary terms for offenders as old as sixteen. This legislation required magistrates and judges to make such sentences for at least two but for no more than five years; youngsters sentenced to terms longer than five years still had to serve them in a penitentiary.[26] During his term as Ontario's Inspector of Prisons, Asylums, and Public Charities, J.W. Langmuir expanded the facilities for potential or actual young offenders in that province. On the basis of his recommendations, in 1879 the province set aside part of the Andrew Mercer Reformatory to care for girls under the age of fourteen. Langmuir also made great efforts to change the existing Reformatory for Boys from what was essentially a prison into a place which would truly reform its young inmates.[27]

Voluntary organizations also provided institutional care for neglected and dependent children. In Toronto, for example, the Protestant Orphans' Home opened in 1849 and the Boys' Home in 1859. During Langmuir's inspectorship and afterward, under its Charity Aid Act of 1874, the Ontario government encouraged voluntary societies to set up and expand institutions designed to care for orphaned, neglected, dependent, and refractory children. While its motives in this work were partly humanitarian, the government no doubt also saw the force of Langmuir's argument that, if left to themselves, the children looked after in these institutions would 'become inmates of our gaols, reformatories, and penitentiary,' and therefore a constant public charge.[28] While Ontario took the lead in work to prevent and cure juvenile crime, other parts of Canada also made some efforts along these lines. In 1866, Halifax established an industrial school for boys, and in 1870 the federal government passed legislation permitting Protestant juvenile offenders to be sentenced to the school for periods of not less than two and not more than five years. When the city's Roman Catholics founded a similar institution in 1884, Parliament extended the legislation to cover children of that faith.[29]

Further blurring the distinctions between the neglected and delinquent, Canadians also sorted out by statute for special treatment those considered 'predelinquent.' Thus some young people who were at least technically innocent of any law-breaking could be incarcerated and treated in exactly the same way as if they had been found guilty of an offence. Under Ontario legislation passed in 1880, the parent or guardian of a boy between the ages of ten and thirteen could complain to a county or district court or police magistrate that 'by reason of incorrigible or vicious conduct' the boy was beyond the control of the parent or guardian. If the judge saw 'due proof' of such a complaint, then he could confine the boy in the reformatory for up to five years.[30] Society could also take such action on its own behalf. Under the Ontario Act for the Protection and Reformation of Neglected Children, a judge could order a neglected child under fourteen committed to 'any Industrial School or Refuge for boys or girls, or other institution' subject to provincial inspection for a period up to his or her eighteenth birthday.[31]

Where reformers of the late 1880s and 1890s really differed with their predecessors was on where society should place the children it had removed from their unsatisfactory homes and families. As their legislation amply demonstrated, the older group generally believed that only a long period of compulsory and segregated training, discipline, and schooling – preferably a minimum of two years spent in a special home-like but reforming institution – would change the character of the predelinquent or delinquent young person. Superintendent Donald J. McKinnon of Ontario's Victoria Industrial School characteristically argued that 'the quickest and safest' way to bring back a boy who was a confirmed truant, or insubordinate to his parents or teachers, was 'to put him in some well disciplined institution where every boy must obey.'[32] In justifying long-term institutional treatment, its Protestant chaplain explained that he had followed what had happened to the 221 boys discharged over a three-year period from the Ontario Reformatory for Boys. Since only 56 of them had gone astray again, he concluded, the institution had reformed about 75 per cent of them.[33]

In sharp contrast to their predecessors, the new generation of reformers looked to a wholesome family environment – a rehabilitated natural family or a suitable foster home – to deflect from their path those who were likely to drift into a life of crime. Explaining the Ontario legislation of 1893 to his colleagues, Senator G.W. Allan pointed out that the new Children's Aid societies could place a ward in a foster home so that the 'family tie' and the 'wholesome influences' that went with it would not be broken in the same way as when the youngster was placed in a charitable institution where it was 'only one of fifty or sixty others' and lost all 'the influences of a home ...'[34] In addition to preventing delinquency, a healthy family might also provide the healing therapy to reform those who had already drifted into a life of crime. Kelso was Canada's most eloquent and persistent exponent of this point of view. In all sections of the province, he wrote in 1895, good homes were looking for the services of growing boys. These homes provided schooling for half the year for younger lads and moderate wages for those who were older. It was a question, he continued, whether many of the boys in the industrial school or the reformatory 'would not do well in one of these homes, and be better prepared there for the real work of life than they could possibly be in the best reform school ever established.' Delinquent children, he concluded, 'should be committed on the indeterminate plan, and then there should be a generous sending out on parole of lads who could fairly be trusted to do well.'[35]

Both groups shared, however, the deeply engrained belief of English Canadians that corporal punishment could cure delinquency.[36] At the Ontario Child-Saving Conference in 1894 Senator Allan, the Reverend J.R. Black, secretary and agent of the Kingston Children's Aid Society, the Reverend S. Card, chaplain of the reformatory, and other delegates spoke in favour of, as Card put it, 'the reformative power in the end of a birch.'[37] Even Kelso thought corporal punishment a reasonable idea when it was clearly the only alternative to imprisonment. As a general rule, however, he argued that whipping was not needed 'so much as love of the right sort, discernment of child-character, individual attention, patience and self-control.' Most of the children he dealt with had learned hardship and cruelty 'all too soon' and 'to try to beat them into goodness would only be to follow out the course of their former treatment' and 'to harden instead of mollify their dispositions.'[38]

III

When they saw what actually happened to youngsters enmeshed in them, reformers demanded changes in existing ideas, practices, and institutions. Not only did they look at theory, they also looked around carefully and saw children who were not being taken care of satisfactorily by the system their predecessors had put together and, particularly, that too many youngsters were finding their way into the adult prison system.

What, then, did Canadians do to children who got into trouble? For many children, an appearance in the police court was the first product of their transgressions. In the first nine months of 1886, 8570 people were committed for trial in Toronto. Of these, 361 were between ten and fifteen years of age, and 698 between fifteen and twenty.[39] According to Kelso, the Toronto police reported that in 1890 they had arrested 653 boys between the ages of ten and fifteen and 971 between the ages of fifteen and twenty.[40] Canadian courts of the time handled the children appearing before them with little consistency from one court to another and one appearance to the next. Some youngsters were lectured or let off with a warning, others were given suspended sentences, and many were sent to gaols, reformatories, industrial schools, or even penitentiaries for sentences of greatly varying lengths.

Consider the cases of some youthful criminals and other problem youngsters of the 1890s. The rector of St Matthew's parish in Hamilton, the Reverend Thomas Geoghegan, explained to the Ontario Royal Commission in 1890 that boys who broke city by-laws were often arrested and taken to the local lock-up.

He knew 'three boys under ten years of age who were seen walking on the Grand Trunk track outside the city.' A constable took their names and 'the patrol waggon went round to their homes at night after they were in bed and took them to the police station.'[41] While stating that his officers would summons rather than arrest boys for swimming or playing on the street, or 'any offences against the by-laws,' Hamilton's police chief responded that his force did confine to the lock-up before trial boys charged with 'larcenies and misdemeanors.'[42]

W.H. Howland told the commissioners the grim saga of a family that he had known for over a decade. From about 1879 to 1882, the older boy was 'in the common gaol ... for small petty offence[s], for which he would receive ten, three and five days, and so on ...' There he received a thorough education in crime, 'graduated rapidly,' and 'began to consort with a harlot at fifteen.' At this time his mother was dying in a wretched hovel with two children, one hers and the other belonging to another woman, 'crawling over her.' Outside, the boy and two women lived in a shed which formed 'the congregating place for about a dozen boys ...' At fifteen, he was sentenced to the penitentiary for three years. Soon after his release, he was sentenced to the Central Prison for a year, then to Penetanguishene for three years, and was at that time serving a further six-year term in the penitentiary. Beginning his criminal career at ten, the younger boy 'went in and out of gaol' until he was twelve 'for periods varying from ten, twenty to thirty days.' At this age, he was sent to Penetanguishene for four years and later to the Central Prison for two. While Howland did not know at exactly what age their sister became a prostitute, he thought it was 'before she was eleven years old.' She was sent to the Mercer Refuge. Between 1879 and 1890 'the total time of this family in gaol,' Howland summarized, had been twenty-two years.[43]

Senator Allan told his colleagues what happened to two Toronto girls who were charged with petty theft. The fifteen year old was accused of stealing a hat from her sister and the thirteen year old of stealing sixty-five cents and a brush and comb from her employer. Despite the fact that neither girl had come to the attention of the police before, they 'were arrested on Saturday night, kept in the police cells all night, carted to the jail on Sunday, and placed with some pretty bad characters.' On Monday they were 'taken from the jail in a van, crowded with the very worst class of men and women.' There, despite the pleas of E.E.A. DuVernet, acting for the superintendent of neglected and dependent children, that the cases be heard privately, the magistrate ordered the girls brought into open court where he remanded the thirteen year old on bail and let the fifteen year old go on a remanded sentence.[44]

The list of new arrivals in Dorchester Penitentiary in New Brunswick for 1887–8 included twelve-year-old Herbert Smith who was to serve five years for breaking and entering, thirteen-year-old Enos Medley who was to serve three years for compound larceny, eleven-year-old Edward Chambers who was to serve two years for burglary and larceny, and fourteen-year-old Robert Welsh who was to serve seven years for manslaughter. The Protestant chaplain of Dorchester was pleased that that year there had been 'no increase in the number of "boy convicts"' and that those then in the penitentiary were 'looked after with special care.'[45]

Newspaper accounts and public records also told Canadians much about young lawbreakers. In March 1891, a New Westminster newspaper reported that a fourteen-year-old Indian girl was sentenced to six months at hard labour for stealing twenty dollars and some clothes.[46] Later the same year, two Kamloops boys accused of stealing some flower pots had their sentence suspended when they promised to be on good behaviour for the next six months.[47] In late April and May 1897, a gang of six boys, led by fourteen-year-old Willie Oleson, broke into nine Vancouver business establishments and stole, amongst other things, some boots, shoes, cameras, and a watch. The boys then sold the stolen goods to a cook at the Ottawa Hotel. Out of his share of the proceeds, young Oleson bought himself a revolver. The magistrate sentenced the cook to two years, the businessman who sold Oleson the revolver to five dollars or ten days, and Oleson himself 'to 30 days' imprisonment, to be kept away from the other prisoners and fed on bread and water as much as possible.' Since British Columbia had no reformatory, the other boys 'were discharged on being well lectured.'[48]

In addition to their delinquents, late-nineteenth-century Toronto and other Canadian cities had a host of abused and neglected children. In 1889, Kelso estimated that Toronto had 'between six and seven hundred boys and about one hundred girls' who were sent out on the streets 'by drunken and avaricious parents to earn money by the precarious selling of newspapers, pencils, etc.,' but who more frequently used their work 'as a cloak for begging and pilfering.'[49] That same year, the Toronto Police Station gave shelter to 539 waifs who were 'not classed as offenders.'[50] Even after the city placed newsboys under municipal regulation and supervision, Kelso reported in 1890 that there were no less than '592 boys licensed to sell papers in the streets of Toronto, and ... a couple of hundred' who had not applied for licenses. At least two hundred amongst the licensed boys had 'no responsible guardians or parents.'[51]

Some of these lads stayed in the Toronto Newsboys' Home. There they were charged ten cents a day for supper, bed, and breakfast or $1.30 a week for full room and board. Except for two nights a week, when they could remain out until nine, the boys had to be in by seven o'clock. Others lived in cheap lodgings.[52] A worker out of the Jarvis Street Mission described the latter sort of place. 'In a small cellar with low ceilings, dimly lighted, the air reeking with fumes of tobacco and whiskey,' he and his fellow workers would find '100 or 125 men and boys; some playing cards, others drinking and smoking.' Around the sides 'of this den was a shelf, on which the men slept, heads to the wall, feet outward, with no pillow or clothing to cover them other than the rags they wore.' Some also slept on the floor. The nightly charge to stay in such a place was five cents.[53] Although no friend to missionaries and reformers, C.S. Clark generally confirmed their description of the lives of newsboys and other lads of the Toronto streets. While some 'of the more careful ones' did well, for most the lives they pursued led to 'miserable results.'[54]

As to 'incorrigible' youngsters, Superintendent McKinnon of the Victoria Industrial School reported that most of those sent to his institution fell into this category; that is, they slept out at night, ran away from home, refused to go to, or were suspended from school, and had 'proved unmanageable by the parents or teachers.'[55] The school's records show that of its first fifty boys, twenty-five were 'sent on the application of a parent or guardian, who charged them with being uncontrollable, and drifting into criminal habits.'[56] Of the seventy-four boys entering in 1903, thirty-seven were committed for incorrigibility.[57]

How representative were these case histories and reports? Since Ontario was the only province with a full range of institutions, it provides the best example of how Canadians put prevailing theory into practice: troublesome boys and girls there were more likely than elsewhere to be treated as people thought was best for them. In 1889, Ontario courts committed eighty-five boys to the Ontario Reformatory at Penetanguishene. Of these, one was seven, five were nine, six were ten, six were eleven, seventeen were twelve, and twelve were thirteen years old.[58] In the same year, the Ontario Industrial Refuge for Girls admitted nineteen girls. Of these, one was four, two were eight, two were nine, three were ten, two were eleven, three were twelve, and two were thirteen years old.[59] At the end of 1889, Ontario's only industrial school contained upwards of 140 boys. Nine of these were from seven to nine years of age, 46 were from ten to twelve and 53 were thirteen to fifteen.[60] In the same year 451 boys and 46 girls under sixteen were committed for varying periods to the common gaols.[61] The federal penitentiary in the province also contained a number of young persons. In the year ending 30 June 1889, Kingston Penitentiary contained 100 males and 1 female under twenty years of age. Of the new arrivals in the previous year seven were sixteen, four were seventeen, four were eighteen and eight were nineteen years old.[62]

These figures, however, give an incomplete picture of the number of children who were actually incarcerated in Ontario in 1889. They do not, for example, include those children who were picked up, lodged in the cells for an hour or two, overnight, or over a weekend, and then let go with an informal warning from sheriffs, gaolers, police officers, or even magistrates. Neither do they include children whose parents or guardians committed them to a home of one kind or another at the suggestion of the police or magistrate. On 30 September 1889, Ontario children's institutions which received provincial grants held 1855 children – many of whom, of course, were there because they were orphaned or had only one working parent to support them – and 3706 different youngsters resided in them at some time or another over the whole year.[63]

In addition to the number of children being institutionalized, the new reformers were also very much concerned about what happened to children once they were put behind the walls. Their remarks to the Prison Congress displayed some of the anguish of reformers – both of old and new schools – over what children and young people learned from adult prisoners and hardened criminals. For this reason, some lock-ups and common gaols, such as that in Hamilton, tried to segregate prisoners.[64] Chatham's gaoler believed that his institution's imperfect classification system contaminated younger prisoners. While he thought they did it 'through bravado more than malice,' older, more hardened prisoners not uncommonly taught criminal ways to boys in their midst.[65] The nation's former chairman of the Board of Inspectors of Asylums and Prisons, E.A. Meredith, expressed himself much more strongly. In his experience, the association of prisoners in county gaols was a 'frightful cruelty and injustice to the innocent prisoner or the novice in crime' and a 'corrupting influence of the worst kind to all.'[66]

Special institutions for children also provided an unsatisfactory setting for their clients. The family-like quality that its founders had envisioned as the central characteristic of the Ontario Reformatory for Boys at Penetanguishene did not survive the test of time.[67] Although it was, in the opinion of the Ontario royal commissioners of 1890, 'equal if not superior to any they had seen in the best institutions visited by them in the United States,' it was, nonetheless, primarily a prison for boys. Partly because of a poor site, and partly because of inadequate or insufficient equipment, the objections of trade unions, and other limitations, its inmates did not leave it well-trained in any trade or occupation.[68] Even with its reasonably able staff and fair facilities, the fact was that in dormitory, in the dining room, and on the playing fields youngsters less than ten years old mingled with and learned from hardened boys, some with long criminal records – such as those in Howland's sample family – of sixteen or older.[69] In a way its 'Dormitory System' was representative of the whole institution. Under this arrangement, the Protestant chaplain explained, the 300 boys were divided between two dimly lighted dormitories. Each night, five guards 'shod with noiseless slippers' made constant patrols so that it was 'quite impossible for anything bad to be done by the boys.'[70]

At that time the beliefs and teaching on sexual practices held that masturbation was extremely harmful to those who indulged in it.[71] Middle-class parents and managers of institutions for boys, therefore, were constantly on the watch to prevent it. Thus this fear structured the whole character of over a third of each and every day that a boy spent in the reformatory. In the opinion of its superintendent, 'half the boys throughout the towns and villages in the country' were masturbators.[72] He also believed that the 'cottage system' being promoted by some reformers to provide inmates in institutions with a family-like environment was wrong because it could not provide proper surveillance. On the other hand, Superintendent McKinnon of the Victoria Industrial School – which was organized on the 'cottage system' – stated that, while he would not claim he had 'succeeded in stamping out masturbation completely' in his school, he thought it was 'nearly at an end.'[73]

In the view of its promoters and supporters, McKinnon's school and others like it provided the best custodial and curative treatment to pre-delinquent and delinquent youngsters available in late-nineteenth- and early twentieth-century Canada.[74] In 1874, the Ontario legislature passed an act which, in its 1884 amended version, permitted school boards or philanthropic organizations to establish industrial schools to lodge, clothe, feed, and teach neglected, incorrigible, and truant youngsters who were under the age of fourteen.[75] In consequence, a thoroughly distinguished group of Torontonians and other Ontarians – the vice presidents and governors alone numbered over sixty well-known businessmen, politicians, and other community leaders – banded together to build an industrial school for boys at Mimico, near Toronto.[76] Opened by the governor general, the Marquess of Lansdowne, on 16 May 1887, the Victoria Industrial School enrolled its first boy a month later. 'The objects of the institution,' explained its superintendent in 1894, Thomas Hassard, were 'to provide the children with a home and suitable employment.' Its boys lived under 'the "Family Plan," or "Cottage System,"' residing 'in a cottage home, under the care of a matron and guard,' who acted as '"mother" and "father" of the "family"' and who worked to have 'the home feeling restored and implanted in the breast of each boy.' The Ontario commissioners found that, while the cottages were 'very neat structures,' the 'only supervision of the boys at night' was provided by the officer who slept in an adjoining room. In their cottages, the boys learned the simple tasks of housekeeping – cooking, baking, mending, and housework. In this work and in all other aspects of the program school officials tried to keep the boys busy all the time. They attended day and Sunday school, took trades training in farming, printing, tailoring, and shoe-making, and participated in a drill and sports program. As long as a boy was kept busy, Hassard explained, he kept out of trouble.[77]

By the turn of the century, Ontario had established three more industrial schools – the Alexandra School for Girls in East Toronto, the St John's School for Catholic Boys in East Toronto, and the St Mary's School for Catholic Girls in Toronto. On 30 December 1901, the four schools enrolled a total population of 226.[78] Other provinces followed suit; before 1910, for example, both British Columbia and Manitoba had established their own industrial schools.

As the nineteenth century drew to a close, Canadians looked both backward and forward in their treatment of neglected, dependent, and delinquent boys and girls. Most of the middle class shared a belief in the need for a higher standard of civic order and in flogging as a preventive and cure. In looking for the causes of bad behaviour they seized upon environment, and especially the narrowest environment, that of the family itself, as their prime target. English Canada's all-pervasive commitment to the assumption that the family was the best – meaning most efficient, effective, economical, and 'natural' – method of child-rearing produced the characteristic supporting custom and legislation underlying nineteenth-century social structure. As an unstated corollary to this belief they also considered that, indeed, most Canadian children were already reasonably well-reared by traditional means. On the other hand, since Canadians had to support through their gifts and their taxes a whole cluster of institutions ranging from county workhouses and gaols through children's homes and lunatic asylums to reformatories, prisons, and penitentiaries, they saw that, obviously, some families in the past had not done their jobs properly and that some presently in their midst were failing to do so. Bad families made the next generation of those whose behaviour would pose a social threat to the rest. In particular, the class that the respectable saw bound together by the closely interconnected evils of pauperism, alcoholism, and crime replicated itself, generation upon generation, through its children; unless society intervened, such youngsters would follow their parents in a route which began in neglect and moved through childhood and youthful delinquency towards its grim and inevitable terminus. The principal difference between the generations in the English-speaking middle class was how the state should insert itself into this situation. Despite the failure of Penetanguishene and similar establishments elsewhere, in putting their faith in industrial schools some people showed that they still believed that it was possible to incorporate into an institution many of the characteristics of a well-run – and perhaps nostalgically old-fashioned – family that also had the task of educating its younger members. The next chapter examines the efforts of other Canadians to replace this belief with one that focused on care and rehabilitation in a family home.

8

Towards 'Intelligent and Progressive Legislation for the Prevention of Crime': Preparing the Way for the Juvenile Delinquents Act, 1886-1908

In the years immediately following the Toronto Prison Congress, many English Canadians tried to come to grips with the problem of juvenile delinquency in their society. As part of this task, promoters of family-focused care had to demonstrate the greater efficacy of their approach over more traditional practices. Since their plans for preventing delinquency dovetailed into other aspects of child-centred reform, they found this part of their effort relatively easy to accomplish. In a remarkably short period of time, many people, and particularly some of those most able to facilitate change, came to believe that the best preventive for delinquency was to place neglected and dependent children in a proper home environment. This idea drove a devoted band of men and women – mostly volunteers, including a wide range of community leaders – to spread with great rapidity a network of Children's Aid societies across Ontario and other parts of Canada in the 1890s and the early years of the twentieth century. Advocates of change found their second job – that of demonstrating the value of home and family care for the already delinquent – more difficult. Not until they had their preventive machinery reasonably well established could Canadian child-savers give much systematic attention to their curative program. At this point, Canadian reformers examined the contemporary children's court movement in the United States. They experimented with and adapted the complex organizational, administrative, and legal machinery developed across the border to work in the Canadian constitutional setting. In 1908, Parliament crowned their efforts by passing the Juvenile Delinquents Act.

I

Men and women in Ontario, particularly in Toronto, were the first to advocate the family-centred method of preventing juvenile delinquency and to develop new procedures and practices for implementing it. In the years between 1886 and 1893, a group of Toronto organizations established or promoted, in rapid succession, playgrounds, the Victoria Industrial School, the Toronto Humane Society (which initially concerned itself with children as well as animals), a new lodging-house for newsboys, a school for truants, 'fresh air' and 'Christmas' funds for poor children and their families, and a Children's Aid Society. They cajoled Toronto and then Ontario to regulate newsboys and to institute separate trials for youthful offenders. They held a conference to promote prison reform and brought to their city the annual meetings of the National Prison Association and the American Humane Society.[2] Their most important single achievement, however, was to persuade the provincial government to set up in 1890 a five-man Royal Commission on the Prison and Reformatory System of Ontario, chaired by the province's former inspector of prisons, asylums, and public charities, J.W. Langmuir. 'All the moral forces of the community,' Kelso later wrote, were 'actively united in the demand for intelligent and progressive legislation for the prevention of crime.'[3]

Langmuir and the other commissioners believed that the subjects of preventing and curing juvenile delinquency were their 'most important' tasks. In their open hearings, which they conducted all over Ontario, they regularly asked their witnesses for the causes of vice and crime in children and for suggestions as to how to prevent them. In visits to nearby American institutions they thoroughly examined practices and procedures. They read widely and thoughtfully about developments in Britain, other European countries, and Australia. The commissioners produced a detailed and practical report that was characterized by an obvious sympathy for young people in trouble.[4] For these reasons, and because it came along at exactly the right time, the report had an enormous influence in changing Canadian practices in caring for neglected, dependent, and delinquent children.

The commissioners first spelled out means to prevent children from drifting into a life of delinquency. In their view, the 'baneful influence of bad homes' was one of the most serious causes of crime. For this reason, they argued that the traditional 'rights of parents' could be 'forfeited by gross, willful neglect or by such continued gross misconduct as must work the ruin of their children.' In many cases, 'the only means of saving the child' was 'its immediate and complete removal from parental control and parental influence.' The commissioners criticized Ontario for making no legal provision except through industrial schools for placing children in homes other than their own. They recommended that compulsory school attendance laws be rigorously enforced. They called for all parts of the province to establish day industrial schools to control and teach disorderly and habitually truant children. They favoured a curfew for boys and girls, the regulation of second-hand, pawn, and junk shops, and an end to the importation of immigrant children. They called for authorities to establish and supervise playgrounds and gymnasia and to give more generous support to charitable organizations supporting children.[5]

The commissioners then considered children who had already committed offences. They recommended that, whenever it was possible to do so, those under the age of fourteen should be summoned rather than arrested. If an arrest was necessary, the youngster should be detained but in a place 'entirely separate and away from a police station.' No matter what the charge, children should be tried with no one present 'except the officers of the court, the necessary witnesses, the truant or probation officer' and parents or guardians. 'Under no circumstances,' they argued, should the province commit those found guilty to a common gaol, nor even to a refuge or reformatory 'until all other means of correcting or reclaiming' them had been tried. The commissioners insisted that courts should be empowered to make the widest possible use of admonitions, suspended sentences, and supervised probation. When young people had to be confined, the commissioners recommended they be sent to industrial schools, remaining there only as long as 'absolutely necessary to render them fit to be placed in a private family, either as apprentices or boarders.' Youngsters 'not thoroughly vicious,' should be placed almost immediately. The commissioners also recommended that the Ontario reformatory be moved to a more suitable location, that it adopt the 'cottage system,' and that its atmosphere be changed from that of a prison to a school – 'a hive of active, earnest, unremitting industry' – in which boys should learn to work at least as hard and as well as their contemporaries on the farm and in the factory. More important, the report suggested that sentences to the reformatory be indeterminate so that a boy 'by his industry, his diligence and general good conduct' could earn a remission of his penalty, or be allowed to leave on parole. To supervise those apprenticed or boarded out from the industrial schools and paroled from the reformatory the investigators suggested that the province set up local voluntary boards all over the province.[6]

Obviously, the commissioners envisaged that Ontario would expand both its institutional and non-institutional arrangements for child care. For a number of reasons, however, this did not take place. Most important, their ringing endorsement of family-centred care closely accorded with the notions of the new generation of reformers and administrators in the province. Further, the idea worked effectively in practice and could be implemented quite cheaply. Over the next few years, therefore, Ontarians and other Canadians gave earnest attention to ways by which neglected, dependent, and then delinquent children could be cared for outside refuges, industrial schools, and other institutions.

Prodded by the reformers, the Ontario government began to translate some of the commissioners' recommendations into practice. In April 1893, the provincial secretary, J.M. Gibson, introduced in the Legislature a bill which soon came to be called 'The Children's Charter' or the 'Gibson Act.'[7] Gibson explained that the bill reflected not only the recommendations of the royal commission but law and practice elsewhere. Imperial legislation passed in 1889 provided the basis of those sections dealing with cruelty to children. These forbade a parent or guardian to ill-treat, neglect, abandon, or expose a boy under fourteen or a girl under sixteen in a way 'likely to cause ... unnecessary suffering, or serious injury to its health.'[8] This and related provisions, Gibson explained, reduced parents' right of property in their children and affirmed that, from infancy, children possessed 'the rights of citizenship.' Cruelty to children, he went on, was more than merely a matter of inflicting physical injury or suffering; his officials designed the act to protect children from being taught to steal or, by example, to become prostitutes.[9]

Laws passed as early as 1872 in South Australia inspired those parts of the bill establishing a new system of caring for orphans and waifs, and existing practice in Michigan and Massachusetts provided the model for administering it. Rather than being raised in institutions, the children were to be placed in 'the care of motherly and fatherly people' who would give them 'wholesome family influences.' The bill assigned two tasks to privately organized Children's Aid societies in cities and to voluntary 'visiting' committees in rural areas. They were to search out needy children, 'rescuing them from pernicious influences and surroundings,' and to find suitable foster homes over which they were to maintain 'a watchful and kindly interest.' To oversee the operation of the whole system the provincial government was to appoint a superintendent of neglected and dependent children.[10]

Finally, the bill implemented as much as a provincial legislature could of the recommendations of the commission regarding young people already charged with delinquent behaviour. Children charged with offences against provincial statutes and municipal ordinances were to be confined separately from adults, to be tried in private, and, as far as possible, in places other than police courts.

Ontarians greeted the bill favourably. It was commended both inside the Legislature and without, and the 'Gibson Act' received royal assent on 27 May 1893.[11] The government promptly implemented its provisions. It appointed J.J.

Kelso as superintendent of neglected and dependent children. By the end of that year, Kelso and interested local citizens had organized Children's Aid or similar societies in Ottawa, Toronto, Peterborough, London, and Guelph.[12] For most of the next decade, the legislation stimulated voluntary organizations and their professional staffs to give their main attention to its preventive rather than its curative provisions. Kelso and others secured the establishment of thirty Children's Aid societies in Ontario alone by the end of 1901.[13] Manitoba passed legislation modelled on the Ontario act in 1898, and British Columbia followed suit in 1901. Thereafter, interested people in those provinces established societies in Winnipeg, Vancouver, and Victoria.[14]

Although he by no means laboured alone, John Joseph Kelso was the key person in this early activity.[15] As a young journalist in Toronto, Kelso discovered the miserable conditions afflicting the children of the street in that city. He resolved to devote his life to 'plead for these little ones' who perished by the wayside 'in a land abounding in Christian activities.'[16] With the help, advice, and support of Toronto merchants and businessmen, such as J.H. Pearce, J.W. Langmuir, John Ross Robertson, William Gooderham, and J.K. Macdonald, of politicians such as W.H. Howland, E.F. Clarke, and Senator G.W. Allan, and of professional men and reformers such as Goldwin Smith, Beverley Jones, J.G. Hodgins, and Dr A.M. Rosebrugh, Kelso sparked the organization of the Toronto Humane Society, the Children's Fresh Air Fund, and the Toronto Children's Aid Society. He presented an influential brief in 1890 to the Ontario royal commission.[17] Despite Lady Aberdeen's observation that he was 'too afraid of calling a spade a spade,' Kelso had the journalist's knack of writing and speaking in a way which immediately touched the emotions of his readers and listeners.[18] From his early articles in the Toronto *World* and then in the *Globe*, through his widely distributed annual reports, magazine articles, letters to editors, press interviews, and by means of his numerous speeches across Ontario and the rest of Canada, Kelso eloquently preached the gospel of child-saving and of nurturing youngsters in a loving family. He displayed administrative abilities of a high order. That he persuaded communities all over Ontario to found Children's Aid societies – over sixty by 1907 – is but one example of this quality in action.[19]

Like their colleagues in public health and in education, Kelso and his associates were able to harness to their cause much of the interest in moral and social reform which was flourishing at this time. In Toronto Kelso brought together a broad cross-section of the reform community in the city to help organize the Toronto society.[20] Its first major task was to lobby the provincial government to pass the child welfare legislation called for in the report of the Langmuir royal commission. Thereafter, the society undertook the full range of tasks assigned to it by the Gibson act. Its work attracted support at the highest level. At the annual meeting in October 1893, the speakers included the governor general, Lord Aberdeen, Senator Allan, and Gibson. On the platform as well were the lieutenant governor of Ontario, a provincial cabinet minister, eight prominent clergymen, and other local notables.[21] Such support greatly assisted the Toronto and other societies to move quickly into the front rank of voluntary agencies in their communities.[22] In Vancouver, the president of the society for a number of years was Sir Charles Hibbert Tupper, son of the former prime minister and himself a former federal cabinet minister. As in Toronto, Ottawa, Winnipeg, and other cities, the Vancouver society's board of directors also included a wide range of the city's businessmen, clergy, and professional men and their wives.[23]

The activities of individual Children's Aid societies show how they handled a variety of actual cases. In its annual report for 1906–7, the Ottawa society commented very briefly on the present condition of each of the 563 children who had, since 1894, been entrusted to its care. Of the initial 7 cases, the first, a boy taken and placed in 1894, was still with the paternal uncle who had adopted him. The second, an imbecile girl taken in 1895, had died of consumption at the age of eight in the Orillia Asylum. The third, a woman of twenty-one when the report was made, after being 'cruelly treated by a relative,' was taken in 1896 and placed with her paternal grandparents where she was 'quite satisfactory.' In July 1905, the fourth, a girl, had ended her connection with the society by marrying 'a respectable young man.' The fifth, a boy by now aged fourteen and recently moved to a new foster family, had 'a good home' but was still 'restless and unsettled.' Finally, two sisters who had been taken and placed out in 1896 were still with the paternal uncle who had adopted them.[24]

Some societies became far more involved in their buildings and shelters than did others. In its first twelve years, the Ottawa society took control of 431 children. Of the 93 taken in 1904–5, it found 'domestic homes' for 58 – including 14 re-placings – sent 14 to industrial schools, placed 9 with parents and, at the time of the annual meeting, had 12 children awaiting homes.[25] Over its first twelve years, the Vancouver Children's Aid Society had taken charge of 475 children. Of these boys and girls, 130 had been adopted 'into good homes,' 46 were 'at service, supporting themselves,' 12 had been 'discharged,' 74 had been returned to their parents, 15 had died, 9 had run away, 19 had married, 9 had 'transferred,' and 12 had entered a vocation. Nevertheless, 149 wards of the society remained in its home, together with 19 'temporary boarders.' Indeed, up to the 1920s, the Vancouver society spent an enormous amount of time, effort, and money on building and operating its home, becoming as much a traditional child-care as a child-placing agency.[26]

While societies generally tried to support, bolster, restructure, and ameliorate the natural families of problem children, their officers also put considerable faith in placing such young people into a new environment. Over the first nine years, societies in the province had, Kelso explained, found 'homes and situations' for 'over two thousand children.' In 1905, he proudly reported that the province no longer tolerated evils which had been quite common when he began his work. There was, he said, 'an entire absence of begging on the part of children,' and there were no more of 'the ragged and barefoot children who used to excite the sympathy of good people and cause money to be generously given for soup kitchens and Christmas dinners.' There were, as well, no more 'homeless newsboys sleeping in odd corners,' nor 'children carrying beer cans.' Instead, he reported, 'bright well-dressed children' played 'merrily' on their way to school and public men everywhere advocated 'more play grounds, sanitary homes, good wages, the Saturday half-holiday,' and other philanthropic measures.[27] In 1909, the president of the Ottawa Children's Aid Society, W.L. Scott, boasted to the Canadian Conference of Charities and Correction that of the seven thousand children 'transplanted' under the provisions of the Gibson act, 'less than 2 per cent' had turned out failures. He also claimed probably a much larger number had been 'saved in their own homes' by improving home conditions. 'What an army of future criminals,' Scott continued, had 'this work transformed into good citizens!'[28]

While the Gibson act and its duplicates in other provinces undoubtedly improved the lives of many children, sometimes Kelso, Scott, and Children's Aid Society members and supporters overstated their case. At the Charities Conference, no one asked Scott to prove that, had the Children's Aid societies not come to their rescue, the pauper, drunkard, and criminal classes would have added to their ranks most or all of the thousands of children he mentioned in his speech. Perhaps, as well, Torontonians had not swept their streets quite so clean as Kelso claimed. In 1910, the Toronto Children's Aid Society 'instituted a campaign against boys under eight years of age selling newspapers and smallwares in the streets late at night.'[29] Two years later, the commissioner of the Toronto Juvenile Court claimed that, due to the efforts of one of his probation officers, the 'down-town streets have been practically cleared of "weeping Jimmies," the "swiping gangs" ... broken up, and the pocket picking of the big stores stopped.'[30]

Despite the best efforts of Kelso and Children's Aid societies to place youngsters in foster homes, child-care institutions continued to thrive in Ontario. They reported 1855 inmates in residence in September 1889, 1832 in the same month in 1900, and 2082 in September 1910.[31] As Gibson explained to Lady Aberdeen, the ladies who managed and supported these agencies did 'not like their charges to be scattered away from their eyes.'[32] Kelso took issue with institutions that did not send out youngsters until they were between ten and fourteen. If a home kept a girl until she was thirteen, her character was then developed and she did not attract people in the same way as would a five to seven-year-old 'full of those nice little traits' that appealed to people's 'love and sympathy.' Treating the older girl as a servant, families often restricted her 'to the kitchen and a back room upstairs' and gave her 'no advice of sympathy at that most trying period of life.' Institutions also made it possible for negligent parents to have their little children cared for 'at a trifling expense' and then resume their guardianship when the youngsters were 'old enough to earn wages.'[33]

Kelso was also acutely conscious of how institutions changed over time. Originally, he argued, orphanages had been founded by people 'inspired with a love of humanity and a desire to do some good in the world,' and boys and girls brought up there 'were blest by the tender compassionate love of men and women who sought to give them the best possible substitute for father and mother care.' When such persons passed away, however, their places were taken by those asked to take office or because they wanted 'to be associated with persons of good social standing.' As a result, Kelso concluded, at a time when he had far more foster homes than he could fill, 'hundreds of clean, well-fed children' were growing up in institutions who did not know and never could know 'the ordinary joys of childhood and the endearments of home ties.'[34]

II

Reformers also endeavoured to change the treatment of children already adjudged delinquent. In 1892, the federal government amended the Criminal Code so that, where 'expedient and practicable,' offenders apparently under the age of sixteen were to be tried separately and without publicity.[35] Two years later, the Ontario government and influential citizens of that province persuaded the federal government to sponsor a bill which provided for the 'separation of youthful offenders from contact with older offenders and habitual criminals during their arrest and trial' and for their commitment to places where they might be 'reformed and trained to useful lives instead of being in prison.'[36] As Ontario was at that time the only province that had the court committees necessary for placing out convicted juveniles, these provisions of the act applied in the first instance only in that province. Since magistrates and judges had not generally found it 'expedient and practicable' to follow this practice when it was left to their discretion, Parliament also changed the Criminal Code to make it mandatory that those apparently under sixteen be tried separately and without publicity.[37]

Indeed, the most important task of these early years was to persuade magistrates and municipalities to implement in both letter and spirit the new provincial and federal legislation. As Kelso explained in his report for 1894, while Ontario legislation specifically prohibited the reformatory from receiving boys under thirteen, magistrates tried 'in every possible way' to circumvent the law. They did so because, while the provincial treasury paid the full costs of the reformatory, the industrial school assessed each boy's costs to his home municipality. The situation gradually improved. While, in 1889, 47 boys thirteen and under entered the Ontario Reformatory and 497 boys and girls under sixteen spent some time in the common gaols of the province, the comparable figures for 1895 were 21 and 314.[38]

It was, however, only after they had their preventive machinery well established that Ontario reformers could give thorough attention to rehabilitating the delinquent. By the turn of the century they started to work on a broad front to achieve their ends. Children's Aid societies in Ontario began to take greater advantage of the 1894 federal requirements that they should be notified whenever an information had been made against a child and that permitted them to make recommendations regarding sentence. In 1894, the Toronto Children's Aid Society made recommendations on the cases of only 54 youthful offenders. Eleven years later, after its officers had investigated 587 cases, only 56 of these youngsters were committed to an industrial school.[39]

Kelso and others also gave their attention to industrial schools and the reformatory. While he commended industrial school staffs for their 'enthusiastic sense of the importance and responsibility of the work' and the 'high moral atmosphere' of their schools, Kelso did not conceal his belief that they were a poor alternative to foster homes. There might be, he admitted, a 'danger of going too far in the work of home-finding' but 'in view of past experience' he was convinced that many more lads 'would be far better off and have greater scope for their activities, in the farm homes of the Province.' Children in reform schools needed 'the advantages and privileges of well-ordered family homes far more than the discipline of an institution.' For this reason, he joined members and staffs of Children's Aid societies in enthusiastic support of all schemes which would result in shorter stays in industrial schools, particularly parole and the indeterminate sentence. Children's institutions, Kelso argued, should promise all their inmates that 'just as soon as their conduct' warranted it they would be 'returned on parole to the natural life of the community.' In contrast to the practice of the schools, Kelso also believed that a child on parole or released from custody should be visited regularly to ensure that he or she was not slipping into old habits.[40]

For entirely different reasons, the staffs of industrial schools also gave their enthusiastic support to the idea of indeterminate sentences. Like the trustees and employees of other child-care institutions, industrial schools workers naturally had a stake in what they did. They also reflected the persistence of the older view of rehabilitation. They tended to believe that only well-regulated institutions could do the job and therefore tried to hang onto a child as long as possible. They were also concerned that parents who had committed their own youngsters could not always be persuaded to leave their boys and girls in as long as the staff felt necessary. This difference between the 'Children's Aid' and the 'Industrial School' positions was clearly displayed when, in 1900, Ontario provided that all sentences to industrial schools for infringements of provincial and municipal statutes be indeterminate and that children so committed be under the guardianship of the school until they were eighteen.[41] In commending this development, Kelso drew particular attention to the provision that 'every child must be given an opportunity outside the institution within a period of three years.' The superintendent of the Victoria Industrial School, C. Ferrier, welcomed the change because it removed 'all cause of misunderstanding, both in children and parents, as to the power the school may exercise.' During 1903, well after the new legislation had gone into effect, of the 248 boys who had been in the Victoria Industrial School at some time or other over the year, 70 departed. Of this number, 32 went to their own homes, 28 to other homes, 7 escaped, 1 transferred to St John's, and 1 went to the reformatory. Kelso obviously had much persuading yet to do.[42]

As they expanded their placement work, Kelso and Children's Aid societies also made greater efforts to intercept children before they were sent to institutions and particularly to gaol. Kelso argued, with the complete agreement of Ontario's sheriffs and gaolers, whose opinions he carefully surveyed on the matter, that boys who had once been inside a gaol, if only for a week or so, constituted 'a different class from the ordinary boy offender' not yet committed. Since such youngsters had already 'learned so much about the prison system,' they were 'no longer deterred from wrong doing by fear of consequences.'[43] Kelso also complained that police officials showed 'a great lack of patience' with boys who had broken municipal ordinances. These functionaries saw the reformatory as 'the easiest way to get rid of a troublesome lad' and thus gave more weight to 'the spirit of revenge and punishment' than to a consideration of the boy's future welfare.[44] Kelso and some of his compatriots worked along the very edge or even beyond what the law permitted. One day the warden of Central Prison in Toronto told Kelso that the prison then held two boys, one ten and the other eleven, who 'had been sentenced to five years each in the Reformatory.' Without consulting anyone, Kelso took charge of the boys and placed them in farm homes. Although he 'waited with bated breath ... no one showed the least concern or even enquired as to what had become of the children.' Emboldened by this success, Kelso boasted that in the next two years he 'successfully waylaid or intercepted some forty boys, all under sentence to the Reformatory, and all spirited away ... before they reached their legal destination.' When the provincial attorney general eventually discovered this scheme, he 'kindly consented to shut his eyes to what was going on.'[45]

As its most effective example of the efficacy of home over institutional care for juvenile delinquents, Ontario closed its Reformatory for Boys at Penetanguishene in 1904.[46] For a time, the provincial government responded to the criticism of the Langmuir commission by planning a more up-to-date reformatory in a more appropriate location. Amidst such uncertainty, Penetanguishene gave minimal consideration to new ideas and changed very little over the 1890s. In 1898, it apprenticed only 5 of the 175 boys who were in residence at some time during the year, in 1899, 3 out of 188 and, in 1900, 5 out of 194. In response to Kelso's persuasion, the government decided, instead of replacing the reformatory, to place out all the boys already in it and to take care of future cases through Children's Aid societies and industrial schools.[47] Despite the substantial reservations of some magistrates, police officials, and some of the reformatory staff, all eighty-eight inmates were parolled and carefully placed either in the care of a family or in a job. Although the lads 'seemed a tough crowd,' Kelso later explained, they obviously responded 'to sympathetic treatment, friendship and implicit trust in their word.' At the end of four years, Kelso reported that, at that moment, none of the boys was in the penitentiary in the province, that the three who had been in the provincial gaol had been there for short sentences only, and that one boy of twenty who had moved west was in prison for theft. These four boys comprised the only serious cases.[48]

Encouraged by the success of this venture, in 1905 the Ontario government reduced the population of the Ontario Refuge for Girls from sixty-five to five with about the same measure of success. In February 1908, Kelso reported that, because they were 'weak-minded,' eight or ten of the girls were in institutions; of those sent out to homes, 'four were brought back for immoral conduct, and five others caused great anxiety before they finally settled down.' No less than twenty-one, however, had since 'married well.'[49]

To any who might miss it, Kelso went on to state the moral of these two stories: it was not 'law, or system or institution' that saved, 'but only the personal influence of good men and women thoroughly embued with the spirit of love and compassion for the children of misfortune and temptation.'[50] Fifteen years of enormous effort had paid a handsome return.

III

In the years after Penetanguishene released all its inmates, the central thrust of the effort to keep delinquent children out of institutions turned into what was called the 'Children's Court Movement.' In turn, this activity led very quickly and directly to the passage of the federal juvenile delinquency legislation of 1908. As early as 1887, Toronto had informally, though not very successfully, instituted private trials for children.[51] Both the Ontario act of 1893 and the federal legislation of 1892 and 1894 had provided for such trials for youngsters under sixteen. While Toronto and, later, Montreal met this requirement through separate children's courts, most places put it into effect by conducting the trials of youngsters either in the magistrate's chambers or the usual courtroom at a time when police court was not in session. Influenced by American experiments, those in the juvenile court movement sought to establish special courts with separate judges, detention homes, and probation officers. The latter could investigate and make recommendations on children before the courts prior to sentencing. Further, because these officers would be able to supervise the boys and girls closely, juvenile courts would be able to dispose of most cases through probation. This movement, in short, wanted to separate children entirely from the whole police and assize court systems and place them in the hands of people whose main interest was in reforming youngsters.

Some Chicago citizens – especially members of the Woman's Club of that city – had taken the lead in introducing children's courts in the United States. In 1899, they persuaded the Illinois legislature to pass a Juvenile Court act and the first court sat in Cook County on 1 July that year. In the next few years, the idea spread with great rapidity; by 1909, twenty-two states had juvenile court laws.[52]

Canadians interested in child welfare quickly familiarized themselves with the ways in which both American and English communities conducted children's courts and operated supervised probation schemes.[53] Kelso was a long-time acquaintance and correspondent of Judge Harvey B. Hurd, who drafted the Illinois legislation[54] Judge Ben Lindsay's Denver, Colorado, juvenile court was undoubtedly the most famous of these years, and he visited Canada on a number of his many speaking tours. Canadians, however, turned neither to Chicago nor to Denver but to Philadelphia for the model for their first systematic effort to put the notion into practice.[55] In May 1906, W.L. Scott, president of the Ottawa Children's Aid Society, and John Keane, its paid secretary, attended the annual meeting of the National Conference of Charities and Correction in Philadelphia. Scott and Keane were so impressed with what they saw of the Philadelphia probation system that, on their return from the conference, they persuaded the executive committee of the Ottawa society to adopt the scheme in their city. In August that same year, the society appointed two probation officers and sent them to Philadelphia to observe the work there.[56]

In its first year, probation work in Ottawa exceeded the expectations of the society. 'Juvenile probation no longer rests for us on theory,' Scott reported enthusiastically at the next annual meeting: 'Its efficiency has been amply proved by over a year of practical work.' While he and the board had initially considered 'extravagant' the claim of Philadelphia and other American cities that the combination of the juvenile court and supervised probation had reformed all but 5 per cent of delinquent children in their own or in foster homes, Ottawa made a 'still better showing.' Of the 240 cases handled since the system was begun, Scott reported, 'only three or not 2 per cent' had been sent to industrial schools and two of these youngsters were sent there not by the courts but by their parents.[57]

Scott and the two probation officers clearly recognized the immensely difficult task which they faced. One of the officers explained that some of the boys under her charge were 'very hard to manage.' Five of them never worked for 'more than two or three weeks at a time.' One left his job and boarding house 'owing ten dollars for his board' and nobody knew where he now was. Another was sent away to a special school, was returned 'on account of his conduct' and since then had stayed at home both 'unwilling to work or study.' Still, there were cases where the officers were somewhat more successful. One boy of thirteen, from an 'idle' family, who 'had never been willing to study and was completely ignorant,' was severely reprimanded for stealing and then put on probation. After his officer persuaded him to return to school, he 'attended classes regularly and reported every week to the Probation Officer.' Moreover 'he worked part of the vacation' and returned to school the following September. Despite its difficulties and disappointments, therefore, the society generally shared the gratitude of its other probation officer, 'for the legislation we have to keep our children from being sent to jails and reformatories.'[58] Although the Ottawa society believed that its new probation work could be carried out under the federal legislation of 1894, it soon discovered that 'new legislation was absolutely essential.'[59] In particular, since probation officers had no legal status, they were unable to gain admission into homes where they were not welcomed. In trying to change this situation, Scott and the Ottawa Children's Aid Society transformed their pioneering work from local into national importance. Through the discussion their campaign aroused, many Canadians became aware both of the new ideas regarding children's courts and probation services and of the fact that they had been implemented with great success in a Canadian setting. This favourable publicity in turn stimulated other communities to consider beginning the work themselves.[60]

Scott undoubtedly played the central role in the rapid passage of the Juvenile Delinquents Act. Not only was he an able lawyer and social reformer but he also had excellent political connections. In drafting the proposed bill he had the help of Liberal Senator F.L. Béique, and of his father, Senator R.W. Scott, secretary of state in Sir Wilfrid Laurier's government and associated in the past with such reforms as the Canada Temperance Act ('the Scott Act'). The Scotts were able to arrange that Mrs Hannah Kent Schoff, chairman of the Philadelphia Court Committee, address a special meeting of senators and members of Parliament when she visited Ottawa under the sponsorship of the Children's Aid Society in December 1906.[61] In the spring of 1907, the elder Scott introduced the juvenile delinquents bill into the Senate in hope of encouraging both parliamentary and public discussion. After what the younger Scott described as 'much agitation,' the Senate gave the bill unanimous second reading.[62] At this point Senator Scott withdrew it at the request of the minister of justice in order to give the government time to consider it carefully. Clearly the Scotts and others hoped that the bill would either become a government measure or at the very least receive cabinet support. They immediately began to organize a campaign to pressure Parliament to pass the bill at the next session. Kelso and the younger Scott persuaded numerous organizations, including WCTU branches, Children's Aid societies, Local Councils of Women, the boards of orphan homes, and church groups, to send letters and petitions to Parliament.[63]

In May 1908, Senator Béique introduced into the Senate a bill very similar to that of the year before. He prepared his brief for it with care; he presented British, American, and Canadian precedents and practices and effectively argued the practical case for non-institutional care of delinquents. After considerable debate and examination of the measure in committee, it passed third reading in the Senate on 16 June 1908.[64] From there the bill went to the House of Commons, where A.D. Aylesworth, minister of justice, presented it as a government measure and, after a brief debate, it passed its third reading on 8 July 1908.[65]

What did the new Juvenile Delinquents Act accomplish?[66] One of its most important aims was to deal with the complex problem of jurisdiction.[67] While constitutionally Parliament has exclusive jurisdiction over crime in Canada, provincial legislatures have jurisdiction over the civil status of persons. Parliament was therefore unable to follow American precedent, which was based upon the chancery court tradition, and define delinquency as a state or condition.[68] Instead, the act defined the offence of delinquency as an act performed by any boy or girl apparently under the age of sixteen that violated any federal, provincial, or municipal ordinance for which a fine or imprisonment was the punishment, or any other act for which he or she was liable to be committed to an industrial school or a reformatory. Since provinces alone have the constitutional right to set up courts, the application of the new federal legislation depended upon their cooperation. The act therefore provided that it should be put in force in any province, or part of a province, only after the provincial or the relevant municipal government had established detention homes and had designated or established juvenile courts.

When a province or municipality had met these conditions, section 16 of the act gave the juvenile court the widest possible powers in dealing with cases of juvenile delinquency. First, no matter how serious the case, the juvenile court had exclusive jurisdiction over it. Only the court itself could decide to order that an indictable offence be tried before an adult court. Second, once it found a child guilty of delinquency, the court had a very wide range of options in dealing with the culprit. Within the broad framework that it must act as required by 'the child's own good and the best interests of the community,' the court could adjourn the hearing, could impose a fine up to ten dollars, could commit the child to the care or custody of a probation officer or other suitable person, could supervise the child through a probation officer in its own home, or could place him in a foster home. Further, it could commit the child to the care of a Children's Aid society or of a superintendent of neglected and dependent children, or send him to an industrial school, refuge, or reformatory. The act, however, specifically forbade that a juvenile delinquent be sentenced to, or incarcerated in, any gaol, penitentiary, or police station that also held adults. Even after the court had disposed of the case, the child remained its ward and subject to it until the court itself terminated the relationship or the child became twenty-one years of age. The act made it an offence for any adult to encourage or otherwise cause a child to commit a delinquent act and for parents and guardians to so neglect a child that he became or was likely to become a delinquent.

The act provided for juvenile court committees and probation officers to investigate and advise the juvenile court judge on how best to deal with a child and, if necessary, to take charge of him after sentence. In a clause which echoed the Illinois statute, the act enjoined judges, court committees, and all others involved in the care and treatment of delinquent boys and girls to construe its provisions 'liberally': the 'care and custody and discipline' of a juvenile delinquent was to 'approximate as nearly as may be' that given by parents and, as far as was practicable, each child was to be treated 'not as a criminal, but as a misdirected and misguided child, and one needing aid, encouragement, help and assistance.'[69]

IV

As a rule, commented Senator L.G. Power of Halifax during debate on the Juvenile Delinquents Act, governments did not go about looking for legislation to undertake, 'particularly legislation of a philanthropic kind.' Indeed, in enacting the statute, the federal government was clearly responding to the immediate, practical needs of the Ottawa Children's Aid Society. Two broader characteristics of the passage of the act, however, deserve particular comment. First, Senators Scott and Béique, with the concurrence of the government, introduced both bills in the Senate rather than in the House of Commons, and Parliament conducted its main debate in the upper House.[70] In taking this step its sponsors and the government clearly indicated that, in their opinion, the proposals were of limited interest to all but a small minority of Canadians and not a subject of much controversy amongst this group. With the major exception of some senior members of the Toronto police force, and some hesitation on the part of persons associated with industrial schools and similar institutions, both the petitions and the parliamentary debate indicated that Canadians working in or concerned about child welfare approved of the measure.[71] Although they did so for a variety of reasons, the majority of senators and members clearly supported the measure. A few expressed concern over what they saw as the wide powers accorded to probation officers and over the deprivation of certain youngsters of their right to trial by jury. Nevertheless the only formal division over the measure in either House in the session of 1907 and that of 1907–8 took place in the Senate over the constitutional issue as to whether the federal government could proclaim the act in a municipality without the appropriate provincial government taking steps to permit it to do so. Both Houses of Parliament, therefore, generally concurred with Senator Béique that the bill met 'a public demand which should be satisfied without further delay.'[72]

Over a period of about two decades, then, Kelso, Gibson, the Scotts, and others concerned with social improvement had convinced themselves and had persuaded many members of the relatively small group of Canadians who influenced or decided social policy that their new ideas for the prevention and cure of delinquency were workable propositions. In a very real sense, therefore, those responsible for its passage could look upon the new Juvenile Delinquents Act as a great triumph for the idea of family-centred care of problem children. The kind of treatment which they had found worked so effectively with thousands of neglected and dependent children could now be applied systematically to the care of delinquent children as well. As W.L. Scott explained to the National Council of Women in October 1908, the spread of Children's Aid societies, and the passage of the Act, demonstrated belief in the idea that a child was a product of its surroundings and that the home was 'the best place' for his development.[73] Child-centred reformers were now ready to turn to the formidable task of transforming their essentially pilot projects into nation-wide practice.

9

Trying to Make a 'Child into What a Child Should Be': Implementing the Juvenile Delinquents Act, 1908-1925

In her report to the fifth Canadian Conference on Child Welfare in September 1925, Charlotte Whitton boasted of the 'advanced state' of the way that Canada cared for its juvenile delinquents.[2] She thus celebrated the fact that, a generation after they had embarked on the task, Canadians had moved a long way towards institutionalizing those ideas on the use of family-centred means of preventing and curing juvenile and adult crime which some had found so novel and so exciting in the late 1880s and 1890s. Although Miss Whitton would have been the first to point out that reformers had yet to prod many parts of the nation into implementing the new standards, during the preceding three decades institutions had certainly given way to the family as the agency chiefly responsible for keeping youngsters from entering upon a life of crime. While an earlier generation of Canadian child welfare workers had devoted its efforts to building and supporting infant homes, orphanages, and industrial schools, the group active from the 1890s to the 1920s and beyond gave most of its attention to schemes that placed problem children in a family setting.

After Parliament passed the Juvenile Delinquents Act, reformers found they had to undertake three important jobs. First, they had to get the law implemented all across the nation. Since they had designed it to be proclaimed piecemeal – only after provinces or municipalities had met certain conditions – its advocates had to persuade each community to take the necessary action.[3] Second, judges, court committees, and probation officers had to design procedures for conducting their work effectively. Third, reformers had to explain their failures. Social workers, probation officers, judges, and communities discovered that, while the new notions might be more effective than the old, they did not eliminate juvenile delinquency. Further, courts found it necessary to continue to confine some children for fairly long periods of time. At this point many committed to the new practices felt obliged to find a way of explaining their failures without endangering their fundamental belief in family cures. As a result, some of them abandoned for a time their basically optimistic and increasingly sophisticated environmentalism to embrace the crude genetic determinism of the early mental hygienists.

As Miss Whitton explained, by the 1920s reformers had gone some way towards accomplishing these tasks. In a fashion similar to other contemporary efforts for child and family, what they had accomplished was not so much that all delinquent or potentially delinquent youngsters were being cared for under the preventive procedures of the Juvenile Delinquency Act and related provincial legislation, but that these practices had become the Canadian norm. Pioneers had laid out and standardized a new pattern of treatment and had started to professionalize the staffs that carried it out. They began to see more clearly their connection with efforts in health and in education and to come together in joint enterprises and organizations with their compatriots in these fields. Finally, as they testified by embracing mental hygiene, most of those in this vanguard generation were far too committed to the ideology of their program to begin to use their accumulating experience as a basis for a critical assessment of their fundamental assumptions.

I

In the dining room of a house on Simcoe Street in February 1909, Winnipeg opened the first court under the Juvenile Delinquents Act. The distinguished barrister, politician, and police magistrate, the Honourable T. Mayne Daly, acted as judge. In the first case, Judge Daly suspended sentence and assigned four runaway girls to the care of the superintendent of neglected and dependent children.[4] Five months later a dominion parole officer reported that his investigation revealed that only 2 out of the initial 198 youngsters who had passed through the court had proved to be 'unsatisfactory cases.'[5] Winnipeg's prompt action was not typical; other Canadian communities proceeded very slowly to implement the new legislation. Over the act's first five years, in addition to Winnipeg, only Halifax, Charlottetown, Montreal, Ottawa, Toronto, Vancouver, and Victoria set up juvenile courts. By 1917, eight more communities or areas – including the whole province of Alberta – had joined the original group. By 1922, Nova Scotia had set up two courts, Prince Edward Island one, Quebec one, Ontario thirteen, and British Columbia three or four. On the prairies, Manitoba had extended the act to two court districts and Saskatchewan and Alberta had passed general legislation extending it over the whole of each province. Thus, although most of the major cities of the nation applied the act over its first decade and a half, provincial and municipal authorities were very slow to implement it in the smaller cities, towns, and rural areas.[6]

Most courts were established only after concerned citizens made the same sort of effort as the Ottawa Children's Aid Society had earlier undertaken. In an order-in-council in September 1908, the government announced that it would not proclaim the act in a city or district until it had provided a proper temporary detention home, had an industrial school available, had found a judge willing to serve in the juvenile court, had provided for a probation staff, and had the agreement of an organization or some individuals to serve as Juvenile Court Committee.[7] In urban centres local organizations such as Children's Aid societies, Local Councils of Women, WCTU branches, and child protection societies conducted campaigns to ensure that their communities met these conditions. In Vancouver the passage of the act stimulated discussion, and public opinion, including that of members of the city council, appears to have agreed with the local Juvenile Protection Association on the need for a juvenile court and detention home in that city. Vancouver, however, took two full years – and the enthusiasm generated by a visit from Kelso himself – to meet all the conditions; its juvenile court did not actually begin work until June 1910.[8] On the prairies, where rural municipal organization was weak, provincial governments extended the act outside of the cities by using existing courts and provincial child care facilities.

Over this same time, juvenile court workers created what they believed to be effective judicial, professional, and administrative practices. Vancouver's Judge Helen Gregory MacGill wrote that an effective juvenile court must recognize certain fundamental principles: that its function was not punishment but treatment; that each case required preliminary investigation; that supervised probation was the 'very essence' of rehabilitation; and that children must not be incarcerated with adults.[9] Despite considerable local and regional variations, most tried to put these principles into practice by dealing with delinquents in three stages: preliminary investigation, a court appearance or appearances, and follow-up activities.

In the critical first and third of these steps, the probation officer occupied the key position. He was, Scott explained, 'the first essential.'[10] In the investigative stage, he tried to make it unnecessary for most children in trouble to make even an initial appearance before the judge. In most instances Commissioner J. Edward Starr of the Toronto Court passed cases to one of the probation officers for investigation, and found that often 'kindly advice or warning' were sufficient and no further action was necessary.[11] In enforcing truancy laws, the superintendent of neglected children in Winnipeg directed his officers to patrol the streets and department stores during school hours. In this way, and usually with the support of parents, he prodded most truants and unregistered youngsters into classes without having to undertake court proceedings against either them or their parents.[12] In Vancouver, a probation officer made a nightly round of downtown sections to find juveniles who walked the streets late at night or who attended theatres or pool rooms unaccompanied.[13]

When these informal and basically persuasive efforts did not correct a child's behaviour or when one had been formally charged with an offence, then judges required their probation officers to conduct a thorough investigation of the case before bringing it before them. Sometimes police, probation officers, and judges placed children in a shelter or detention home for a period of observation and testing. In Vancouver, the detention home, with accommodation for fifteen boys and five girls, was in the same building as the juvenile court. While children were never kept in the home for more than a few weeks, during the time they were in residence they attended school in the company of a number of supervised children who came daily from their own homes. When not in school, the children played games or kept occupied doing the housework of the home. Each was also, of course, carefully observed by the staff.[14]

As they grew in experience, juvenile courts began to use both volunteers and specialists to help them. In addition to probation and school attendance officers, Judge D.W. McKerchar of the Winnipeg court called on the business community for help in finding jobs, asked missions and other organizations to provide 'Big Brothers' and 'Big Sisters,' arranged for physicians to give medical examinations, and in March 1919 opened a psychopathic department for special counselling and diagnosis. Whenever a youngster repeated an offence, the clinic staff visited his home, school, and neighbourhood to obtain information about the family and its environment, and they examined and tested the child. Judge McKerchar then used this information, as he explained, 'in deciding the best form of treatment' and in disposing of the case 'in the best interests of the delinquent.'[15] By 1921, the Toronto court had on its staff a psychiatrist, five probation officers, one social investigator, one social investigator-stenographer, one stenographer, and three court clerks. The judge could also consult three psychiatrists and three psychologists.[16] In Halifax, the judge could call on the Children's Aid Society's full-time probation officer and, from the police force, the city's truant officer and two policewomen.[17]

Children and young people who appeared before juvenile courts found them somewhat more relaxed and less formal than other courts. In the carpeted Toronto courtroom of Commissioner Starr the 'Bench' consisted of an armchair behind a long table, at one end of which sat the agent of the Toronto Children's Aid Society, at the other the agent of the St Vincent de Paul Children's Aid

Society and, on either side of the commissioner, the chief probation officer and the clerk.[18] Starr apparently modelled some of his practices – such as having boys report to him each week – on those of the famous Ben Lindsay.[19] Partly because of their own temperaments and partly because many of them were drawn from the ranks of those already on the bench, other juvenile court judges, including Starr's successors in Toronto, did not take so strong and Lindsay-like a personal involvement in each case.[20] In 1920, an outside observer commented that although the Vancouver court was 'conducted with due regard to legal formalities' as far as the taking of evidence was concerned, he 'noted with pleasure that both Judges dealt with each case in a common sense parental fashion.'[21]

After establishing guilt, the juvenile court judge was ready to dispose of the case. He listened carefully to what the probation officer and others of the advisory staff had to report on the youngster's physical and mental condition, and his home and school environment. In all courts, the preferred choice was to put the child on probation in his own home or, failing that, to place him on probation in a foster home. As a last resort the judge could place him or her in an industrial school or other child-care institution. For judges to follow either of the latter options with girls posed special problems. Foster homes for girls, argued Judge MacGill, needed to be scouted out more carefully than those for boys. Further, and strongly if unconsciously underlining a double standard, although boys' offences were joy-riding and breaking and entering, 'only too frequently' those of the girls were sexual and often resulted in pregnancy. In these cases, the court had to consider both the expected child and the mother.[22]

In dealing with those children whom the court decided to rehabilitate either in their own or in foster homes probation officers took on a job even more difficult than their preventive and investigative tasks. As W.L. Scott explained to the Canadian Conference of Charities and Correction, making a child 'into what a child should be' was a particularly slow process because the probation officer had to start by undoing what it had taken years to do. It was 'the loving and unsparing personal effort, fresh with every new case as with the first that alone could save.'[23] In many cases their real problem was more with parents than with youngsters. Probation officers had to try to reconcile mothers and fathers who were separated, to arrange for financial support for deserted wives, and to attempt to modify the habits of severe, cruel, or drunken parents.[24] Some probation officers regularly visited the child in his natural or foster home. Others required the youngster to report in on a regular basis. In some cities, such as Vancouver, Winnipeg, and Toronto, the probation officer could also call on a corps of volunteers to help in the rehabilitation process.

Two circumstances tended to circumscribe the general effectiveness of probation work. Either from the size of his case load or their other police, truant, inspectorial, or child placement responsibilities, many officers were not able to give individual cases very much time. Moreover, during the first decades the position never developed into a career demanding special training or providing opportunity for advancement. Juvenile courts therefore found it difficult to attract to their staffs the bright, able, committed men and women which Scott and other initiators of the scheme felt were absolutely essential to make probation a success.[25]

Juvenile courts in small towns and rural areas were less likely than their urban counterparts to put all of Judge MacGill's principles into practice. Outside the cities, the local police magistrate often acted as judge of the juvenile court and conducted its proceedings in his office.[26] In some places these magistrates could call upon probation officers for assistance. Manitoba made its school attendance officers ex officio probation officers, Alberta did the same with officers of its Department of Neglected and Dependent Children, Saskatchewan with its inspectors of foster homes, and Ontario with the paid agents of local Children's Aid societies. Such expedients, however, merely added to the already onerous work load of these officers. In consequence, rural probation workers tended to concentrate most of their limited time on investigation and gave minimal time to rehabilitation. Indeed, some rural juvenile courts carried out their duties without any of the necessary machinery. Until some provinces began in the late 1920s to send travelling mental health clinics and other diagnostic services to rural areas the nature and quality of the treatment given a rural or small town delinquent depended very much on the personal character of the judge. In practice, proclamation of the Juvenile Delinquents Act in such circumstances probably made little real difference over what had prevailed earlier under the 1894 federal legislation. If rural practice differed little in the 1920s from that of the 1890s, however, the standards by which it was judged had changed enormously.

The family-centred care which was at the heart of the juvenile court idea had taken but one generation to become the principal policy in English-speaking Canada for preventing and curing juvenile delinquency. It not only governed the thought and work of the growing professional child welfare community in the years after the First World War but also framed in the efforts of a further generation of workers. As late as 1961, the 'intake' procedures followed by the Vancouver Juvenile Court were but a more thorough version of the activities undertaken forty years earlier by Judges Shaw and MacGill and Chief Probation Officer H.W. Collier.[27]

What one believer called 'social optimism' was also a central characteristic of the new notions of child welfare.[28] What comes through strongly in the early accounts of child-saving, and not merely from lay reformers but from those actually labouring with erring children, is the obvious realism with which they tackled their duties and the generally hopeful view they had of the outcome. After serving twelve years as a police magistrate and juvenile court judge, H.C. Shaw of Vancouver still felt that 'the majority of those in our penitentiaries and jails' could be made into 'good citizens.'[29] After the same number of years as Vancouver's chief probation officer, during which he and his family had lived right in the detention home, H.W. Collier expressed a strong preference for probation over custodial care. He proudly described the efforts he and his staff made to 'cure' children in their homes and the high rate of success they had achieved.[30]

In this generally optimistic framework, juvenile court officers of the 1920s naturally tried to extend the scope of their efforts. The future was their concern; their 'bounden duty,' explained Judge Shaw, was 'to try to make the public generally, and our Legislators in particular, see what we see and catch our "vision." '[31] To enable their movement to salvage a greater proportion of delinquent Canadian children they first asked for more of what they already had. They argued that the act should be extended to cover a greater proportion of the Canadian population and a wider range of Canadian youth. Despite their pleas, however, the juvenile court system spread very slowly in the 1920s and 1930s.[32] On the other hand, reformers and court workers achieved their latter goal when, in 1921, Parliament amended the Juvenile Delinquents Act to permit juvenile courts in those provinces requesting such a change to deal with young people up to eighteen instead of sixteen years of age.[33] By 1925 three provinces had taken advantage of this provision. To culminate their efforts to improve the law, in October 1928, representatives of courts, child welfare agencies, and industrial schools convened in a round table conference with federal officials to draft a new bill.[34] In 1929 the federal government repealed the 1908 statute and enacted a new Juvenile Delinquents Act that incorporated much of what the professional workers proposed.[35]

The child welfare movement also called on governments and the judicial system to enforce more effectively other appropriate legislation. In her compilation of provincial statutes which had a bearing on the matter, Judge MacGill discovered in 1925 that their total ranged from two enactments by New Brunswick's Legislature to thirty-nine by Alberta's.[36] The courts, however, did not always interpret legislation to the liking of child welfare officers. Under an amendment to the Criminal Code passed in 1918, to expose a child to the danger of becoming immoral, dissolute, or criminal by indulging in 'sexual immorality' became an offence.[37] Judges MacGill and MacLauchlan argued that, in some provinces, 'strained interpretations' of this provision had made it impossible to convict under it partners of common law marriages 'with several children of the parties in the same house.'[38]

In the early 1920s, some of the professionals and their lay supporters suggested extending the jurisdiction of the juvenile court to cover the entire family.

Two separate strains in the movement came together in this particular effort. On the one hand, the court's supporters continued to believe that a child's family was the origin of his or her delinquency problem. On the other, the professionally trained social workers who were beginning to appear in Canada at the time were using the technique of family casework with some effect.[39] Judge Emily Murphy of Edmonton and others therefore argued that the juvenile court should grow into a court of domestic relations.[40] Over the next two decades, indeed, many juvenile courts gradually extended their jurisdiction to include much of the related provincial legislation regarding children and families and many of them in practice became family courts.[41]

Despite their optimistic faith, juvenile court judges, probation officers, and Children's Aid officials had to come to grips with the problem that they were not salvaging all pre-delinquent and delinquent children. In the first bloom of the 'mental hygiene' movement, therefore, some judges and probation officers began to blame most of their failures on the fact that the children involved were too mentally incompetent to be saved.[42] To diagnose the consistent troublemaker who did not respond easily to the patient care of judge and probation officer as mentally defective and then pop him into a custodial institution was a tempting solution to a difficult problem. It was, explained Saskatchewan's superintendent of child protection, F.J. Reynolds, 'an imposition on foster parents as well as a detriment to the child to try to keep the troublesome feeble-minded class in foster homes.'[43]

To their credit, judges and other professionals were generally able to resist the easy way out that the mental hygienists provided. Those present at the delinquency sessions of the Canadian Conference on Child Welfare in Winnipeg in September 1923 did not quarrel with Judge D.D. Harkness of that city when he strongly reaffirmed the principle on which a whole generation of workers had based their work. There was, Harkness argued 'scarcely a single child' amongst the 1600 to 1800 juveniles in institutions in Manitoba 'whose needs would not be better served by the rehabilitation of his own family home, or the provision of a foster home or of a boarding home.' What was needed, he continued, was 'a larger use of the family home, a broader application of the parental spirit, a profounder faith in the power of affection to chasten and discipline.'[44]

II

Such, then, were the procedures, practices, and beliefs regarding delinquent youngsters that the professionals – judges, probation officers, Children's Aid officials, and provincial superintendents – borrowed or developed over the early years of the Canadian juvenile court. In order to see the new system as a whole,

TABLE 1
Summary of cases brought before the Winnipeg Juvenile Court,
1 July 1917 to 30 June 1920

Year	1917–18	1918–19	1919–20
Cases brought before the Court			
Boys and youths	789	844	1143
Girls and maidens	76	82	101
Adults	14	43	45
Total	879	969	1289
Charges laid			
Theft	338	332	267
Shopbreaking and theft	110	125	84
Disorderly conduct	76	115	70
Wilful damage	81	83	80
Breach of city bylaws	111	81	403
Incorrigibility and vagrancy	73	79	93
Trespass (common and on railway property)	49	52	27
Truancy	50	50	64
Contributing to delinquency	11	36	30
Neglect and dependency	37	14	52
Carrying and discharging firearms in the city	10	13	11
Selling papers during prohibited hours	17	11	46
Assault	9	11	12
Breach of Motor Act	0	11	13
Gambling	0	11	11
Breach of Tobacco Act	16	10	4
Escaping from custody	6	10	2
Breach of probation rules	10	8	40
Using obscene language	0	8	6
Indecent acts and assault	0	7	3
Stealing rides on cars	0	6	0
Receiving stolen goods	8	4	17
Arson	0	4	0
Forgery	4	3	4
Giving liquor to minors	0	0	6
Cruelty to animals	0	0	11
Slander	0	0	2
Material witnesses	0	0	2
False pretenses	3	0	5
Endangering life	8	0	0
Sending in false fire alarms	5	0	0
Miscellaneous (minor offences)	15	6	10
Total	1047	1130	1375

TABLE 1
(continued)

Year	1917–18	1918–19	1919–20
Disposition of cases			
Fined	32	92	417
Placed under probationary supervision	530	548	380
Detained in detention home	178	176	152
Warned and discharged	128	104	111
Dismissed and withdrawn	64	39	99
Ordered to compensate parties injured	53	62	57
Made wards of Children's Aid Society	27	18	46
Sent to industrial school at Portage la Prairie	12	23	20
Sent to work on farms and to homes in country	38	27	19
Sentences suspended	15	18	16
Placed in institutions by parents at request of court	15	14	8
Sent to Home of Good Shepherd	2	4	7
Released on bonds for good conduct given by parents	0	4	7
Returned to parents	0	0	5
Newsboys badges cancelled	13	4	3
Sent to penitentiary (wards over 16)	0	2	0
Miscellanous	1	2	4
Total	1108	1090	1351
Fines imposed			$2,104.00

CALCULATED FROM: Manitoba, Department of Education, *Report*, 1919–20, 122, 126–7. The number of charges laid and the number of dispositions exceeds the number of offenders because some of the latter were charged with more than one offence and received more than one form of treatment.

however, one must also look at it from the point of view of its clients: what actually happened to the youngsters who became caught up in its workings?

Early records make clear that many youngsters who ran afoul of the law never appeared before the courts at all. Indeed some juvenile court systems dealt with a majority of cases through the informal persuasion or coercion of its probation officers. As Winnipeg's Juvenile Court heard 2306 cases in its first eight years, probation and other officers disposed of 2511 without proceeding to this stage. Of these over 4800 children, the court committed only 156 to industrial schools.[45] In 1921 the Toronto Juvenile Court handled 2384 'unofficial' cases, of which only 100 were eventually brought into the court. Through its probation officers, the court 'tried to assist the home to meet its full obligations' to each youngster and eventually discharged them without recording their involvement in the judicial process. In the same year, the court dealt with 1663 officially delinquent children.[46] In her report for 1921, Judge Ethel MacLachlan of the Regina Judicial District explained that, with increasing experience in the use of warnings and investigations, officials were bringing fewer and fewer cases before her court: over its first four years cases declined from 169 in 1918 to 104 in 1919, to 101 in 1920 to 88 in 1921.[47]

An examination of statistics included in the report of the Winnipeg Juvenile Court over a three-year period (Table 1) shows both the kinds of offences that brought children to court and how they were treated there. Although the laconic nature of the records makes it more difficult to classify offences than their disposition, one can roughly divide the charges into three groups. Some, such as stealing rides on cars, selling papers during prohibited hours, breaking probation rules, breaches of the Tobacco Act, and truancy, together with some examples of theft, disorderly conduct, trespass, and wilful damage, were peculiarly 'youthful' – what Judge MacGill described as 'boys ... in "gangs"' – offences.[48] Others, such as breaches of the city by-laws and of the Motor Act were clearly non-criminal in any but a technical sense, and the offending youngsters were treated in much the same way as if they had been adults committing the same acts. Judge McKerchar explained that 'the vigilance of the police in the enforcement of traffic regulations' accounted for the rise in cases from 1918–19 to 1919–20.[49] As the table shows, over these two years breaches of by-laws – presumably mostly those concerned with automobiles – rose from 81 to 403 and fines from 92 to 417. In the last group were the cases of theft, shop-breaking, assault, disorderly conduct, indecent acts, and the like which, if they had been committed by adults, were serious breaches of the Criminal Code. During the 1920s the Dominion Bureau of Statistics would classify these crimes when they were committed by a juvenile as 'major' offences.[50]

After youngsters were tried, Judge McKerchar left the vast majority of them in their own homes, some under the supervision of a probation officer and others not. Since many of those placed in the detention home were soon released on probation, only those sent to the penitentiary or to the Home of the Good Shepherd, placed in institutions or the industrial school, sent to the country or made wards of the Children's Aid Society were actually removed from their home environments. In 1917–18, the court took this step with 94 of the 865 youngsters appearing before it, in 1918–19, with 88 out of 926, and in 1919–20 with 100 out of 1098. In turn, however, since approximately two-thirds of those youngsters whom the judge removed from their homes were sent not to the industrial school but to the country or to the Home, or were made wards of the Children's

Aid Society, one may assume that many of these boys and girls either had no home to go to or, if they had, were badly neglected by their parents. In his early reports, Judge McKerchar also commented on 'repeaters' – the group he described as the 'test of the Court's efficiency.' For the year ending 30 June 1917, 22 per cent had been before the court in former years, while a year later the percentage had dropped to 18.[51]

In his report for 1920–1, Judge McKerchar provided practical examples in support of Kelso's and Scott's case for the non-institutional care of even hard core young offenders. In one instance, he reported, over the past four years he had sent seventy delinquent boys to work on farms 'where they would be properly cared for and trained' and 'would receive reasonable compensation for their services.' He placed six through the superintendent of the detention home, the other sixty-four through the Reverend Harry Atkinson, boy's work secretary of the Stella Avenue Mission. Of the latter group, eight were first offenders or orphans, eleven had appeared before the court twice, nineteen had appeared three times, twelve had appeared four times, five had appeared five times, one had appeared six times, three had appeared seven times, one had appeared eight times, and one no less than fourteen times.[52] All six placed out by the superintendent were 'doing well.' As to the rest, employers had given seven 'splendid' reports; thirty-one, good reports; fourteen, fair reports; and twelve, poor reports. Of the twelve reported as poor, ten came again before the courts, which sent eight to the industrial school and one to gaol for three months. One other boy from the group went on to serve over two years in Stony Mountain Penitentiary. Thirty-six were still on the farm. Underlining the positive results of this practice, McKerchar pointed out that sixty of the seventy boys taken from unsatisfactory homes had 'not again transgressed.'[53]

As the Winnipeg and other court records indicate, juvenile courts sent some youngsters to industrial schools and even to the penitentiary. As to the latter, the Canadian Association of Child Protection Officers' committee on juveniles in penitentiaries, chaired by W.L. Scott, reported in 1923 that of the 388 inmates in Kingston Penitentiary twenty years of age and younger, 18 were sixteen years old, 63 were seventeen years old, 82 were eighteen years old, and 225 were from nineteen to twenty years old. Scott's committee concluded that there was 'not adequate classification and segregation of young persons' in penitentiaries such as would be available in separate institutions, nor were their 'individual characters, personalities and needs' studied. Further, such institutions had no adequate facilities for vocational training, employment, and other aids to help inmates become good citizens.[54] Although the committee and the association requested that the government change the situation, Canadian courts persisted in committing youths to penitentiaries: in 1938, one boy under sixteen, and seventeen sixteen-year-old boys entered Canadian penitentiaries; in 1960, thirty boys under sixteen and fifty-nine sixteen year olds took the same grim step.[55]

The boys and girls who attended some industrial schools undoubtedly found them not very different from the reformatories of an earlier generation. Industrial schools in Canada found it very difficult to maintain themselves as institutions whose prime purpose was education. Their task had a considerable hazard built right into it; as Scott aptly put it, industrial schools collected 'bad children from all over a Province' and endeavoured 'to reform them together.'[56] Other judges probably did as Toronto's Commissioner Starr who, when discussing fifteen-year-old 'Jack's' problem with him, said: 'Jack, you have to obey this Court. Now which will you do? Go to work and report here, or go to Mimico?'[57]

Those boys whom Judge McKerchar and other Manitoba magistrates sent to the Industrial Training School at Portage la Prairie were probably more fortunate than some of their counterparts elsewhere in Canada. The principal, F.W. McKinnon, explained that, for half the day, his boys attended a provincially inspected school under regularly qualified teachers. Indeed, McKinnon boasted, the school was so organized that it was able 'to teach the boy all the work of his grade as well as a trade.' In 1919–20, 6 of the approximately 100 boys in attendance wrote the high school entrance examination.[58] Although the school taught its boys farming skills, tailoring, carpentry, and shoe-repairing, McKinnon and his staff were probably less successful with trades training than they were in the classroom. In the opinion of Saskatchewan's Superintendent Reynolds, the work of McKinnon's tailor and shoe shops was 'meagre.' Because the 'chief operation' at Portage la Prairie was 'farming and stock raising,' which boys could secure by having them 'fostered out to farmers,' Reynolds had removed all Saskatchewan boys from the Manitoba school.[59] McKinnon was well aware of the problem. He wrote that parents pleaded 'that their sons be taught some kind of mechanical trade.' Arguing that some trades were dying out as others came to life, McKinnon pressed the government to install a printing press and urged that the blacksmith shop be fitted up 'as an Automobile and Gas Tractor School.' He could, he explained, 'place a dozen boys in up-to-date garages and each boy could earn at least $100 per month.'[60]

The Manitoba school displayed other positive characteristics. McKinnon encouraged parents 'to visit at any time' and he set aside 'a special dining room and parlor for their use.' In a typical year, 'scores' of parents visited their boys. In addition, under an honour system, boys merited such privileges as 'visits to park, picture shows, and short visits home.'[61] In addition to its educational accomplishments, and as a further indication of the success of the school, in his 1917–18 report, McKinnon explained that no less than 135 of the boys who had attended the school since it opened had enlisted in the Canadian army. Many had obtained commissions – at least three were captains and five were lieutenants – and most served overseas.[62]

In the context of his apparently liberal administration of the school, however, McKinnon repeatedly called for longer sentences. Echoing the sentiments of the previous generation of heads of industrial schools and reformatories, McKinnon wrote that it was 'foolishness' to send a boy to an industrial school for a period of only three or four months; the school could not change a boy's character in six months or a year. If, however, he was 'given a sentence of three years' he would be able 'to learn a trade,' and in that time the school could 'leave an impression upon the life of a boy.'[63]

Other schools shared many of Portage la Prairie's characteristics. In British Columbia, the Industrial School for Boys followed roughly the same routine as that in Manitoba; half the day in school and half in trades training. According to Superintendent D. Donaldson, the school taught its boys tailoring, shoe-making, carpentering, cooking and baking, and farm and garden work.[64] However, on an official visit to the school, the British Columbia mental hygiene surveyors found that it had 'no equipment for suitable industrial training' and that it had not operated its carpenter shop for the previous two years. For out-of-school employment, the boys could learn only farming and shoe-making.[65] The Monastery of the Good Shepherd, the industrial school for Roman Catholic girls in Halifax, gave each youngster, in addition to school work up to the grade six level, the chance to learn 'sewing, knitting, crocheting work, dressmaking, shoe making, and domestic science.' When a 'normal' girl finished the six grades, the school tested her and then provided her with an opportunity to prepare for 'a commercial, domestic or industrial' career. If mentally handicapped youngsters showed 'special aptitudes for gardening, boot making, tending hens, chickens, etc.' the monastery gave them 'ample opportunity to follow their bent.'[66] At the Maritime Home for Girls, at Truro, Nova Scotia – a new institution which was managed by the Presbyterian and Methodist churches – all the girls attended school under a qualified teacher. In addition, they entered 'into all branches of domestic work, gardening, shoe repairing, etc.' In the opinion of the Nova Scotia Mental Hygiene Survey, the home's inmates were 'happy and industrious, and appreciative of all that was being done for them.' It was 'an admirably conducted institution' with a proper follow-up system – it had thirty-five girls out on supervised parole – and made 'most intelligent endeavours ... to reform children' who were capable of being reformed.[67]

In his report for 1911, British Columbia's Superintendent Donaldson gave further evidence that some industrial schools were as much prisons as schools.

He commended the 'splendid' work of the newly opened Vancouver Juvenile Court and Detention Home which saved many youngsters from being committed to his school. In consequence, however, Donaldson continued, a more difficult class of client came to his institution. A boy reached the school only after the home, the school, the Church, a suspended sentence, and probation had all failed; he was often 'in the last stages of juvenile crime.'[68] In an era when parents, teachers, and principals still practised a considerable amount of corporal punishment, one of the staff of the British Columbia Industrial School described to the Vancouver Trades and Labor Council the 'brutal' floggings Donaldson and his staff administered to runaways. After failing to persuade the attorney general to investigate the matter, the council dropped it.[69] In his report for the following year, however, Donaldson noted that some new inmates were 'more than usually trying.' With the exception, however, of those boys 'who made their escape and were recaptured,' Donaldson explained that he had not ordered a single boy whipped over the whole school year. Further, while he had found it necessary 'to demand and enforce a somewhat strict discipline,' he 'tried as far as possible to eliminate the idea of a prison and prison surroundings.'[70]

Donaldson, of course, was not alone in employing corporal punishment. According to the Nova Scotia Mental Hygiene investigators, a majority of the boys, who ranged in age from eight to sixteen, in the Halifax Boy's Industrial School were what they described as 'defective.' Nevertheless, the school employed corporal punishment, 'with a strap for first offences,' as its 'routine' punishment for misdemeanours. Boys guilty of 'repeated misconduct' were confined in cells, seven by twelve feet, 'with boarded walls and barred windows' on 'bread and water rations.' The school sent its incorrigibles to Dorchester Penitentiary.[71]

When she took over as superintendent of British Columbia's Industrial School for Girls in 1918, Margaret W. Bayne was determined to show its inmates that it was 'not so much a place of punishment' as one where they were 'given another chance to make good.' After a physician's examination of each girl showed that about half of them needed treatment for venereal disease, Miss Bayne segregated each new arrival 'until the doctor ... pronounced her free from contagion.'[72] On the positive side, Miss Bayne changed the staff and abolished such existing rules as those requiring that hair be worn in 'prison style' and that meals be eaten in complete silence. She improved on the uniform and instituted an honour system. She lengthened the daily time devoted to schooling, trained the girls in all aspects of housework, and instituted a commercial course. By the end of the first year, Miss Bayne explained, five of the approximately forty inmates would be able to fill positions as stenographers and another had gone out to a course at a business college in Vancouver. In 1920, ten of the twenty-eight residents were taking the commercial course.[73] Most girls, however, seemed destined for domestic service. By the end of her first eleven months in the position, Miss Bayne claimed that she and her staff had effected 'a harmonious home atmosphere in the school.'[74] In the opinion of the mental hygiene survey of British Columbia, Miss Bayne understood 'the nature of the problem of juvenile delinquency' and dealt 'with her charges in a most kindly and intelligent fashion.' Nonetheless, some girls were difficult to control. An unruly inmate, reported the mental hygiene surveyors, slept in a basement room where there was 'an iron prison cell of the same type as that utilized at Oakalla Jail.' The first night, the girl slept on a bed outside the cell under the threat that if her behaviour did not improve she would be placed in the cell itself. The threat was effective enough: up to the time of the survey the school had not actually placed any girl in the cell.[75]

Two other characteristics of industrial schools in the early years after the passage of the Juvenile Delinquents Act deserve comment – the sleeping arrangements and the ages of their inmates. Although early advocates of industrial schools promised that boys and girls would live like 'families' under the 'cottage system,' other provinces were little more successful than Ontario had been in fulfiling this pledge. The industrial schools for boys in Manitoba, British Columbia, and Halifax housed their inmates in dormitories. Those in British Columbia held a minimum of twenty-five to thirty in each large room, while those in Halifax had from fourteen to seventeen beds in each.[76] The industrial school for girls in British Columbia also housed its youngsters in dormitories, as did Halifax's Monastery of the Good Shepherd. The Maritime Home for Girls divided its approximately sixty inmates amongst three cottages. Some institutions without cottages agitated for them. Although Manitoba's Superintendent McKinnon wrote that he would like to segregate certain types of boys, especially those whom he called 'degenerates' and 'mental defectives,' such a system was impossible in his present building.[77] The superintendents of both the Halifax Industrial School and St Patrick's Home in that city repeatedly stated their desire for better accommodation.[78]

Despite the efforts of reformers, courts and parents continued to commit some very young children to institutions. Although the published records are far from complete – those of the Manitoba school did not give the ages or the age range of its inmates – others hint at what was going on. In some years British Columbia gave very complete information (Table 2) that showed boys as young as nine being confined with youths twice their age. In 1921, the fifty-seven girls in residence at the Maritime Home for Girls in Truro ranged in age from seven to sixteen. The Halifax Industrial School included boys from eight to sixteen and the Monastery of the Good Shepherd girls from five to over sixteen.[79]

TABLE 2

Ages of inmates in British Columbia industrial schools

Age	9	10	11	12	13	14	15	16	17	18	19	Total
Boy's Industrial School												
1911	–	–	2	5	9	9	7	15	6	–	–	53
1914	2	1	2	7	9	15	20	20	11	2	1	90
1923	1	1	5	8	11	19	25	34	9	5	–	118
Girl's Industrial School												
1914	–	–	–	2	1	7	10	2	–	–	–	22
1918*	–	–	1	1	2	6	8	11	7	–	–	36

*Age at entry
SOURCE: British Columbia, *Sessional Papers*, 1912, p. N25; *ibid.*, 1915, pp. S5 and S13; *ibid.*, 1918, p. M49; *ibid.*, 1923, p. J6

III

Although the 1920s were appropriate years to do so, those who worked in the field did not take the opportunity to examine critically the effects of a generation of work to prevent and cure juvenile delinquency. Did the new theories and the practices which grew out of them, indeed fulfil the promises which Kelso, Scott, and so many others made for them?

Recent criticism of the effects of the juvenile court movement in the United States and of the present treatment of juvenile delinquents in Canada suggests that one must use considerable caution in answering this question. In applying present standards to past conditions one must, first, be careful to sort out what, given earlier states of knowledge and social conditions, was actually possible at the time. Obviously, one cannot hold professionals of the 1920s responsible for not knowing what a further half-century of study and experience has revealed to their successors. Although modern social scientists appear almost as far from explaining the causes of juvenile delinquency as were the delegates to Kelso's 'child-saving' conference in 1894, the former have nonetheless moved far beyond the simple formulations which characterized the earlier era.[80] Second, one must try to distinguish between the short- and the long-term effects of the reform movement. Early juvenile courts may well have treated child offenders more justly and humanely than did contemporary magistrates courts. However, if Canadians then went on to improve other aspects of their judicial system while leaving the juvenile court essentially unchanged, then the time might come when juvenile offenders would be better treated in an adult rather than a juvenile court.[81] In short, in evaluating the effects of the new procedures developed between the 1880s and the 1920s, one must apply to the criticisms of recent investigators the same scepticism that they have so rightly used to assess the claims of the child savers.

In a recent study, Anthony Platt judged that 'in no sense' could the originators of the juvenile court movement in the United States be 'considered libertarians or humanists.'[82] In fact, Platt concluded, their reforms did not represent anything really 'new' but rather expedited a traditional, increasingly repressive policy that had developed over the nineteenth century. Reformers assumed that adolescents were naturally dependent and therefore 'created a special court to impose sanctions on premature independence and behaviour unbecoming to youth.' In turn, this court deprived the children who appeared before it of the safeguards built into the rest of the judicial system. Further, the 'child savers' had 'paternalistic and romantic' attitudes to delinquent youth which they backed up with force. Finally, they 'promoted correctional programs requiring longer terms of imprisonment, long hours of labor and militaristic discipline, and the inculcation of middle-class values and lower-class skills.'[83] Recently, too, the Canadian sociologist Lynn McDonald has challenged what she describes as the 'conventional wisdom' that juvenile crime in Canada is rising sharply. Using data for the period 1950 to 1966, she argues, on the contrary, that the rising rates of juvenile delinquency as reported by police are a product of the fact that Canadian authorities 'are permitting progressively less deviance on the part of citizens, especially juveniles.' Thus law enforcers are increasingly inclined to prosecute even trivial infractions, especially if they are committed by juveniles. The net effect of this early identification – or 'labelling' – of people as delinquents, she concludes, may actually stimulate 'their development as deviants' and thus 'this increased apprehension of juveniles' may 'eventually result in more adult crime.'[84] While their criticisms are perhaps more sharply focused on issues raised in this study, Platt and McDonald are not, of course, the only modern critics of the juvenile court. In the early 1960s, the majority of submissions to the Department of Justice Committee on Juvenile Delinquency recommended, with the concurrence of the committee, that the jurisdiction of the juvenile court be narrowed both as to the definition of prohibited conduct and in the power of disposition given to the judge.[85]

Does Platt's evaluation of American child savers apply to their contemporary Canadian counterparts? Do McDonald's conclusions, which she draws from recent developments in the field, also apply to this earlier era of intense interest in young offenders? One cannot give a simple 'yes' or 'no' answer to either question. Indeed, out of the incomplete nature of the evidence available on the matter, one can assemble data which both support much of what Canadian child savers did and, as well, confirm some of what their modern critics say about them.[86] In addition, then, to noting their most important accomplishment up to the 1920s – that of making their ideas into English Canada's 'conventional wisdom' for preventing and treating juvenile delinquency – one can, in the context of modern investigations, come to three general conclusions about the intense effort which reformers put into the previous thirty years.

First, the reform movement led English Canadians to change – mostly for the better – their treatment of neglected and dependent children. While reformers exaggerated the proportion of such youngsters who, but for official intervention, were destined for the class of paupers, drunkards, and criminals, early apprehension or other treatment undoubtedly deflected some from following this sort of life. In the 1890s there really were many Canadian children who, if society had not taken a hand, faced an extremely bleak future. Even discounting their self-serving nature, the early records of Children's Aid societies make very clear that their officers discovered badly abused and neglected children which an earlier generation might never have helped or even identified.[87] In turn, these agencies were less likely than their predecessors to lump the more unruly of the neglected in with the already delinquent. Further, for those children in this group who, for lack of relatives or friends to care for them, the courts would have committed to orphanages or even gaols and reformatories, Children's Aid officials and provincial superintendents of neglected and dependent children found alternative care in foster homes. Over the decade and a half between 1875 and 1889, the number of youngsters resident on a single day in Ontario's grant-receiving child care institutions more than doubled from 970 to 1855 and those resident at some time during the year grew at roughly the same rate from 1727 to 3706.[88] The latter figure represented less than 0.5 per cent of the over 775,000 Ontarians then under sixteen.[89] On the other hand, over the three decades between 1889 and 1920, those resident on a single day increased by a little over 300 to 2188 and those resident at some time over the year by less than a third to 4951.[90] In 1921, the provincial superintendent of neglected children reported that since 1893 legal orders had made over 18,900 children wards of his office or Children's Aid societies in the province. These agencies had also provided a further 1000 children with homes when requested by relatives to do so. In 1921 alone, Kelso explained, societies had added 936 new wards to their rolls while they or his office had released 459 from future supervision. This left a total of 11,500 children in the province – or roughly 1 per cent of those under sixteen – still 'subject to continued care and oversight.'[91] The long-term reports of Children's Aid societies on their wards, the results of Kelso's disposal of the inmates of the Ontario Reformatory, the work of the English child-placing societies in Canada, and the success of McKerchar's efforts to place out his hard core cases provided its proponents with considerable evidence of the merits of a non-institutional approach. And, to the social returns from this system – such as a reduction in the number of potential delinquents – one must also add the benefits acquired by some of the youngsters themselves. Certain of them were fortunate enough to be incorporated into a loving family, rather than a 'professional' foster home, an orphanage, or an industrial school.

In the early years of the work, child welfare and court workers were sometimes too hasty in removing youngsters from their own homes. This initial over-enthusiasm for apprehension, however, gradually declined. The extension of probation services, the use of the techniques of family case work, the introduction of workmen's compensation and mother's pensions, together with the professional workers' growing experience on the job, helped them to handle a larger proportion of potential and actual problem cases in their own homes. In the years between 1905 and 1918, the Vancouver Children's Aid Society gradually increased the number of children committed to its care each year from twenty-nine in 1905 to fifty in 1910 to a peak of seventy-nine in 1913.[92] Over the next five years, however, the number declined to forty-six in 1914, thirty-nine in 1915, fifty-four in 1916, thirty-nine in 1917, and nineteen in 1918.[93] Over the year 1920–1, Manitoba's superintendent of the Children's Act reported that his office personally investigated nearly 200 cases involving over 400 children. He was, however, 'pleased to say that nearly ninety per cent of these cases were adjusted without removing the children.'[94]

In addition to reducing the proportion of apprehensions, Children's Aid societies worked hard to improve the quality of the placements it made. In the early stages of the work, reported Robert Mills of the Toronto Children's Aid Society, the youngsters placed in free homes were 'necessarily of one of two classes': those 'wanted for their own sakes as members of the family – usually young infants – and those wanted for the services they could give, – usually children eleven or over.' The society therefore rarely placed abnormal children; further, above the age of toddlers, boys were 'almost invariably' forced into becoming farm labourers and girls into becoming domestic servants 'quite regardless of their background or training and experience, their individual aptitudes and preferences.' In order to save them from long residency in institutions, and because such children needed a home 'even more than a normal' youngster, in the 1920s the Toronto society began placing out in boarding homes both its non-ward youngsters and its wards who were 'unattractive in physique or disposition, ... infants of dangerous heredity, and ... mentally subnormal children.' In September 1925, Mills reported, the society had 674 children placed in free homes, 53 children boarded out under its own supervision, and a further 21 babies boarded out through the Infant's Home.[95]

Second, child welfare reformers helped middle-class English Canadians bring about the more ordered society towards which many of them worked so assiduously. Although the measures one can use to prove this assertion are quite crude, they nevertheless indicate that Canadian communities permitted less deviant behaviour in the early 1920s than they had a generation before. While increasingly close regulation of Canadian drinking practices – capped for a time by prohibition – provides the most obvious example, other indicators suggest the same trend. Criminal statistics show that those charged, convicted, and sentenced for various offences increased at a rate far more rapidly than did the population.[96] Between 1889 and 1920, while the population of Canada less than doubled, those convicted of indictable offences more than quadrupled.[97] Perhaps a surge in criminal behaviour accounted for part of this growth. Probably also, however, increasingly thorough, efficient, and sometimes less tolerant policing netted a larger proportion of law-breakers than had been customary in the past.[98] As some of the more astute observers in the Senate debate on the 1908 act had observed, the cumulative effect of a host of federal and provincial statutes and municipal ordinances was to make illegal much behaviour which had not been so before.

Moral reformers and others concerned with social improvement gave much of their attention to juvenile behaviour. As we have seen in their efforts to regulate newsboys and other street traders, to enforce school attendance legislation, to curtail smoking, and to prevent girls from being recruited into a life of prostitution, Canadians definitely set tighter limits on how they would permit youngsters to behave. In some such efforts, they did indeed, as Platt asserts, both assume and enforce a longer period of youthful dependency. In describing the early effects of British Columbia's raising the age of those coming under the Juvenile Delinquents Act to eighteen, D.B. Brankin, superintendent of neglected children and of the Industrial School, noted that some boys who as adults had already served one or two months for an offence found themselves, now restored to juvenile status, sentenced to two or three years in the Industrial School for repeating the same misdemeanour.[99]

However, while undoubtedly some of this ordering of youngsters' lives was negative in intent – that is, society stated that, for their own good, it would not permit children and young people to behave in certain perhaps disagreeable but nonetheless long-accustomed ways – other aspects of it were more positive. Federal, provincial, and municipal governments intervened protectively between children and many aspects of the environment in which they were reared. Just as the introduction and enforcement of public health regulations brought about a sharp rise in the life-chances of the young, so child welfare legislation made it increasingly difficult for parents, guardians, and employers to abuse or dangerously over-work children and young people. Youngsters generally benefitted from changes making the legal position of the mother regarding her children more closely equal to those of the father. Some provinces also greatly improved the legal status and rights of illegitimate and adopted children.

Certainly, as Platt notes in considering some of the negative aspects of the effort, both the positive and negative dimensions of the tightening control of the young continued and strengthened trends which began early in the nineteenth century. As the discussion in chapter 7 has already made clear, however, this persistent pursuit of the goal of order was accompanied in the generation under review by so fundamental a change in theory and practice that to describe the events of this era solely in terms of its continuity with the previous one is to miss the greater part of its significance. Canadians had decided to give improved homes and families a major role in improving their society. They included the family life of neglected, dependent, pre-delinquent, and delinquent children as a part of this much broader effort.

Third, the records of early and even later efforts of Canadians to try in new ways to prevent some youngsters from turning into adult criminals do not provide enough evidence for one to make an accurate evaluation of the effectiveness of their program. As the enormous literature on juvenile delinquency testifies,

TABLE 3

A selection of statistics related to juvenile delinquency, 1875–1920

Year	1875	1889	1900	1903	1910	1920
Canada						
Population (in thousands)*	3954	4729	5301	5651	6988	8556
Population under 16 (in thousands)*	–	1864	1960	–	2513	3192
Convictions for indictable offences of those 16 and older†	n.a.‡	3521	4853	5483	10327	15088
Convictions for indictable offences of those under 16†	n.a.	687	915	1038	1373	3355
Number of prisoners in penitentiaries	848	1195	1424	1250	1859	1931
Ontario						
Population (in thousands)*	1746	2075	2172	2217	2482	2863
Population under 16 (in thousands)*	–	778	731	–	789	938
Convictions for indictable offences of those 16 and older†	n.a.	1927	2260	2344	4539	6707
Convictions for indictable offences of those under 16†	n.a.	391	509	540	834	1707
Ontario Reformatory for Boys						
Committed that year	71	85	66	44	–	–
Present on a single day	173	210	145	86	–	–
Ontario Industrial Refuge for Girls						
Committed that year	–	19	32	8	–	–
Present on a single day	–	49	48	70	–	–
Ontario provincial gaols						
Boys 16 and under committed that year	389**	451	298	225	87	106
Girls 16 and under committed that year	70**	46	42	21	13	9
Present on a single day	–	14	10	5	11	2
Ontario Industrial Schools						
Victoria						
Committed that year	–	n.a.	65	74	164	156
Present on a single day	–	140	140	178	289	n.a.

St John's						
Committed that year	–	–	20	25	67	n.a.
Present on a single day	–	–	48	55	76	n.a.
Alexandra						
Committed that year	–	–	8	n.a.	40	n.a.
Present on a single day	–	–	31	25	90	n.a.
St Mary's						
Committed that year	–	–	–	3	10	n.a.
Present on a single day	–	–	–	8	25	n.a.
Kingston Penitentiary						
Children 16 and under	–	7	3	21††	28††	0##
Ontario children's institutions receiving provincial grants						
Total resident at some time during that year	1727	3706	4178	4116	4779	4951
Present on a single day	970	1855	1832	1887	2082	2188
Ontario children under supervision of supt of neglected and dependent children						
Number of new entries that year	–	–	247	239	604	936
Total number on books	–	–	1318	2030	n.a.	11500

CALCULATED FROM: Canada, *Sessional Papers*, 1890, no. 9, facing p. 114; *ibid.*, 1901, no. 34, pp. 84, 87; *ibid.*, 1904, no. 34, p. 86; *ibid.*, 1911, no. 24, p. 102; *ibid.*, no. 31, p. 105; *ibid.*, 1922, no. 10B, p. 282; Ontario, *Sessional Papers*, 1890, no. 11, pp. 13, 120-1, 138; *ibid.*, 1896, no. 12, p. 5; *ibid.*, 1900, no. 36, pp. 11, 23, 68, 72, 81, 84; *ibid.*, no. 37, pp. 102, 104; *ibid.*, no. 40, pp. 19, 71, 75-6; *ibid.*, 1903, no. 39, pp. 18-9, 47-50, 64-5; *ibid.*, no. 43, pp. 6, 58, 61-2; *ibid.*, 1904, no. 40, p. 88; *ibid.*, 1911, no. 25, pp. 15-27; *ibid.*, no. 26, pp. 50, 107, 110-12; *ibid.*, 1912, no. 26, p. 9; *ibid.*, 1921, no. 25, p. 131; *ibid.*, no. 26, pp. 26-7; *Report … into the Prison and Reformatory System*, pp. 19, 22, 102; *Canada Year Book*, 1932, p. 110; Urquhart and Buckley, *Historical Statistics of Canada*, pp. 14, 643-4, 651, 655; Splane, *Social Welfare in Ontario*, p. 232; *Handbook*, p. 145

* From nearest census year: 1891, 1901, 1911, 1921

† These figures are based on offences, not persons. Thus if a person were found guilty of three cases of burglary at the same time then each would be entered in the statistics for that year.

‡ Figures not available

** Under 16

†† Under 20

Information discussed on p 135 casts some doubt on this figure.

the matter is an extremely complex one which can only be touched on very briefly here. The members of the Department of Justice committee which analysed the subject in the early 1960s, however, went right to the heart of the problem: there had been, their report explained, 'no adequate research' to determine whether juvenile court proceedings had 'a positive value in terms of a child's behavior problem.'[100] What follows, then, merely hints at what more sophisticated research in the history of the work of many individual juvenile courts might reveal.

Let us examine this data first of all. As Table 3 indicates, between 1889 and 1920 Ontario's population increased by just under 40 per cent. Over the same period the number of those over sixteen convicted of indictable offences increased over three-fold and those under sixteen by about four-fold. Obviously both adults and young people felt the effects of Ontarians' desire for a greater measure of orderly behaviour. On the other hand, the number of youngsters who found themselves at any time over the year in the common gaols dropped to a quarter of its earlier level. Probably the most important figures displayed in the table, however, are those showing the number of youngsters present in the institutions for long-term custody – the reformatory, the refuge, and the industrial schools. When one puts these data into the context of the number of youngsters convicted of indictable offences, its significance becomes evident. Between 1889 and 1900, as the population of Ontario increased by about 4 per cent, that of industrial schools and the like went up by 3 per cent. Convictions of those under sixteen for indictable offences rose over the same period by 30 per cent. By 1903 – the last year of the reformatory – the population of the province had risen by about 7 per cent over 1889, that of the institutions – including Penetanguishene – by about 6 per cent, and convictions by about 38 per cent. Again, between 1889 and 1910, the increase in population of the province and in industrial schools and the like grew at roughly the same rate; each by about 20 per cent. Over the same two decades, however, convictions rose by 113 per cent. Because the method of computing the data changed, and some of it is not available, one cannot make similar comparisons over the whole of the first generation of the work. Between 1889 and 1927, however, as Ontario's population grew by 65 per cent, that of its custodial institutions for youngsters increased from 399 to 628, or by 57 per cent. For those under sixteen, Ontario recorded 391 convictions for indictable offences in 1889, and 2282 convictions for 'major' offences in 1926, a more than five-fold increase.[101]

Clearly, any effort to interpret these data and measure the effects of the new legislation – especially over the early years of its implementation – must consider both in the context of the increasingly ordered society. In this regard, one must emphasize, child welfare reformers and workers did not themselves decide upon the amount of order to be required in English Canada, but merely shared in the half-conscious search for a social consensus on the matter. As we have seen, to the child-centred group the more immediate and more urgent question was what agency would place the tighter limits around the behaviour of the young and how it would do so. Through the use of much hard work and resourcefulness, they succeeded in having much of the responsibility placed in their own hands rather than those of the agencies traditionally responsible for law and order. Given McDonald's thesis, it might well have been better if English Canadians of the time had left troublesome young people alone to grow up and out of their problems. On the other hand, given the social climate of the time, the real question one must ask at this point is whether, after the reformers took control, their new system imposed the new standards more effectively – that is, to the long-term benefit of the youngsters caught up in it – than the traditional police, legal, and court systems would have done.

In attempting to answer this question, one must first consider the case of the pre-delinquent. What happened to that broad group of children living at the edge of serious trouble and those youngsters who, although they had broken the law, had not reached the stage in which delinquency had become a persistent condition or way of life? For these probably one-time offenders or accidental delinquents, the judicial process changed in a number of ways. With tighter policing and supervision, they were perhaps more likely to be caught in or after their transgressions. When caught, however, they were much less likely to spend even a day or two in the common gaol in the sometimes harrowing company of adult prisoners. On the other hand, changes in how Canadians actually disposed of these cases were probably more apparent than real. While traditional Canadian courts could and did deal harshly with some youngsters, nineteenth-century magistrates frequently let first offenders off with a warning or a suspended sentence. Under the new arrangements, such a child was, through the preliminary work of the probation officer, less likely to appear in court at all. In addition, if the probation officer conducted a tactful and discreet investigation, the child may well have avoided being 'labelled,' which was a likely fate for the youngster who appeared in open court. If, however, he did appear before a judge, his chances of being incarcerated for a first offence were probably about the same as those of his predecessor under the traditional system. Finally, court workers and the other new welfare agencies may sometimes have been able to help the child and his family – morally, emotionally, or physically – to cope with the crisis and sometimes to assist in rectifying root causes.

The judicial process also changed for those youngsters more committed to or more deeply involved in a delinquent style of life – those who had not been deflected or deterred by the preliminary efforts of the juvenile court system. When they seriously misbehaved, the net of the law was more likely than before to gather up such young people. Through the persistent efforts of Kelso, Scott, and all the other court and community workers who shared their deep aversion for any sort of incarceration, a somewhat greater proportion of such boys and girls appear to have avoided the gaols, reformatories, or industrial schools and instead were treated in their own or foster homes. If one accepts the reformers' assumption that non-institutional care – even that of 'professional' foster homes – was preferable to that provided by reformatories, industrial schools, and the like, then the reforms definitely benefitted these young people; penal institutions were deprived of the chance of labelling them and of socializing them into the criminal class. Others in this second group, perhaps those who had received less patient care or whose behaviour or condition had pushed him or her beyond what the non-institutional resources of society could, or felt they could, cope with, went to institutions, sometimes for long periods of time. Whether these latter boys and girls as they appeared before the juvenile court judge who sentenced them were better or worse off than they would have been in a magistrate's court is a question which also needs thorough investigation. Under the traditional system, however, very few poor youngsters seem to have had counsel; like the rest of those charged in the police court, most children appearing there received the brisk, perfunctory justice then characteristic of that institution. The evidence examined in these chapters suggests that, at the very least, the humane and sensible men and women who formed the first generation of juvenile court judges treated youngsters with as much fairness and equity as a magistrate's court would have done. If this conclusion is accurate, then those looking for the roots of the growing concern over due process, self-incrimination, and the like, which became serious concerns in Canada by the early 1960s, may well find them in changes which took place both in social standards as to what was fair and just and in the practices of juvenile and other courts after the 1920s.[102]

In the move from the old system to the new, the institutional stage in the treatment of young offenders probably changed the least. Under the traditional system, courts had sentenced youngsters to terms which ranged from a few days to two to five years in reformatory and sometimes even longer terms in the penitentiary. Again, only thorough investigation can reveal in what direction and to what degree juvenile courts actually changed the pattern of imprisonment of young people in comparison with earlier practices and then current ones for adults. In making such comparisons over the short term, should one consider a few weeks of 'observation' in a detention home as being roughly equivalent to a similar period of time served in a common gaol? When one examines the nature of long-term incarceration, however, the picture is much clearer. While the rhetoric of those who promoted and operated these new institutions argued that an industrial school was, as W.H. Howland put it, much more analagous to a boarding school than to a prison, our brief examination of them indicates that this hope rarely became a reality. In his account of the closing of Penetanguishene, Kelso explained that all the boys alluded to it as a prison and to themselves as prisoners; they 'laughed incredulously when it was referred to as an educational institution.'[103] It seems very likely that many inmates of Canadian industrial schools, both then and later on, would have joined in this laughter.

PART IV

'The School Must Be
the Agent': Using the New Education
to Make the New Society

10

Changing Albert School:
The Institutional Context
for Education Reform in Canada,
1890-1920

On Monday, 24 June 1889, the last school day before the eight-week summer vacation, the elementary schools of Saint John, New Brunswick, conducted their closing exercises of the first term of the year. While most rural and some urban schools in Canada still customarily centred such affairs around the oral examination of the pupils, the Saint John elementary schools gave a more modern air to their two-part programs. In the opinion of the local newspaper, Albert School always put on an interesting program. There the children first presented their parents and other guests with a twenty-five item entertainment during which, twenty-five girls from grades one and two sang the 'Chorus of Flowers,' fourteen girls of grades six, seven, and eight sang 'The Bouquet of Rose Spirits,' Frank Hartley recited 'Entertaining Sister's Beau,' Emily McDuffee declaimed 'Little Cy Downer's Ride,' William R. Montgomery recited 'The Dutiful Boy,' nine girls performed some 'Motion Exercises,' and the whole school sang 'Vacation is Coming' and 'Nearer My God to Thee.' Following the entertainment, Alderman A.C. Smith, Alderman Israel Smith, and J.V. Ellis, the local member of Parliament, addressed the children and parents and presented to their winners a wide range of prizes. In Miss Bertha A. Brittain's class of grades one and two boys, Edward Lawson and John R. Fox won prizes for attendance and percentage, Thomas Nichols and Archie Wilmot for diligence, Charles Montgomery for percentage, and eight boys for attendance. At the end of the day's proceedings, parents and visitors congratulated the staff 'on the fine exhibition.'[2]

From the 1880s to the 1920s, Canadians wrought enormous changes in the schooling of their children. As they moved into the empty West and into the growing cities and suburbs, they took their schools with them. As their standard of living rose, they increased their commitment to the formal education of their youngsters. In some provinces, English-speaking and French-speaking Canadians wrangled with even greater vehemence than usual over the religious form or ethnic identity of public and separate school systems. More important, as schools lured and coerced children to stay for longer and longer periods in their charge, two bands of reformers, mostly though not entirely drawn from outside the educational system, prodded, pushed, and cajoled Canadian schools to change what they were trying to do with their charges. One group, as they came to a new view of child, family, and the process of schooling in Canadian society, tried to make schools more humane, more child-centred, and more responsive to the way in which children grew. The other, as they examined the effects of the rapidly changing nature of work in rural and urban Canada attempted to make schools more practical and relevant to the later lives of their inmates. Later on, these groups came together in an effort to 'Canadianize' the growing band of immigrants entering the nation. Over the span of a generation this loose confederation of peoples, interests, and organizations gradually forged their ideas into a new public consensus on what English-Canadian education should be. In addition, in an activity which profoundly transformed the context in which all other change took place, school systems themselves worked to increase the length and regularity of their pupils' attendance and to improve the quality of their teaching staffs. Change, and the talk of change, in turn led some to look fondly back through the rosy haze of memory at their own schooling and to argue that reformers and schoolmen were destroying a wonderful Canadian institution.[3]

What was the nature of the late nineteenth-century schooling which some wanted to preserve and so many others wanted to make over? While there were certain characteristics common to the nation as a whole – education was generally free and centralized – obviously there is no simple answer to this question. No one year formed a 'great divide' between the old and the new. School systems were not cold and static enterprises. Especially in the cities and towns, teachers, school inspectors, and school trustees tried to improve the effectiveness of the schools; they added new topics to the curriculum and experimented with new teaching techniques. From classroom to classroom, from school to school, from town to town, from province to province, there were immense differences in the schooling given to Canadian children. Within the framework of such differences, however, there was something of a common experience of going to school late in the nineteenth century which was very different from going to school late in the twentieth. Since this common feeling existed, perhaps a vignette of a single city school in its setting might give more of the characteristic flavour of what it was that Canadian children then experienced in their schools than would a broad survey of Canadian education as it was at that time.

Albert School and the Saint John school system as they were in 1890 together provide a good example of urban schooling of the period. With a population of 39,000, or about one-eighth of the provincial population of 321,000, Saint John was the largest city in the Maritime provinces and sixth largest in Canada. Although not the political capital of New Brunswick, the city, with its concentration of population, finance, and labour, was the metropolitan centre of the province. Despite a relative decline in importance in the years after Confederation, the city's shipping and other transportation interests provided the means for the entry of ideas and practices from such larger centres as Liverpool and Boston.[4] The establishment of free schooling in the province in 1871 engendered, especially in Fredericton and Saint John, enthusiasm for creating the system which was to grow out of the legislation.[5] Twenty years later, accounts of Saint John schools displayed pride in what had already been done together with a sense of liveliness about the work under way at the moment and planned for the future. Saint John's pride was probably justified: in a period when most Canadians attended one-room rural schools, that city exemplified the best schooling available to Canadian children at the time.

Located at the corner of Duke and Watson Streets, Albert School was a two-storey frame building containing 'ten school-rooms, ten cloak-rooms, ten teachers' rooms' and an 'exhibition hall.' In the basement there were two play rooms and a janitor's apartment and at the rear of the school an annex fitted with latrines.[6] Under the terms of the Compromise of 1875, which provided that in populous places New Brunswick school boards could organize separate schools for Protestant and Roman Catholic children, most of the pupils and teachers who walked to Albert School each morning belonged to Protestant denominations.[7] As Table 4 indicates, the school observed the then customary practice of dividing its pupils into classes on the basis of both sex and grade. Except in very large schools, therefore, most teachers faced classes which contained more than one grade. The fact that Miss Brittain's class was two and a half times as large as Mr Montgomery's reveals two other common characteristics of schooling of the time: classes varied widely in size from one to another and those for younger children were generally larger than those for older ones. Indeed, of the twenty-two grade one and grade two classes in Saint John in the first term of 1889, a majority contained over sixty pupils each. The smallest class enrolled forty-four grade one and two pupils in it and the largest 101 grade ones.[8]

Although the table shows that all the teachers in Albert School possessed either first or second class licenses, in this characteristic they were typical neither of their province nor of the nation. Because Saint John then paid the highest teachers' salaries in New Brunswick, only 8 of the 129 teachers who enrolled classes in the spring term of 1889 had third class licenses. Of the province's total

TABLE 4

Albert School, Saint John, N.B., first term, 7 January – 25 June, 1889

Teacher	Class of certificate	Grades taught	Number enrolled	Average attendance*	Percentage attendance*
John Montgomery, principal	I	7 and 8 boys	30	21	71
Agnes Livingstone	I	6, 7, and 8 girls	46	36	77
John McKinnon	II	5 and 6 boys	36	27	75
Clara E. Burridge	I	5 girls	45	32	72
Enoch Thompson	I	4 boys	38	26	69
Lydia J. Fullerton	I	4 girls	46	31	68
Annie Montgomery	II	3 boys	41	29	72
Lizzie G. Corbett	I	2 and 3 girls	48	36	74
Bertha A. Brittain	I	1 and 2 boys	75	57	76
Annie B. Allen	II	1 and 2 girls	64	40	62
The school as a whole			469	335	72

CALCULATED FROM: New Brunswick, *Journals*, 1889, pp. A134, A142–143, A147–151 force of 1566 teachers, however, 491, or almost one-third, held this lowest class of license, which indicated that although they had probably attended the Normal School for one term, they had not reached their junior matriculation. Of the rest, fourteen of the province's staff were fully qualified grammar school teachers, 264 had Class I, and 797 held Class II licenses.[9]

In its average and percentage attendance columns, the table indicates that many Albert School pupils attended irregularly. Indeed, in Saint John and in the rest of Canada at this time teachers could sort school-aged children into four reasonably distinct attendance groups. First, there were the majority of children who, except when they were ill, attended every school day. At the end of each school term in Saint John and across Canada, local newspaper columns were filled with lists of pupils, such as those in Miss Brittain's class, who had received awards for perfect attendance. Second, there were those children who, because their parents believed that their labour was essential to the family well-being, entered school late in the autumn, attended reasonably regularly over the winter, and left again early in the spring. In the second term of 1889, the Saint John board reported that 828 pupils left school before the end of term. Out of this total, it described 137 children, mostly drawn from the upper grades, as having 'gone to work,' and listed a further 278 under 'cause unknown.' No doubt many of the latter were also at home working on farm or in shop for their parents.[10] Third, there were the children who were sent or came to school very irregularly. In the second term of 1890, 456 of the 6786 pupils enrolled in the Saint John schools attended for 25 or less of the 85.5 days the schools were open.[11] Finally, many children did not attend school at all. From the 1881 census and other indications, the school board believed that there was a school population in Saint John 'in excess of 12,000, or more than 4,000 above our school enrollment for the year.'[12]

In common with many other Canadians of the time, Saint John teachers and school trustees showed a growing interest in the whole matter of regular school attendance. While perhaps a majority of Canadian educators then might have echoed the slogan 'schools for all, and all at school' proclaimed by New Brunswick's superintendent of education, T H Rand, in fact they and the trustees for many years put much more effort into achieving the first part of the saying rather than the second.[13] In 1889, the Saint John trustees said they believed that all children 'between the ages of seven and fourteen' should be compelled to attend school regularly 'during a certain period of the year.'[14] At their Institutes in the fall of 1889 and again in 1890, the Saint John teachers discussed attendance, lateness, and early dismissal. At the latter meeting, indeed, they passed a cautious resolution which 'fully' endorsed 'the principle embodied in compulsory attendance at school.'[15] At the meeting the previous year, however, John

Montgomery, principal of Albert School, pointed out that 'schools were made for the people and not the teachers' and that 'if parents wished their children excused the teacher could not very well refuse.' Two other principals supported this general notion and the superintendent explained that he was opposed only 'to the practice of dismissing children immediately after roll call.'[16] After making compulsory attendance a matter for local option in 1906, two years later the province made attendance compulsory for Saint John boys and girls between the ages of six and fourteen.[17]

What went on in Albert and other schools of the city? From such materials as the Saint John school curriculum, texts, descriptions of demonstration lessons, proceedings of teachers' institutes, inspectors' reports, questions on the provincial teachers' examination, and accounts of the local fair one can coax out some of the flavour of what the teachers and pupils did together in the classrooms of Albert and other schools in 1890. Of the 6700 pupils enrolled in the city's schools that year, over 6000 studied 'Temperance Teachings of Science,' 'Morals and Manners,' 'Reading, Spelling, and Recitation,' 'Composition,' 'Form and Drawing,' 'Singing,' 'Numbers and Arithmetic,' 'Geography,' 'Minerals, Plants and Animals,' and did some 'Physical Exercises.' Varying numbers of pupils also worked at sewing, knitting, 'Grammar and Analysis,' 'Printing and Print-Script,' history, physics, physiology, French, and Latin.[18] While most of this curriculum was typical of English Canada of the time, because of the influence of Loring W. Bailey, a professor at the University of New Brunswick, pupils in the schools of that province were more likely than most Canadian children to study their environment.[19] Bailey's work with teachers, particularly through the Maritime Summer School of Science, established in 1887, encouraged them to try practical activities in geography and scientific temperance and to conduct field studies of local plants, animals, and minerals.

A version of what was called 'object' or 'oral and object' teaching was also exciting the interest of the Saint John board and many of its teachers. In its original form, object teaching grew out of Johann Heinrich Pestalozzi's efforts to develop teaching methods which would train not only the mind of the child but his hand and heart as well. While Pestalozzi's ideas were known in both Canada and the United States from earlier in the century, they began to have a major impact in North America only after 1859. In that year, Edward A. Sheldon, superintendent of schools and principal of the State Normal School at Oswego, New York, was inspired by some English Pestalozzian materials which he examined in Egerton Ryerson's educational museum in Toronto. Sheldon and others at his Normal School developed techniques of oral and object teaching and how to teach them to student teachers. Over the next thirty years, the ideas of what came to be called the 'Oswego Movement' evolved, were applied to many school subjects, and spread all over North America. While in the hands of the movement's practitioners Pestalozzi's subtle suggestions for using all the senses in learning were transformed into a somewhat mechanical process, often they were a great improvement over the recitation techniques which they replaced. Except when they became rigidly stylized, oral and object lessons made schoolrooms into much more active and interesting places for children to be and improved the quality of learning which took place in them.[20]

In September 1889, teachers attending the Saint John County Teachers' Institute saw an example of object teaching. In her 'illustrative' lesson, which probably reviewed rather than taught the skills it demonstrated, Miss Grace Orr of Victoria School, Saint John, worked with her class of kindergarten pupils. After giving each youngster a smooth board and a bit of clay, Miss Orr showed a small sphere to the class. Through 'questions and answers' she 'acquainted' the children with its characteristics and then asked each child to model one in clay. Teacher and pupils 'worked in unison, talking and singing cheerfully.' When the sphere was finished the class next studied the cube and cylinder in the same way. As Miss Orr explained, the process of modeling brought into play 'all the primary movements of which the fingers are capable' and was thus 'an excellent manual training.'[21]

Its display for the International Exhibition held in Saint John in late September and early October, 1890, provided the School Board with a chance to explain and to illustrate its new method.[22] In this new style of teaching, a child was 'taught to recognize a sphere or ball by handling it, and to tell what he observes with regard to it.' Then he was required 'to reproduce the form in clay.' Next, he drew 'its outline on blackboard, slate or paper.' He then cut a number of the forms out of paper, arranged them in such patterns as his 'taste or knowledge' suggested, and pasted them on cardboard. As soon as possible, his teacher also asked him to print or write 'a simple description' of what he had done. As his powers of observation developed, the child came to recognize 'the same form as the basis of other figures (apples, oranges, etc.)' and was able to reproduce these 'in clay, and paper, and by drawing, and descriptive writing.' The child therefore proceeded 'through the several forms and up through the respective standards of instruction.' Contained in these processes, the trustees concluded, were such benefits as 'the quickening of the powers of observation, the training of eye and hand for the purposes of reproduction or description, and the general application of knowledge to practical uses.'[23]

Teachers in Albert School also taught the more traditional school subjects. Most of them probably agreed with John Lawson of Andover, New Brunswick, that the 'first essential in the education of a child' was 'to teach him to read.'[24] Although a few teachers were beginning to argue that effective silent reading was

the principal end of their teaching of this subject, most gave their major emphasis to oral reading.[25] After introducing the subject to beginners through a 'look-
say' technique, teachers quickly turned to a method which combined a long
study of phonics with a great deal of individual and group oral reading.[26] Through
phonic exercises, teachers believed, they would teach children to define accurately and spell correctly both the words they had studied and other words encountered in reading. By the careful and frequent practice of pronunciation,
enunciation, articulation, inflection, and emphasis, explained the introduction to
a widely used Canadian reader of the time, children would 'acquire the power of
reading with expression.'[27] The best method for teaching inflection, John Lawson explained, was that of 'simultaneous class-reading, after the teacher's pattern,
in daily exercise.'[28] To prepare themselves for this kind of teaching, students at
the New Brunswick Normal School learned how to answer such questions as
those for Class II and Class III certificates in 1890 in which candidates had to
describe 'the proper bodily posture for reading,' name 'the characteristic excel-
lencies of good reading,' give the rules 'for selecting emphatic words,' and mark
the emphatic words in the first five lines of Othello's speech as he enters the
room to murder Desdemona.[29]

A series of demonstration lessons which accompanied the day-long closing
activities of the provincial Normal School, in June 1889, provided other examples of what sorts of lessons Albert School and other New Brunswick teachers
strove to teach to their charges. Miss M. Gertrude Hannington, governor general's
medallist in the school's junior division, began the day with a lesson to grade six
pupils on the human heart. 'By the aid of a large drawing she elicited intelligent
answers from her pupils respecting the vital parts of the human frame.' Next,
Miss Simmons taught a class of grade one pupils in 'Number.' Through her 'win-
ning manner, she held the close attention of the little tots and received prompt
answers' to every question. The pupils 'were tried with 13 cents, these were distributed in the class, then divided, etc. and quick ready replies always given.'
Then Miss Sarah H. Shenton, BA, governor general's medallist in the senior division, taught a grade eight class a lesson on the Magna Charta and the reign of
King John. Through 'a liberal use of the blackboard she obtained from her class
a thorough knowledge of Magna Charta, its date, the benefit conferred upon
every Englishman, etc.' Concluding the morning's activities, John Brittain, a new
instructor on the Normal School staff, taught the Seniors 'a very interesting lesson upon the flowers' and then 'examined the Juniors in agriculture.' In the
afternoon, the visitors observed, in what the local paper said was probably the
'most interesting exercise of the day,' Miss Clark examine both classes 'in reading
and recitation.' Miss Clark's pupils 'did her great credit, and the young lady who
"broke down" towards the close of her recitation was fully to the front with her

peers.' Mr Creed then closed the examination with 'a pretty keen test' of both classes in 'Geometry and natural philosophy.'[30]

Pupils in Albert School were promoted from one grade to the next 'chiefly upon the estimate of the teacher.' To provide them with the data on which to make such decisions teachers maintained a 'merit book' in which they entered a daily mark for each pupil. In its report for 1889, the Saint John School Board justified this practice with the argument that the time had arrived 'when an examination, whether oral or written, should cease to be the evidence of a child's ability for promotion.'[31] This practice represented a considerable change in procedure from that prevailing in the city earlier in the decade. After he had established a complete and graded course of instruction, based on common text-books, for New Brunswick in 1879, Superintendent Rand experimented for about four years with a system of evaluating teachers that he based on the English model of payment by results.[32]

Each year the provincial school inspector evaluated the work of the Saint John school system. In 1889, although he made generally favourable comments on its work, William S. Carter expressed a concern shared by the province's chief superintendent, that Saint John was considering using a 'graded system of teachers' salaries' and had returned to the 'Merit Book' system of daily marking of pupils. In Carter's opinion, the former was 'repressive' of the best teaching talent, while the latter had been 'discarded by all progressive education' for the whole system was 'inaccurate and unjust.'[33] The following year, Carter commended the trustees for their work in repairing and improving school buildings. He criticised them for 'the very unsatisfactory state of the music in the schools,' the fact that, as to apparatus, the schools were not 'yet supplied with lesson sheets, and weights and measures,' and that the Board had prohibited 'the study of Latin in Grades VII and VIII.'[34]

Despite these professional criticisms, the citizens of Saint John apparently approved the work of Albert and other schools in their community. The local newspaper reported favourably on school affairs. The enthusiasm of the parents for the activities which closed Albert School in June 1889 was characteristic of those who attended the exercises that day at the other schools as well. Probably most people in Saint John would have agreed with their school trustees who reported that, 'with some exception,' their schools were institutions of which both they and citizens generally could 'feel justly proud.'[35] In this climate of public regard, neither Saint John teachers nor their less involved fellow citizens were able to foresee the effects that two sorts of changes, already under way, would have on their school system.

Between the 1880s and the 1920s the reformers did not change the school system nearly so much as it changed itself.[36] The managers of Canadian schooling

– ministers and officials in departments of education, school inspectors, urban school trustees, and career school principals – worked to better the quality of what they did through such means as improving school attendance and upgrading the qualification of teachers. When the effects of the gradual implementation of these policies came together with those stemming from the great growth of the Canadian population and the spread of settlement, they had a dynamic effect on Canadian educational systems. In turn, these mainly institutional changes greatly influenced the thinking of reformers and helped to shape the proposals which they put forward. Although most of the important story of these developments lies outside the scope of this study, a brief examination of key changes is necessary to suggest the improving context in which the reformers operated.[37]

The most obvious change was the enormous growth of the educational establishment. Between 1891 and 1923, total enrolment in publicly controlled elementary and secondary schools in Canada more than doubled from 942,500 to 1,939,700 pupils. Increasing at an even sharper rate, the number of teachers grew more than two and a half times, from 21,149 in 1890 to 54,691 in 1920. While growth was a characteristic of nearly all provinces, some areas and dimensions of the educational enterprise grew much more rapidly than did others. The slow decline in enrolment in mostly rural Prince Edward Island, from 22,500 in 1891 to 17,800 in 1921, was more than offset by the sharp rise in rural schooling which settlement produced in Manitoba, Saskatchewan, and Alberta. The enrolment in Manitoba went from 23,900 in 1891 to 129,000 in 1921.[38] In the decade 1906–16 the number of organized school districts in Saskatchewan increased from 1190 to 3878.[39] Many urban school systems also showed dramatic growth. Between 1890 and 1920, the daily pupil attendance in Toronto increased from 20,000 to 41,800.[40] Over the same period enrolment in Vancouver went from 1750 to 19,000.[41] In Winnipeg, enrolment increased from 5750 in December 1899 to 35,700 in 1920–1.[42]

Canadian secondary education expanded much more rapidly than did schooling as a whole. In New Brunswick, as enrolment in elementary schools increased only marginally, from 58,250 pupils in 1890 to 62,785 in 1920, that of secondary schools more than quadrupled, from 439 to 2265. While enrolment in publicly controlled elementary schools in Ontario rose from 484,181 in 1890 to 574,532 in 1925, that in secondary schools almost tripled from 31,779 to 82,502. Such growth was not confined to the long-settled parts of the nation; while only 244 of the 8039 public school pupils in British Columbia were in secondary schools in 1890, by 1920 the proportion had grown to 6636 out of 79,174.[43]

English-speaking Canadians also improved the quality of their educational enterprise. Children and families made a greater investment in the time and effort they devoted to formal education. School systems improved the quality of their teachers, the teaching materials they worked with, and the physical environment their pupils worked in. In turn, teachers improved their methods and became much more adept in their handling of a wider range of children. Compared to the situation which had existed thirty years before, by 1921 a greater proportion of school-aged children went to school, and a greater proportion of those in school attended more regularly each year, stayed in school for a longer number of years, and were taught by teachers who were both better educated and better trained than their predecessors.

Canadian schools and Canadian communities worked together through many separate developments to effect these changes. Provincial governments opened schools in newly settled areas and extended and more effectively enforced school attendance legislation. Provincial and federal governments passed laws to regulate the employment of children in mines, shops, and factories.[44] Ministers and officials of provincial departments of education improved the selection procedures and training practices of teachers. They rationalized and professionalized the rapidly growing systems they administered. Trustees made great improvements in school accommodation. Perhaps most important, as a rising standard of living reduced the need of many families for the income of their youngsters, a greater proportion of Canadians made a deeper commitment to the education of their children.

Since the information is both complex and incomplete, one must look in two ways at the matter of the growing proportion of school-aged children who were actually attending school. First, census figures show that there was a substantial decline in the proportion of young people in the work force. While enumerators in 1891 discovered that 13.8 per cent of all Canadian children between the ages of 10 and 14 were gainfully employed, their counterparts in 1921 reported only 3.2 per cent of such children as working. In agriculture, the decline was from 11.4 to 1.9 per cent and that in all other industries from 2.3 to 1.4 per cent.[45] As experience in both Britain and the United States had already shown, however, to legislate or otherwise push children and young people out of the work force was not necessarily to put them into school.[46] Nevertheless, census returns of a type available for only part of the period provide proof that at least some of those no longer working did indeed end up in a classroom. Between the census of 1911 and that of 1921, the Dominion Bureau of Statistics calculated that the proportion of children not attending school at any time was reduced by half.[47] This decline varied greatly from province to province. For eleven year olds – the age that had the highest level of school attendance – the national drop was from 13.1 to 5.3 per cent, while that in Nova Scotia was from 10.6 to 6.6 per cent, in Ontario from 9.9 to 3.9 per cent, in Alberta from 30.9 to 5.9 per cent, and in British Columbia from 20.5 to 4.3 per cent.[48]

School officials expected that increasing the proportion of the young at school would handicap their efforts to improve regularity of attendance. Reluctant attenders, custom held, were irregular attenders. It is therefore noteworthy that the greater proportion of children attending school did so more regularly as well. Over the decade 1911 to 1921, the census showed that the percentage of those enrolled in school who actually attended for between seven and nine months of the school year rose significantly. For seven year olds, the increase between 1911 and 1921 was from 80.0 to 84.2 per cent, for nine year olds from 88.7 to 91.3 per cent, for eleven year olds from 90.0 to 92.0 per cent, and for thirteen year olds from 87.6 to 91.0 per cent.[49] Although school attendance data is less complete and exact than that of the census, it provides further proof of this trend towards more regular attendance and also indicates that it extended over the whole thirty-year period.[50] Between 1891 and 1921, the percentage average daily attendance made the least gain in Prince Edward Island. There it rose from 57.3 per cent in 1891 to 64.0 in 1921. In Manitoba, it rose from 51.9 per cent in 1891 to 66.7 in 1921. British Columbia showed the sharpest rise from 54.8 per cent in 1891 to 79.8 in 1921.[51] Attendance rose most sharply in the cities. In Winnipeg in 1899, out of an enrolment of about 6000, 3657 attended for 150 or more days in the year, 1495 attended between 100 and 150 days, and 2020 attended for less than 100 days. Two decades later, out of an enrolment of about 36,000 in the 1920–1 term, 951 attended for over 200 of the 202 days of the school year, 16,017 attended between 175 and 200 days, 7268 attended between 150 and 175 days, 4995 attended between 100 and 150 days, 3166 attended between 50 and 100 days, and 3369 attended for less than 50 days.[52]

More regular attendance, in turn, led children to stay in school longer and to complete more grades. Traditionally, those who left school before the age of fourteen came in greater proportions from the lower grades than the upper. In other words, the closer in grade a child stayed with his peers the more likely he was to continue in school.[53] Again, the records provide satisfactory information for only the latter years of this period. In 1923, M.C. MacLean of the Dominion Bureau of Statistics estimated that the average child on leaving school at about grade six was at least one grade further on than he would have been a decade earlier.[54] The bureau's later illiteracy and school attendance study indicated that because of the improvement in attendance between the census of 1911 and that of 1921, 'about half as many again ... attended long enough to complete the common school course in 1921 as in 1911,' and there was 'a similar though diminishing difference in each grade below the last grade of the common school course.'[55]

Despite these important improvements in pupil attendance, it was probably the teaching force which underwent the most wide-ranging changes over these years. Although the whole complex matter needs much careful examination before the exact nature and significance of the changes in teachers can be clearly understood, one can describe some of the more obvious developments.[56] First, there was a sharp improvement in quality; both in their general education and in their professional training teachers in 1920 were very much better than they had been in 1890. While Ontario's teaching force grew in size from 8 394 teachers to 14,829 between 1890 and 1920, the proportion of those whose certificates indicated that they had not completed junior matriculation dropped from over half to less than 10 per cent. Meanwhile, those with at least junior matriculation and a year of professional training grew from less than 10 to over 80 per cent of the teaching body. Even in the West, where the very rapid growth of rural schooling made such improvement more difficult than in the long-settled areas, a parallel though less extensive change took place. Between 1910 and 1920 in Saskatchewan, the percentage of teachers with less than junior matriculation declined from slightly over 50 to slightly less than 40 per cent.[57]

A major shift in the balance between men and women in teaching accompanied this improvement in quality. The number of men teaching in New Brunswick declined from 394 out of a total of 1573 teachers in 1890 to 141 out of 1975 in 1920. While 139, or almost half, of the 285 teachers in British Columbia in 1890 were men, they constituted only one-fifth or 572 of the 2557 teachers in the province by 1920.[58] Undoubtedly, many men who once might have become teachers went into the growing number of jobs offered by an expanding economy. Also, as the qualifications necessary to enter the profession went up, the lure to young men on the rise of a year or two of school-keeping may well have gone down. Finally, as elementary teaching increasingly became a profession for women, school boards found that they could generally get a more highly qualified and committed young woman for the same price or less than that of a man.

Paradoxically, the actual opportunities for men and women who made a career commitment to teaching rose sharply. Not only did the number of teachers increase even more extensively than the number of pupils, but, unlike the pupils, the teaching force was mostly drawn from the Canadian population. The great host of immigrants brought substantially more pupils than they provided teachers, principals, and school inspectors from their own ranks. Increasing average attendance also added to the demand for teachers. As children attended more regularly fewer of them could conveniently be enrolled in each class. Primary classrooms most clearly displayed this change. The increase in schools with more than one teacher also opened up opportunities for promotion for ambitious young men. The decline in the proportion who attended one-room schools in Canada provides one crude measure of the effect of this process. In Nova Scotia, the proportion of pupils in graded schools rose from 48.1 per cent in 1903 to 60.8 in 1919. In Alberta between 1905 and 1919, the total number of pupils in graded schools grew from 10,635 to 68,329 while those in ungraded schools went from 13,619 to 53,238.[59]

Changes in enrolment and in attendance, the growth of the system, and the quality of those in their ranks had, in turn, a major effect on the teaching profession itself. Many teachers played an important role in the reform movement. Others took part in an effort characteristic of many professions and semi-professions of the time, to upgrade, to formalize educational and admission requirements, and to bring their ranks into a fully organized profession. Teachers were also caught up in the sense of excitement engendered by rapid growth and change.[60] While the initiative and much of the leadership for major changes in Canadian education came from outside the ranks of the profession, the great enthusiasm of many teachers brought success to many of the pilot projects of the new education.

One gross measure of the effects of these great efforts put into education was the very sharp decline in illiteracy in Canada. While the assembling and interpretation of such figures is a notably complex operation, involving such variables as nativity, sex, and rural and urban residence, in a census monograph the Dominion Bureau of Statistics explained that the reduction in illiteracy between 1891 and 1921 was 'accomplished by the school alone, in the face of increasingly unfavourable conditions.' The principal 'unfavourable' condition to which the monograph drew attention was the increasing proportion of the Canadian population who were 'foreign' (that is, who were neither Canadian-born nor from the British empire).[61]

Hidden in all these changing figures, of course, was an enormous and by 1920 as yet uncompleted effort. Teachers, truant officers, social welfare workers, school trustees, and school officials became preoccupied and occasionally obsessed with the matter of prompt and regular school attendance. Not only did they have to persuade or coerce reluctant parents to send their children to school, they also had to persuade often unwilling local school trustees to open their schools for the required number of days in the school year. As late as 1909 in Saskatchewan, 208 of the 1691 elementary schools were open for 100 or less of the school year of 210 days.[62] Provinces passed compulsory attendance laws and then they and the local school board had to establish the necessary enforcement machinery: school censuses, accurate records, work permits, and truant officers. Out of all these efforts on the one hand and growing community pressure to conform on the other came first the idea, then the belief, and finally the ingrained social habit that going to school was not only what all children did as a normal part of their childhood but that they did so as a matter of course promptly every day over the whole school year for a gradually increasing number of years.

The bureaucratic aspect of all of this activity affecting Albert and other schools in English-speaking Canada calls for some comment. To carry out these internal changes and to try out and introduce new programs the managers of Canadian education had to specify what trustees, teachers, and pupils must do and perhaps add modestly to the rolls of supervisors to ensure that they did so. Some see this gradual bureaucratization as the most important change in education in the latter years of the nineteenth century.[63] As early as 1918, Peter Sandiford argued that the day of centralized authority in education, so necessary in the pioneering stage of Canadian society, had passed.[64] While the matter is peripheral rather than central to the main interest of this study – which is the making of the new program of what society *ought* to do with children rather than the way in which this program was implemented – a brief survey of the evidence suggests three tentative conclusions on the matter.

First, the supervisory staff of Canadian education did not grow substantially between the 1880s and the 1920s. In 1890, Ontario maintained a staff of 81 school inspectors to supervise 9201 teachers, or roughly 113 teachers per inspector; thirty years later, 125 inspectors supervised 15,331 teachers, or about 122 teachers each. Over the same period, the number of headmasters of collegiate institutes and high schools in the province increased from about 120 to about 170, while the number of assistants in such schools rose from 332 to 1207.[65] Urban staffs grew more rapidly. In 1913, James Collins Miller discovered that the median number of schools per inspector ranged upward from 75 in Ontario, through 83 in Manitoba, 117 in Alberta, 139 in Nova Scotia, 152 in Quebec, to between 181 and 239 in New Brunswick.[66] Since his examples do not show the growth of municipal supervisory staffs, such as Vancouver's, they are by no means definitive.[67] What they do suggest, however, is that in much of Canada the growth of the administrative staff in education barely kept pace with the growth in the system as a whole.

Second, in the latter part of the twentieth century, English Canadians may well be able to argue that bureaucracy is the dead hand on the system. In a period characterized by well-trained and well-organized teachers, of parents and parent groups with the initiative and the affluence to demand and to subsidize a range of alternative styles of education, and of self-confident students who insist on a share in the making and implementing of educational policy, an elaborate compulsory apparatus may no longer be necessary. One must not, however, apply these as yet not proven conclusions retrospectively to an earlier period of Canadian history without a very rigorous examination of the actual situation as it then was.

For English-speaking Canada between 1890 and 1920, one cannot make a clear-cut case on the matter of the bureaucratization of education. On one side, officials used their control of finance, teacher supply, and curriculum to effect a very gradual improvement in the quality of rural schooling in Canada. In doing so they had to work with a very inexperienced corps of teachers. In his study of rural education Miller determined that in 1913 the great majority of rural teachers were between seventeen and twenty-three years of age.[68] School inspectors and supervisors gradually transformed the central, graded curriculum from a pious hope into a reasonably accurate guide as to what actually went on in the schools. With the help of their compatriots in the growing public health service, they began to enforce minimum standards of sanitation and preventive medicine to the benefit of children attending both rural and urban schools. A small body of specialists in civic and provincial education offices laid out, explained, and demonstrated the new elements being introduced into the curriculum.

On the other side, professional educators carried out the wishes of the majority in dragooning the foreign-born and their children into chauvinistic displays which must have given great offence to parents who had already committed themselves to the Canadianization of their families. Many educational administrators and other professionals also accepted innovative schemes uncritically. They showed themselves reluctant to remove any element of the new education once it had embedded itself in the curriculum.

Third, in urban areas before the First World War, school superintendents were very much under the control of their boards of education. If the immensely prestigious James L. Hughes was able to persuade the Toronto board to institute kindergartens and other reforms, he also had to follow their lead in such matters as the introduction of medical inspection. Leadership in the prewar period in Vancouver came not from the superintendent and supervisors but from board members. By using its professional staff, the board helped Vancouver to escape from the mediocre levels of schooling then prevailing in the rural areas of the province.[69]

These comments suggest that in this critical period in the history of Canadian education the issue is not so much the bureaucratization of education but the use to which the new machinery was put. Those who hired the administrators and supervisors and wrote the regulations saw these actions as the only available means of effecting the broad range of changes which many Canadians thought were necessary to improve the lives of their children. Contemporary opposition to increasing centralization and regulation was not an alternative strategy for effecting change but a device for doing nothing at all. In rural areas, as the very slow growth of consolidation eloquently testified, provincial bureaucrats, and especially local school inspectors, prodded the 'kickers,' to use James W. Robertson's term for them, who made up the majority of rural school boards into hiring better teachers, providing minimum sanitary facilities, putting schools into reasonable repair, keeping them open for a moderate length of time, and building teacherages. In the ebb and flow of rural teachers, observed a Manitoba report, the local school inspector was the one person who was relatively permanent in the rural school system.[70] Different routes to educational change probably had to wait until other sources of power came together in such organizations and pressure groups as teachers, parents, and community associations and, later still, in the combinations of activist students.

11

'A Very Strong Undercurrent of Dissatisfaction': Setting the Stage for the 'New' Education, 1885-1900

As they gave increasing attention to their children, a growing band of English-speaking Canadians in the 1880s and 1890s came to believe that schools were not doing all they ought to prepare children for the future. Mrs Adelaide Hoodless of Hamilton, Ontario, said that she saw growing in Canada 'a very strong undercurrent of dissatisfaction' with the educational system, 'a sort of unsatisfied want, so vague that its existence could scarcely be accounted for, but very real and unsettling in its effects.'[2] Canadian and Imperial patriots called for the schools to produce a generation with deeper loyalties to nation, monarch, and empire. Protestant and Roman Catholics alike looked, in a time of change, to the schools to inculcate the traditional faith and values more effectively. Since it seemed 'a hopeless task' to get schools out of politics, or to 'introduce into them the idea of Christian morals as part of the education of a human being,' argued the New Westminster *British Columbian*, then 'the only recourse' was to 'pay more attention to church, private and parish schools.'[3] Those who saw rural decay spreading like a blight across the Canadian countryside called on schools to effect a cure. Those working to establish a new kind of childhood and family wanted teachers to conduct their classes in ways that would help children develop their physical, intellectual, and emotional potential to the full. Industrialists and manufacturers demanded that schools be reorganized to train an efficient work force. Others deplored, as did the Calgary *Herald*, methods of teacher education which taught students that it was 'nothing short of criminal to take a strap to a boy.'[4]

Further, as reformers decided that the surest way to bring about reform in the future was through children, the essential features of the school inevitably drew their attention. If Canadians were to improve social conditions, explained Mrs Hoodless, then they had to 'go to the root' which was 'the HOME.' The school, she continued, must become the agent that shaped 'the homes of the next generation.'[5] If they could only make the institution work in the way they wanted it to, reformers believed, then they had in the school a ready-made engine of enormous power. Unlike social agencies which dealt with such small proportions of the total population of boys and girls as the sick, or the dependent, or the delinquent, schools in modern society could be made to contain the whole of the next generation within their walls. Public employees controlled and directed Canadian children for a growing portion of their lives. Moreover, schools assembled children in a way that one could get at them conveniently; educational authorities had already gathered, organized, and roughly classified them according to such criteria as age, sex, ability, and the neighbourhood in which they lived.

While they looked to teachers for help in applying their new ideas to the young, reformers generally believed that the 'pressure must come from outside the teaching body.'[6] Some teachers, however, were sceptical of the new ideas being forced on them. You could not 'open your schoolroom door for a breath of fresh air without having someone with a mission fall in,' explained Miss Agnes Deans Cameron, principal of the South Park School in Victoria.[7]

From their initially vague dissatisfactions with contemporary education, reformers moved on to specify how they would change the schools. Two major strains in the growing discussion and debate about education – one which wanted schooling to be more practical and one which wanted it to be more child- and family-centred – brought forth specific programs for change. Although one can make too much of the distinctiveness of each group – there was, after all, a great deal of overlap in membership, rhetoric, and activity between them – they were nonetheless separate entities. In what they had already individually accomplished by the turn of the century in changing Canadian education one can see most clearly the differences between them. In their efforts to protect and improve Canadian families, the child-centred workers had accomplished two things in the schools: they had demonstrated that kindergartens made a useful addition to the school system and they had added temperance education to the curriculum. In their attempts to improve the quality of the Canadian work force, the practical-minded had introduced some vocational and technical training into Canadian education. By about 1900, however, their interests temporarily converged: both groups believed that what they called 'manual training' was the necessary next phase of school reform. To understand why these two strains came together at this time, one must first consider the pioneering educational activities of both.

In the late 1870s and 1880s such influential Ontarians as Egerton Ryerson, his assistant J. George Hodgins, school inspector and later University of Toronto professor George Paxton Young, Adam Crooks, minister of education from 1876 to 1882, his successor George W. Ross, minister from 1883 to 1889, and James L. Hughes, the Toronto school inspector, began to promote the cause of the Froebelian kindergarten in that province. As his visits to the United States and his reading stimulated his interest in the kindergarten movement, Hughes capitalized on opportunities for experimentation which his position made possible.[8] Devoting his enormous energy and highly developed powers of persuasion to the task, he talked the Toronto School Board into opening, in January 1883, the first public school kindergarten in Canada. As its director, the board appointed Miss Ada Marean, who had operated a private kindergarten in the city since 1878. When they later married, Ada Marean and James L. Hughes became the most important Canadian exponents of the kindergarten idea both in their own country and as a part of the international kindergarten movement. As a result of their efforts and those of other supporters of the kindergarten, in 1885 the provincial government permitted Ontario school boards to provide schooling for children who were five years old. Two years later, the province formally accepted the kindergarten as part of the public school system. By 1893, Ontario had sixty-six kindergartens, all in urban areas, which enrolled a total of 6375 children.[9] The movement also spread to other provinces. In Nova Scotia, the supervisor of the Halifax schools, Alexander McKay, recommended that kindergarten principles be introduced in the schools of that city.[10]

The proponents of Froebelian kindergartens believed, in Hughes' words, in 'reverent love for the child, profound respect for his individuality as the element of divinity in him, and freedom and self-activity as the conditions of most perfect growth physically, intellectually, and spiritually.'[11] To put these beliefs into practice, they directed their efforts to enrolling as many youngsters as possible in their 'gardens of children.' Although they agreed that the centre of their interest was thus in the growing child, North American kindergarten supporters tended to separate into two groups on the matter of how they wanted to use their institution. One party saw the kindergarten primarily as an agency which used young children as agents to improve the family life of the poor. Promoters of the Free Kindergarten Association in Winnipeg believed that 'the proper education of children during the first seven years of their lives' did 'much to reduce poverty and crime in any community.' Association members got acquainted 'with the homes of the little ones,' tended the sick, organized meetings for the 'improvement' of mothers, and sometimes even invited them to tea.[12]

Others directed their efforts to use Froebelian ideas to reform the whole school system. From 'catacombs' in which 'the self-hood, the originality and the executive tendency of childhood' were buried, schools must become 'gardens,' Hughes argued, in which 'each child' grew 'to be its grandest, most complete self.'[13] The postulates upon which kindergarten processes were built were 'fundamental principles that should guide the teacher in the work of teaching and training the child throughout its school course.'[14] In part because of the enormous influence of Hughes, the latter emphasis prevailed in Canada even more completely than it did in the United States.[15] As the first bloom of their enthusiasm wore off and as public interest shifted to manual training, most Canadian proponents of kindergartens withdrew from the role of missionaries of a new gospel of family life and education. As they centred their efforts on freeing the early years of schooling from many of its constraints, they were gradually absorbed by the education system and became merely a special kind of primary teacher.

Although kindergarten ideas were of greater long-term significance in Canadian education, in the late nineteenth century temperance education reached far more children than did kindergartens. From the mid-1880s until well into the twentieth century the rapidly growing Canadian temperance movement conducted a major campaign to have its principles thoroughly and universally taught in schools. Strongly rooted as it was amongst those who wanted to protect childhood and preserve and strengthen family life – for years the watchword of the Canadian WCTU was 'Save the Young People and Children' – the movement gave much of its characteristic passion and a great deal of its attention to the nurture of the young. To combat such evil influences of the liquor traffic as 'its invasion of our homes' and 'its corruption of our women and youth,' Christians had to 'fight like soldiers brave and true, and cry unto the God of heaven for strength and victory.'[16]

As a first step in their efforts with the young, the temperance movement worked through families. Through them, it turned to existing voluntary organizations, especially Sunday schools, and set up special temperance groups like Bands of Hope and Juvenile Lodges. At its second meeting, the Richmond Hill, Ontario, WCTU decided that 'the first work taken up be the forming of a Band of Hope among the children.'[17] Within a year of its founding, the New Westminster, British Columbia, WCTU sponsored a Band of Hope with 126 members. Through singing, marching, recitation and signing of pledges, special talks and lessons, temperance revival meetings, essay contests, picnics, and prize-givings, both Sunday school and temperance organizations carried out effective programs of indoctrination. In April 1893, sixty children in New Westminster presented a concert entitled 'Temperance Mother Goose.'[18] Successful as all such activities were, however, temperance advocates discovered that Sunday schools and Bands of Hope attracted to their ranks mostly the children of those who were already committed to the goals of the movement.

If they were ever to free the nation from the scourge of alcohol, the movement believed that it would have to get at the Canadian population as a whole. According to the president of the Halifax WCTU, however, persuading adults of the merits of abstinence was 'throwing pebbles against stone walls.'[19] Thus temperance groups pledged themselves, as did the annual meeting of the Ontario WCTU in October 1886, 'not to rest satisfied' until compulsory temperance instruction was 'given to all grades of pupils in our Schools.'[20]

To persuade provincial departments and local school boards to add their subject to the school's program, the temperance movement brought to bear the same broad array of techniques that it used in its wider battle for prohibition.[21] Through its own crusading organizations, through those of churches such as the Methodist and Presbyterian who embraced their cause, and with the help of more widely based organizations such as the Local Councils of Women, temperance believers waited on and petitioned members of provincial legislatures, ministers of education, and provincial cabinets.[22] In 1893 alone, the New Brunswick legislature received nineteen petitions favouring compulsory temperance teaching.[23] In addition, a steady stream of delegations attended local school board meetings to plead their cause, to suggest appropriate textbooks and methods of teaching, and to promote their ideas amongst board members, school inspectors, and teachers. As the movement grew in strength, an increasing number of legislators and school board members themselves embraced the cause and in turn campaigned for school temperance instruction.

Teachers therefore made a major contribution to the eventual success of this campaign. Halifax's Supervisor McKay explained that the 'great majority of teachers' had found that pupil progress was hindered by the poverty brought on by drinking habits, and the fact that 'children from the homes of the intemperate ... frequently possessed ... cloudy intellects and demoralized habits.'[24] In the 1890s, teachers' meetings and institutes frequently discussed two aspects of temperance education: whether the subject should be a compulsory part of the curriculum and how best to teach it to school children. In January 1892, members of the Mainland Teachers Institute resolved that temperance be made a compulsory subject in the elementary school curriculum and an option on the province's high school entrance examination; the marks gained by those writing this paper were to be added as a bonus to those earned on the rest.[25] Indeed, how best to teach the subject was for some years the central issue of the whole matter. Although some trustees and school officials argued, as did one in Vancouver when presented with a temperance petition, that the public schools had 'become the scapegoats upon which to place the sins of people,' most agreed with the Victoria and New Westminster school boards that scientific temperance must be made a compulsory subject.[26] However sceptical they might feel privately about either the ends or the means of the temperance movement, by the 1890s it became well-nigh impossible for teachers or school board members to argue against the idea that children should be taught to shun the evils of drink.

Temperance advocates differed as to the best way of teaching their principles to children. At one extreme, the WCTU and others whose major commitment was to the crusade itself made temperance education into a new school subject. In a manner not unlike more recent efforts at anti-smoking and anti-drug education, they put together under the general heading of 'scientific temperance' an amalgam of physiology, chemistry, nutrition, and history. From a course in scientific temperance, argued its advocates, children learned the scientific basis for not drinking. Most of those who argued for the temperance course also insisted that it be 'put upon exactly the same level as other subjects in our school curriculum.' Experience in the Maritime provinces, explained the president of the Halifax Local Council of Women, showed that unless scientific temperance were 'given as much consideration and as honourable a place as geography, grammar or any other study,' it stood 'a very poor chance of being taught at all.'[27] Many who favoured the separate course went on to argue, as did the WCTU convention in Victoria, in November 1893, that a pass mark in scientific temperance should be made a condition for promotion from grade to grade and a compulsory subject on the high school entrance examination.[28]

Others who generally supported the temperance idea questioned whether it should be taught as a separate school subject. Those who saw prohibition as one of a range of necessary social changes, such as some members of Councils of Women, took this position. To these people, temperance education was but part of a wider curriculum: 'we should,' explained Mrs Hoodless, 'have temperance, domestic science, and chemistry of food combined in one textbook.'[29] Some, such as the General Assembly of Canadian Presbyterians, insisted that the school must 'give instruction on the moral, as well as the scientific bearing' of temperance.[30] Others were sceptical of an academic approach to the teaching of behaviour. School Inspector William Burns suggested that teachers take advantage of situations that came up naturally in their lessons to spread the temperance message and, most important, ensure 'that every word and action of theirs' tended 'towards urging their pupils to lead a moral life.'[31] In his concern for the teacher's behaviour, Burns shared common ground with Mrs C.D. Bigelow, dominion superintendent of scientific temperance instruction for the WCTU, who insisted that 'no teacher should tipple, and no tippler should teach.'[32]

For a time the separate-subject point of view prevailed. In 1884, Ontario included temperance as one of the compulsory subjects in its new elementary curriculum.[33] In 1893, the New Brunswick Legislature enacted that temperance instruction must 'be given orally from a suitable textbook in the hands of the teacher, to all pupils unable to read' and 'to all others with text-books in the hands of the pupils.'[34] In 1895, the Nova Scotia legislature also required that both pupils and teachers study scientific temperance.[35] Ontario school regulations also prescribed that 100 of the possible 1100 marks on the high school entrance examination and 50 out of the 1650 possible in the Normal School program were to be based on an examination in temperance.[36]

In the early years of the new century, however, more and more members of the temperance movement became convinced that they could achieve their goal through provincial or even national legislation. While continuing to support temperance education, they gave most of their energy to politics.[37] In consequence, the increasingly influential public health movement supplanted temperance organizations in shaping the form which temperance education took in schools. Public health workers, most of whom strongly supported temperance principles, gradually changed the focus of the health curriculum from the study of physiology to that of hygiene and of good personal health habits. Since temperance fitted quite naturally into this context, health curricula and textbooks gave considerable emphasis to the topic. Schools then gradually abandoned separate courses in scientific temperance.

In the latter half of the nineteenth century many Canadians also expressed dissatisfaction with the way in which education prepared boys and girls for the world of work. As early as 1848, the *Agricultural and Canadian Journal* called for the education of farmers' sons 'in their profession.'[38] In its earlier phases, the main tenor of arguments for practical education was that schools should teach farming and agriculture. Later, the gradual growth of industry in Canada stimulated a parallel concern to train an efficient managerial and working force. In 1889, both 'the manufacturers and the mechanics alike' expressed to the federal Royal Commission on the Relations of Labor and Capital their belief that the 'State should extend the present school system by providing technical and industrial training for the youth of our working classes.'[39]

Local and provincial educators and politicians responded to these demands for practical training. In 1871, Ontario made agriculture a compulsory subject in the elementary school course of study. Three years later, it established the Ontario Agricultural College in Guelph. In 1885, Nova Scotia passed an 'Act to Encourage Agricultural Education' which called for the appointment of a lecturer in agriculture at the Truro Normal School and extra grants to teachers who taught agriculture. First established in Canada in the 1820s, mechanics institutes gave a wide range of practical lectures and courses in technical subjects. In 1855, McGill added applied science to its curriculum. From the winter of 1866-7 onward, the Board of Arts and Manufacturers conducted practical classes in Montreal. In 1877, Ontario established a school of practical science. In 1884, Nova

Scotia opened a mining school. In 1892, Toronto established an evening technical school. Two years later Ontario opened a school of mining and agriculture in
Kingston.[40] In the late 1880s, industrial schools began to give some practical
training to Indian boys and white delinquents.[41]

Since they were generally designed to teach the more highly skilled levels of
practical work, most of these and other pioneering efforts were directed at adolescents or adults. Only a very few elementary school pupils learned skills like
sewing and industrial drawing, or read in an agricultural textbook about proper
farming practices. In the 1890s, however, Canadians began to change this whole
situation. Advocates or practical education joined the child-centred in looking
upon manual training as a means of bringing about needed changes in schooling.
In turn, when circumstances pushed the federal government into helping train
Canadian farmers, the man it picked to direct the effort took a leading role in
reshaping Canadian education along lines which accorded with the wishes of
both groups.

In the late 1880s and early 1890s some Canadians began to use 'manual training' in place of 'industrial' or 'practical education' when referring to this dimension of elementary schooling. Reflecting the dual roots of the subject, advocates
of manual training used the term in two generally distinct ways. Since handwork
accorded with their ideas on child development, those working out of child-
centred and Froebelian contexts saw manual activities in the school as an integral part of the general education of all youngsters: 'a means for the development
of brain, eye and hand, through handicraft' to produce men 'whose every power'
was 'fully developed and nobly guided.'[42] To others, manual training was clearly
pre-vocational or frankly vocational in intent; through 'free mechanical drawing,
modelling in clay, working in wood for boys and sewing for girls' children would
learn rudimentary tool-handling skills and the principles underlying mechanical
operations.[43]

While favouring manual training, however, its pioneer advocates seldom agreed
as to what activities they included in their new subject. Throughout the 1890s,
its various proponents suggested that the schools teach a very wide range of
'manual' activities, including playing 'house' in kindergartens and the primary
grades, teaching and demonstrating gardening and farming skills, English and
Swedish sloyd and other forms of woodworking, the use of tools, mechanical
drawing, cardboard, clay, and paper handicrafts, and cooking and sewing. En-
compassing even more in the term, in 1898 the Nova Scotia superintendent of
education reported that all teachers in training in that province took short
courses 'in several forms of manual training, such as drawing, modelling, woodwork, chemical and physical experimentation, biological work (including use of
the microscope),' and that trustees could provide all of these activities in their

schools.[44] Actually, it was not until about 1910 that Canadians came to a rough consensus as to what they meant by 'manual training.'

The fact that a senior member of the federal civil service became a leading educational reformer was a central part of the process through which Canadians began to define with some precision manual training and other branches of what they came to call the 'new' education. In the 1880s and 1890s, farmers in eastern Canada had to shift at an ever accelerating rate from grain growing to specialized mixed farming. In response to such conditions as soil exhaustion, the virtual disappearance of an eastern agricultural frontier, a growing use of substitutes for barley malt, a rise in American tariffs, and the extremely rapid increase in wheat production elsewhere, they abandoned wheat and barley and turned instead to such more intensive agriculture as fruit and vegetable farming, stock raising, feed growing, and dairying.[45] To accomplish with a minimum of difficulty such a sharp shift in the way in which they earned their living, farmers had to master quickly a whole new package of knowledge and skills. In doing so they both helped themselves through their own organizations and drew extensively on a rapidly growing range of assistance which the provincial and federal governments provided for them.[46] Responding to pressure from a growing number of agricultural organizations, to members of Parliament from rural areas, and to the real needs of a growing industry, in 1890 the federal government established the office of Dairy Commissioner – later Commissioner for Agriculture and Dairying – in the Department of Agriculture.[47] To the new position the government appointed one of the principal spokesmen in the effort to persuade it to enter the work, James Wilson Robertson.

In carrying out his tasks as commissioner of agriculture, Robertson formed opinions which prompted him to take a leading role in making Canadian schooling more practical. Born in Scotland in 1857, he emigrated to Canada with his family in 1875 when he was seventeen years old. Although he had been apprenticed to a leather firm at the age of fourteen, in Canada Robertson entered cheese manufacturing. After successfully managing a number of cheese factories in western Ontario, in 1886 the Ontario Agricultural College appointed him to the position of dairy professor. Defining education as that which 'helps to fit a man to bring things to pass,' in his teaching at Guelph, at Cornell University, and in his work as dairy commissioner, Robertson tried to help farmers learn to do their job better. Throughout the 1890s he used speeches, travelling dairies, dairy inspectors, dairy schools, bulletins, experimental dairy stations, and the inspection of cheese factories to ensure that the farmer 'should thoroughly *understand* his business.'[48] He also assisted the dairy industry by improving cold storage and transportation facilities and by developing markets for its products.[49] Both as part of their vice-regal duties and as owners of agricultural land in British Columbia, Lord and Lady Aberdeen had many opportunities to observe Robertson's work. He was, Lady Aberdeen confided to her journal, 'a capital man, full of enthusiasm for his work and of real zeal for the development and building up of the country.'[50] Fifteen years later, the journalist Herbert Francis Sherwood shrewdly observed that Robertson was 'essentially a pioneer.' Having 'planted the seed, demonstrated how to make it fruitful, and won friends for it,' he left the harvest to others and pressed on to a fresh field. 'One forward step each year' was his aim.[51] He was also a very persuasive speaker; in 1966, one of Robertson's compatriots in educational reform, H.B. MacLean, recalled that Robertson could hold an audience spellbound.[52] In the 1890s he became well known in Canada for his professional activities and for such public service as assisting in the founding of the Victorian Order of Nurses and the Canadian Association for the Prevention of Consumption.

By the turn of the century, Robertson's work with rural Canadians brought him to the conclusion that formed the rationale of the educational reform enterprise which was called the Macdonald-Robertson Movement. Conditions of rural life, Robertson argued, could be improved in two ways. First, Canadians must make farming more attractive and profitable by the 'spread of knowledge and the giving of practicable and economical illustrations of application of that knowledge to local conditions.' Second, they had to change their schooling and other training so that children would be 'attracted to rural occupations' and be 'qualified to be successful in them.' Canada's best asset, he concluded, was 'an intelligent, prosperous and contented population, with the children being brought up for life at its best' in their home locality.[53]

Robertson drew ideas from both roots of the 'new' education. In advocating practical studies, he attacked what he described as 'the too exclusive book and language studies of the common schools.'[54] While conceding that a few youngsters might have to study Latin and Greek to equip them for professions, the study of these subjects, as usually conducted in Canadian elementary and secondary schools, could not compare 'in culture value, or in forming and strengthening the character and developing the intelligence of the children, or in fitting them for the work of life' with the 'training of their faculties by means of Nature Study work, Manual Training and Household Science.'[55] Robertson also adopted ideas from the child-centred reformers. He deplored the 'present arrangement of a school with its children in even ranks, its lack of physical motion, its silence and its attempts to make character by hearing instead of doing.'[56] The 'whole child goes to school – body, mind and spirit,' he explained to a Charlottetown audience, 'and the training of hand, head and heart, should go on harmoniously.'[57] In a broadly defined and widely implemented manual training program, Robertson believed, Canadians could respond effectively to the educational needs which the new era in their history demanded. In 1899, he took the first step towards giving his ideas a practical expression.

12

'The Common Centre from which Radiated Plans and Labours': The Macdonald-Robertson Movement Demonstrates the New Education to Canadians, 1900-1913

As a product of his growing concern for the learning of farm children and of the difficulties he found in teaching their parents, in 1899 James W. Robertson organized a contest for youngsters to select choice heads of grain from one year's crop to be used as seed in the next. Robertson later explained to the National Education Association that, as commissioner of dairying and agriculture, he had discovered that farm families often failed to appreciate the advantages 'of a plan or scheme set out in a written statement.' He therefore designed the contest to counter this lack of understanding and to help improve Canadian crops through the use of better seeds. In the task of selecting choice heads of grain for seed 'was something,' Robertson explained, 'which would be so helpful and instructive to boys and girls that they would go on with it, and the habits of observation and thought and study would remain with them.'[2]

In this modest effort at 'leavening the system,' Robertson embarked on a course of action which, more than any other event, changed turn-of-the-century school reform in English Canada from a heterogeneous collection of people and ideas into an organized movement. As a result of the seed contest, Robertson teamed up with the Canadian tobacco merchant and philanthropist, Sir William Macdonald. Over the 1890s Macdonald had made generous donations to McGill University. He shared with Robertson a desire to improve the quality of rural life in Canada, especially in the English-speaking parts of Quebec and in his native Prince Edward Island.[3] To broaden the scope of the seed-growing contest and keep it going for a three-year term, Macdonald therefore provided $10,000 for prizes. The two men then went on to conduct a campaign, called the 'Macdonald' or the 'Macdonald-Robertson Movement,' which formed a core around which many others worked to improve Canadian schooling. Except for the seed-growing contest, neither Robertson nor Macdonald invented the educational ideas which they incorporated into their movement. Gradually and eclectically, they put together a program out of public discussion of education over the 1890s, work going on elsewhere, and their growing experience with what they were doing. Over the first decade of the twentieth century they gave Canadians practical demonstrations of such elements of the 'new' education as manual training, school gardening, nature study, domestic science, consolidated schools, and better methods of training teachers.[4] They also incorporated into their demonstration schools the results of separate efforts to introduce kindergartens and systematic physical training into Canadian education. The Macdonald-Robertson movement culminated in 1910 when the federal government named Robertson as chairman of its Royal Commission on Industrial Training and Technical Education.

After the seed contest was under way, their quest for a means to improve rural life through rural schooling led Robertson and Macdonald to the subject of manual training. While it did not have exactly the effect which its two sponsors had in mind, their efforts to introduce manual training into Canadian schools was remarkably successful. Reasoning that all educational movements 'begin in cities and spread into the country districts,' Robertson decided that the place to start encouraging manual training was in the schools of the cities and towns 'in places where newspapers were published and to which the country people looked for guidance.'[5] The man in the country, went one of Robertson's more dubious judgments, was 'not willing to take a lower grade of education for his boy than the town or city man.'[6]

They followed a model developed by James Huff Stout to improve the schools of Menominie, Wisconsin. Macdonald offered to 'pay for the equipment required for educational manual training in one place in every province in the Dominion, and also to meet the expenses of qualified teachers, and of maintenance for three years in all those places.'[7] The response to the offer was so overwhelming that Macdonald eventually agreed to finance demonstrations in seventeen centres. Robertson travelled to England to visit various institutions offering manual training and to hire instructors. By the summer of 1900 he had recruited a band of twenty-four; one from Sweden, one from the United States, and the other twenty-two from the British Isles. After a summer's indoctrination into the principles of the movement, these men spread out across Canada to set up twenty-four manual training centres for the autumn term.[8] Before the period of Macdonald maintenance ceased in 1903 there were forty-five fully qualified manual training teachers in Canada, half of them native Canadians, receiving assistance from the Macdonald funds and training over 700 boys each week.[9]

In the next few years the manual training idea spread rapidly. In 1904, Ontario made manual training an option in the elementary school curriculum and appointed the Macdonald fund director for that province, Albert H. Leake, as provincial inspector of technical education.[10] In 1908, the province made it possible for those teachers-in-training who passed their examinations at Easter to attend a special course at Guelph, with travel, room, and board paid for by the Department of Education. Significantly, the course was directed at potential city teachers who would be able 'to give such instruction in drawing and woodwork' as would lay 'a proper foundation for real industrial training.' By 1911, manual training was taught in 26 of Ontario's 279 urban municipalities and in one township.[11] By 1909, Robertson estimated that over twenty thousand Canadian boys and girls annually received 'the benefits of Manual Training Education.'[12]

While the new subject was more popular in central and western Canada than in the Maritimes, Orville H. White's careful calculations show that there was some growth in manual training all across the nation. From four manual training teachers in 1900–1, British Columbia expanded its force to sixteen in 1909–10 and to fifty-eight in 1918–19. Saskatchewan had one such teacher in 1901, one in 1910, and twelve in 1917. Ontario extended its initial seven manual training centres in 1900 to sixty in 1910 and to one hundred in 1919. New Brunswick's centres increased from three in 1900 to eighteen in 1910 and to twenty-one by 1917. On the other hand, Prince Edward Island started three centres in 1900, reached a peak of five in 1905, and declined to one by 1912. This last centre closed in 1919.[13]

Canadian educational reformers also sorted out the various elements of practical education. They came to define more sharply what they meant by what they variously called manual training (in the wide sense in which they used the term), hand work, hand-and-eye training, constructive work, and industrial education. By 1910, they had divided the broad territory of practical education into five relatively distinct areas; 'manual arts' for younger children, manual training in the narrower sense of the term, vocational and technical education for adolescents and young adults, domestic science, and nature study and school gardening.[14]

For kindergarten and younger elementary pupils, both practical and child-centred reformers called for handicrafts, plasticene modelling, needlework, raffia crafting, scissor work, basketry, clay modelling, and cardboard work.[15] These 'manual arts,' their proponents argued, were a 'means of developing the sense organs and of training faculties and powers to meet the things and forces of the outer world with intelligent discriminations.'[16] As such, they were both prevocational and part of general education.[17] They also accorded with the active practices developed by the proponents of kindergartens, the child study movement, and other pioneers in teaching methods.[18] Since classroom teachers could conduct most of these activities with little in the way of special training or equipment, by the 1920s they had secured a permanent position in the practices of many Canadian elementary school classrooms.[19]

By 1910, most English Canadians had narrowed their use of the term 'manual training' to refer to a one-, two-, or three-year course taught to boys in the upper grades of the eight-year elementary program. Reflecting the English, American, Swedish, and Canadian origins of its early teachers and their freedom to develop their own courses, what boys did under this heading initially varied from teacher to teacher and region to region. As local and provincial authorities made the subject compulsory, included it in teacher education, and added special directors and inspectors to help practising teachers, the content became quite astonishingly uniform and was to remain unchanged for a generation or even longer. This standard curriculum, which was roughly based on English and Swedish sloyd, combined mechanical drawing, introduction to hand tools, and the making of such useful objects out of wood as watch holders and plant stands.[20] By this time, too, both groups of proponents of manual training had come together in the view that it could both be pre-vocational and serve general educational purposes.[21] In order to assuage the fears of trade unions that it was a device to undermine tradesmen and mechanics, the subject's supporters were careful to downplay the practical side of the work. The aims of the manual training teacher, explained T.B. Kidner, Macdonald fund supervisor in Nova Scotia and then manual training supervisor in New Brunswick, were 'quite different from those of a craftsman.' While the latter's goal was to produce an article, the teacher's was that of 'training and developing a human being'; in this task the article was 'simply the *means* and not the *end*.'[22] Through such rhetoric, and the rudimentary level of skills built into the course, the advocates of manual training were eventually able to persuade organized labour to give wary support for its introduction in the schools.[23]

In its Canadian form, however, manual training failed to fulfil its promised role of integrator of the curriculum. While Robertson had assured the sceptical that manual training was not another subject but a means of integrating what youngsters did in school, in practice specialist teachers, mostly with a craft rather than a teaching background, taught batches of boys for a half a day a week in a manual training centre.[24] In consequence, the subject turned into a sterile, mechanical progression which, White argues, even boys failed to enjoy.[25] Despite these facts – and expert critics like Albert Leake forcefully pointed them out – advocates of the new education continued to promote manual training vigorously.[26] Putman and Weir also noted a characteristic of both manual training and domestic science that would have dismayed Macdonald and Robertson: outside of the large urban centres, the subjects had 'precarious standing.'[27] Rural parents were, apparently, slower in demanding urban-style schooling for their youngsters than Robertson had expected.

Manual training therefore soon ceased to have much connection with efforts to extend Canadian vocational training and technical education. Although the first flush of interest in an ill-defined manual training led some to see hand-and-eye work as directly training Canadian workmen, this attitude quickly waned as the Macdonald and other pioneering ventures demonstrated their real nature.[28] In his report to the Ontario government in 1911, John Seath separated manual training and domestic science, which he described as 'cultural and practical,' from industrial and technical education. He defined industrial education as 'general courses which prepare for any trade, as well as the special courses which prepare for individual trades,' and technical education as 'courses provided for those who are designed for the higher directive positions' in industry.[29] By 1922, two decades of experience with both manual training and various styles of vocational education showed, explained L.W. Gill, director of technical education in the federal Department of Labour, that while helpful in developing 'manipulative skill of a general character,' manual training had 'no well-defined objective' such as was present in industrial training. Well-grounded in a theoretical framework, manual exercises in vocational education illustrated 'the principles and methods underlying occupational work' and assisted in establishing them 'firmly in the mind of the pupil.'[30]

In consequence, those who wanted Canada to establish institutions to teach skilled levels of practical education gave their energies to a separate campaign.[31] Although proponents of specialized vocational programs for adolescents and young adults lost interest in handwork programs, they indirectly assisted those promoting the new schooling by establishing a context of discussion and activity that made manual training a welcome addition to general education.[32]

In the third phase of their joint effort, school gardening, Macdonald and Robertson turned more directly to the problems of rural education. In their most original contribution to the movement they supported a scheme whereby one or two children tended and experimented with a small plot of land on or near the school ground.[33] Macdonald movement school gardening was a blend of three separate educational ideas: nature study, manual training for rural pupils, and agricultural education for elementary pupils.[34] Nature study, which began in a small way in Canada in the late nineteenth century, was the result of an effort to introduce some elementary principles of science into the school curriculum. In nature study, teachers were supposed to conduct field studies on local plants, animals, and minerals with their classes. Until it was combined with the school garden, however, nature study in the lower grades often consisted of planting a tree or a flower bed on Arbor Day or taking a class walk to the woods on a fine spring day. In the upper grades it frequently emphasized 'committing to memory a mass of terms descriptive of the various modifications which the organs of plants' underwent, a practice that provincial curricula encouraged.[35] Most teachers, observed a Manitoba school inspector in 1905, ignored nature study; of those who attempted it, most went no further than 'reading such books as "Wild Animals I Have Known" or futile little stories about flowers.'[36] When, however, school gardening was coordinated with nature study teachers took their charges outside regularly to give them a systematic course.

The Macdonald-Robertson movement gave its characteristic practical demonstration of school gardening. Robertson recruited eight teachers with wide experience in rural schooling and in 1903–4 sent them on a year's study tour of Chicago, Cornell, Columbia, and Clark universities in the United States and to the Ontario Agricultural College. These teachers then established twenty-five 'object lesson' school gardens, five each in Ontario, Quebec, New Brunswick, Nova Scotia, and Prince Edward Island. In Carleton County, Ontario, J.W. Gibson set up gardens at the schools at Carp, Galetta, Richmond, North Gower, and Bowesville.[37] During the gardening season, Gibson visited each school one day a week to assist pupils and teachers. At the end of the first year, one of the teachers reported that because the school garden had 'relieved much of the drudgery of the school work' it had been his 'pleasantest year' of teaching.[38]

School gardening gradually became an important aspect of rural education in Canada. For the minority of rural children who received any benefits from the new education, it was more likely to take this form than any other. After adding the subject to the school curriculum in 1904, three years later Ontario began to make special grants to schools and teachers for conducting school gardening. In 1910, fifteen schools qualified for the grant and the next year thirty-three schools did so. At this time, the province appointed S.B. McCready of the Ontario Agricultural College as director of elementary agricultural education.[39] In 1904, McCready had begun a series of special courses at the Macdonald Institute in nature study which gave great emphasis to school gardening.[40] In the first nine years, over eight hundred teachers took this course.[41] Not all of these teachers, however, actually taught their new specialty. In the spring of 1909, McCready had ninety-seven teachers in his class. When he polled them all a year later only sixteen had started school gardens and, because sometimes trustees and even inspectors were 'not favourable,' many were not doing any sort of nature study at all.[42]

Nevertheless, the growing concern for the quality of rural life continued to have some effect on schooling. In an address to a New York YMCA gathering in 1911, Robertson expressed the naive belief which characterized many of those who talked about what they called the 'rural problem' in Canada: 'our vast areas of good lands,' he said, 'could and should carry happy homes for millions more people and not have them huddled into big towns where the children cannot play.'[43] Efforts to improve rural schooling through agricultural education, school gardening, nature study, and school consolidation were one result of this interest. Another was that, under the pressure of representations from farm organizations, Women's Institutes, church organizations, and members of Parliament for rural ridings, the federal government began to take a financial interest in rural improvement.[44] In 1912, Parliament passed the Agricultural Aid Act which distributed half a million dollars to the provinces for the general improvement of rural economic, social, and educational conditions.[45] The next year it enacted the Agricultural Instruction Act that provided provincial departments of agriculture and education with ten million dollars to be spent over a ten-year period, some of which could be spent on the 'amelioration of the conditions of rural life, particularly in so far as women and children are concerned.'[46] Research sponsored by the Commission of Conservation provided information of great value to provincial departments planning programs under the act. In the summer of 1916, the commission's Committee on Lands, which Robertson chaired, conducted a detailed survey of 400 farms in Dundas County, Ontario, that discovered that 98 per cent of farmers and 92 per cent of their wives had attended only elementary school. To F.C. Nunnick, an agriculturalist on the staff of the commission, these figures indicated 'the wisdom and advisability' of making rural elementary schooling 'as efficient, adequate and suitable as possible to prepare the young men and young women for real life in the country.'[47]

Each province, however, had sole authority to decide how it would spend its annual share of the federal funds. In Prince Edward Island, the government increased the number of school inspectors, provided a summer school in agricultural education at Prince of Wales College, and bonuses for teachers who developed school gardens and provided agricultural instruction to their pupils.[48] British Columbia hired J.W. Gibson from the Ottawa Normal School as provincial director of agricultural education. Gibson taught agricultural education and school gardening at summer schools, supervised school gardening and distributed grants to teachers, and organized agricultural courses in high schools.[49] By 1924, about one-third of the public and separate schools in Ontario gave instruction in elementary agriculture. About two-fifths of them had school gardens and four-fifths had home gardens.[50]

School gardening and agriculture varied greatly in quantity and quality. Its chairman, Sir Clifford Sifton, proudly reported to the Commission of Conservation that its work in Dundas, the illustration county in Ontario, was having some remarkable effects. By 1917, seventy-six of the seventy-eight schools in the county taught agriculture, twenty-eight of the county's teachers had attended the summer course in Guelph, rural pupils had attended four 'very successful' school fairs, and teachers had effected a 'considerable increase in the number of home-gardens and school-gardens in the county.'[51] Harold Foght found great variation in school gardening and agricultural teaching in Saskatchewan, as did Gibson in British Columbia.[52] An Alberta inspector noted that there were 'too many cases' where little mounds of earth served 'but to mark the grave of the seed or of the early-departed plants.'[53] Some teachers did only barely enough work to collect their grants, provincial departments were slow in adapting courses to local conditions, frequent changes of teachers broke the continuity of the work, and teachers encountered great difficulties in pruning needless repetition from the course and bringing it to bear on the local district and its possibilities.[54] In his evaluation of Nova Scotia education in 1919, James Bingay judged school gardens a failure in that province.[55]

Although Macdonald and Robertson incorporated domestic science as a major strain in their movement, others were more central in demonstrating its effectiveness. Throughout the 1890s, a growing band of influential and mostly urban women, many associated with the YWCA, the Local Councils of Women, the WCTU, and Women's Institutes, conducted a campaign for girls to receive this kind of manual training. While their ranks included Lady Aberdeen and Mrs Lillian Massey-Treble of Toronto, Adelaide Hoodless was undoubtedly the most effective campaigner for domestic science in Canada. Working through the Hamilton YWCA, of which she was president from 1890 to 1900, the National Council of Women, of which she was treasurer for ten years, and the Women's Institutes, which she helped to found, Mrs Hoodless preached what she sometimes called the 'message' of domestic science.[56] While a kind, personable woman – one obituary described her as 'large-hearted and whole-souled' – Mrs Hoodless was also efficient, tough minded, and determined. As with the many other causes for which she fought, she argued the case of domestic science with clarity and passion.

Domestic science found favour amongst both child-centred and practical educational reformers. The subject was not, explained Mrs Hoodless, 'Cookery' but 'the application of scientific principles to the management of a Home, or briefly – correct living.'[57] Like other manual training enthusiasts, those who favoured domestic science believed that it served 'a general educational purpose' in that 'the cultivation of manual dexterity' reacted 'advantageously upon the intellectual faculties' and might even 'act as a stimulant in the pursuit of other studies.'[58] Others argued its practical merits. To some, domestic science had a two-fold function: to teach housewifely duties to those in 'humbler homes' and to provide proper vocational training for potential domestic servants.[59] The most widely used argument for domestic science, however, was that in a time of rapid change and consequent social stress, society had to come to the support of the home.[60] The 'influence of the home on the children,' explained the report of the Royal Commission on Industrial Training and Technical Education in its advocacy of domestic science, was 'direct and continuous.' Good homes ministered to the welfare of the people 'by ensuring conditions under which the children may be healthy, wholesome and happy.' Since the effect of the home was 'like the influence of the moon on the level of the sea,' good homes kept 'the tide of life high for the whole community and the state.'[61]

Whatever wider educational implications others saw in it, however, domestic science teachers quickly made the subject a practical experience for the girls who took it.[62] In her domestic science classes in Winnipeg in 1908–9, Dora Dibney learned about such matters as air in relation to life and fire, cleaning with powders, brooms, and dishcloths, general rules for canning and preserving, and she made baked apples, bread, salads, and ice cream.[63] Although Mrs Hoodless always argued the wider case for domestic science, her own textbook focused on practical and useful information.[64] By 1920, British Columbia's thirty-nine domestic science teachers and forty-nine domestic science centres provided a three-year course that began in grade six. Visiting a centre for a half-day each week, girls studied and practised household sewing, home management, personal hygiene, laundry work, and theoretical and practical cooking. The province required that girls able to take the course had to complete it satisfactorily in order to be eligible to write the high school entrance examinations. For the few rural schools that cooked hot lunches for their pupils, the province also outlined a course of forty half-hour lessons entitled 'Nature Study Course in Foods.'[65]

Since the subject retained its practical dimension and changed its content with changing times, domestic science rarely degenerated into the sterile form which came to characterize much of the rest of manual training. The fact that teaching the subject quickly grew into a fully professional activity probably strengthened its more lively and relevant characteristics. University graduates gradually came to do most of the teaching and many universities set up schools of household or domestic science.[66]

It was indeed through training teachers for the subject that the Macdonald-Robertson movement entered the effort to introduce domestic science in Canadian schools. Because they worked with older girls and women, the Hamilton, Ottawa, and Toronto branches of the YWCA directed their domestic science programs of the 1890s at those who had already left school and designed them to train domestic servants.[67] As Mrs Hoodless and others came to believe that the best age for such instruction was from twelve to fifteen years, the focus of the work soon shifted to the education of school girls.[68] In Hamilton, she worked to have domestic science taught in the local schools, in Toronto to persuade the provincial government to include the subject in the school curriculum, and at national meetings to encourage women elsewhere to take up the promotional work. As a result of her efforts, the Hamilton School Board permitted the YWCA to teach domestic science in its schools in 1896-7 and 1897-8. In 1897, the Ontario Department of Education decided to permit school boards to introduce the subject in their schools. For a time, domestic science teachers were trained by the Ottawa YWCA and by the Hamilton Normal School of Domestic Science and Art. To put this work on a more permanent basis, however, Mrs Hoodless determined to enlist Macdonald's support. When he provided the two institutions, discussed below, for training of domestic science and other teachers, his movement helped promote the rapid spread of the subject in Canadian schools.

Growing concern for the physical condition of school pupils produced another constituent of the prewar 'new' education.[69] Physical activity, body training, physical training, physical culture, calisthenics, and physical education – to cite some of the names which Canadians used when they talked about this topic – had a variety of roots. As a part of preventive medicine, public health workers insisted that hygiene teaching and fitness exercises be included in the school program. Others believed that regular exercise helped in maintaining good school discipline. The 'proper use of drill and calisthenic exercises' argued James L. Hughes, gave 'an erect, graceful figure and easy carriage,' benefitted the health, and aided 'in securing effective discipline.'[70] Canadians also shared the growing public interest in the western world in physical fitness, games, and other sports. This development, which was related to contemporary attitudes to sex, produced an almost mystical aura about games and play. In turn, it shifted the YMCA and, to a lesser extent, the YWCA to their characteristic concern with fitness as an element in the development of Christian character.[71] Play, explained the director of physical training for the Montreal YMCA, was 'the spirit of immortality made manifest.'[72] Finally, as an expression of contemporary militarism, some Canadians called for general fitness, military drill, and cadet corps to be included in the school program.[73] What he wanted, explained the minister of militia and defence, Sir Frederick Borden, was 'not only the bodily development of children of all classes and both sexes' but also that all boys acquire 'an elementary knowledge of military drill and rifle practice,' so that they could if necessary 'take part in the defence of their homes and country.'[74]

Despite official encouragement, few turn-of-the-century Canadian teachers followed any systematic program of physical activity with their charges.[75] After 1900, however, some urban youngsters were able to use a growing number of supervised and unsupervised playgrounds.[76] Nevertheless, the combined efforts of schools, voluntary associations, and playgrounds reached only a small proportion of Canadian children. To remedy this situation, Borden's Militia Department began in 1907 to assist provincial departments of education by providing some drill instruction in schools and courses for interested teachers.[77] Capitalizing on Lord Strathcona's long interest in military affairs and preparedness training, Borden persuaded him in 1909 to establish a fund to support physical and military training in the schools.[78] Its constitution stated the two aims of the Strathcona Trust: 'to improve the physical and intellectual capabilities of the children, by inculcating habits of alertness, orderliness and prompt obedience' and 'to bring up the boys to patriotism.'[79]

Not all Canadians approved of the militaristic trend in physical education. 'True patriotism' did not consist 'in presenting a warlike front to other nations' wrote a Saskatchewan school inspector, 'but in maintaining a spirit of justice, fairness and kindliness towards our fellow citizens.' Patriotism, he argued, could be taught better through literature, history, civics, and geography.[80] Elements in the labour movement also expressed vehement opposition. 'The child,' argued the B.C. Federationist, was 'an easy victim' of militaristic propaganda.[81] Such Christian pacifists as British Columbia's Doukhobors expressed their distaste for Strathcona-style physical education.[82] In the midst of the war, Harold Foght, an American, cautiously commented on the daily military gymnastics that the Saskatchewan normal schools gave their students. While admitting the value of such exercises, Foght argued that a much better curriculum 'would be a kind of physical education beginning with a study of personal health, and simple exercises practicable for the schoolroom and playground, non-competitive athletics, volley ball, indoor baseball, etc.'[83]

Despite such opposition, most provincial departments of education, in accepting Strathcona grants, cast their physical education programs in a 'preparedness' mould.[84] In response to what it described as an often expressed need for a graded program of exercises that could be performed with little or no equipment under the direction of someone with little or no training in the subject, the Trust prepared a Canadian edition of a British syllabus of exercises. Based on a Swedish system of gymnastics, the exercises in the Syllabus, claimed its preface, had 'been most admirably selected and arranged in proper progression with a view to the promotion of the harmonious development of all parts of the body, and their suitability for children.' Further, it included 'games and dancing steps' to ensure some 'freedom of movement and a certain degree of exhilaration' that were essentials 'of all true physical education.'[85]

In fact, however, very little 'exhilaration' was built into what James L. Hughes described as the very 'dry biscuits' style of physical education teaching which entered Canadian schools through the Trust.[86] Commands, which 'should always be given in a cheerful, lively manner,' explained the Syllabus, consisted 'of two parts, the *explanatory* and the *executive*.' In heel raising and knee bending, these took the form of: '"Heels – *raise*, Knees – *bend*, Knees – *stretch*, Heels – *lower*, Re-*peat*, 1, 2, 3, 4."'[87] In 1910, Vancouver's supervisor of drill, Sergeant-Major A.C. Bundy, explained that the 'Daily Movements of the pupils' of the city were 'now uniform, so far as it is possible, and while of a military nature' had been arranged 'from a school point of view.'[88] All across Canada, student teachers studied the *Syllabus* at normal schools and practising teachers absorbed the techniques in after-school classes, at summer schools, and militia camps.[89] Even untrained teachers could, with a minimum of preparation, follow a great deal of the *Syllabus* in their classrooms. For these reasons, while a play focus continued to motivate YMCA workers and some teachers, military-style calisthenics became and remained a central element in physical education in Canadian schools until after the Second World War.

In another phase of their movement Macdonald and Robertson established four 'object-lesson' consolidated rural schools. Unlike their other activities, these schools were more means than ends, a way to demonstrate that rural children could partake in all aspects of the new education. Under this scheme, which was modelled on some already under way in Iowa, Ohio, and Indiana, a number of weak local rural schools were consolidated into one strong district school.[90] 'Placed in some central locality,' the new schools could 'employ efficient, well-paid teachers, and increase the value of the educational system in many other ways.'[91] If milk and cream could be brought regularly to one central place, Robertson characteristically argued, then it should not be more difficult to collect children in one central school.[92] Consolidated schools could make manual training, domestic science, nature study, school gardening, and physical education integral parts of their curriculum. This improved quality of education in turn would arouse the interest of pupils so much that the 'attractiveness' of consolidated schools would itself become 'a form of compulsory education.' Consolidated schools would also benefit children in other rural schools; since many of their graduates would go on to be teachers themselves they would, Robertson explained, display the influence of their training in their own one-room schools.[93]

Robertson set up the schools in the characteristic fashion of the movement. Macdonald offered to buy the land, provide and equip the buildings and vans, and pay the teachers' salaries and other expenses above current tax rates for a period of three years. On sites selected by the provincial departments of education, the Macdonald Funds built a Macdonald Consolidated School at Middleton, Nova Scotia, which opened in September 1903, at Kingston, New Brunswick, which opened in September 1904, at Guelph, Ontario (next to the Agricultural College), which opened in November 1904, and at Hillsborough, Prince Edward Island, which opened in May 1905. To staff the schools, Robertson recruited competent teachers and principals, sent them to various places in Canada and the United States for training, and paid them well.[94] To draw public attention to their merits, Robertson surrounded them with as much publicity and fanfare as possible.[95] At the formal opening of the Hillsborough School, the speakers included the lieutenant governor and the premier of the province. The next day, the governor general visited the school with a large party of guests.[96]

Macdonald schools were amongst the best in their day. They were housed in fine buildings, staffed by young, capable, and enthusiastic teachers, and incorporated all the latest ideas in curriculum and methods. In addition to the regular range of school subjects taught along the lines of a first-class urban school of the time, Hillsborough had a kindergarten, taught manual arts in the lower grades, music and drawing to all pupils, and manual training, domestic science, nature study, and physical drill to the upper grades. Each pupil had his or her own garden and, as well, the girls shared a kitchen garden and the boys experimental farm crop plots.[97] In 1910, the school added a special high school course in agriculture for farmers. Each attracted fee-paying children from other districts. At each, when compared to the schools they replaced, enrolment of school-aged children was more complete, they attended more regularly, and stayed in school longer.[98] While the six old schools which the Hillsborough School replaced had together managed to matriculate only one pupil in the previous five years, in its first five years the new institution matriculated twenty pupils from its own district and twenty of the twenty-seven who attended from elsewhere for the purpose.[99] Indeed, the evidence suggests that Robertson could well be pardoned his boast that the Macdonald Consolidated Schools were the best rural schools in the world.

Nonetheless, while each accomplished with its pupils what its proponents had promised it would, the four consolidated schools were the least successful ventures of the Macdonald-Robertson movement. Although transportation costs and the poor conditions of rural roads were factors in their failure, the principal cause was the extreme reluctance of rural ratepayers to bear the extra costs of consolidation. As Albert Leake later explained, despite some initial arguments that consolidation might reduce costs, experience in both Canada and the United States generally showed that the gross costs of consolidated schools were higher than the small district schools they replaced. Although, due to their much better attendance records, the cost per pupil per month was often lower in consolidated schools, the actual taxes paid by the local ratepayers were considerably higher.[100] Before consolidation and over the three-year experimental period, the tax rate in the Hillsborough district was eleven cents per $100 of valuation with individual school taxes in the area ranging from twenty cents to $5.20 per year. After the experiment was over and three of the six districts withdrew from the arrangement, the rate became forty cents per $100 and individual taxes ranged from eighty cents to $20.80.[101] This sharp increase was perhaps lower than that faced by districts embarking on consolidation on the Macdonald scale without outside help. Macdonald had provided the building and equipment, and he, Robertson, and the provincial government continued to give some extra support to the school. Costs were also pruned by replacing farmers with senior school boys as van drivers and by parents agreeing to pay small fees for their children.[102]

Very few school districts in eastern Canada followed the Macdonald-Robertson model of rural school reform. As one commentator explained, the demonstrations did not generate 'a sufficient force of enlightened public sentiment ... to sustain and expand' the movement.[103] Thus, while parents were enthusiastic about the obvious advantages of Macdonald schools – only one parent amongst the ratepayers in the three withdrawing districts in Guelph voted to do so – they were not able to convince their neighbours of the extra worth of consolidation. In perhaps the best example of local attitudes in central and eastern Canada, New Brunswick's Special Agricultural Commission, set up in 1908, polled trustees of 1420 school districts for their opinion on the matter. Of the 219 districts which replied, only twenty-four favoured consolidated schools and only twenty-two were willing to pay higher taxes for them.[104] By 1919, New Brunswick had only five consolidated schools.[105] Even in Ontario, where the Department of Education had recommended rural school consolidation as early as 1904, the province had effected only twenty-seven consolidations by 1925 and, as late as 1940, had only twenty-eight.[106]

In these years, the idea of consolidating schools took root most effectively in western Canada. In Manitoba, consolidation got underway in 1905 when the town of Virden began to draw pupils to its school from the adjacent rural district. Despite the fact that the province had, as the special inspector for consolidations carefully explained, no 'Macdonald manna' to assist it, the Department of Education gave vigorous leadership to capitalize on favourable public sentiment. Although the Macdonald movement did not provide funds in this part of Canada, it did give an example for the West to discuss. By 1909, the demand for information on the subject in Manitoba had become so great that the province assigned a full-time inspector to promote consolidation. By 1911, the province had fourteen consolidated schools in operation. Some, like the one-teacher school with twenty-two pupils at St Patrick, were rural or rural-village consolidations. Others, like that at Dauphin, conveyed thirty-eight rural pupils to the thirteen classrooms in town.[107]

Manitoba discovered, however, that while conveying children solved 'the problem of irregular attendance in the rural districts,' and was clearly practicable even in that province's extreme climate, it did not automatically lead to 'school work better suited to rural life.' Only two of the fourteen consolidated schools included any of the new education in their programs.[108] Some Manitoba consolidated schools nonetheless came close to the Macdonald ideal. One day during the school year 1914–15, the local school inspector reported that 'over a hundred people, consisting of teachers, trustees and parents visited the famous consolidated school' in Roblin. There they 'viewed the regular work of the seven teachers, as well as the special features such as: cadet drill, bench and forge work, sewing, raffia work, and the agricultural studies.'[109] By 1921, Manitoba had effected 110 consolidations, which enrolled over one-sixth of the total rural school population.[110]

Saskatchewan consolidated its first school in 1913 as did Alberta the next year. School consolidations were strongly supported by the provincial survey of education made by Harold W. Foght in 1918.[111] By the end of 1920, Saskatchewan had thirty-nine consolidations.[112] In the previous year, the provincial department reported that the average attendance in its consolidated schools was about 90 per cent in contrast to the 60 per cent for all the public and separate schools in the province.[113] By 1919, Alberta had consolidated 209 districts into 63, and the province was second only to Manitoba in the number of rural school consolidations on the prairies.[114] By the same year, British Columbia had carried 'centralization' and what was 'virtually consolidation to a greater degree of perfection than any other province.'[115]

The most important permanent monuments to the Macdonald-Robertson movement were the Macdonald Institute at Guelph, Ontario, and Macdonald College of McGill University at Ste-Anne-de-Bellevue, Quebec.[116] As Robertson explained, as a product of the school garden, consolidated schools, manual training, and domestic science movements, Macdonald established these institutions to train leaders needed for rural regeneration and educational reform.[117] More than anyone else, Adelaide Hoodless encouraged Macdonald to put up the money for the institute at Guelph. In 1900, she had persuaded Lord Strathcona and the Ontario provincial government to help transform the YWCA domestic science operation in Hamilton into the Normal School of Domestic Science and Art.[118] Mrs Hoodless was convinced, however, that because of its excellent laboratory and other facilities, the Ontario Agricultural College in Guelph was the most appropriate permanent location for such a school. After persuading Macdonald and Robertson of the merits of this arrangement, the latter conducted the necessary negotiations with the college and the Ontario government.[119] At a cost of $182,500, Macdonald built and equipped the institute which was formally opened in December 1904.[120] In addition to teaching manual training and household science teachers, most of whom went to urban schools, the institute conducted short courses for farmers' daughters and other women in cooking, sewing, and 'domestic art' and courses in nature study and school gardens, without fees, for rural school teachers. Unlike Macdonald College, however, the institute did not offer a full training program for teachers. Macdonald and some provincial governments provided scholarships for teachers to attend. In 1904, the institute held its first summer school for teachers and that fall it conducted its first inter-provincial teachers class. By 1908, Mrs Hoodless was able to claim, 'without fear of contradiction,' that the Macdonald Institute stood 'at the top of the list for practical, earnest effort in organizing and placing the study of Home Economics on a solid basis.'[121]

Although Macdonald College – 'Sir William's greatest yeast cake [and] ... the supreme illustration of Dr. Robertson's methods of leavening' – was a much more substantial project than the Macdonald Institute, its aims were similar.[122] Robertson, who organized the college, supervised its building, and became its first principal, declared that its instruction was to be 'vocational for the three fundamental, mothering occupations' which nurtured the race: first, farming, where man became 'a partner with the Almighty'; second, 'the making of homes'; and third, 'the teaching of children.' Together 'the homes, the schools, and the farms' were finding the 'common centre from which radiated plans and labours; "A little child shall lead them."'[123] The project was announced in November 1904, work began in 1905, and the college opened in November 1907. At a cost of about a million and a half dollars, Macdonald bought the site and erected and equipped the buildings. In 1906, he turned over the site, the buildings, and a two million dollar endowment to McGill.[124] The provincial government then amalgamated the McGill Normal School with the new college.[125] In addition to its schools of agriculture, household science, and teacher education, the college included facilities for short courses of the sort which had been initiated at the Macdonald Institute. In 1914, Macdonald increased the endowment by a further one million dollars, and, on his death in 1917, he left the college a similar amount.[126]

Graduates of the two Macdonald institutions quickly spread out across the nation, training their new colleagues in the principles of the movement. In the nature study course at the institute which ended in June 1905, there were four teachers from Prince Edward Island, nine from Nova Scotia, seven from New Brunswick, twelve from Quebec, and nineteen from Ontario.[127] Vancouver appointed Miss Elizabeth Berry, a graduate of the institute, as its first teacher and supervisor of domestic science.[128] Abigail DeLury went from the institute to the staff of Macdonald College to Moose Jaw to teach domestic science and then to the faculty of the University of Saskatchewan.[129] Henry MacLean went from the institute to be a teacher at and then principal of the Hillsborough school, to Victoria, BC, as a school principal and an instructor at the Provincial Summer School for Teachers and, finally, to the Provincial Normal School in Vancouver.[130]

Partly as a product of Macdonald-Robertson and other activities, Canadian interest in education rose sharply over the first decade of the new century. In 1898 and 1899, the Ottawa and Toronto boards of trade appointed committees to consider ways and means of establishing technical education in Canada.[131] In 1902, Nova Scotia's Legislative Committee on Education reported that the schools, in seeking 'to train memory only,' failed 'to fit the pupil for skilled labour or practical life.'[132] In the same year, Macdonald paid the expenses for John Adams, later professor of education at the University of London, to investigate the Protestant educational system in Quebec.[133] In 1904, Ontario introduced a new elementary school curriculum that included nature study, art, music, and physical education and listed manual training, domestic science, and agriculture as optional subjects. The same year, the Montreal convention of the Canadian Manufacturers Association set up a committee on technical education.[134] In 1906, Ontario sent Albert H. Leake to examine industrial education in the United States.[135] In 1907, the National Council of Women set up a permanent committee on education.[136] In 1908, Prince Edward Island appointed a royal commission on education that recommended nature study, school gardens, manual training, and rural school consolidation.[137] In the same year, Alberta established a committee to revise the curriculum in that province which strongly supported the introduction and extension of music, art, physical education, manual training, domestic science, and other elements of modern education.[138] At their triennial meeting in Victoria in July 1909, over 400 members of the Dominion Educational Association discussed the 'new' education and elected James W. Robertson as their new president.[139] Manitoba set up a royal commission in 1910 to study technical education for agriculture and industry in the province that recommended technical schools, 'hand-and-eye' work in the elementary grades, and better training of teachers for the 'new' education.[140] In the same year Dr John Seath, superintendent of education for Ontario, published a special report on industrial education in Britain, France, Switzerland, and the United States that made extensive recommendations for such education in Ontario.[141] While each of these events had important regional implications and some, such as the DEA meeting and the Seath report, were discussed by interested people across the nation, the federal Royal Commission on Industrial Training and Technical Education had the greatest national influence.[142]

On the first of June 1910, Sir Wilfrid Laurier's government passed an Order-in-Council establishing a royal commission to enquire into the 'needs and present equipment of ... Canada respecting industrial training and technical education, and into the systems and methods of technical instruction obtaining in other countries.'[143] While business, labour, and educational interests had promoted the idea, the ambitious minister of labour, W.L. Mackenzie King, deserved the major credit for persuading a reluctant cabinet to venture into territory which was constitutionally reserved to the provinces.[144] Although King reassured the provincial premiers that the commission was 'solely for the purpose of gathering information ... to be at the disposal of the provinces and available for general distribution,' provincial response ranged from grudging to enthusiastic.[145] To chair the royal commission the government selected James W. Robertson and appointed a distinguished group of Canadians to serve with him: the Honourable J.N. Armstrong from Nova Scotia, Reverend George Bryce (Peter H.'s older brother) from Manitoba, Gaspard de Serres from Quebec, and Gilbert M. Murray, David Forsyth, and James Simpson from Ontario.[146]

Robertson wasted no time in getting to work. On 6 July 1910, the commissioners met with Mackenzie King in Ottawa. By 18 July they were in the Maritimes on the beginning of a nation-wide tour which lasted until February 1911. The commission travelled extensively in Canada, the United States, and Europe, visited over one hundred places, held 174 sessions to hear testimony, took transcripts of evidence from 1470 men and women, and requested 180 written memoranda. In March 1911, they submitted a preliminary statement to the minister.[147] The final report of the commission, in four volumes, was published in 1913 and 1914. Although differences which led to Robertson's abrupt resignation as principal of Macdonald College in 1909 had formally ended both the relationship between the two men and the Macdonald-Robertson movement, in a very real sense the royal commission was the climax of the latter.[148] The ideas and demonstrations of the movement were a central theme of the evidence, of the briefs, and of the commission's recommendations.

Since the commissioners stretched their terms of reference to the very limit, their report was far more than a narrow study of industrial training and technical education. It was, first of all, a thorough account of the current state of Canadian education at the time. In addition, its comments and recommendations made the report into a blueprint for the implementation in Canada of the 'new' education. The commissioners opened their report with a survey of 'the present Equipment' for industrial training and technical education. They reported on universities, technical and trade schools, agricultural colleges and extension work, normal schools, high schools, elementary schools, evening classes, correspondence courses, apprenticeship programs, playgrounds, and physical culture and drill.

The commissioners then discussed 'Elementary education in relation to industrial training and technical education.' The tenor of their recommendations for this level of schooling was well summarized in their comment that the 'experience of the school should tend more directly towards the inculcation and conservation of a love of productive, constructive and conserving labour.' Such prevocational and trade-preparatory work, they continued, 'in no way' hindered 'progress in general education of a cultural sort.' They recommended more 'hand-and-eye' training, drawing, physical culture, nature study, experimental science, singing, supervised games and play, and manual training from kindergarten through to ages eleven or twelve. To make room for these studies in what they described as an already crowded time-table, they suggested that the 'work of the school day be arranged less and less on subjects' and 'more and more on occupations, projects and interests' as a centre 'for the correlated study of general subjects such as reading, composition, number work, writing and drawing.' To assist the provinces in reforming elementary education, the commissioners suggested that the federal government spend $350,000 per year over a ten-year period, as a 'carrot,' to encourage provinces to provide drawing, manual training, nature study, experimental science, pre-vocational work, and domestic science.[149]

The commissioners called for similar sorts of reforms in secondary education. They criticized high schools for their focus on college preparation. They proposed a much broader secondary curriculum, suggesting pre-vocational work, continuation programs for school 'drop-outs,' shop work, and home economics. 'Making homes,' they argued, was 'much more than building houses and providing furniture, food, clothing and things.' It was 'creating a temple, not made with the hands, as a place of culture for the best in human life.' For the development of secondary and postsecondary education the commission recommended what it called 'a Dominion Development Fund' that would spend three million dollars a year for ten years to encourage the provinces to expand industrial, technical, and rural education, home economics, and vocational guidance. For both the elementary and secondary funds, the commissioners argued, the federal government had set itself an ample precedent in the Agricultural Education Act of 1913.[150]

Four years of war intervened before the federal government took any action on the report.[151] Ignoring all suggestions regarding elementary education, the Technical Education Act of 1919 allocated ten million dollars to be spent on a matching basis with provincial governments over ten years.[152] In most provinces, this money stimulated projects already under way and brought a number of new or expanded technical schools and vocational programs. Between 1919 and 1927, the number of day teachers in vocational schools in Canada increased from 384 to 1515, the number of day students from 8512 to 34,703, the number of evening teachers from 1423 to 2129, and the number of evening students from 51,827 to 60,313. Central Canada, and particularly Ontario, made most use of the legislation. In the fiscal year 1926–7, only Ontario took the full amount of funds available to it under the act.[153]

In retrospect, one can see that the central function that the royal commission served was an educational one. Its hearings and report helped the English-Canadian community to accept the ideas of the new education as desirable and reasonable goals for its schools. The progression of the commission across the nation was accompanied by wide publicity. In each city it visited its meetings were well attended and reported in detail in the local press. In many places, Robertson, already a well-known and persuasive speaker – was called upon to make an address and to tour the local schools with his fellow commissioners.

The commission's two-and-a-half day visit to Vancouver and vicinity exemplifies its educational role. The commissioners spent their first day touring public elementary, secondary, and night schools and the BC Electric Railway's training school. The next day they visited Vancouver industries in the morning, heard Robertson address the luncheon meeting of the Canadian Club, and heard briefs in the afternoon and evening. Before leaving for Victoria the following afternoon they listened to other witnesses. In all, eighteen Vancouver organizations and individuals, including the Board of Trade, an iron works, a probation officer, the Trades and Labour Council, the Local Council of Women, and two products of the Macdonald movement, the supervisors of domestic science and of manual training, presented their views to the commission. The tours, Robertson's speech, and the briefs all received thorough coverage in the local press.[154] As the Vancouver school board chairman remarked, the widely reported visit of the commission would 'tend towards bringing the public more in sympathy with this part of our work,' and would 'eventually force our hands, so that very soon' Canadians would have in their midst 'Technical Education, as it is known in Germany, England and the United States.'[155]

In fact, of course, the commission did this task for more than merely technical education. To those already experimenting with new dimensions of schooling, the commission's visit gave them the chance to tell their fellow citizens what they were doing and to exhort their communities to further efforts. To those looking for change in their schools, Robertson's speeches and the commission's *Report* provided both a new program and a coherent rationale as to why it should be implemented. Finally, the sessions and the *Report* of the commission were amongst the most important of the events which gradually shifted opinion in English speaking Canada to the view that their new society demanded a new kind of education. Had Robertson been of an ironic turn of mind he might have been amused by the fact that the movement which he began to regenerate rural Canada had its major impact in the cities which he sometimes scorned.

13

From Proposals to Policy: The 'New' Education Enters the Main Stream, 1910–1920

In September 1915, the Reverend Edmund H. Oliver, PHD, principal of Presbyterian Theological College in Saskatoon, spoke to the founding meeting of the Saskatchewan Public Education League on 'The Country School in Non-English Speaking Communities.' He argued that the solution to the difficulties he saw arising from such schools did not lie 'in making concessions' but in 'a programme of reform.' Such a program would include larger administrative units, medical inspection, a uniform treatment of all non-English languages, strict enforcement of the regulations governing the teaching of other languages, use of the direct rather than the indirect method of teaching English, and substantial encouragement of school gardening and school fairs.[1]

The league was a product of growing public concern about the state of education in Saskatchewan. The previous June, the Honourable Walter Scott, premier and minister of education, told the provincial legislature that perhaps the time had come for a thorough overhaul of the Saskatchewan educational system and called for a non-partisan, province-wide discussion of the matter.[2] Under Scott's general leadership, the league, departmental officials, and Dr Norman F. Black, a former school inspector and currently a teacher at the Regina Collegiate Institute, campaigned for better schools in the province.[3] Most Saskatchewan newspapers gave the campaign thorough coverage and strong support; the league distributed thousands of pamphlets in English, German, French, and Ruthenian, and Black and others spoke to a great variety of local and provincial organizations.[4] To culminate the year's events, the government proclaimed Friday, 30 June 1916, as 'Better Schools Day' when, with the children dismissed, parents and other citizens could come together in all the schoolhouses in the province to discuss improving the educational system.

Scott and his fellow campaigners must have been disappointed by the results. The Department of Education received only about one hundred letters reporting resolutions passed at meetings. In his analysis of these returns, Morley Toombs noted that, while some meetings endorsed many aspects of the new education, others strongly, even unanimously, opposed such innovations as agriculture as a school subject, school gardens, manual training, domestic science, and consolidated schools.[5] Perhaps as much as anything else, the day revealed the truth of a lament made a year earlier by A. Kennedy, school inspector at Weyburn, that most people in his district had a 'tremendous lack of interest' in all school matters except the tax rate.[6]

The Saskatchewan School Campaign in fact demonstrated in microcosm much of what happened to the new education in the second decade of the twentieth century. In the years following the grand progression of Robertson and his fellow commissioners across the nation, English Canadians accomplished three things with the cluster of ideas, devices, and techniques which they grouped together under the general heading of the new education. First, in many parts of the nation, they added an aggressive policy of 'Canadianization' to their program for forming and reforming society through the school. Second, they made many of their ideas a part of official educational policy in many provinces. Finally, they learned that the real obstacle in the way of implementing their plans was not the opposition of those who took issue with their ideas but the widespread indifference of communities, of school trustees, and of many teachers.

I

From the mid-1890s, immigration added to the Canadian population an increasing proportion of people whose mother tongue was neither English nor French. In 1891, only 153,000, or 3 per cent, of the total Canadian population of 4,833,000 were neither Canadian born nor British born. By 1901, the 278,000 foreign-born made up about 5 per cent of the population. In 1911, 753,000 foreign-born out of 7,207,000 and, in 1921, 890,000 out of 8,788,000 made up about 10 per cent of the total Canadian population.[7] Since these figures do not show the Canadian-born children of the foreign born, they actually underestimate this element in the Canadian population. The 1921 census showed that, for the whole of Canada, 7 per cent of the Canadian born had both parents of alien birth. In the western provinces, the proportions were much higher: in 1921 only about 40 per cent of their population had both parents born in Canada. There, foreign-born parentage was particularly high amongst young Canadians. In 1921, persons 'having both parents alien born' formed 34 per cent of the total population of Canadian birth under ten years in Manitoba, 42 per cent in Saskatchewan, and 41 in Alberta.[8]

Not all immigrants moved to the western agricultural frontier: urban centres of eastern as well as western Canada also attracted large numbers of new Canadians. In 1921, out of a total population of 619,000, Montreal had 80,000 people whom census authorities classified as neither British or French by 'racial origin.' This group included 43,000 Jews, 14,000 Italians, 2400 Poles, and 1100 Ukrainians. In the same year, Toronto's total population of 522,000 included 35,000 Jews, 8200 Italians, 2100 Chinese, and 1400 Poles. In Winnipeg, the proportion was much higher: 55,000, or nearly one-third, of the 179,000 people in the city, were in the non-British, non-French category, including 14,000 Jews, 6800 Austrians, 6400 Ukrainians, 5700 Poles, 4800 Germans, and 2300 Icelanders. In Regina, 8200, or about one-quarter of the total population of 34,000, gave the census-taker the same wide range of ethnic origins.[9]

In the early stages of this great movement of people, English-Canadian efforts to assimilate the immigrant formed but small parts of two of their other concerns. Until just before the First World War, many people saw Canadianization as one dimension of the wider problem of extending educational opportunities to all children by overcoming the traditional reluctance of rural communities to provide good schools. Others looked on the immigrant from the context of their efforts to prevent separate French-speaking communities developing in Ontario and in the West, which they expressed in the intricate and continuing controversy over the 'school question.'[10] As the proportion of French Canadians in western Canada declined and that of the immigrants rose, however, some English Canadians, especially on the prairies, began to give direct attention to the growing 'third force' element in their society. In the strongly emotional atmosphere aroused by the First World War, they made the assimilation of immigrant children into a major political issue in each of the prairie provinces.

English Canadians battled with immigrant parents over what sorts of adults the children of the latter were to become. On the one hand, most ethnic groups apparently envisioned a society in which their children, while taking a full part in the wider Canadian community, would retain through their language and their faith the best of what their parents had brought with them from the old world. On the other hand, English Canadians wanted to build through their own children and those of the immigrant a society which improved upon the best elements of the English-Canadian and British traditions. A cultural mosaic had no place in their vision of the future. Even those Canadians who were most sympathetic to the social and cultural problems of emigration shared with the most rabid proponents of rapid assimilation the same goal: for English Canada, the debate was over means, not ends. Thus, while our central interest is how English Canadians made Canadianization into an important element of their social policy regarding children, to understand some of the bitterness which this issue generated, we must first look briefly at the subjects of their growing interest.

Although historians and social scientists have not yet done much cross-cultural analysis of the many ethnic communities that comprise the 'third force' in Canadian society, one can nonetheless make a number of tentative statements about the immigrants' views on childhood and schooling in the new environment. Even a superficial examination of third-force history, for example, makes clear that many of those who made the matter of immigrant education into a social crisis did not understand what was going on within the various immigrant communities. Through his examination of similar groups at this same time in the United States, Timothy L. Smith discovered that, in fact, an intensified concern for schooling was 'an integral part of the social experience of migration.' Immigrants coming to the United States, Smith explains, had three interlocking motives for their obvious interest in education: it was a means whereby they could get ahead in the new world; it provided a core around which they could shape their families and communal life in the new environment; and, finally, it helped them to create for themselves a new ethnic identity.[11] While there may well be important differences between what Professor Smith discovered in the American situation and what actually happened in Canada – the subjects of his research, for example, mainly settled in urban areas and those causing Canadians the most concern were in rural areas – some evidence suggests that his broad conclusions apply to Canadian immigrants as well.[12]

First, one can amply document the fact that immigrants were very interested in the education of their children. The literature about ethnic settlements reveals that one of the first activities of a new body of settlers was to establish churches and schools. In August 1885, Hungarians from the coalfields of Pennsylvania established a new settlement at Hun's Valley, Manitoba. Their first year's work included surveying the land, building their houses and stables, putting a few acres into cultivation, and starting on the building of a church and school. To the 'great satisfaction' of the colonists the provincial government granted a teaching permit to one of their number, Michael Ruby.[13] By 1889, four years after establishing their colony, the German settlers at New Toulcha in Assiniboia, duplicating the experience of countless bands before them, had erected 'a very compact and solid building' which was 'used as a school during the week and as a church on Sundays.'[14] While children in the New Finland colony, established in Assiniboia about 1890, were first taught in the home of Antti Myllymaki, in 1896 the community organized the New Finland School District No. 435. Although the ratepayers authorized $300 for the erection of the school, they did not borrow the money because 'most of the building had been done by the ratepayers.'[15] Almost without exception, the Ukrainian settlers discussed in Vladimir Kaye's study showed the same interest in an English-speaking education for their children as did the people of Dauphin, Manitoba, who, in February 1901, reported in a petition to the Department of the Interior that since establishing their colony in 1896, 'we have built a good house and stables and give You a list how many money We spend here and how menny we have cleared and broken land (each of us) and we have a school building up for purpose of our children.'[16] Some colonists, such as the Finns at Sointula, British Columbia, had to work hard to get English taught to their children.[17]

In urban areas, immigrants established their own schools and used the public schools to learn English. In 1883, the Toronto Public School Board provided a school room 'for the purpose of teaching Italians and other Foreigners the English Language.'[18] In 1901, Roman Catholics in Edmonton established a night school for Ukrainian girls working in the city. There they learned English, reading, and writing and had the opportunity to converse and sing in their own language.[19] In 1907, Winnipeg's superintendent of public schools reported that 'non-English speaking citizens of the northern part of the city' applied for night schools to learn 'the language of the country in which they had cast their lot.' Six hundred students quickly enrolled in classes that met three evenings a week for twenty weeks and another 200 put themselves on the waiting list.[20] The demand for such schooling persisted: in the 1913–14 school term, of the 1901 students enrolled in the city's night classes, a 'large proportion' were recent immigrants learning English.[21]

Immigrants to Canada apparently wanted the same chances to get ahead as did their counterparts in the United States. While some Canadian immigrants fled persecution elsewhere, or came, as did the Doukhobors in Saskatchewan and British Columbia and the Finns at Sointula, to create a society based on some ideal model, most immigrated to better their own lot and that of their children. In 'getting ahead,' education and family were closely intertwined; two generations worked together to achieve success. When Father Nestor Dmytriw, the first Ukrainian priest to visit the settlements in Manitoba, talked to a poor man in his 'modest' house in Stuartburn, the settler explained that 'at least my children will have it better.' Dmytriw agreed: the children were 'a soothing hope, quiet comfort for the bedraggled and poverty-stricken parents.' Indeed, some of the Stuartburn children had in only two years already made remarkable progress. While the older boys and girls were serving in well-to-do English-Canadian households to assist their own families and to learn Canadian customs and manners, the younger ones went to school where their progress astounded 'even English neighbours.' The children, Dmytriw concluded, were 'our future' and were 'already exercising a beneficial influence over their parents.'[22] In support of learning the ways of the host society, ethnic periodicals such as the *Ukrainian Voice* regularly reported the educational achievements of the group and exhorted parents to keep their children in school. 'To uplift us from our lower position,' argued an article in 1914, 'we need leaders, educated leaders.'[23] Many immigrant families saw, just as clearly as did their English-speaking compatriots, that the rural school provided a way by which one could escape from the farm. Ambitious Ukrainian boys and girls in Manitoba used schools to make their way into a broad range of middle-class occupations, becoming thereby a source of leadership for their compatriots and a cause of community pride.[24] With the exception, perhaps, of some Mennonite and Doukhobor communal settlements, where economic advancement in the new environment was neither an individual nor a group goal, successive ethnic groups in Canada repeated this story.[25] Not all youngsters, however, were successful. Investigations of prairie schooling showed that perhaps thousands of immigrant children 'at a time when their bright, young minds might be moulded' were 'drudges for helpless or short-sighted parents, or for greedy employers.'[26]

To meet both the needs of the old identity and the new environment, however, third-force parents wanted their children to grow up as bilingual and bicultural Canadians. As the *Ukrainian Voice* insisted in the midst of the school crisis during the First World War: 'We wish to know and speak our language, but not only our own. English is our first language here.'[27] In British Columbia, Japanese immigrants made great efforts to ensure that their children learned both English and Japanese.[28] Obviously speaking for more than his own group, Ole Hjelt wrote that while the 'Anglo-Saxon's greatest desire' was that the immigrant 'forsake his mother tongue and culture to make way for the English language and the Anglo-Saxon culture,' the ordinary Norwegian did not understand why it was necessary 'to give up either his language or his cultural heritage in order to be a good citizen.'[29]

As Cornelius Jaenen has demonstrated in the case of the Ukrainians, many third-force settlers in western Canada believed that bilingual schooling was the best means for fostering bilingualism and biculturalism.[30] Throughout the early years in the West, and especially in rural settlements where they formed most or all of the population, Ukrainian Canadians tried to provide bilingual schools. They did so legally in Manitoba where the Laurier-Greenway Agreement of 1896 allowed bilingual instruction wherever ten pupils spoke French or any language other than English.[31] Elsewhere they adopted less formal methods. In many parts of Saskatchewan, they took advantage of regulations issued under the 1901 ordinance that permitted school boards to provide one hour of instruction each day in a language other than English.[32] The means they favoured, however, was to try to ensure that local schools were informally bilingual. In practice homogeneous or almost homogeneous ethnic settlements hired as the local teacher – and often community leader and spokesman – one of their own group who also spoke English. In the face of a general unwillingness on the part of native Canadian teachers – in short supply anyway – to isolate themselves in an 'alien' environment, provincial education authorities at first hesitantly cooperated in this practice and then tried to impose some standards on it. They provided the appropriate grants to those districts which organized themselves on their own or under the prodding of the school inspector. Both Manitoba and Saskatchewan experimented with special teacher training programs. In Manitoba, the provincial department operated the Ruthenian Training School from 1905 to 1916 and, in Saskatchewan, the education department conducted its Training School for Teachers for Foreign Speaking Communities from 1909 to 1914 and special classes in the Regina Normal School from 1914 to 1917.[33]

Until the crisis in bilingual schooling developed during the First World War, some new Canadians in rural areas succeeded in achieving their goal. In the school year 1914–15, A. Weidenhammer, the province's inspector of German-English bilingual schools, made generally favourable reports on the classrooms of eighty public school teachers who enrolled 2576 pupils.[34] By the end of 1915, Fr J. Skwarok estimated, there were about 400 Ukrainian schools in operation in western Canada.[35] In Saskatchewan in 1918, Toombs calculated, 246 out of a total of 6062 teachers had 'foreign names.'[36] Even before the war, Alberta's policy was, as the minister of education, J.R. Boyle, stated, to 'have no Bi-lingual schools' and that English was 'the only language permitted to be used as the medium of instruction in our schools.'[37] New Canadians, and especially the Ukrainians, responded vigorously to this policy.[38] Inspectors reported that, rather than accept all-English schooling, some districts hired uncertified teachers, operated private bilingual schools, or refused to open schools at all. In 1913, H.R. Parker, inspector at Vermilion, explained that seven districts 'each having from 12 to 40 children of school age ... made practically no progress.' Eight others with buildings did not operate. Parker found a 'strong sentiment that their schools should be conducted by Ruthenian teachers and in the Ruthenian language' developing amongst the settlers.[39] In urban and other ethnically mixed areas immigrants used such measures to maintain their language and culture as insisting that the mother tongue be the language of the home, private schools, Saturday and Sunday schools, and student hostels and boarding houses.[40]

In the early years of the large non-English, non-French immigration to Canada, few Canadians expressed much concern about assimilation or Canadianization. In May 1899, the deputy minister of the interior, James A. Smart, believed that the 'one aim and desire' of Galician settlers seemed to be 'to speak the language and to become Canadians.' Since immigrants appeared to associate the two together, Smart continued, 'from all accounts' they promised 'to acquire Canadian citizenship and the language very rapidly.'[41] Less optimistically, *The Canadian Magazine* believed it would take two generations before immigrants could be 'fitly prepared for the life they are to live in the land of their adoption.'[42]

Smart, however, apparently expressed the dominant view. Initially, English Canadians saw the immigrant as one who was determined to assimilate to their society through an almost mechanical process. As late as 1914, the Manitoba Department of Education believed that the problem of language, 'though sufficiently difficult' at that time, would 'vanish with this generation.'[43] Up until almost the beginning of the First World War, English Canadians, even in the prairie provinces, gave much more attention to the French–English, Catholic–Protestant 'school question' than they did to the assimilation and education of immigrants.[44]

Over the decade after 1910, many English Canadians moved from a reasonably relaxed position on Canadianization to an aggressive policy of assimilation. Beneath this shift in emphasis lay a cluster of complex and closely related issues and events. First, a growing band of critics argued that bilingual schooling was a dismal failure; that such schools did not teach English nearly as effectively as did unilingual schools. Embedded in this argument were two further issues: a paedagogical controversy over the best method of teaching English to the non-English and a wider policy question as to the real function of bilingual schooling. The policy question in turn formed but one dimension of the more fundamental concern of many English Canadians over the long-term nature of western Canadian society. Further, intensely partisan provincial politics, especially in Manitoba, the approaching crisis over French language rights with which Canadianization became inextricably intertwined, and the strong passions aroused by the war added considerably to the heat of already volatile debates.

In January 1913, the Winnipeg *Free Press*, which supported the provincial Liberal party, began a series of sixty-four articles dealing with 'the Bilingual situation, with school attendance, with school management and conditions in all parts of the Province.' Although these articles were, in the opinion of the *Canadian Annual Review*, hostile towards the Conservative government of the province, they also indicated 'the serious difficulties which any Government would have to face in treating a problem born of divergent races, languages, customs and even natures.'[45] These articles were but one of a series of unofficial and official reports showing that the bilingual school was failing in what English Canadians saw as its prime task, that of teaching immigrant children to speak, read, and write English.[46] In 1916, Manitoba's new Liberal government directed the superintendent of education to prepare a special report on the state of bilingual schooling. His report showed that about one-sixth of the pupils in Manitoba attended bilingual schools, that many children in them had slight knowledge of English, that children in these schools did not progress nearly as far nor as rapidly up the ladder of grades as did those in unilingually English schools, and that, in nearly one-fourth of the bilingual schools, groups of French, German, Polish, or

Ruthenian children were taught 'in some other non-English tongue but not in their own.'[47] In wartime Manitoba, the *Free Press* was particularly indignant about this latter condition where, it argued, 'an actual majority of the children, but composed of several different nationalities, including English-speaking children' had to 'submit to a Ruthenian teacher, or a Polish teacher or a German or a French teacher.'[48] In 1918, the Saskatchewan survey of education confirmed the general conclusions of the Manitoba investigation.[49]

Most of these reports, investigators, and critics focused their concern on rural communities. In Winnipeg, where there was a large and highly concentrated immigrant population, schools placed children who came to them with no knowledge of English into special classes where all work was 'subservient to instruction in English.' As soon as the child learned the language, he was transferred to the 'grade suited to his general education and stage of development.'[50] Toronto followed the same practice.

As a result of such discoveries, most opponents of the bilingual system began to argue that the issue was primarily a paedagogical one.[51] Ignoring such matters as the low level of public support rural communities often gave to their schools and the insufficient training of bilingual teachers, they merely asked whether the 'direct' or the 'indirect' method was the most effective way to teach English as a second language.[52] Saskatchewan school inspector J.T.M. Anderson, who became one of the most influential writers on the topic, explained that the evidence showed that the 'greatest success' was obtained 'in the teaching of English by the Direct Method.' It was, he argued, the *'natural* method' by which little children learned to speak.[53] In addition to their own field work, Anderson and other advocates of the direct method cited both contemporary French experience and historical precedents as proof of the superiority of their approach.[54]

Others took issue with this conclusion. The Ukrainian-Canadian historian Vera Lysenko later argued that bilingual teachers found that when they took over schools from those who did not understand the native tongue of the pupils, that the youngsters were 'unable to make any real use of the English tongue in their every day life or to absorb any information which would widen the horizons of their existence.'[55] For a time, some English Canadians supported the latter approach. Sir Rodmond Roblin's Conservative government in Manitoba consistently defended the bilingual method.[56] There were, explained Premier Walter Scott to the Toronto *Globe* in 1913, 'no Bi-lingual schools in Saskatchewan.' Nevertheless, he continued, there were cases where the teachers had 'to use the mother tongue of the children in primary instruction.'[57]

While Scott's statement supported the indirect method, it also indicated that English-Canadian concern over immigrant education had deeper roots than any apparent failure of bilingual schools. In contrast to the immigrants, who saw bilingualism as the end product of bilingual schooling, English Canadians, as Jae-nen has demonstrated, looked upon such schools as but a necessary evil, a transi-tional phase on the road to a unilingually English-speaking school system in a unilingually English-speaking society.[58] To accept bilingual schools as a perma-nent part of the educational system would be to agree to a multilingual society in western Canada. In their continuing crusade against the French language on the prairies, English Canadians had already demonstrated that they would not will-ingly accept this sort of future. At the very minimum they insisted that, while other languages should not be 'despised or slighted,' English 'must be the com-mon solvent for all.'[59] In 1915, Alberta's Minister Boyle, put the matter more bluntly: in a statement to the provincial Legislature he addressed himself to the foreign settlers in the province. In that they did not know the English language, he said to them, they 'came into this country with a heavy handicap.' They had no right to bring up their children with the same handicap.[60]

Although opposed to a bicultural or multicultural society, English Canadians were unclear about what end they had in mind for the Canadianization they so enthusiastically advocated.[61] They projected their fear for the future much more clearly than they did the vision of it. Because of the immigrants' ignorance, cor-ruptibility, and propensity for violence and crime, George Fisher Chipman wrote in 1909, the 'patriotic people of Winnipeg' were 'on the defensive in endeavour-ing to educate and Canadianize the foreign immigrants.' If this element were not subdued, he continued, it would 'surely leave an indelible mark upon the future citizenship of Winnipeg and consequently upon the entire West.'[62] One 'indelible mark' which English Canadians came to fear more than most was what they called the building of the 'Tower of Babel' in, or the 'Balkanization' of, western Canada. Were Canadians, Edmund Oliver asked the Public Education League, 'to be an homogeneous people' or were they 'to repeat the tragic sufferings of poly-glot Austria?'[63]

What, then, did they want of the 'foreigner'? Some English Canadians obvi-ously wanted immigrants to move to what the American sociologist Milton Gor-don calls 'Anglo-conformity.' This condition, Gordon explains, demanded 'the complete renunciation of the immigrant's ancestral culture in favor of the be-havior and values of the Anglo-Saxon core group.'[64] In Winnipeg, Chipman ex-plained the 'fusion of races in the melting pot' was unceasing and that the 'blast furnaces' were 'developing the new Canadian.' Chipman and others made clear, however, that their new Canadian was but an English Canadian of the traditional sort.[65] In his address on Oriental immigration to the Social Service Congress in Ottawa in 1914, H.H. Stevens, a member of Parliament from Vancouver, argued a Canadian's duty to preserve the national type in Canada. If he 'wanted to find a typical Canadian' Stevens would 'go to some of the older sections of Canada' where he would locate 'the very finest type of manhood' that could be 'found on the face of the globe.' Canadians must keep this manhood 'pure and free from the taint of other peoples.'[66] Some saw the national type as incorporating both Canadian and British qualities. In his justification for the abolition of the bilingual clause in Manitoba, the minister of education, Dr R.S. Thornton, saw Canadians building 'under the British flag, a new nationality' which would be 'simply Canadian and British.'[67] Commenting on this sense of 'dual-nationality,' Charles W. Peterson observed that the status of Canadians was 'beclouded and intangible.' Could we, he went on, 'readily assimilate foreign populations on such a basis?'[68]

Some English Canadians took a somewhat broader view of the future. Although immigration greatly intensified the problem of developing a sense of community in the city, the Church of England's Social Service Chaplain in Toronto explained that, in the public school, acting as a social centre, Canadians had 'the melting pot for the fusion of our race, the creation of citizenship on this continent.'[69] While favouring the teaching of English to the immigrant – with 'a little training many of them would make much more efficient workmen; some of them would be enabled to perform an altogether higher grade of service' – J.S. Woodsworth did not want to press them all into one mould.[70] 'Some of us,' he wrote in his preface to C.B. Sissons' book, 'never quite understood that the older Ontario type of Canadian, however admirable,' had 'not been the only type of Canadian.' If ever one type were to evolve, Woodsworth went on, it would 'be catholic enough to incorporate in itself the best elements in the various peoples' who were making their home in Canada.[71] While in logic full Anglo-conformity probably leads to what Gordon describes as 'structural' assimilation – that is, the dominant group completely absorbs the minority – in their excluding and often prejudicial actions if not always in their public statements, English Canadians revealed that they had 'behavioural' assimilation in mind. After the Alberta legislature unanimously passed a resolution opposing 'bi-lingualism in any form' in the school system of that province, Sissons explained that this and similar statements meant that the 'prevailing opinion in western Canada' was that in 'the home, in societies, in churches,' and in efficiently maintained private schools 'German or Polish or Ruthenian or any other of the score of languages in our cosmopolitian West might be perpetuated – but not in the public schools.'[72]

The First World War brought the language issue to a head. Responding to the alarming reports about rural schooling, the sentiments aroused by two bitterly fought election campaigns, a growing concern about the shape of the future, and the rising passions generated by the war, the new Manitoba government took drastic action. In 1916, and in the face of vigorous French-Canadian, Polish, Mennonite, and Ruthenian opposition, the province abolished all bilingual schooling and enacted a compulsory attendance law.[73] This decision, restrictions on the French language in the schools of Ontario, the way that the war revived the never too deeply buried anti-French Canadian feeling in English Canada and, at the same time, generated strong anti-foreign sentiments made the matter of minority language rights into a national as well as regional issue.[74] By 1918, reported the *Canadian Annual Review*, the school language question was 'the chief issue' of the year in Saskatchewan. During and after the 1916 'Better Schools' campaign an increasingly wide range of groups, including the Grain Growers' Association, the Church of England Synod, the Rural Municipalities Association, the Orange Order, the Sons of England, and the provincial School Trustees Association called for completely unilingual schooling in the province.[75] In 1918, the government responded by sharply curtailing French language rights, by making it compulsory to fly the flag and sing the national anthem on each school day, by making Dr J.T.M. Anderson director of education for schools of the foreign and mixed language districts, by compelling trustees to take an oath of allegiance, and by eliminating the indirect method of teaching English.[76] The following year it required that trustees not only take the oath but also produce a declaration of naturalization.[77]

Throughout the 1920s and beyond, Alberta, Saskatchewan, and Manitoba followed an aggressive assimilation policy in their common schools.[78] Provincial education departments applied a whole series of special measures in 'foreign' districts. They persuaded these areas to appoint properly qualified teachers, provided opportunities for bilingual teachers to improve their qualifications, appointed official trustees over difficult or recalcitrant districts, demanded that school boards conduct their business in English, insisted that schools fly the flag and sing the national anthem, and placed 'missionary' teachers amongst the foreign population. In 1920, the special school organizer for Manitoba, Ira Stratton, reported that over the previous year he had arranged for the building of twenty new schools and nineteen teacherages, organized a circuit for a travelling instructor in household arts and, with the help of volunteer groups, experimented with newspapers, talking machines, and motion pictures. He saw an increasing, although insufficient, number of candidates attempt the grade eight examinations. He also discovered some of the 'old bi-lingual teachers ... still at work in the schools' and argued that in all cases where they had 'not materially improved their English and taken additional training,' they should be dropped.[79] In 1921, in his report as director of such activities in Saskatchewan, Anderson gave an example of how he applied persuasion. In one district where the majority were of a 'foreign' nationality and the minority English-speaking, the school board, which 'knew very little English,' appointed 'an unqualified teacher of their own nationality.' When the minority complained, Anderson visited the district, 'advised the teacher to leave at once and suggested to the trustees that they resign, which they were quite willing to do.' That the 'foreigners' wanted to cooperate, Anderson went on, 'was shown by the fact that a few days later they elected a new board of trustees – all English-speaking.' The new board hired a highly qualified teacher and the district then had 'one of the most up-to-date rural schools in the province.'[80]

Stratton, Anderson, and their Alberta colleague, Robert Fletcher, were assisted by a combination of the sharp decline in immigration after 1913 and improved teacher education. Ironically, many of their 'missionary teachers' were recruited from the ranks of the children of immigrants who had worked their way through the school system to a teaching certificate. Anderson calculated, for example, that 666 'New Canadians' obtained non-professional teaching diplomas in Saskatchewan between 1912 and 1915.[81] In Manitoba, the department's summer session provided a special course in the best methods of teaching English to non-English-speaking children. In 1918, sixty students enrolled for the course.[82]

In the long run, however, educational authorities pursued Canadianization most effectively by improving the quality of the whole school experience of rural Canadian children. By raising teacher qualifications, improving attendance, re-making the curriculum, building modern schools and teacherages, raising salaries, and turning schools into community centres, the prairie provinces gradually brought virtually all children into schools where English was the sole language. As early as 1923, Peter H. Bryce argued that a single generation of immigrants 'under the influence of modern educational institutions' had already made themselves 'in many ways into good Canadians.'[83] Census data gave strong support to Bryce's conclusion. Although the Dominion Bureau of Statistics study of 1921 census data noted that the 'element of race' was 'the strongest factor in illiteracy in Canada,' and that 'racial characteristics in respect of illiteracy' persisted, there was nonetheless a very sharp decline in such illiteracy from one generation to the next.[84]

To look ahead into the 1920s, the 1930s, and beyond and to put the matter into Gordon's framework, one can see that many third-force Canadians 'behaviiourally' integrated into English-Canadian society. Most gradually made of themselves something that was neither an old 'Ontario-type' English Canadian nor a European or Asian who lived in but not of the new world. Family, congregation, ethnic association, and schools were powerful agencies in creating new sorts of people who were both Ukrainian and Canadian, or German and Canadian, or Chinese and Canadian.[85] As we have seen, many such people themselves took the first steps in this process. Even discounting their alarmist tones, however, the various reports on the weaknesses of bilingual schools demonstrated that the prairie provinces had to make greater efforts to improve schooling in immigrant and other rural and pioneer districts. With the inestimable advantage of hindsight, one can also look backward and see that the 'problem' of the immigrant child was not a special case but one important aspect of the need to improve the schooling of all rural children. Aggressive and chauvinistic Canadianization campaigns were unnecessary.

II

On 31 January and 1 and 2 February 1917, the ninth convention of the Dominion Educational Association assembled at the Ottawa Normal School. Probably because of the difficulties posed by the war, now in its third, grim winter, only thirty-one members attended the session.[86] Nevertheless, the association cooperated with the Ottawa Teachers' Association in presenting an interesting program. On the evening of Wednesday, 31 January a large crowd gathered in the Assembly Hall of the Collegiate Institute to listen to the famous school superintendent of Gary, Indiana, William Wirt, comment on motion pictures of school activities in his city. Next morning, Wirt addressed Ottawa teachers and delegates on the topic 'Progress in Education Through School Administration.' In the afternoon, Professor John Dewey of Columbia University spoke to both groups on 'Observation and Thinking.' That evening, everyone assembled again at the collegiate institute for a public session at which Professor Dewey gave an address entitled 'Socializing the Schools.' The governor general, the Duke of Devonshire, then warmly thanked the speaker. At its Friday session, the association created its first honorary members – John Dewey, the Honourable P. Boucher de la Bruère, and James W. Robertson.[87]

The warm welcome which Ottawa extended to distinguished American advocates of school reform suggests how far promoters of change had moved the discussion – if not the practices – of Canadian education since the 1890s. In his presidential address to the association, which rounded out his two terms in that office, James W. Robertson referred to this distance. Fifteen years before, he reminded the delegates, he had asked the 1901 convention of the association to help him prepare a program which would, Robertson quoted himself, 'serve for education a purpose somewhat similar to that which illustration stations, dairy stations and experimental farms' had done for agriculture in Canada. It was not too much to say, Robertson went on, that in consequence of the efforts of the resulting Macdonald movement, 'elementary education in every Province' had 'immensely advanced, particularly in rural schools.'[88] While perhaps Robertson exaggerated the movement's effects on rural Canada, certainly English Canadians had, over about two decades, made many changes in both their urban and rural schools. Again, as in the case of schooling in the 1890s, a reasonably detailed discussion of conditions in a single place – in this instance the province of Manitoba – suggests the extent of change more effectively than would a brief province-by-province national survey.

'The course of study,' explained Manitoba's deputy minister and superintendent of education in their 1914 report, was a 'temporary treaty of peace between the conservative thinker and the educational reformer.' An examination of this report reveals that, by the outbreak of the First World War, reformers had managed to firmly embed much of the 'new' education into the 'treaty of peace' then prevailing in this province. Clearly, the province's educational officials – the deputy minister, the superintendent of education, the principals and teachers of the normal schools, and the inspectorial staff – were committed to changing traditional practices. The 'function of the elementary school,' the deputy minister and the superintendent pointed out, in a good example of how popular educational theory was beginning to combine the old and the new, was 'to furnish the keys of knowledge.' The child learned to read that he might 'be put in touch with the accumulated wisdom of the race.' He grappled with arithmetic in order to 'interpret the relations of time and space.' He mastered writing, spelling, and composition to 'impress his thoughts upon others' and geography and history to know 'something of the world ... and something of the country' to which he owed 'the duties of citizenship.' His teachers taught him 'to observe the changing phenomena of nature,' gave him some instruction in drawing, and lightened 'his labours with song.' He studied the 'value of a sound physique' and supplemented the 'healthful exercise' of the playground with 'well-chosen drill.' City boys attained 'some facility in the use of tools' and country boys 'the lore of the farm.' City girls learned 'something of Home Economics' while the country lass served 'her apprenticeship in the home.' Finally, through moral education, the child gained 'some conception of the duties' he owed 'to himself, his fellows and his Maker.'[89]

In his annual report, Inspector T.M. Maguire, who was based in Portage la Prairie, demonstrated how much of this theory was implemented in one of the better-organized rural areas of the province. Maguire supervised forty-five schools, forty-four of which contained but one room. Of these, one was closed and another consolidated with a school in the neighbouring inspectorate. Of the remainder 'twenty-three schools kept the same teacher throughout; seventeen had two teachers, and three had three teachers during the year.' Despite these handicaps, many of the schools had successful school gardens and competed in Strathcona physical drill competitions that took place at local annual picnics. In preparation for a school fair, a music teacher spent a month touring the schools. In the teaching of other subjects, Maguire explained that, while 'much good work' was done, there was a 'lack of systematic and persistent drill in fundamentals.'[90]

While the new ideas had but tenuous hold in Maguire's territory, prewar Winnipeg had incorporated into its schools much that had been highly theoretical as recently as the turn of the century. In addition to the standard subjects, pupils in the first four grades did handwork 'in plasticene, raffia, clay and wood-carving.' From grades five to seven, girls took sewing lessons and boys did 'bench work.' In their final elementary year, the girls switched to cooking and the boys 'to the forge and wood-turning rooms of the technical high schools.' In addition, in the northern part of the city, where the immigrants had mainly settled, the Department of Medical Inspection organized instruction in child hygiene. A nurse from the Margaret Scott Nursing Mission established a Little Nurses' League that taught girls to care for children and encouraged them to put this knowledge into effect in their crowded part of the city. Of the 419 elementary teachers on the staff in 1912–13, 392 did ordinary classroom work, 12 taught manual training, and 15 directed 'the work of special departments.'[91] In the next school year, and in addition to Superintendent Daniel McIntyre and his assistant, the school board employed one director of technical education, three primary supervisors, two drawing supervisors, two physical drill supervisors, two music supervisors, two sewing supervisors, one cadet band supervisor, two medical practitioners, and four nurses.[92] Like his provincial superiors, McIntyre warned 'that the enthusiastic reception given on all hands to the newer subjects' must not be allowed to 'obscure the view of the primary purpose of the elementary school.'[93]

The new education, however, required properly trained teachers. In 1913, the province's deputy minister expressed the hope that elementary schools would no longer need specialist teachers. 'So large a part' did domestic science, music, art, and physical education take up in modern education that before long no 'progressive' teacher could 'afford to omit them from the list of his accomplishments.' Manitoba also needed 'a special type of teacher inspired with the missionary spirit in very abundant measure' to serve the non-English portions of the population. In that year, however, of the 2964 teachers employed in the province, 1153 held third class certificates – at best, grade ten education plus eleven weeks in a normal school – and a further 1278 held second class certificates.[94] For the provincial department to put the new 'treaty' between tradition and reform into practice using such a poorly prepared rank and file required that the province do more than merely tinker with its curriculum.

Manitoba therefore took a number of practical steps to improve the quality of its teaching force. In the 1914–15 school year, the department lengthened the normal school term for third class certificates from eleven to fifteen weeks, gave increased emphasis to 'practical' subjects in the training curriculum, and decided to require, as of 1 July 1916, three rather than two years high school as a prerequisite for entrance to normal school. In addition, the province expanded its summer school offerings, which it focused on such practical subjects as woodcarving and construction, forging, drawing, basketry, design, nature study, elementary agriculture, and school gardening.[95] Not all changes in teacher training, however, brought the results that the department desired. The province insisted that students enrolled in the advanced course at the normal schools take one month's training at the agricultural college. The principal of the Winnipeg Normal School explained, however, that in fact about 85 per cent of those who took the course never went back to rural schools and therefore made no practical use of much of the instruction the college had given them.[96]

Although Ontario and western Canada generally moved more quickly than did the eastern provinces, school systems across the nation duplicated the two most obvious characteristics which the Manitoba situation revealed. First, they formulated a view of schooling which incorporated into a curriculum that continued to stress 'fundamentals' some of the educational ideas of both child-centred and work-centred educational reformers. Second, outside of the larger cities, they moved very slowly in putting the new ideas into practice. Even systematic Canadianization programs, which the prairie provinces mainly directed at their rural areas, were only just getting under way.

In 1917, Nova Scotia's superintendent of education, Dr A.H. MacKay, accurately observed that his province was 'pretty conservative.' It had, he went on, 'the old academic system from grade 1 right up to the high school.' Nevertheless, the curriculum contained 'the manual training addition' which included manual training, domestic science, and rural science. The Normal College, MacKay explained, ensured that all its graduates were trained to teach at least one of these subjects.[97] The fact that Superintendent MacKay faced problems similar to those in Manitoba suggests, however, that Nova Scotia had a considerable way to go before it could implement effectively even its modest foray into the new education. In 1917, an opposition newspaper argued that over one-third of the pupils enrolled in the schools attended for less than ninety-nine days. Much of MacKay's teaching force was poorly trained and inexperienced. His report for 1918–19, showed that only 1640 of the province's 3012 teachers had normal school training, that 942 of them had one year or less teaching experience, and that a further 668 had only one to three years experience.[98] In his contemporary evaluation of the Nova Scotia school system, Glace Bay's supervisor of schools, James Bingay, criticized teacher-training in his province. 'Judged only by results,' he argued, the Normal College's training methods 'would be condemned as unsatisfactory.' In Bingay's opinion, however, the college failed because it had to admit immature and ignorant students and had far too brief a time to make them over. 'Under present conditions,' he concluded, Nova Scotia made 'teachers enough' but they were 'not good.'[99]

At the other end of the country, the 1920 edition of British Columbia's *Courses of Study* called for public school children to study, over part or all of their elementary program, reading, writing, language and literature, arithmetic, geography, history, drawing, music, nature study, manual training or domestic science, and physical training.[100] As in Manitoba and Nova Scotia, as both George Hindle's survey and the Putman-Weir evaluation reported, the new subjects were generally confined to the urban areas of the province.[101] As Bingay had done in Nova Scotia, Putman and Weir criticized the training of teachers in British Columbia. Although, chronologically, both of the province's normal schools belonged in the twentieth century, judged 'by their ideals as expressed in practice' they were, in the opinion of the two investigators, decidedly less modern.[102]

In justifying this charge Putman and Weir made clear that what they described as 'formalism' was a third central characteristic of the 'treaty' between the new and the old as Canadians actually put it into practice in their schools. Although Robertson and other proponents of the new education had insisted that what they proposed was a new way of organizing and especially of integrating children's learning, those mostly urban school systems which by 1920 had incorporated some or all of the new into their programs had merely added manual training or domestic science or nature study as separate items to the regular subject-upon-subject fare of their pupils. Further, in their concern for material for 'school experiences,' Putman and Weir pointed out, school officials and teachers had forgotten the child. Elaborate manuals and detailed curricula 'designed to assist the young teacher' became instead, as they turned her attention from children to things, 'the principal agent in her destruction.' Foght explained that formalism was a major characteristic of Saskatchewan schools. Putman and Weir observed that it held 'supreme sway' in most of the assisted schools in British Columbia. An overemphasis on examinations, they felt, was responsible for 'the deadening formalism and narrow uninteresting content of lesson topics' in the intermediate grades of district and municipal schools as well.[103]

Some primary classrooms were the major exception to this general situation. While they found no kindergartens in British Columbia, wrote Putman and Weir, they saw 'the kindergarten spirit in scores of primary classes,' especially those in Vancouver. In them they witnessed such practices as kindergarten songs, the use of sand tables, modelling in plasticene, paper cutting and folding, and the making of doll house furniture out of paper and cardboard. In addition, and reflecting 'much credit on the supervisor of primary work,' the primary teachers of the city taught reading, especially silent reading, 'remarkably well.'[104] Foght observed 'many bright spots in Saskatchewan.' Now and again he had come upon in the junior class 'the happy wholesome looking teacher' whom the children loved and had confidence in; the teacher who dramatised much of her work, who used local materials, who had games of all kinds, who invited visitors – 'especially younger brothers and sisters, the latter with their dolls' – and maintained blackboard honour rolls of the children who saw the first flowers or birds of spring.[105]

What was called the Kindergarten-Primary Movement took the lead in introducing the freer, more active kindergarten methods of learning into the early years of formal schooling. Although the 'old-fashioned Froebelian kindergarten teachers,' Putman and Weir stated, looked upon this development as 'treason to the memory of their Patron Saint,' the commissioners suggested that, on the basis of their observations, the idea deserved to be extended. In 1915, the Ontario Department of Education instituted a kindergarten-primary class at the Toronto Normal School and began to teach the movement's ideas at summer schools. The province awarded a special Kindergarten-Primary certificate to kindergarten teachers who attended one such summer class and to primary teachers who attended two.[106] By 1921, Ontario had awarded 258 such certificates.[107] In addition, some urban areas – most notably Winnipeg – were beginning to use primary consultants and supervisors to spread progressive primary education in their areas.[108]

III

Reminiscing late in life about his first year as a Macdonald-Robertson teacher in Canada in 1900, Albert H. Leake recalled how much propaganda work 'had to be done ... to convince the public and many educational authorities that Manual Training was a desirable subject to be introduced into the schools.'[109] Like Leake, advocates of other branches of educational change felt that one of their main tasks was to preach to and convert those who expressed scepticism about either the rationale for or the content of the new education.

Especially over the first decade of the new century, they had much well-articulated opposition to respond to. Unions had been extremely wary of manual training. Carrie Derick of McGill University argued that those who saw in domestic science – which in practice, she explained, meant 'cooking, sewing and laundry work' – a 'universal panacea' and therefore extended it 'to include every part of a liberal education, with the domestic arts as the centre of the curriculum from the kindergarten to the university,' were making claims which were at the least unproven.[110] In 1904, the Senate of Victoria College, University of Toronto, expressed its continued support for Latin in the schools and opposed the inclusion of both nature study and manual training in the elementary curriculum.[111] The Macdonald-Robertson movement itself was attacked. While commending Robertson for his efforts 'as an organizer of practical or technical education,' James Cappon of Queen's University argued that Robertson was 'under the influence of fallacies' derived both from the utilitarians and the new paedagogy which put concrete methods in 'opposition to literary and abstract methods of intellectual training.'[112]

Of special concern to some critics were what appeared to be the limiting quality of some of the new educational proposals. Dr George Parmalee, secretary of the Protestant Committee of the Council of Public Instruction of Quebec, noted that some people 'would determine a child's future calling at birth, training the children of farmers to spend their lives upon the farm by special teaching of agriculture.' Not only was this undemocratic but the 'loss to the country of preventing each child from developing his highest qualities would be incalculable.' For these reasons, rural schools should not differ materially from city schools; nature study, music, calesthenics, and, above, all literature' were 'equally essential to both.'[113] While assuring his listeners that British Columbia was 'in the current,' the province's superintendent of education, Dr Alexander Robinson, asked those attending the 1913 meeting of the Dominion Educational Association a number of rhetorical questions about the direction the current was flowing. Was the type of young man entering the university or a bank 'with manual training of a better class than the young man of twelve or fifteen years ago who went in without it?' When he went to a new country, such as British Columbia, was 'he more observant of the trees and the birds and the geological formation of the country?' Robinson agreed that one could teach children 'to produce wonderful results in raffia work and so on; but to what good?'[114] In 1920, the editor of *Saturday Night* complained that the product of Toronto's schools could 'dress dolls and "fry" beef steaks' but could not 'write decent hands, nor add up a column of figures.'[115]

Clearly, those who wanted to change the school gradually overcame much of this theoretical opposition. A wide variety of lay groups urged departments of education and school boards to commit themselves to educational innovation. The provinces gradually incorporated new ideas into their school curricula. Normal school instructors indoctrinated their charges into the theory and practices of child-centred and practical education. Teachers' institutes and summer sessions featured courses on teaching the new subjects. Some provinces and boards offered financial incentives and rewards to those who would learn and then teach elements of the new education. School inspectors prodded their subordinates and local school boards to implement change. Despite all these efforts, most Canadian teachers in 1920 provided their pupils with a schooling which was at best an improved version of what Saint John and other cities and towns had given their parents a generation before: better trained teachers taught a greater proportion of Canadian children for a longer portion of their lives. Reformers and school officials alike had discovered that apathy, indifference, and inertia were the most potent enemies of the transformation of the school.

Naturally, a great deal of the malaise was located in rural areas. In his 1909 report, Saskatchewan School Inspector F.V. Reilly noted that his teachers did their weakest work in nature study.[116] Although financial grants and compulsory courses at normal schools had trained many Canadian teachers in physical education, Inspector R. Goulet of St Boniface noted that teachers displayed 'an evident lack of interest in physical training.' About half of them 'occasionally' taught the subject.[117] 'The greatest drawback to educational progress' in his area, reported Inspector F.H. Belton of Roblin, was 'not opposition on the part of trustees and ratepayers, but indifference' which was more difficult to deal with. He found that annual meetings were always sparsely attended and the secretary-treasurers frequently did most of the school boards' business.[118] The Mason School District responded, perhaps sardonically, to the Saskatchewan Better Schools Day meeting in their area by unanimously deciding that 'the only way to keep the rising generation on the land' was 'to do away with education altogether' so that when the children grew up they would be 'incapable of filling any other walk of life.'[119]

Urban school systems also gave problems to those who wanted to make them over.[120] As part of their survey of British Columbia education, Putman and Weir made a detailed examination of the Vancouver school system. They charged the city's school board with wasting money on 'repairs, upkeep of grounds, overlapping in instruction, inefficient and unnecessary supervision, small classes in senior grades, and especially in paying salaries to mediocre and – in a few cases – positively inefficient teachers.' They found that while men taught small classes women taught large ones. They criticized the elaborate organization for the teaching of subnormal pupils and the conduct of physical training, games, and cadet companies. They discovered that the board sometimes appointed teachers on a basis other than their professional competence. They praised the primary supervisor and the medical, dental, and nursing services. They recommended that the whole administration of the city's system be reorganized. To improve the quality of teaching in the city, they suggested that the board put an end to slipshod methods of appointing teachers and introduce a competently and thoroughly organized system of supervision.[121] In Vancouver, as in the rest of the province, Putman and Weir firmly believed that the child 'should be taught, as a child, in terms of the life about him' in ways that he was 'an active and interested participant,' and not merely for his future life as an adult.[122]

By the early 1920s, school reformers had placed before Canadians a reasonably clear program as to what the 'new' education in Canada should be like. Such sophisticated blueprints as British Columbia's Putman-Weir report culminated a long and complex process of discussion, trial and error in the schools, and observation of experience elsewhere. In the 1880s, the child-centred reformers introduced the kindergarten and temperance education into the schools. In the same years, the work-centred reformers gradually developed a few vocational programs for Canadian youth and a program of adult education for Canadian farmers. In the 1890s and the first decade of the new century the two groups came together to promote such basic elements of the 'new' education as manual training, vocational and technical education, domestic science, nature study, school gardening, physical education, school medical inspection, and school consolidation. In the second decade they added the Canadianization of immigrants and the isolation of mental defectives to the list of their concerns. They also discovered the real nature and strength of the opposition to what they wanted to do. Like their counterparts in child health and child welfare, educational reformers had put together a program which, they believed, came to grips with the problems posed for children and young people in a society which was changing and had changed in many fundamental ways. To educational reformers and, increasingly, to the band of professional educators who had more or less adopted their ideas, the next phase of the task was to bring the benefits of their program to all Canadian children.

The American historian Joel Spring takes issue with Lawrence Cremin's supposed failure to give a coherent statement of the nature of progressive education in the United States before the First World War. What, in his *Transformation of the School*, Cremin called 'progressive education' in this period, seems, writes Spring, to be 'a conglomeration of educational changes with no particular common bonds except that they represented something new.'[123] What Spring says about what Americans called 'progressive' education one can also say about what Canadians called the 'new' education. One must also say, however, that the two overlapping groups of Canadian reformers came up with a cluster of ideas that they believed would help Canadian children live happy, useful lives in the industrializing cities and the regenerated countryside. With the advantages of hindsight we can quickly identify the naïvete of the theory behind hand-and-eye training, the repetitive drudgery of school gardening, and the excesses of Canadianization. We can also see some of the merits in smaller classes, better trained teachers, and a curriculum which teachers tried to relate to the physical and emotional development of youngsters and to the community in which they lived. If we now can see and criticize the generally ramshackle quality of the *ad hoc* bits and pieces Canadians called the 'new' education then our quarrel surely is less with those who put it together than with the school boards, schoolmen, and others who, as they actually implemented it between the 1920s and 1950s, should have discerned its weaknesses and turned to something better.

PART V

Children in English-Canadian Society in the Twentieth Century

14

'Launch a Generation': Organizing to Implement the New Consensus

One of the duties the nation owed its many young men 'doing their bit at the front,' explained Ontario's provincial secretary, W.J. Hanna, to the first meeting of the Civic Improvement League of Canada in January 1916, was 'to make home life ... better worth fighting for, better worth returning to ...'[1] To accomplish this worthwhile goal, Hanna insisted that Canadians should pass labour laws that would ensure each child a healthy mother and, if necessary, provide her with free prenatal and hospital care. They must make certain that all infants had pure milk and germ-free water and regular attention from a visiting nurse. Through town planning, they must arrange that each home had 'sunshine and fresh air on all sides,' proper sewage disposal, garbage collection, and fire protection, and had access to a nearby supervised playground. Moreover, they must organize the school system so that a child entered his proper class, did not have to sit beside a defective or consumptive classmate, and had a school bank to teach the merits of thrift. Boys should receive manual training there and take compulsory military instruction, and girls should learn 'mothercraft, cooking and sewing,' as well as some skills necessary for wage earning. Canadians were obliged to provide a public library and to ensure that motion pictures were properly censored. 'Launch a generation' with these advantages, Hanna exhorted, and Canadians would solve their civic problems.

The fact that a politician assembled these separate elements into a coherent program suggests how far advocates of change had gone in making their ideas the basis for Canadian social policy. The establishment of a Canadian Council on Child Welfare in 1920 gave further confirmation to this situation. There was, Helen MacMurchy wrote in 1923, 'perhaps no effort for child welfare' that had been 'neglected or untried in Canada.'[2] By the 1920s, however, reformers had done much more than merely try out a long list of discrete projects for the young. When they started out in the 1880s and 1890s only a very few Canadians – Adelaide Hoodless perhaps more than most – saw Canadian childhood in a way that would have appealed to those at the founding meeting of the council. For the rest, the process of arriving at the broad view was a long-term one: a number of laymen or professionals, or both, came to believe that Canadian society would benefit from the teaching of mothercraft, or kindergartens, or hand-and-eye training, or foster-home care, or a reduction in high rates of cholera infantum, or some other service to youngsters. After turning the ideas into a series of specific tasks, they laboured away at each. In so doing, those in one part of a single field came to see how intimately connected their problem was with that of their colleagues in another. Thus Canadians trying to reduce infant mortality tied their efforts to the pure-milk, anti-tuberculosis, school medical, and other campaigns of the public health movement. In the next stage, specialists in child health, child and family welfare, and education discovered points at which their separate interests intersected. To take the same example a step further, health groups trying to reduce infant deaths saw that they would more closely approach their goal if they cooperated with those endeavouring to raise standards of child care in the family, to improve housing, to hold distressed families together, and to persuade the school to teach the next generation to be better parents.

Over a period of forty years, a dedicated band of English Canadians transformed certain crude notions into a new social consensus on how the young should be reared. By establishing the Council on Child Welfare, workers in each branch of the reform movement testified that they knew how closely tied in their own efforts were with those under way in other fields. Although they had already brought about some official action, they thereby declared that they were going to insist that all levels of government assume their appropriate responsibilities for implementing the new program. In the management of the council they also demonstrated the shift from amateur to professional control over policy and an accompanying lack of interest in looking critically at its components.

The appearance of the new national consensus provides an appropriate opportunity to show more precisely the relationship that Canadian developments had with those elsewhere. One can, as well, use the occasion to probe a little further into the motives of those who marched in the crusade for Canadian children.

I

Events in British Columbia exemplified that many Canadians were coming to see that a variety of separate efforts for youngsters could be tied together into a single package. In 1907, a group of Vancouver citizens trying to change the city's treatment of youthful delinquents set up the Vancouver Juvenile Protective Association. Reflecting a widening of their interests, eight years later its members changed the organization's name to the Vancouver Child Welfare Association. In turn, in 1918, this society formed the nucleus of the Child Welfare Association of British Columbia. The first convention of the provincial association drew representatives from its Vancouver branch, Councils of Women, Women's Institutes, the IODE, the Women's Missionary Society, the St Andrew's and Caledonian Society, and Vancouver's Adult School. Delegates passed resolutions calling for more technical education, for Doukhobor and Mennonite children to attend school, for mothers' pensions, for regulation of child pedlars, for the establishment of institutions to care for deficient and defective youngsters, for higher standards of school sanitation, for curfews, and for the extension of the jurisdiction of juvenile courts to eighteen year olds and to rural areas of the province.[3]

English Canadians also used national organizations to demonstrate the growing strength and unity of the reform movement. With Methodists in the vanguard, from the 1890s onward many Protestants displayed an increasing interest in solving social problems. Although preoccupied with the temperance question, they also took an active interest in health, welfare, and educational issues. In 1907, many 'progressive churchmen' – to use Richard Allen's phrase for them – banded together into the Moral and Social Reform Council of Canada.[4] In March 1914, this organization, now called the Social Service Council of Canada, sponsored a great Social Service Congress in Ottawa. There, speaker after speaker pleaded for measures which would improve the lives of Canadian children.[5] The First World War accelerated this drive for social and moral reform. Between 1914 and 1918 many Canadians came to believe that only a re-made society could justify the enormous cost of the conflict. Delegates attending the three wartime conferences on civic improvement, for example, tied the betterment of child health and family welfare to the war effort.[6] In 1917, the Canadian Public Health Association set up a Child Welfare Section.

In 1920, the newly established federal Department of Health appointed Helen MacMurchy as first chief of its Division of Child Welfare.[7] The same year, the department helped organize and finance the first national conference on child welfare.[8] The over two hundred delegates represented many municipal and provincial health and welfare agencies, the Social Service Congress, the Public Health Association, and the National Council of Women. After sharp debate over whether the Child Welfare Division, the Canadian Public Health Association, or an entirely new organization should undertake the necessary national coordination, the delegates decided to establish a broadly based Canadian National Council on Child Welfare.[9] Dr MacMurchy's office thereafter gave secretarial support and some financing for the council's annual Canadian Conference on Child Welfare and related meetings. In its *Handbook*, the division provided workers with the first thorough national survey of local, provincial, and national arrangements for child welfare. It distributed hundreds of thousands of copies of books and pamphlets on child care and family life.[10]

Although initially little more than a loose federation whose principal function was to arrange an annual conference, the Canadian National Council on Child Welfare soon became the most important national organization in the field. At the urgings of its honorary secretary, Charlotte Whitton, in the mid1920s the council adopted an ample budget, established a national office, and selected Miss Whitton as its full-time executive secretary.[11] Through its annual conferences, the publication of *The Canadian Child Welfare News*, its briefs, reports, and other publications, and Miss Whitton's strong leadership, the council assumed a central role in Canadian child health and welfare work. When, early in the 1930s, Dr MacMurchy retired from the Division of Child Welfare, the council absorbed its functions as well.[12]

Although they united in many joint ventures, each reform organization also retained its separate identity. Even the council divided itself into separate sections for child health, for the child in industry, for education and recreation, for the ethical and spiritual development of the child, for the mentally and physically handicapped child, and for French-speaking child welfare workers. Although it refused to become an official section, the Association of Child Protection Officers customarily held its meetings in conjunction with those of the council and arranged those parts of the council's program dealing with neglected, dependent, and delinquent young people. Nevertheless, the council spoke to the nation with an increasingly authoritative voice on behalf of all children. It collected information, set standards towards which municipal and provincial organizations could work, and nudged the federal government to extend its action to the limits of its constitutional jurisdiction.

Despite the central part the Child Welfare Council assigned to the new schooling in the campaign to transform Canadian childhood, those changing education had but loose ties with the rest of the reform movement. Except for serious cases, health inspectors and welfare officers spent only brief periods of time with individual youngsters. Teachers, however, had to work with virtually all the children of Canada, and over long periods of time. In relation, then, to the apparatus of child health and welfare, that of education was enormous. More so than their compatriots in other fields, proponents of the new education were also trying to change the direction of an already ongoing enterprise. Once those working from the outside had persuaded municipal and provincial school officials to incorporate the new ideas into their educational policies, these reformers lost much of the influence they had temporarily acquired. Assisted by some school board members and parent groups, the school establishment itself took charge of making over Canadian education. Two important reports illustrate what happened; the Royal Commission on Industrial Training and Technical Education gave the best prewar statement of what the 'new' education in Canada should look like, and Putman and Weir provided the best in the postwar years. Although both documents had roughly the same intent, they differed greatly in tone and style. The first shows that it was written by well-educated laymen, the latter by competent professionals. In contrast to Robertson's rough and ready theory, Putman and Weir used all the latest conclusions in child development, psychology, administration, and educational theory.

This shift from amateur to professional control also characterized child health and welfare. With a few outstanding exceptions, notably Peter H. Bryce, J.J. Kelso, and James L. Hughes, in prewar Canada laymen ran most health, education, and welfare enterprises. In Vancouver, the school board itself introduced medical inspection, manual training, physical drill, and other health and educational changes into its schools. The executive and board of directors of the city's Children's Aid Society decided to build and maintain the large children's home. The very success of the reform movement, however, eventually and perhaps inevitably brought amateur control to an end. Dr MacMurchy's *Handbook* lays bare the product of four decades of labour; it lists dozens of federal, provincial, and municipal laws, and the many organizations set up to put their provisions into effect. It shows hundreds of doctors, nurses, probation officers, child and family welfare workers, and manual training, physical drill, and domestic science teachers working in full-time positions that had not existed a generation before. A combination of their increasing numbers with their growing expertise enabled these men and women to take a greater and greater share of policy-making into their own hands. A comparison between Kelso's Child Saving Conference in 1894 with the Canadian Conference on Child Welfare in 1925 suggests the extent of this trend. At the first gathering, less than a fifth of the over 160 persons present were employed in child health, education, or welfare. At the second, nearly half of the 130 there had professional positions in these fields.[13]

Like their prewar predecessors, members of the council and other proponents of modern childhood displayed enormous confidence in the rightness of what they were doing. Although she saw 'no limit to the ramifications of child welfare work,' Mrs Charles Thorburn, president of the council in 1925, justified its continued growth on the basis that the motive power behind it was the strongest in the world: '"Love for children."'[14] Within the health, welfare, and educational communities, sharp differences which once had raged over basic issues such as the merits of youthful immigrants, whether to care for problem youngsters in homes or in institutions, or whether education should be 'practical' or not, almost disappeared. Reformers' awareness that in some areas they had begun to make substantial gains reinforced the vigour, the determination, the arrogance, and the single-mindedness which characterized their pursuit of their goals. The pride of the public health movement in what it had achieved spilled over into education and welfare. The analogy, however, was not really appropriate.

Although medical researchers faced and met extremely difficult challenges, investigators in child care and schooling confronted far more complex problems than did public health officers. Since minds are much more difficult to deal with than bodies, child study, psychology, criminology, and sociology did not provide schools and welfare agencies with either precise or precisely applicable knowledge of the sort that came from medical laboratories. When, therefore, those who tried to create a new kind of childhood or family life made a wrong diagnosis or failed to solve a problem that they had correctly perceived, often it was not that they lacked the will to do so or did not work at it hard enough, but that they did not know how to accomplish what they wanted to do.

It is at this point that we must fault their professional successors. The latter seldom asked themselves about the appropriateness of the programs they fought for and came to administer. With rare exceptions, they neither called for nor sponsored investigations or research which examined the validity of their fundamental assumptions or the actual effects of the work that they did. Until the 1950s, few members of the Canadian educational establishment doubted the wisdom of policies enunciated by the Putman-Weir Report and later statements and programs in its genre. Those in child welfare waited even longer to probe into the hypotheses that underlay the Juvenile Delinquents Act. For a generation or more, many Canadians who spent their lives working with and for children remained satisfied with the cluster of ideas that had been laid out by the early 1920s.

Professionalization and the new, more personal kinds of child care forced the state – especially the provinces – to take a much more direct role in the lives of the young. Although it operated normal schools, a reformatory, and schools for the deaf and blind, nineteenth-century Ontario, for example, usually helped children in indirect rather than direct ways. The province set minimum standards for schools and orphanages, provided supporting financial grants and, through its inspectorial staffs, ensured that institutions met the requirements and spent the money properly. In the new century, all three levels of government expanded their indirect help through grants to Children's Aid societies, to Red Cross and VON, child health activities, to church-run homes of various sorts, and to new national organizations like the Canadian Council on Child Welfare. They also became much more deeply involved in such direct services for children as school and public health nursing, offices for neglected, dependent, and immigrant children, and in curriculum planning for the schools. While both indirect and direct aid would continue to grow in the years to come, the latter rather than the former would take the lion's share of the increments.

Thus, although by the 1920s reformers had made many of their goals into national ones, they also paid a price for their success. A generation characterized by a great deal of creative social experimentation gave way to one characterized by a single-minded pursuit of its program.

II

Our examination of changes in health, welfare, and education suggests another major question: to what degree did these new ways of caring for Canadian children stem simply from the application of ideas that other nations had already found to be effective? The development of the Ontario Board of Health after 1882 was perhaps an early manifestation of this pattern. In its first year alone, the board copied its forms from those used in Michigan, assembled a library of reports of foreign boards of health, sent two of its members to a sanitary conference in Michigan, others to visit boards of health in nearby American cities, and one to Europe to attend the International Congress of Hygiene in Geneva and to examine sanitary affairs in Britain. The Ontario Public Health Act of 1884, which established the basic framework for the administration of provincial public health programs for the next forty years, was based on the English Public Health Act of 1875. In subsequent years foreign and particularly American models, examples, and statistics made up much of the literature of Canadian public health, welfare, and education, and trips abroad for observation and study were routine. Indeed, Hilda Neatby argues that Canadian professional educators who studied in the United States imposed 'progressive' education on Canadian schools.[15]

As I suggested earlier, this explanation is too simple. On the one hand, the implication that when Canadians became aware of a problem in their own society they looked elsewhere for its solution underestimates prior influences from abroad. In some instances, in fact, Canadians sometimes discovered that they had a problem as a result of learning that people elsewhere had already identified and attempted to solve it. Both they and the Americans learned from French medical research that traditionally high rates of infant mortality were not inevitable but a problem in public health. On the other hand, this explanation also overestimates outside influence. It does not take into account that developments in one part of Canada shaped those in another, that some parts of the country quickly equalled or surpassed foreign standards of child care, and that Canadians themselves contributed to the international stockpile of knowledge and practices in health, welfare, and education. Most provinces modelled their systems of public health and welfare on Ontario's Public Health Act of 1884 and its Children's Protection Act of 1893. In 1910, Peter H. Bryce claimed that, 'compared to a similar number of neighbouring American states,' health work in Canada was 'at least as far advanced, and of as high a scientific character.'[16]

Drawing lines from one development here to another there also overemphasizes uniqueness and the importance of being first and underestimates the internal logic of some social change. Once Canadians accepted certain premises about public health, or child welfare, or education there were only a limited number of ways in which they could respond. They began their efforts to improve child health, for example, through such diverse projects as milk stations, mothers' meetings, school inspections, and anti-tuberculosis crusades, not only in imitation of others but out of the natural tendency towards a direct and voluntary response. In the long run, however, they turned over most of the responsibility to that new professional, the public health nurse, again from the logic of necessity as well as example.

Furthermore, a search for influence draws attention away from the role played by the national and international communities in public health, social welfare, and education which formed in the latter years of the nineteenth century. Many Canadian reformers came together regularly at regional or national conferences and through the medium of journals and proceedings. In these ways they put together loosely structured networks of men and women who began to build a common sense of identity and purpose around the occupations that they shared.[17] Until well into the new century, however, Canadians belonging to international organizations often thought them of greater importance than their own national ones. Nonetheless, they clearly looked upon themselves not as consumers of ideas produced elsewhere but as contributing members of a worldwide community devoted to improving conditions in their special fields. As such, they served as full members in what modern investigators describe as the 'transnational' process of building the structure of knowledge, and creating the procedures and practices in each field.[18] The part played by Canadians in the American Public Health Association provides an excellent illustration of this point. After the association decided in 1884 to open its membership to Canadians, the latter treated it as a continental rather than primarily an American organization. Thus six Canadians served as its president over these years: Frederick Montizambert in 1891, Emmanual Persillier Lachapelle in 1894, Peter H. Bryce in 1900, Frank Wesbrook in 1905, R.M. Simpson in 1911, and C.J.O. Hastings in 1918. The association held its annual meeting in Toronto in 1886, Montreal in 1894, Ottawa in 1898, and Winnipeg in 1908.[19] At a representative session of the association, its thirty-eighth meeting in Milwaukee in September 1910, at least five Canadians presented papers.[20]

Canadians in education and in welfare similarly participated in international professional communities.[21] James L. Hughes spoke frequently in the United States and was active in the affairs of the National Educational Association.[22] Both he and his wife, who was a charter member of the International Kindergarten Union and its president in 1906, were important figures in the kindergarten movement.[23] James W. Robertson's speaking engagements in Britain and the United States, his visiting lectureships and offers of permanent positions in the latter country, and his professional friendships with such people as W.H. Hoard, Gifford Pinchot, and Sir Horace Plunkett all testified to his international influence among those who had banded together to regenerate rural life.[24] Albert H. Leake published three major works on practical education in the United States, two of which appeared as prize essays in economics.[25] In the late nineteenth century, J.W. Langmuir took part in the affairs of the American National Congress of Charities and Correction as Warden James Massie did in those of the American Prison Association. Over most of an extended career lasting until the early 1930s, J.J. Kelso was invited to such meetings as the White House Conference on Child Welfare, spoke frequently in the United States, and served in executive positions in the Federation of Humane Societies, the American National Conference of Charities and Correction, and the American Prison Congress.[26]

Despite their many and often important individual efforts, however, we must not overestimate the Canadian contribution to 'transnational' health, welfare, and education. As events described throughout this study make plain, we must also apply to public health and to schooling Tamara Haraven's conclusion that the formative period in Canadian public welfare was characterized by a blending of American experience with Canadian traditions.[27] Clearly, whether lay or professional Canadian reformers borrowed, modified, or invented an approach or procedure in child welfare or education, they did so in accordance with their assessment of Canadian conditions. They often displayed pride in their accomplishments. As early as 1880, Langmuir told the National Conference of Charities and Correction that Ontario's institutions formed 'one of the most complete charitable and correctional systems on the continent.'[28] In 1920, while describing the deplorable state of Canadian birth statistics, the president of the Child Welfare Section of the Canadian Public Health Association quickly explained that, bad as the Canadian situation might be, conditions were substantially worse in much of the United States.[29]

In short, those who tried to improve the lot of Canadian youngsters looked upon the rest of the world selectively; with their characteristic self-assurance they took one idea from here, another from there, and added their own modifications and inventions. They were sure that they knew how each element fitted into the over-all and, in their opinion, superior systems that they were constructing. We must, therefore, give them the credit for what went well and assign them the blame for what went badly.

III

Why did so many Canadians enlist in the campaign to improve the lot of the nation's youngsters? While only a few of them fit neatly into a single group, we can, I believe, sort reformers into three somewhat separate clusters: Christians imbued with the 'social passion'; those of the urban middle class who saw a reconstructed childhood as part of their effort to make the new environment a place of order and prosperity for themselves and their offspring; and ambitious men and women building careers in the new professions. All three groups shared a common although unexamined premise. They believed that if men of good will tried hard enough they could indeed 'launch a generation' that would be free of the age-old problems of society.

Christian 'social passion' was at the root of much of the reform work for children and young people. In his superb study of the role of the social gospel in Canadian society, Richard Allen argues that, while one can view the reform movement from many vantage points, 'only when it is looked on as a religious expression, striving to embed ultimate human goals in the social, economic, and political order' can one fully appreciate its success and its failure.[30] Preachers and publicists in denominational and interdenominational Christian organizations exhorted parents towards a more loving nurture of their youngsters. The WCTU magazine, for example, carried regular articles on child care under such titles as 'Ten Commandments for the Mother,' 'The Mother Who Laughs,' 'Mother and Child,' 'Our Neglected Children,' 'Work as Punishment,' and 'A Word to Parents.'[31] Religious beliefs undoubtedly motivated many to take leading roles in reform organizations. Of the 424 men serving on the executives of Children's Aid societies in Ontario in 1895, 55 were ministers.[32] In 1896, church-based organizations made up well over half (181 of 307) of the societies federated into the twenty Local Councils of Women in Canada.[33] Social gospellers like the Methodist minister J.S. Woodsworth of All Peoples' Mission in Winnipeg pleaded for or established kindergartens, fresh air camps, playgrounds, juvenile courts, compulsory schooling, and a reformed educational system.[34] Presbyterians and Methodists cooperated on urban and rural social surveys in which the plight of children and families figured prominently.[35] Practical concern for children was a major theme of the interdenominational Social Service Congress in 1914. In 1920, the

Social Service Council sent representatives to the meeting that established the Canadian Council on Child Welfare.

The desire of middle-class English Canadians for a more disciplined society, though often articulated by those who also expressed a strong sense of Christian mission, was another source of inspiration to seek new ways of caring for children. In justifying and administering mothers' pensions, English Canadians emphasized their strong desire to use the family as a means of ensuring social stability. 'Every child,' argued a group advocating mothers' allowances in 1918, was 'entitled to home life and care of a suitable character,' and 'the best interests of the state' required the government to make sure that he receive it. To this end the committee recommended that Ontario grant an allowance sufficient to provide 'satisfactory home care' beginning with the children of widows and then extending the service to include those whose fathers were in prisons or asylums, or chronically incapacitated, or who had permanently deserted their families.[36] Before the Ontario Mothers' Allowances Commission granted a pension, explained its first annual report, an investigator's assessment, together with one from a local advisory board, informed the commission 'as to the fitness of the mother to bring up her children and to maintain proper standards in the home ...' Nevertheless, the commission boasted that, by such means as paying allowances by cheque, it fostered family pride, and that most recipients looked upon the pension as 'a reward for service, not a form of public relief.'[37]

A similar concern for order appeared in the movement for educational reform. In 1915, the Ontario Department of Education issued a manual for teachers, one purpose of which was to show through historical evidence how the teacher was 'a necessary and, potentially, an influential factor in determining the direction and strength of social movements.' In a key chapter entitled 'Education for Social Efficiency,' the author examined the social change he saw then under way in Canada. In education lay the 'hope for a better distribution of all classes of workers over the varied fields of industry' that would bring Canada 'to the front of nations in industrial progress and in intellectual development.' In practice, the writer continued, modern education had four purposes. First, taxpayers relied on schools to teach youngsters the means of 'social control': appreciation of liberty, respect for institutions, and the need for voting intelligently. If anyone doubted 'the advantages of education for social control, let him contrast the conditions in Mexico with the conditions in those countries' where education was 'not only free but compulsory.' Second, the school must disseminate knowledge, for upon knowledge depended 'intelligence, social progress, and happiness.' Third, 'by free education for all in our public schools' society met the demand for 'social improvement.' Taxpayers cared 'little for the advantage of individual pupils'; they were 'preoccupied mainly with the welfare of society.' Finally, through practical subjects, the school met the demand for 'industrial efficiency'; it thereby responded to the need 'to make each individual a productive social unit.'[38]

Propagandists of the child health movement echoed such appeals for social utility and efficiency. In 1913, the editor of the *Public Health Journal* urged the Toronto city council to make a grant to a campaign against infant mortality with the argument that while it cost '$50 a head' to bury the four infants who died in Toronto each day, 'it would not cost $5 a head to save their lives.'[39] Nor did the national loss end 'with the long line of white hearses' that deposited 'their tiny contents in our cemeteries.' The conditions that produced a high mortality rate also reduced the vitality and increased the liability to disease of those who survived, making them unable 'to make the best of life's chances.'[40] Mme Jules Tessier explained that, according to political economists, each individual was 'worth about $1000 to the country.' Therefore, what 'wealth to the nation would not the annual saving of even a few hundred lives mean ...?'[41]

The life-long zeal of a third group of Canadians for child welfare grew out of the rewards they found in the work that they did. Many of the reformers, Peter H. Bryce, Helen MacMurchy, C.J.O. Hastings, C.K. Clarke, Alan Brown, Lina Rogers Struthers, J.J. Kelso, W.L. Scott, Helen MacGill, James L. Hughes, Ada Marean Hughes, Adelaide Hoodless, and James W. Robertson, displayed a passionate commitment to one or another reform. Some moved back and forth easily from their own particular interest to the social gospel. As active laymen Kelso, Hastings, Scott, and MacMurchy took part in the 1914 Social Service Congress. Although they rarely gave it verbal expression, many of the professional workers also displayed the personal ambition that was one of the driving forces in the reform movement. Public health, for example, was rapidly expanding and offered an attractive and even romantic career to a physician who did not feel called to be a country doctor or to a nurse who wanted to escape from the drudgery of a hospital routine. Since reform was the raison d'être of their professions, the next generation of public health workers, child welfare officials, and those schoolmen and teachers who promoted the new education were reformers, not cynically and usually enthusiastically, but sometimes without the real fervour for change which drove the pioneers.

IV

From the very moment of their birth, many of the over a quarter of a million Canadian babies of 1921 stood a better chance of surviving than had infants of any earlier generation. The cumulative effects of school health courses, domestic science training, 'little mothers'' classes, discussion in women's groups, prenatal counselling by physicians and public health nurses, and a stream of information in newspapers, magazines, and pamphlets made it probable that the young mothers of the 1920s were, as the *Western Women's Weekly* put it, not only 'just as good' as the old-fashioned ones but 'a great deal better.'[42] A public health nurse might visit these infants, or their mothers might take them to a well-baby clinic in the neighbourhood or at a fall fair. If these children grew up in the city, they were apt to drink safe milk and pure water. Their houses were more likely than those of earlier generations to have water closets, ice boxes, and screen doors. Streetcars, automobiles, and better sanitation reduced the likelihood of their contracting fly-borne ailments, and they were less liable to catch such diseases as tuberculosis, scarlet fever, or diphtheria. If they did become ill both their mothers and their physicians knew more about caring for them properly.

These youngsters also had the chance of a fuller, richer life. The effects of the rise in the standard of living over the previous generation made it possible for their parents to feed and clothe them better and to keep them out of the work force for a longer period of time.[43] Fewer boys and girls had to struggle through the bitterly hard-working childhoods that had characterized earlier eras. Families that planned carefully were able to use an expanded educational system to widen the life-time options and opportunities available to their youngsters. The new standard of living, improved public health, better safety measures in industry, workmen's compensation, minimum wage legislation, and a lower mortality rate for adults helped to make Canadian families more stable and permanent than they had ever been before.[44] With a gradual decline in hours of work and an increase in electrical and other labour-saving devices in the home, many families were able to spend more time doing things that went beyond ensuring their mere survival; as Brother Barnabas put it, Canadians of the 'new era' had wrung a great deal of enriching leisure time from the 'business of living.'[45] If accident or tragedy struck, increased insurance benefits, workmen's compensation, and mothers' pensions reduced the likelihood that families would break up or that youngsters would have to go to work prematurely. Between 1890 and 1926, the annual total of all insurance claims – death, matured endowment, and disability – paid out in Canada rose from $3.1 million to $35 million. In the latter year, the five provinces that had introduced mothers' and dependents' allowances – Manitoba, British Columbia, Alberta, Saskatchewan, and Ontario – dispersed $4 million under their schemes. In 1926, as well, provincial workmen's compensation funds spent $11 million in medical aid, hospitalization, and cash benefits.[46]

Even the really unfortunate amongst those born in 1921 – the illegitimate, the deserted, the orphaned, the neglected, and the delinquent – probably spent their early years very differently from similarly placed young people in preceeding generations. Children of unmarried parents started to benefit from three kinds of legislative change.[47] Beginning in 1921 with Ontario's Children of Unmarried Parents Act, a number of provinces sharply increased the state's interest in such children, making it much easier, for example, for mothers to get maintenance from fathers.[48] In 1917, New Brunswick became the first of a number of English-speaking provinces to follow Quebec's long-standing practice of legitimizing births when the parents subsequently married each other.[49] Canadians also began to transform adoption from a form of indenture under which the family rights of the youngster involved had to be laid out legally into the modern practice that makes such children full members of the adopting family.[50] The increasing popularity of adoption and the trend towards family rather than institutional care for neglected, dependent, and delinquent youngsters strongly reduced the chances of infants spending more than a short time in a foundling home and that of older boys and girls living out their childhoods in orphanages or other institutions for children. In 1925, for example, Robert E. Mills, director of Toronto's Children's Aid Society, reported that a recent survey of three large children's homes in that city showed that although 'when Toronto's population was much smaller all three institutions had been crowded to capacity, together they could now muster only enough inmates to fill one ...'[51] Only those juvenile delinquents whom Canadians looked upon as being the most difficult to handle were as likely as their earlier counterparts to spend long periods of time in institutions.

Many boys and girls who started school in 1921 found their experience considerably different from that of their parents and grandparents. They were more likely to go to a graded school and be taught there in smaller classes by a woman teacher. The teacher of the 1920s was both better educated and better trained than her predecessors. In addition to teaching the three Rs more effectively, she usually followed a curriculum consciously geared to modern life. Her pupils took nature study, health, manual arts, manual training or domestic science, and they followed a systematic program of calisthenics. Some secondary students found vocational classes or schools available to them. The new intelligence and standardized tests classified many pupils into different groups, and some found themselves sorted out from their peers and placed in special classes or schools. Changing custom, backed up by more thorough law enforcement, made it likely that youngsters would attend school regularly and progress further. Some who worked through the usual eight grades found that they did not have to hurdle the dreaded entrance examinations to get credit for completing grade school or to go on to high school. A nurse or doctor visited the school regularly to survey its sanitary condition, to search for cases of infectious diseases, and to examine the general physical condition of the pupils. For some youngsters, the health service also arranged for the treatment of chronic ailments which parents could not or would not attend to.

Most children born in 1921 found the world treated them more tenderly than it had their predecessors. Books and articles on child care advised parents to use kindness and love to develop their children's character.[52] Although it is impossible to tell whether such exhortations reduced the amount of physical punishment used in the home, we have some direct evidence that it changed the treatment of children elsewhere in society. In his study of concepts of discipline in Canadian education, F. Henry Johnson discovered that the use of corporal punishment in Canadian schools declined considerably between 1885 and 1920.[53] Juvenile court judges dealt with youngsters somewhat less severely than did police magistrates. Although the situation varied considerably from institution to institution, even industrial schools apparently treated their youthful inmates less brutally than the prisons and reformatories of an earlier era.

Despite the changes we have examined, many boys and girls born in 1921 grew up in ways very similar to those experienced by their parents and grandparents. Of those born over the next three decades, however, a growing proportion lived through childhoods very different from those of the generations that preceded them. What by the 1920s many English Canadians had made into their policy, and which they exemplified through lives of some of their children, gradually became the norm for bringing up all Canadian youngsters. The reformers surveyed in this study did not, of course, single-handedly effect all of the many differences in either policy or practice in rearing the young. Wide-reaching changes in Canadian society – industrialization and the movement from farm to town, for example – made it certain that more and more Canadian children would mature in ways very different from previous generations. If other forces, however, made a new sort of growing up inevitable, they did not prescribe its shape and form. What the reform movement did accomplish was to draw the plans for and rough in many of the dimensions of a transformed childhood.

Notes

Canada, *Journals* / *Journals* of the House of Commons
CHA / Canadian Historical Association
CHR / *Canadian Historical Review*
CJMH / *Canadian Journal of Mental Hygiene*
CYB / *Canada Yearbook* (although the title changed over the years, it will be referred to as CYB throughout)
DBS / Dominion Bureau of Statistics
DDJ / *Dominion Dental Journal*
Handbook / Canada, Department of Health, *Handbook of Child Welfare Work in Canada for the Year, March 31, 1922*
HEQ / *History of Education Quarterly*
HMSO / His Majesty's Stationery Office
NCW / National Council of Women
PAC / Public Archives of Canada
PC / Privy Council
PHJ / *The Public Health Journal*
RCITTE / *Report of the Commissioners*, Royal Commission on Industrial Training and Technical Education
WCTU / Woman's Christian Temperance Union

CHAPTER 1

1 The quotation in the title of Part I is from Ontario, *Sessional Papers*, 1903, p. 28.

2 The sources for this story are in PAC, MG29/B43, vols 1 and 2, Charlotte Alexander Papers

3 Canada, *Sessional Papers*, 1871, no. 61, p. 2; *ibid.*, 1920, no. 18, pp. 4; 46

4 See Ivy Pinchbeck and Margaret Hewitt, *Children in English Society*, vol. I, *From Tudor Times to the Eighteenth Century* (Toronto: University of Toronto Press, 1969), pp. 105–9, vol. II, *From the Eighteenth Century to the Children Act 1948* (Toronto: University of Toronto Press, 1973), pp. 546–81; Alex. G. Scholes, *Education For Empire Settlement: A Study of Juvenile Migration* (London: Longmans, 1932).

5 Canada, *Sessional Papers*, 1870, no. 80, pp. 6–7; Canada, *Journals*, 1875, app. 4, p. 22. The term Canada, *Journals*, used here and throughout this study refers only to the Journals of the House of Commons.

6 Niagara *Mail*, 10 November 1869; 17 November 1869

7 Canada, *Journals*, 1875, app. 4, p. 22; Leslie Stephen and Sidney Lea, eds., *The Dictionary of National Biography* (London: Oxford University Press, 1937–8), Supplement no. 2, vol. II, pp. 245–6

8 For an account of the work of Charles Loring Brace see Emma Brace, ed., *The Life of Charles Loring Brace, Chiefly Told Through His Own Letters* (London: Samson, Low, Marston and Co., 1894); Miriam Z. Langsam, *Children West: A History of the Placing-Out System of the New York Children's Aid Society, 1853–1890* (Madison: The State Historical Society for the Department of History, University of Wisconsin, 1964). Richard Wohl gives an interesting interpretation of the context of Brace's work in R. Richard Wohl, ed. Moses Rischlin, 'The "Country Boy" Myth and Its Place in American Urban Culture: The Nineteenth Century Contributions,' Donald Fleming and Bernard Bailyn, eds., *Perspectives in American History*, vol. III (Cambridge: Charles Warren Center for Studies in American History, 1969), pp. 107–21.

9 Canada, *Journals*, 1875, app. 4, pp. 22, 36

10 Canada, Department of Immigration, File #3115, 'Inspection of Children – General File,' vol. 1, Andrew Doyle, *Emigration of Pauper Children to Canada*, 8 February 1875, p. 6

11 Canada, *Journals*, 1875, app. 4, p. 23. These are the figures Miss Rye gave in her testimony to the Select Committee. The Department of Agriculture's figures suggest that the total number might actually have been 1307. See Canada, *Sessional Papers*, 1870, no. 80, pp. 6–7; *ibid.*, 1872, no. 2A, p. 9; *ibid.*, 1873, no. 26, p. 13; *ibid.*, 1878, no. 9, p. xvi.

12 Canada, *Sessional Papers*, 1871, no. 61, pp. 68–9; Doyle, *Emigration*, pp. 4–7. For accounts of the child-rescue movement in England, see Kathleen Heasman, *Evangelicals in Action: An Appraisal of Their Social Work in the Victorian Era* (London: Geoffrey Bles, 1962) and Pinchbeck and Hewitt, *Children in English Society*, vol. II.

13 For an account of Miss Macpherson's life and work, see Lilian M. Birt, *The Children's Home-Finder: The Story of Annie Macpherson and Louisa Birt* (London: Nisbet, 1913).

14 Canada, *Sessional Papers*, 1871, no. 61, p. 68; *ibid.*, 1872, no. 2A, p. 9; Canada, *Journals*, 1875, app. 4, pp. 13–14. This was the figure Miss Macpherson gave to the Select Committee. The cumulative records of the Department of Agriculture show that its agents counted 1907 children. See Canada, *Sessional Papers*, 1872, no. 2A, pp. 9, 83; *ibid.*, 1873, no. 26, p. 13; *ibid.*, 1878, no. 9, p. xvi.

15 Canada, *Journals*, 1875, app. 4, pp. 20–1, 36–7; Doyle, *Emigration*, p. 4

16 Quoted in Doyle, *Emigration*, p. 5; see Stephen and Lea, *Dictionary of National Biography*, Supplement no. 2, vol. II, pp. 146–7.

17 Doyle, *Emigration*, p. 4

18 *Ibid.*, p. 3; Canada, Department of Immigration File #3115, vol. 1, H. Fleming, Secretary, Local Government Board, to Andrew Doyle, 12 June 1874

19 Doyle, *Emigration*, p. 36. See also *Toronto Mail*, 12 March 1875; *Toronto Daily Globe*, 19, 20, 22 March 1875. The *Globe* printed Doyle's report in full.

20 To sample the debate in England, see Pinchbeck and Hewitt, *Children in English Society*, vol. II, pp. 572–5; Great Britain, *Parliamentary Papers*, 1877, 'Letter Addressed by Miss Rye to the President of the Local Government Board, December, 1876' and 'Reply of Mr. Doyle to Miss Rye's Report, 14 May 1877.'

21 Canada, *Sessional Papers*, 1876, no. 8, p. xiii; *ibid.*, 1877, no. 8, p. xv; Canada, Department of Immigration, File #3115, vol. 1, *Report of Committee of Privy Council*, PC 68D, 5 July 1875; *ibid.*, PC 967, 28 September 1875; *ibid.*, PC 5, 4 January 1878.

22 Doyle, *Emigration*, pp. 7–8; Canada, *Journals*, 1875, app. 4, pp. 12–13, 24, 36–41; PAC, MG28/I37, vol. 7, *Seventh Annual Report of Ottawa Orphan's Home*, 1872, p. 6

23 They were, however, a shade more formal than the very cursory early procedures of the New York Children's Aid Society. See Langsam, *Children West*, chaps 3 and 5.

24 Canada, *Journals*, 1875, app. 4, p. 13

25 Doyle, *Emigration*, p. 21

26 Canada, *Journals*, 1875, app. 4, p. 11

27 Niagara *Mail*, 17 November 1869

28 Canada, *Journals*, 1875, app. 4, pp. 27, 32–3; Canada, *Sessional Papers*, 1877, no. 8, p. xvi

29 Canada, *Journals*, 1875, app. 4, p. 30

30 Leroy O. Stone, *Urban Development in Canada* (Ottawa: Dominion Bureau of Statistics, 1967), p. 29

31 Canada, *Sessional Papers*, 1889, no. 5, pp. 108–9

32 *Ibid.*, 1872, no. 2A, pp. 9–10, 66; Halifax *Weekly Citizen*, 6 and 11 November 1871; Halifax *Morning Chronicle*, 7 November 1871; Saint John, N.B., *Daily Morning News*, 10 November 1871

33 Canada, *Sessional Papers*, 1871, no. 64, p. 55; *ibid.*, 1872, no. 2A, pp. 43, 49; *ibid.*, 1876, no. 8, p. 14; *ibid.*, 1883, no. 14, p. 140; *ibid.*, 1885, no. 8, p. 33; see also 'Homestead Venture: 1883–1892: An Ayreshire Man's Letters Home,' *Saskatchewan History*, XV (Winter 1962), p. 31; Manitoba *Morning Free Press*, 2 January 1894.

34 Canada, *Journals*, 1875, app. 4, p. 28

35 See Sophinisba P. Breckinridge, *The Family and the State: Select Documents* (Chicago: University of Chicago Press, 1934), pp. 356–7.

36 Canada, *Statutes*, 1863 (1st session), 1864, c. 63; *ibid.*, 1864, c. 145. See Richard B. Splane, *Social Welfare in Ontario, 1791–1893: A Study of Public Welfare Administration* (Toronto: University of Toronto Press, 1965), p. 225.

37 Canada, *Journals*, 1874, app. 4, pp. 11, 28; Elspeth A. Latimer, 'Methods of Child Care as Reflected in the Infants' Home of Toronto, 1875–1920' MSW thesis, University of Toronto, 1953), pp. 37–41

38 Doyle, *Emigration*, pp. 11–12

39 *Ibid.*, p. 13

40 The Ontario Readers, *Second Reader* (Toronto: W.J. Gage Co., 1884), pp. 132–3

41 See, for example, 'How to be Useful,' and 'Impolite Things,' *Dominion Churchman*, 10 May 1887, p. 227.

42 William I. Shaw, 'The Youth of Christ,' *Canadian Methodist Magazine*, XIII (1881), pp. 162–3

43 C. Clarkson, 'Our Boys,' *ibid.*, V (1877), p. 169

44 Splane, *Social Welfare in Ontario*, pp. 63, 232–3; for the increase in such institutions in the rest of Canada see Canada, *Census*, 1871, p. 104; *ibid.*, 1881, p. 437; *ibid.*, 1891, p. 235.

45 PAC MG28/I37, vol. 7, *Second Annual Report of The Protestant Orphans' Home of Ottawa*, 1867, p. 7; *ibid.*, 1869, p. 6; see Lady Aberdeen's comments on the Protestant Girls Home in Halifax in John T. Saywell, ed.,

The Canadian Journal of Lady Aberdeen, 1893-1898 (Toronto: Champlain Society, 1960), p. 103.

CHAPTER 2

1 The quotation in the title of the chapter is from Rev. Dr [Albert D.] Carman, 'The Sabbath-School as a Centre,' *Canadian Methodist Magazine*, XXV (1887), p. 45.
2 NCW, *Yearbook* (although the title changed a number of times, it will be called throughout NCW *Yearbook*) 1894, pp. 10-14, 121, 138
3 A.J. Pelletier, F.D. Thompson, and A. Rochan, 'The Canadian Family,' *Seventh Census of Canada, 1921: Monographs*, vol. XII (Ottawa: King's Printer, 1942); Enid Charles, *The Changing Size of the Family in Canada*, Eighth Census of Canada, Census Monograph no. 1 (Ottawa: King's Printer, 1948)
4 Pelletier, Thompson, and Rochan, 'Canadian Family,' pp. vi, 4, 10-11, 126-9; Charles, *Changing Size of the Family*, pp. 8-12
5 The historical re-interpretation, which began with Philip Ariès, *Centuries of Childhood: A Social History of Family Life*, trans. Robert Baldick (New York: Knopf, 1962) has been elaborated in a number of settings; see, for example, Theodore K. Rabb and Robert I. Rotberg, ed., *The Family in History: Interdisciplinary Essays* (New York: Harper, 1973). Recent sociological theory and research on the family is summarized in John N. Edwards, *The Family and Change* (New York: Knopf, 1969).
6 *The Family* (Englewood Cliffs, N.J.: Prentice-Hall, 1964), pp. 103-17
7 *The Family, Education and Society* (London: Routledge & Kegan Paul, 1966), pp. 1-15
8 Canadian historians, however, are now actively at work in this field. See, for example, Michael B. Katz, 'Social Structure in Hamilton, Ontario,' in *Nineteenth Century Cities: Essays in The New Urban History*, Stephan Thernstrom and Richard Sennett, eds. (New Haven: Yale University Press, 1969), pp. 209-44; Michael B. Katz, 'The People of a Canadian City: 1851-2,' CHR, LIII (December 1972), 402-26; Frank T. Denton and Peter J. George, 'An Exploratory Statistical Analysis of Some Socioeconomic Characteristics of Families in Hamilton, Ontario, 1871,' *Histoire Sociale/Social History*, 5 (April 1970), 16-43; David Gagan and Herbert Mays, 'Historical Demography and Canadian Social History: Families and Land in Peel County, Ontario,' CHR, LIV (March 1973), 27-47.
9 Henry J. Morgan and Lawrence J. Burpee, *Canadian Life in Town and Country* (London: George Newnes, 1905), p. 148

10 While for many reasons the concept of social class has not been much applied to the historical analysis of Canadian development it is in this particular context a useful tool. See S.R. Mealing, 'The Concept of Social Class and the Interpretation of Canadian History,' CHR, XLVI (September 1965), 201–18, and Katz, 'Social Structure in Hamilton, Ontario.' Those who supported or worked to spread the new ideas of child and family and to implement related changes in health, education, and welfare in many ways resembled the new urban middle class which was becoming important in the United States at roughly the same time. For this reason the description of them by the American historian Robert H. Wiebe was particularly suggestive in framing this brief description of the Canadian middle class. See Robert H. Wiebe, *The Search for Order: 1877-1920* (New York: Hill and Wang, 1967), pp. 111–32. In addition, these people seem to be an earlier manifestation of the modern middle class which John Porter describes in *The Vertical Mosaic: An Analysis of Social Class and Power in Canada* (Toronto: University of Toronto Press, 1965), pp. 126, 130–2. The middle-class style of life, explains Porter, rests on the consumption of a set of values which are intimately connected with the rearing of children.

11 M.C. Urquhart and K.A.H. Buckley, *Historical Statistics of Canada* (Toronto: Macmillan, 1965), pp. 44, 595, 463

12 John Keith Foster, 'Education and Work in a Changing Society: British Columbia, 1870-1930' (MA thesis, University of British Columbia, 1970), pp. 117–20

13 Urquhart and Buckley, *Historical Statistics of Canada*, p. 621

14 *The Canada Yearbook* (although the title changed a number of times, hereafter CYB), 1902, pp. 87–8; *ibid.*, 1912, pp. 9–10

15 Ontario, *Sessional Papers*, 1896, no. 17, p. 29

16 Canada, *Sessional Papers*, 1882, no. 42, 'Report of the Commissioners appointed to enquire into the working of Mills and Factories of the Dominion, and of the labour employed therein,' pp. 4–5

17 Canada, *Report of the Royal Commission on the Relations of Labor and Capital in Canada* (Ottawa: Queen's Printer, 1889), p. 10; see also Charles Lipton, *The Trade Union Movement of Canada, 1827-1959* (Montreal: Canadian Social Publications, 1966), pp. 58–64.

18 H.A. Logan, *Trade Unions in Canada: Their Development and Functioning* (Toronto: Macmillan, 1948), chap. 2

19 *Canadian Churchman*, 3 October 1901, p. 597

20 Ontario, *Sessional Papers*, 1895, no. 29, app., p. 39

21 'The Sabbath-School as a Centre,' *Canadian Methodist Magazine*, XXV (1887), pp. 44–5

22 Ontario, *Sessional Papers*, 1895, no. 29, p. 1

23 NCW, *Yearbook*, 1894, pp. 83, 94

24 Helen Cameron Parker, 'Technical Schools for Women,' *Canadian Magazine*, I (October 1893), 634; see also *Woman's Journal*, XV (September 1900), 8.

25 NCW, *Yearbook*, 1895, p. 269

26 Jean R. Laidlaw, 'Training of Young Children,' NCW, *Yearbook*, 1894, pp. 83–90

27 *Ibid.*, 1895, pp. 3–9; Mrs George Bryce, *Historical Sketch of the Charitable Institutions of Winnipeg*, The Historical and Scientific Society of Manitoba Transaction no. 54 (Winnipeg: Manitoba Free Press, 1899), pp. 24–5

28 Bruce M. Carter, 'James L. Hughes and the Gospel of Education: A Study of the Work and Thought of a Nineteenth Century Educator' (DED dissertation, University of Toronto, 1966), pp. 246–60; see also James L. Hughes, *Froebel's Educational Laws for All Teachers* (New York: Appleton, 1899)

29 New Westminster *British Columbian*, 7 December 1899, p. 3

30 John A. Cooper, 'Editorial Comments,' *Canadian Magazine*, XII (February, 1899), p. 367

31 See NCW, *Yearbook*, 1901, p. 145; PAC, MG28/I47 vol. 1, Minutes, 8 February 1900; New Westminster *British Columbian*, 3 February 1891, p. 3.

32 See, for example, Ontario, *Sessional Papers*, 1895, app., pp. 24–6; Victoria *Daily Colonist*, 20 May – 13 June 1890; New Westminster *British Columbian*, 7 December 1897, p. 3.

33 Ontario, *Sessional Papers*, 1895, no. 29, app., pp. 13–17

34 NCW, *Yearbook*, 1897, p. 95

35 See, for example, New Westminster *British Columbian*, 3 February 1891, p. 3; NCW, *Yearbook*, 1894, pp. 134–5; *ibid.*, 1896, p. 328; PAC MG28/I35 vol. 1, 'Minutes of the Ottawa Local Council of Women,' 2 February 1895; Ontario, *Sessional Papers*, 1895, no. 29, app., p. 64; Royal Commission on the Liquor Traffic, *Report*, Canada, *Sessional Papers*, 1895, no. 21, p. 48.

36 According to Bernard Wishy, this contrast between saving the child of the 'nice' family for his own sake and other children for the sake of society was also present in American writings on child nurture at this time. See *The Child and the Republic: The Dawn of Modern American Child Nurture* (Philadelphia: University of Pennsylvania Press, 1968), pp. 16, 131–5

37 'School-Children's Teeth – Their Universally Unhealthy and Neglected Condition,' *Dental Register*, L (1896), pp. 484–5

38 NCW, *Yearbook*, 1895, pp. 114–15. See also Madge Merton and The Editor, 'Our Children and Their Reading,' *Canadian Magazine*, VI (January 1896), p. 285; 'Ruined by Fiction,' New Westminster *British Columbian*, 2 February 1891, p. 3; 12 August 1895, p. 2.

39 Toronto *Globe*, 11 May 1900, p. 12; 12 May 1900, p. 18; 23 May 1900, p. 8

40 NCW, *Yearbook*, 1896, pp. 340–2; see also PAC MG28/I32, vol. 1, Ottawa Local Council of Women, Minutes, 8 June 1895; New Westminster *British Columbian*, 14 January 1893; NCW, *Yearbook*, 1895, pp. 119–28; *ibid.*, 1896, pp. 335–53; *ibid.*, 1901, pp. 147–8; Merton and The Editor, 'Our Children,' *Canadian Magazine*, VI (January 1896), pp. 282–7.

41 W.A. Mackintosh, *The Economic Background of Dominion-Provincial Relations: Appendix III of the Royal Commission Report on Dominion-Provincial Relations*, ed. J.H. Dales (Toronto: McClelland and Stewart, 1964), pp. 36–9

42 G.W. Bertram, 'Economic Growth in Canadian Industry, 1870–1915: The Staple Model,' in *Approaches to Canadian Economic History*, ed. W.T. Easterbrook and M.H. Watkins (Toronto: McClelland and Stewart, 1967), pp. 74–98; see also the summary in Peter B. Waite, *Canada, 1874–1896: Arduous Destiny* (Toronto: McClelland and Stewart, 1971), pp. 74–83.

43 O.J. Firestone, *Canada's Economic Development, 1867–1953: With Special Reference to Changes in the Country's National Product and National Wealth* (London: Bowes and Bowes, 1958), p. 281; see also Robert Craig Brown and Ramsay Cook, *Canada, 1896–1921: A Nation Transformed* (Toronto: McClelland and Stewart, 1974), esp. chaps 1, 4, 5, and 8.

44 Firestone, *Canada's Economic Development*, pp. 77, 91, 171, 173

45 Canada, *Report of the Royal Commission on the Relations of Labor and Capital in Canada* (Ottawa: Queen's Printer, 1889), pp. 8; see also pp. 17–18.

46 British Columbia, *Report of the Royal Commission on Labour* (Victoria: King's Printer, 1914), p. M3; see also Brown and Cook, *Canada 1896–1921*, chap. 6. On the other hand, J.T. Copp argues that there was a slight decline in working-class income between 1901 and 1920. See his 'The Condition of the Working Class in Montreal, 1897–1920,' CHA, *Historical Papers*, 1972, pp. 157–80

47 Ontario, *Sessional Papers*, 1903, no. 43, p. 73

48 Canada, DBS, 'The Canadian Family,' pp. vi, 10–11, 126–9

49 NCW, *Yearbook*, 1895, p. 129

50 Peter G. Goheen, *Victorian Toronto, 1850 to 1900: Pattern and Process of Growth* (Chicago: University of Chicago Department of Geography Research Paper no. 127, 1970), pp. 128–33, 194–205; Goheen did not re-sample bakers or physicians for 1890.

51 Urquhart and Buckley, *Historical Statistics of Canada*, p. 93. 'Sweated' workers, of course, put in much longer hours.

52 NCW, *Yearbook*, 1898, p. 286

53 *Ibid.*, 1894, pp. 134, 240–1; *ibid.*, 1895, p. 100; for a discussion of the nine-teenth century 'cult of true womanhood,' as it manifested itself in the United States, see William L. O'Neill, *Everyone was Brave: The Rise and Fall of Feminism in America* (Chicago: Quadrangle Books, 1969), pp. 7–9.

54 NCW, *Yearbook*, 1902, p. 76

55 Clara Brett Martin, 'Legal Status of Women in the Provinces of the Dominion of Canada,' *Women of Canada: Their Life and Work*, compiled by the National Council of Women of Canada for distribution at the Paris International Exhibition, 1900 (n.pl.: n. pub., n.d.), pp. 34–5.

56 NCW, *Yearbook*, 1895, pp. 331–2; *ibid.*, 1896, pp. 311–27

57 For the accomplishments of a generation of such work, see Canada, Department of Labour, *Legal Status of Women in Canada* (Ottawa: King's Printer, 1924).

58 Stone, *Urban Development in Canada*, p. 29; urban development in Canada in these years is analysed in Brown and Cook, *Canada, 1896–1921*, chap. 5.

59 Richard E. Caves and Richard H. Holton, *The Canadian Economy: Prospect and Retrospect* (Cambridge: Harvard University Press, 1959), p. 44

60 See, for example, Susan E. Houston, 'Politics, Schools, and Social Change in Upper Canada,' CHR, LIII (September 1972), 249–71; and James M. Whelan, 'Social Welfare in New Brunswick, 1784–1900,' *Acadiensis*, II (Autumn 1972), 54–64.

61 See Paul Rutherford, 'Tomorrow's Metropolis: The Urban Reform Move-ment in Canada, 1880–1920,' CHA, *Historical Papers*, 1971, 203–24; for the wider context of the role of the city in Canadian history, see J.M.S. Careless, 'Somewhat Narrower Horizons,' CHA, *Report*, 1968, pp. 1–10.

62 *Victorian Toronto*, chaps. 7 and 8

63 National Conference of Charities and Correction, *Proceedings*, 1897, p. 3

64 For an account of Toronto's rise to eminence, see D.C. Masters, *The Rise of Toronto, 1850–1890* (Toronto: University of Toronto Press, 1947); see also G.P. de T. Glazebrook, *The Story of Toronto* (Toronto: University of Toronto Press, 1971), chaps 6 0.

65 The phrase is used in G.D.H. Cole and Raymond Postgate, *The Common People* (London: University Paperbacks, 1961), p. 454; see also Brown and Cook, *Canada 1896–1921*, pp. 3–4.

66 NCW, *Yearbook*, 1896, p. 389

67 *Woman's Journal*, XV (1 September 1900), p. 5

68 *Final Report of the McGill Normal School, Being the Report of the Fifty-First Session, Ending May 31st, 1907* (n. pl.: n. pub., n.d.), p. 28

69 *Woman's Journal*, XIV (August 1899), p. 3; *ibid.*, XV (February 1901), p. 3

70 *Women of Canada*, p. 258

71 Canada, *Sessional Papers*, 1884, no. 14, p. 144; see also Pinchbeck and Hewitt, *Children in English Society*, vol. 2, pp. 573–5.

72 *Evangelicals in Action*, p. 104

73 Canada, *Sessional Papers*, 1889, no. 5, p. xxiv

74 Stephen and Lea, *Dictionary of National Biography*, Supplement no. 2, vol. I, pp. 99–100; John Herridge Batt, *Dr. Barnardo: The Foster-Father of "Nobody's Children": A Record and an Interpretation* (London: Partridge, 1904); A.E. Williams, *Barnardo of Stepney: The Father of Nobody's Children* (London: Allen and Unwin, 1966); Canada, *Sessional Papers*, 1884, no. 14, p. xxiv

75 Canada, *Sessional Papers*, 1889, no. 5, p. xxiv; Canada, Department of Interior, *Report*, 1901, p. 105; Canada, Department of Immigration and Colonization, *Report*, 1922–1923, p. 63

76 *Report of the Commissioners Appointed to Enquire into the Prison and Reformatory System of Ontario, 1891* (Toronto: Queen's Printer, 1891), pp. 432–51; Canada, Department of Immigration, File #3115, vol. 1, J.M. McGovern to secretary, Department of the Interior, 25 March 1895; Alfred B. Owen to A.M. Burgess, deputy minister of the interior, 24 April 1895; Canada, *Sessional Papers*, 1898, no. 13, pp. 156–8; Pinchbeck and Hewitt, *Children in English Society*, vol. II, pp. 575–8

77 Canada, *Sessional Papers*, 1887, no. 12, pp. 21, 25, 34–5, 56, 60, 154–6; Saint John, N.B., *Daily Sun*, 25 October 1886; H.D. Barrett and J. Abercrombie, 'Our Emigration Work,' *Our Waifs and Strays* (August 1887), typescript copy

78 Canada, *Sessional Papers*, 1889, no. 5, p. 71

79 See, for example, Canada, *Journals*, 1877, app. 6; *ibid.*, 1879, app. 1; *ibid.*, 1886, app. 6; *ibid.*, 1887, app. 5.

80 *Ibid.*, 1888, app. 5, pp. 3, 10

81 See, for example, *Queen's College Journal* (June 1888), pp. 164–5; *Royal Commission on the Relations of Labor and Capital*, pp. 12, 115

82 *Report ... into the Prison and Reformatory System*, pp. 215, 432–51, 738–42, 540, 729

83 Canada, *Sessional Papers*, 1893, no. 18, p. vii; *ibid.*, 1894, no. 13, p. xxxvii; Manitoba *Morning Free Press*, 15 December 1893, 18 December 1893, 29 December 1893, 2 January 1894

84 See Victoria *Colonist*, 24 December 1893, 21 January 1894; Kamloops *Sentinal*, 8 June 1894.

85 Canada, *Sessional Papers*, 1889, no. 5D, pp. vi–vii; Canada, Department of Immigration, File #3115, vol. 1, A.M. Burgess to T.M. Daly, minister of the interior, 6 February 1894

86 Canada, Department of Immigration, File #3115, vol. 1, Lynwode Pereira to J.G. Colmers, secretary, High Commissioner's Office, London, 21 June 1894; printed circular of regulations distributed by Colmers to 27 agencies sending children to Canada, September, 1893; File #2932, 'W.J. Pady, Immigration of Children'; File #3115, vol. 2, Pereira to Colmers, 24 August 1897

87 *Ibid.*, File #3115, W.F. Boardman to J.A. Smart, 29 March 1897

88 Ontario, *Sessional Papers*, 1895, no. 29, app., p. 63

89 Canada, Department of Immigration, File #3115, vol. 1, Pereira to L.J. Seargeant, 12 January 1895; J.M. McGovern to secretary, Department of the Interior, 25 March 1895; Canada, *Sessional Papers*, 1897, no. 13, pp. 113–14

90 Canada, Department of Immigration, File #3115, vol. 2, Boardman to Smart, 29 March 1897; to sample the criticism, see Ernest Heaton, 'Canada vs. Barnardo *et. al.*: The Plaintiff's Case,' *This Week*, 24 May 1895, pp. 605–6; Ernest Heaton, 'Canada vs. Barnardo: the Defendant Case,' *ibid.*, 7 June 1895, pp. 657–9; Goldwin Smith, 'The Leak in the Barrel,' *ibid.*, 21 June 1895, pp. 711–12; Canada, *Journals*, 1894, app. 4, pp. 206, 211; *ibid.*, 1895, app. 3, pp. xiv–xv; *ibid.*, 1896, (1st Sess.), pp. 223–4.

91 See the evidence of Alfred F. Jury, Toronto Knights of Labor, in Canada, *Journals*, 1888, app. 5, pp. 9–10, and the evidence of T.J. Carey, Knights of Labor, in *ibid.*, 1889, app. 4, pp. 86–92; *Report ... into the Prison and Reformatory System*, p. 738; Ontario, *Sessional Papers*, 1895, no. 29, app., pp. 33–5; Canada, Department of Immigration, File #3115, vol. 2, Pereira to D.J. O'Donoghue, 30 July 1897.

92 Canada, *Journals*, 1888, app. 5, pp. 11–17; *ibid.*, 1889, app. 4, pp. 43–4, 90–2; *ibid.*, 1894, app. 4, p. 208; Mr Justice Street in Toronto *Mail and Empire*, 18 September 1896

93 Ontario, *Sessional Papers*, 1895, no. 29, pp. 2, 30–2; see also Canada, Department of Immigration, File #3115, vol. 2, John MacKrell, senior warden, Cordwainer's Company, to H.F. Wilson, private secretary to Joseph Chamberlain, 29 April 1897; *ibid.*, vol. 1, Florence E.L. Sutton, Marchmount Home, Belleville, to secretary, Department of Interior, 30 March 1895; *ibid.*, vol. 2, E. de M. Rudolph, Church of England Incorporated Society for Providing Homes for Waifs and Strays, to secretary, High Commissioner, 16 March 1897; Maria S. Rye to Burgess, 27 March 1897; *ibid.*, William Quarrier, Orphan Homes of Scotland, and Destitute Children's Immigration Homes, to Joseph Chamberlain, 15 November 1897; Toronto, *Globe*, 28 August 1897, William Quarrier to Premier Arthur S. Hardy, and reply.

94 NCW, *Yearbook*, 1896, pp. 470–86, 505–32

95 PAC, National Council of Women Papers, MG28/I25, vol. 155, 'Memorandum of the business transacted at the National Council of Women of Canada at

Montreal 1896 and Referred to Local Councils and Federated National
Societies by the President' (n.d.), pp. 5–6; NCW, *Yearbook*, 1897, pp. 42,
144, 151, 154, 168, 172.

96 NCW, *Yearbook*, 1897, pp. 166–74; PAC, NCW Papers, vol. 155, 'President's
Memorandum on the Business Transacted at [sic] the National Council of
Women of Canada at Halifax 1897 and referred to Local Councils and Fed-
erated National Societies' (n.d.), pp. 9–10

97 Ontario, *Statutes*, 1897, c. 53; Manitoba, *Journals*, 1897, p. 102

98 Canada, Department of Immigration, File #3115, vol. 2, Local Government
Board, Whitehall, to under-secretary of state, Colonial Office, 30 May 1896;
Great Britain, Local Government Board, Poor Law Schools Committee, *Re-
port of the Departmental Committee Appointed to Enquire into the Existing
Systems for the Maintenance and Education of Children Under the Charge of
Managers of District Schools and Boards of Guardians in the Metropolis and
to Advise as to Any Changes that may be Desirable* (London: Queen's
Printer, 1896)

99 Canada, Department of Immigration, File #3115, vol. 2, deputy minister of
immigration to minister, 15 July 1896; *ibid.*, Burgess to Hon. R.W. Scott,
acting minister, 30 July 1896; *ibid.*, P.C. 1564J., 11 August 1896; *ibid.*,
W.E. Knollys, assistant secretary to under secretary of state, Colonial Office,
to Department of Interior, 22 December 1896; *ibid.*, Sir Donald A. Smith to
minister of interior, 23 December 1896; *ibid.*, Burgess to Smith, 8 February
1897; *ibid.*, Chamberlain to governor general, 16 February 1897; *ibid.*,
deputy minister of interior to Clifford Sifton, 23 February 1897; Canada,
Sessional Papers, 1900, no. 13, p. 6

100 Edward St John, hon. secretary, Canadian Catholic Emigration Society, to
The Empire Review, dated 12 May 1903, typescript; see also letters by E. de
M. Rudolf, May 1903; J.B. Gastaldi, July 1903; and E. Bans and Arthur Chil-
ton Thomas, July 1903. Typescripts of clippings contained in the scrapbooks
of Rev. E. de M. Rudolf, secretary of the Church of England Homes for Waifs
and Strays.

101 NCW, *Yearbook*, 1906, pp. 26–9; *ibid.*, 1907, pp. 35–7; *ibid.*, 1910, pp. 62–3;
ibid., pp. 101–3. In England, discussion continued over the wisdom of sending
children to the colonies. See, for example, Kingsley Fairbridge, 'Child Emigration to British Colonies,' *The Child*, I (December 1910), 251–4; Denis Crane,
John Bull's Surplus Children: A Plea for Giving Them a Fairer Chance (London: Horace Marshall, 1915).

102 Postwar developments are summarized in Scholes, *Education for Empire
Settlement*, chaps 6–9.

103 Heasman, *Evangelicals in Action*, pp. 105–6

104 Ontario, *Sessional Papers*, 1896, no. 17, pp. 25–7

105 *Fifth Annual Canadian Conference on Child Welfare: Proceedings and Papers, Ottawa, 1925* (Ottawa: King's Printer, 1926), p. 183

106 M. Agnes Fitz Gibbon, 'Immigration,' *Report of the International Congress of Women ... 1909*, vol. 2, p. 438

107 Batt, *Dr. Barnardo*, p. 129; *Fifth ... Canadian Conference on Child Welfare*, p. 178

108 W.G. Smith, *A Study in Canadian Immigration* (Toronto: Ryerson, 1920), pp. 68–9, 263–5

109 *Fifth ... Canadian Conference on Child Welfare*, pp. 188–90; *Some Angles of Discussion in the Juvenile Immigration Problem of Canada*, Canadian Council on Child Welfare Publication no. 14 (Ottawa: Canadian Council on Child Welfare, 1924), pp. 6–7; see also *Juvenile Immigration Report No. 2*, Canadian Council on Child Welfare Publication no. 15 (Ottawa: Canadian Council on Child Welfare, 1925).

110 *Fifth ... Canadian Conference on Child Welfare*, pp. 190–1

111 *Ibid.*, pp. 191–4; [Mrs.] J. Breckenridge McGregor, *"Several Years After": An Analysis of the Histories of a Selected Group of Juvenile Immigrants Brought to Canada in 1910, and in 1920, by British Emigration Societies* (Ottawa: Ryerson, 1928), pp. 19–36

CHAPTER 3

1 The quotation in the title of Part II is from James Roberts, 'Insanitary Areas,' PHJ, III (April 1912), p. 182.

2 The quotation in the title of the chapter is from Lina L. Rogers, 'Nursing Side of Medical Inspection of Schools,' PHJ, IV (March 1913), pp. 147–8. A version of this chapter appeared in HEQ, XII (Fall 1972), pp. 304–33.

3 Roberts, 'Insanitary Areas,' *ibid.*, III (April 1912), p. 182

4 Peter H. Bryce, 'History of Public Health in Canada,' *Canadian Therapeutist and Sanitary Engineer*, I (June 1910), 287–91; Ontario, *Statutes*, 1882, c. 29

5 Ontario, *Statutes*, 1884, c. 38

6 R.D. Defries, ed., *The Development of Public Health in Canada: a Review of the History and Organization of the Public Health in the Provinces of Canada, with an Outline of the Present Organization of the National Health Section of the Department of National Pensions and National Health, Canada* (Toronto: Canadian Public Health Association, 1940), pp. 15, 35, 49, 56, 67, 90, 101, 115, 131. For the background to the Ontario legislation, see Bryce

'History of Public Health'; Peter H. Bryce, 'The Story of Public Health in Canada,' in Mazÿck P. Ravenel, ed., *A Half Century of Public Health: Jubilee Historical Volume of the American Public Health Association* (New York: American Public Health Association, 1921), pp. 56–66; R.D. Splane, *Social Welfare in Ontario, 1791–1893: A Study of Public Welfare Administration* (Toronto: University of Toronto Press, 1965), p. 199. For an account of the English Public Health Act of 1875, see W.M. Frazer, *A History of English Public Health, 1834–1939* (London: Bailliere, Tindall and Cox, 1950), pp. 114–25.

7 Ontario Board of Health, *Report*, 1883, p. xlvi; *ibid.*, 1887, p. v; *ibid.*, 1899, pp. 74–5

8 *Ibid.*, 1883, pp. xlvi–xlviii, 243–6, 339–49. Such standards varied greatly from place to place. See, Saskatchewan, Department of Education, *Report*, 1906, p. 73.

9 Ontario Board of Health, *Report*, 1891, p. 38

10 A.C. Jost, 'The Conservation of Child Life,' PHJ, XI (November 1920), pp. 503–12

11 *Victoria Daily Colonist*, 13 April 1897, p. 8; *ibid.*, 14 May 1897, p. 8; Ontario Board of Health, *Report*, 1898, pp. 68–75; Toronto *Globe*, 2 May 1900, p. 7; *ibid.*, 4 May 1900, p. 12

12 Ontario Board of Health, *Report*, 1887, pp. iii–v

13 *Ibid.*, 1885, pp. 29–34

14 New Westminster *British Columbian*, 3 June 1892, p. 4

15 PHJ, II (May 1911), p. 221; *ibid.*, III (May 1912), pp. 249–55

16 Saskatchewan Bureau of Public Health, *Report*, 1919–20, p. 8. For an account of the legal status of compulsory vaccination, see Peter Frank Bargen, *The Legal Status of the Canadian Public School Pupil* (Toronto: Macmillan, 1961), p. 79.

17 See, for example, Ontario Board of Health, *Report*, 1882, pp. 168–76; *ibid.*, 1883, pp. xlv, 400–8.

18 See, for example, *ibid.*, 1883, pp. xlvi, 242–3; *ibid.*, 1890, pp. xiii–xvi, lxxxix–xcvii.

19 *Gage's Health Series for Intermediate Classes, Part II* (Toronto: W.J. Gage Company, 1896), p. 11

20 George Rosen, *A History of Public Health* (New York: MD Publications, 1958), pp. 344–403

21 Ontario Board of Health, *Report*, 1892, p. 19; *ibid.*, 1891, p. 1

22 Privy Council, Medical Research Council, *Diphtheria: Its Bacteriology, Pathology and Immunology* (London: HMSO, 1923), pp. 44–63, 126–9, 232–5; C.-E. Winslow, *The Life of Hermann M. Biggs: Physician and States-*

man of the Public Health (Philadelphia: Lee and Febiger, 1929), pp. 102–30; Rosen, *History of Public Health*, pp. 319–20, 333–6; Ontario Board of Health, *Report*, 1890, pp. lvii–lxii; Wade W. Oliver, *The Man Who Lived For Tomorrow: A Biography of William Hallock Park, M.D.* (New York: Dutton, 1941)

23 Ontario Board of Health, *Report*, 1901, p. lxxviii; Defries, *Development of Public Health in Canada*, pp. 77–88; Hermann Biggs, 'The Development of Research Laboratories,' New York Department of Health, *Monthly Bulletin*, I (March 1911), pp. 54–6

24 See, for example, Ontario Board of Health, *Report*, 1899, p. 12

25 R.H. Mullin, 'Recent Advances in the Control of Diphtheria,' *Canadian Medical Association Journal*, XIV (May 1924), pp. 398–406

26 Ontario Board of Health, *Report*, 1901, p. 93

27 Vancouver Children's Aid Society, *Report*, 1910, p. 18

28 Ontario Board of Health, *Report*, 1907, p. 8

29 *Ibid.*, 1920, pp. 37–8; Defries, *The Development of Public Health in Canada*, pp. 77–88

30 Saskatchewan Bureau of Public Health, *Report*, 1917–18, p. 17; *ibid.*, 1919–20, pp. 7–8

31 Medical Research Council, *Diphtheria*, pp. 349–61

32 Ontario Board of Health, *Report*, 1920, p. 37

33 Rosen, *History of Public Health*, pp. 337–41

34 Urquhart and Buckley, *Historical Statistics of Canada*, p. 45; Canada, Statistics Canada, *Annual Report of Notifiable Diseases*, 1972 (Ottawa: Information Canada, 1972), p. 22

35 NCW, *Yearbook*, 1911, p. 43. Canadians also demonstrated their increasing interest in health matters by establishing organizations – the Canadian St John's Ambulance in 1895, the Canadian Red Cross Society in 1896, the National Sanitarium Association in 1897, the Canadian Association for the Prevention of Tuberculosis in 1900, the Public Health Committee of the National Council of Women in 1905, and the Canadian Public Health Association in 1910 – and in such major efforts at environmental improvement as the rapid introduction across Canada of municipal water and sewer systems. See, for example, Leo G. Denis, *Waterworks and Sewerage Systems of Canada* (Ottawa, Commission of Conservation: Committee on Waters and Waterpowers, 1916).

36 Ontario, Board of Health, *Report*, 1920, p. 167

37 *Ibid.*, 1903, pp. 46, 52; see also the Hamilton officer's report, *ibid.*, p. 82.

38 *Ibid.*, 1899, pp. 72–4; *ibid.*, 1901, pp. 6, 110–11

39 Rosen, *History of Public Health*, p. 365

40 Frazer, *English Public Health*, pp. 256–8, 323–4

41 Rosen, *History of Public Health*, p. 366
42 Winslow, *Biggs*, p. 157
43 Lina Rogers Struthers, *The School Nurse: A Survey of the Duties and Responsibilities of the Nurse in the Maintenance of Health and Physical Perfection
   and the Prevention of Disease Among School Children* (New York: Putnam's,
   1917), pp. 17-28; Winslow, *Biggs*, pp. 186-215; 'Division of Child Hygiene,'
   New York Department of Health, *Monthly Bulletin*, I (January 1911), pp.
   14-16; Ernst J. Lederle, 'The Needs of the Department of Health,' *ibid.*, I
   (October 1911), pp. 236-7
44 Ontario, *Sessional Papers*, 1907, no. 62, pp. 23-6; James Kerr and E.W.
   Wallis, eds., *Transactions of the Second International Congress on School
   Hygiene, London, 1907* (3 vols.; London: William Clowes & Sons, 1908);
   A. Maloine, ed., *IIIe Congrès International D'Hygiène Scolaire, Paris, 2-7
   Aout, 1910*, III (Paris: n. pub., 1911), p. 9
45 George A. Auden, 'School Inspection and the Public Health Service,' PHJ, II
   (May 1911), pp. 207-10; L. Haden Guest, 'Poverty and School Clinics,' *ibid.*,
   II (July 1911), pp. 317-19; L. Haden Guest, 'School Clinics,' *ibid.*, IV (May
   1913), pp. 272-7
46 Canada, Commission of Conservation, *Report*, 1910, p. 132
47 II (June 1911), 276; report of Mrs J.N. Smillie in International Congress of
   Women, *Report of the International Congress of Women, held in Toronto,
   Canada, June 24-30, 1909*, II (Toronto: National Council of Women,
   Canada, 1910), p. 57
48 J. Edouard Laberge, 'Inspection médicale des maisons d'éducation,' *Bulletin
   Sanitaire*, IX (1909), pp. 117-24
49 Ontario, *Statutes*, 1907, c. 51
50 NCW, *Yearbook*, 1910, pp. i-ii
51 Edward Miller Steven, *Medical Supervision in Schools: Being An Account of
   the Systems at Work in Great Britain, Canada, the United States, Germany,
   and Switzerland* (London: Ballière, Tindall and Cox, 1910), pp. 182-3
52 Toronto *Evening Telegram*, 14 January 1910, p. 18; Toronto *Globe*, 28
   January 1910, p. 14
53 Toronto *Globe*, 25 February 1910, p. 16; Toronto *Evening Telegram*,
   25 February 1910, p. 10
54 Struthers, *The School Nurse*, p. 34
55 V (February and March 1914), pp. 91-8, 150-60
56 While the PHJ did not list Fort William, the National Council of Women's
   Public Health Committee in 1911 noted it as one of a number of communities where medical inspection was under way. NCW, *Yearbook*, 1911, pp.
   43-7

57 See also Alice Ravenhill, 'The Health of Public School Children in British Columbia,' *The Child*, IV (June 1914), pp. 697–9.

58 Russell Sage Foundation, *What American Cities are Doing for the Health of School Children: Report Covering Conditions in 1038 Cities* (New York: Department of Child Hygiene, Russell Sage Foundation, 1911). The report was summarized for Canadians in PHJ, II (September 1911), p. 433.

59 'Nursing Side of Medical Inspection,' PHJ, IV (March 1913), pp. 147–8

60 PHJ, II (June 1911), p. 275; see also NCW, *Yearbook*, 1911, pp. 43–7; 'The Health of the Child,' *The Canadian Medical Association Journal*, II (September 1912), pp. 704–5.

61 C.E. Terry, 'School Children and Public Health,' PHJ, I (December 1910), p. 385

62 PHJ, II (December 1911), pp. 588–9; Jean Browne, 'School Nursing in Regina,' *ibid.*, V (February 1914), pp. 91–2; 'Medical Inspection of Schools in the Middle West,' *ibid.*, pp. 94–5; 'Medical Inspection of Schools in Ontario,' *ibid.*, V (March 1914), pp. 159–60

63 'Medical Inspection of Schools in British Columbia,' *ibid.*, V (March 1914), p. 153

64 See, for example, 'Medical Inspection of Schools in Nova Scotia,' PHJ, V (February 1914), p. 98; NCW, *Yearbook*, 1912, p. 102; John J. Heagerty, *Four Centuries of Medical History* (Toronto: Macmillan, 1928), pp. 226–45.

65 Struthers, *The School Nurse*, pp. 132–43; see also Leonard P. Ayres, *Open Air Schools* (New York: Department of Child Hygiene, Russell Sage Foundation, n.d.). For an account of the European origins of fresh air schools and their development in an English city, see David A. Turner, 'The Open Air School Movement in Sheffield,' *History of Education*, I (January 1972), pp. 58–80.

66 Daniel Hockin, 'The Rotary Clinic,' *Twenty-fifth Anniversary of Rotary Club of Vancouver, Canada: 1913–1938* (Vancouver: Rotary Club of Vancouver, 1938), pp. 14–15

67 See, for example, Canada, Department of Health, *Handbook of Child Welfare Work in Canada for the Year March 31 1922* [hereafter *Handbook*], Helen MacMurchy, ed. (Ottawa: King's Printer, 1923), p. 56

68 PHJ, V (March 1914), p. 160

69 Browne, 'School Nursing in Regina,' *ibid.*, V (February 1914), pp. 91–3

70 'Medical Inspection of Schools in British Columbia,' *ibid.*, V (March 1914), p. 150

71 Struthers, *The School Nurse*, pp. 1–4

72 Browne, 'School Nursing in Regina,' PHJ, V (February 1914), p. 91

73 'Medical Inspection in Quebec,' PHJ, V (March 1914), p. 156

74 Rogers, 'Nursing Side of Medical Inspection of Schools,' PHJ, IV (March 1913), p. 147
75 IV (February 1913), p. 94
76 Adams, 'School-Children's Teeth,' *Dental Register*, L (1896), p. 480
77 Adams to P.H. Bryce, 10 February 1896, quoted in NCW, *Yearbook*, 1896, p. 463; A.E. Webster, 'Status of Dentistry,' DDJ, XXII (December 1910), pp. 571-607; D.W. Gullett, *A History of Dentistry in Canada* (Toronto: University of Toronto Press for the Canadian Dental Association, 1971), pp. 94-6; Ontario Board of Health, *Report*, 1896, pp. 76-82; Victoria *Colonist*, 25 July 1896, p. 8.
78 'Editorial Notes,' DDJ, XXII (October 1910), pp. 511-12
79 'Complimentary dinner to John W. Dowd, by the Toronto Dental Society, Nov. 22, 1910,' DDJ, XXII (December 1910), pp. 570-600
80 II (May 1911), p. 221
81 For the origin and development of the oral hygiene crusade, see E.B. Hicks, 'Free Examination of School Children's Teeth: What Oral Hygiene Means to Them,' DDJ, XXII (October 1910), pp. 460-6; Arthur Day, 'What is Being Done Outside of the Dental Office for the Improvement of the Human Mouth,' PHJ, III (May 1912), pp. 235-9; Professor Dr Dieck, 'The Care of the Teeth of School Children in Germany,' *ibid.*, IV (June 1913), pp. 366-9; and Robert M. McCluggage, *A History of the American Dental Association: A Century of Health Service* (Chicago: The American Dental Association, 1959), pp. 248-53. For what dentists saw as the social implications of their work see A.W. Thornton, 'The Dentist as Social Worker,' PHJ, III (September 1912), p. 524; W.D. Cowan, 'Dental Caries in School Children and Dental Inspection,' *ibid.*, IV (November 1913), pp. 602-5
82 Gullett, *Dentistry in Canada*, chaps 7-9
83 PHJ, III (April 1912), p. 222; see also C.P. Kennedy, 'Report on the Mouths and Teeth of the Children in Two Public Schools of Toronto,' DDJ, XXII (December 1910), pp. 571-2; A.E. Webster, 'Dental Inspection of Two Schools in Toronto,' *ibid.*, pp. 600-4.
84 'Dental Inspectors Outline of Toronto School Work,' PHJ, II (November 1911), p. 545; W.H. Doherty, 'The Dental Aspect of Medical Inspection of Schools,' *ibid.*, III (December 1912), pp. 680-3; Toronto *Globe*, 29 September, 1910; Vancouver School Board, *Report*, 1918, p. 43; Struthers, *The School Nurse*, pp. 141-2, 205-25; Browne, 'School Nursing in Regina,' PHJ, V (February 1914), p. 93
85 See, for example, 'Alberta Health Act and its Relation to Medical Inspection,' PHJ, III (March 1912), pp. 153-4.

86 To sample this discussion, see Ontario Board of Health, *Report*, 1903, pp.
   40-1; 'Editorial,' PHJ, I (October 1910), pp. 505-6; W.A. Evans, 'Ventilation
   in Schools,' *ibid.*, II (July 1911), pp. 319-22; J.H. Puntin, 'School Buildings:
   Some Notes on Hygienic Principles Influencing Design,' *ibid.*, IV (December
   1913), pp. 654-60; S.S. Kennedy, 'Heating and Ventilating Modern School
   Buildings,' *ibid.*, pp. 661-4.
87 Vancouver School Board, *Report*, 1906, p. 12
88 Thomas J. McNally, 'Sanitary Conditions in Rural Schools,' PHJ, VII (April
   1916), pp. 190-2
89 *Canadian Therapeutist*, I (July 1910), pp. 374-5
90 J. Halpenny, MA, MD, and Lilian B. Ireland, *How to be Healthy* (Toronto:
   W.J. Gage, 1911), pp. iii-v; PHJ, II (October 1911), p. 479.
91 British Columbia Board of Health, *Report*, 1920, p. 15
92 Canada, Dominion Bureau of Statistics, *Historical Statistical Survey of
   Education in Canada* (Ottawa: King's Printer, 1921), p. 110; British Columbia
   Board of Health, *Report*, 1920, pp. 15-43
93 International Congress of Women, *Report*, 1909, vol. II, p. 58
94 PHJ, III (April 1912), p. 222; *Handbook*, p. 153
95 *Handbook*, pp. 82-3; see also Vancouver School Board, *Report*, 1919, p. 39;
   Ontario Board of Health, *Report*, 1921, p. 317.
96 *Handbook*, p. 78
97 Alan Brown, 'Problems of the Rural Mother in the Feeding of Her Children,'
   PHJ, IX (July 1918), p. 297

CHAPTER 4

1 The quotation in the title of the chapter is from Helen Smith, 'Child Welfare:
   Infant Welfare,' NCW, *Yearbook*, 1912, p. 67.
2 New Westminster *Mainland Guardian*, 3 July 1878
3 See, for example, 'Heavy Mortality Among Infants,' Toronto *Globe*, 3 June
   1900, p. 17.
4 Canada, *Sessional Papers*, 1888, no. 12, p. 87
5 Ontario Board of Health, *Report*, 1887, p. 16; see also Splane, *Social Welfare
   in Ontario*, pp. 242-3.
6 Ontario Board of Health, *Report*, 1901, p. 94; *ibid.*, 1902, p. 93; *ibid.*, 1903,
   pp. 82-6; see, for example, *ibid.*, 1903, pp. 79-105.
7 *Ibid.*, 1910, p. 169

8 *Ibid.*, 1885, pp. 128–32; Ontario, *Statutes*, 1887, c. 36; Splane, *Social Welfare in Ontario*, pp. 264–5; Latimer, 'Methods of Child Care,' pp. 46–9. For a later expression of concern on 'baby farming,' see Saywell, ed., *The Canadian Journal of Lady Aberdeen, 1893–1898*, pp. 35–6.

9 NCW, *Yearbook*, 1895, pp. 280–6; *Canadian Churchman*, 13 October 1898, p. 617

10 See, for example, PAC, MG 28/147, 'Minutes of the Salt Fleet Women's Institute,' 1899.

11 NCW, *Yearbook*, 1896, pp. 43–4

12 *Ibid.*, 1901, pp. iv–v; *ibid.*, 1902, pp. iv–v; *ibid.*, 1905, pp. iii–iv

13 A.D. Blackader, 'The More Important Causes Underlying the Heavy Infantile Death Rate in Large Cities and the Benefits to be Derived from the Establishment of Milk Depots,' PHJ, III (July 1912), p. 370; see also Madame Jules Tessier, 'The Value of Milk Depots,' PHJ, VIII (March 1917), p. 65.

14 NCW, *Yearbook*, 1906, p. 30

15 For a survey of the work to reduce infant mortality in Britain and, to a lesser extent, in France and the United States, see G.F. McCleary, *The Early History of the Infant Welfare Movement* (London: Lewis, 1933).

16 Frazer, *English Public Health*, p. 334

17 Rosen, *History of Public Health*, p. 359; Winslow, *Biggs*, pp. 186–94; Oliver, *Man Who Lived for Tomorrow*, chap. 11

18 Benjamin Broadbent, 'The International Congresses on the Prevention of Infantile Mortality,' *The Child*, I (September 1911), pp. 1048–51; PHJ, II (September 1911), p. 44

19 Frazer explains that the incidence of the disease increases very rapidly once the temperature of the earth according to the four-foot earth thermometer reaches or exceeds 56°F. *English Public Health*, p. 333.

20 Saskatchewan Bureau of Health, *Report*, 1910, pp. 27, 35

21 Robert E. Wodehouse, 'Vital Statistics Pertaining to Infant Mortality,' PHJ, II (August 1911), p. 363

22 *Ibid.*

23 See, for example, Rene Bache, 'Massacre of the Innocents,' *Canadian Therapeutist*, I (August 1910), pp. 405–6; C.J. Fagan, 'Causes of Dysentry,' PHJ, I (October 1910), pp. 512–14; 'Infant Feeding,' Saskatchewan Bureau of Health, *Report*, 1910, pp. 10–15.

24 This paragraph only touches on the highlights of an as yet uninvestigated topic. There was, for example, a long and complex debate between advocates of certified and pasteurized milk. See the literature cited below.

25 'The Milk Commission,' PHJ, I (September 1910), pp. 459–60. For an expression of earlier interest in the matter, see Ontario Board of Health, *Report*,

1907, pp. 17–23; W.T. Shirriff, 'Municipal Milk Supply,' PHJ, III (May 1912), pp. 260–6. For work elsewhere, see Rosen, *History of Public Health*, pp. 358–60; Ernst J. Lederle, 'Sanitary Control of the Milk Supply,' New York Department of Health *Monthly Bulletin*, I (June 1911), pp. 126–34; Hermann M. Biggs, 'Infectious Diseases and the Milk Supply,' *ibid.*, pp. 133–5. For a more general account of the New York work, which Canadians frequently cited as a model to be followed, see Winslow, *Biggs*, chaps 11 and 13.

26 J.H. Elliott, 'Shall We Have Pure Milk in Canada,' PHJ, II (August 1911), pp. 353–7; E.C. Shroeder, 'The Relation of Bovine Tuberculosis to Public Health,' *ibid.* (June 1911), pp. 263–72

27 'Hygiene and the Ontario Legislature,' PHJ, II (April 1911), pp. 170–1; Canada, Commission of Conservation, *Report*, 1911, p. 40; British Columbia, *Report of the Royal Commission on Milk-supply in British Columbia: under "Public Inquiries Act"* (Victoria: King's Printer, 1913)

28 Ontario Board of Health, *Report*, 1910, pp. 137–71; *Canadian Therapeutist*, I (July 1910), p. 366

29 For additional references providing an overview of the efforts of milk campaigners to make their standards effective across the nation, see T.H. Whitelaw, 'Municipal Control of Milk Supplies,' PHJ, III (November 1912), pp. 621–5; Hoyes Lloyd, 'How Toronto Controls Her Milk Supply,' *ibid.*, V (May 1914), pp. 446–50; J.A. Baudouin, 'Pasteurization of Milk Supply,' *ibid.*, IX (January 1918), pp. 11–26; and, from 1910 onward, the reports of the National Council of Women's Public Health Committee.

30 R.Y. Parry, 'Keeping Babies Well,' Canadian Conference of Charities and Correction, *Proceedings*, 1911, pp. 65–70; Helen Smith, 'Keeping Babies Well,' *ibid.*, pp. 70–4

31 Geraldine Steinmetz, 'The Clean Milk Campaign in Hamilton,' *American Journal of Public Hygiene*, VI (October 1909), pp. 98–101

32 J. Heurner Mullen, 'History of the Organization of the Babies Dispensary Guild, Hamilton,' PHJ, VI (November 1915), p. 542

33 Smith, 'Child Welfare,' NCW, *Yearbook*, 1912, p. 67

34 Mullen, 'Babies' Dispensary Guild,' PHJ, VI (November 1915), p. 543; Helen Smith, 'The Possibilities of Women's Work in Relation to the Babies Dispensary, Hamilton,' *ibid.*, 548–9

35 Smith, 'Child Welfare,' NCW, *Yearbook*, 1912, p. 68

36 W.L. Cody, 'The Scope and Function of the Medical Staff of the Babies' Dispensary, Hamilton,' PHJ, VI (November 1915), p. 546.

37 Mullen, 'Babies' Dispensary Guild,' *ibid.*, pp. 543–4

38 Chester S. Walters, 'The Duty of the City to the Child: What Can be Accomplished by a "Baby Week,"' *ibid.*, pp. 540–1; J. Heurner Mullen, 'Child Wel-

fare in a Democracy,' *ibid.*, IX (October 1918), pp. 445–56; *Handbook*, pp. 135–6.

39 Ontario Department of the Provincial Secretary, *Infant Mortality: Special Report by Dr. Helen MacMurchy* (Toronto: King's Printer, 1910); Ontario Department of the Provincial Secretary, *Infant Mortality: Second Special Report, by Dr. Helen MacMurchy* (Toronto: King's Printer, 1911); Ontario Department of the Provincial Secretary, *Infant Mortality: Third Report, by Dr. Helen MacMurchy* (Toronto: King's Printer, 1912). See also 'Infant Mortality,' PHJ, II (October 1911), p. 490.

40 See, for example, C.A. Hodgetts, 'Unsanitary Housing,' Canada, Commission of Conservation, *Report*, 1911, pp. 50–84; 'Committee on the Public Health Report,' *ibid.*, 1913, pp. 3–9; G. Frank Beer, 'Work of the Toronto Housing Company,' *ibid.*, 1914, pp. 116–20; Canada, Commission of Conservation, *Civic Improvement League for Canada: Report of Preliminary Conference held under the Auspices of the Commission ... at Ottawa, November 19, 1915* (Ottawa: Mortimer, 1916); Canada, Commission of Conservation, *Civic Improvement: Report of the Conference of Civic Improvement League of Canada held in Co-operation with the Commission ... Ottawa, January 20th, 1916* (Ottawa: n. pub., 1916); Canada, Commission of Conservation, *Urban and Rural Development in Canada: A Report of a Conference held in Winnipeg, May 28–30, 1917* (Ottawa: n. pub., 1917).

41 Alan Brown, 'Infant and Child Welfare Work,' PHJ, IX (April 1918), p. 148

42 As late as 1930, the Dominion Bureau of Statistics estimated that only 22 per cent of live births occurred in hospitals. CYB, 1952–3, p. 186

43 Horace L. Brittain, 'Administration of the Toronto Department of Public Health,' Part II, PHJ, V (August 1915), p. 375

44 Robert E. Mills, 'Birth Registration and Infant Welfare,' *ibid.*, IX (April 1918), p. 171

45 See, for example, NCW, *Yearbook*, 1904, p. 86; 'Infant Mortality,' PHJ, II (May 1911), p. 220.

46 Mills, 'Birth Registration,' PHJ, IX (April 1918), p. 171; see also, NCW, *Yearbook*, 1906, p. 30

47 Brittain, 'Administration of the Toronto Department of Public Health,' Part I, PHJ, VI (July 1915), p. 323

48 Mills, 'Birth Registration,' PHJ, IX (April 1918), p. 171

49 CYB, 1948–9, pp. 185–8

50 Saskatchewan Bureau of Public Health, *Report*, 1914, p. 110; see also Maurice M. Seymour, 'The Value of Vital Statistics in Public Health Work,' PHJ, VIII (October 1917), pp. 245–51.

51 Blackader, '... Causes Underlying Heavy Infantile Death Rate ...,' PHJ, III (July 1912), p. 369; Robert E. Wodehouse, 'Vital Statistics Pertaining to Infant Mortality,' *ibid.*, II (August 1911), p. 363; C.N. Laurie, 'Sanitary Work Among the Foreign Population,' *ibid.*. IV (August 1913), pp. 455–7; J.S. Woodsworth, 'The Significance of Human Waste in Modern Life and its Causes,' *ibid.*, V (January 1914), pp. 21–5; Brown, 'Infant and Child Welfare Work,' *ibid.*, IX (April 1918), pp. 145–61; J.M. Shaver, 'Civic Problems Caused by the Immigrant,' *ibid.*, VII (October 1916), p. 433

52 Saskatchewan Bureau of Public Health, *Report*, 1914, p. 44

53 See, for example, Maurice M. Seymour, 'Presidential Address,' PHJ, VI (December 1915), pp. 593–605.

54 Saskatchewan Bureau of Public Health, *Report*, 1914, p. 46

55 *Handbook*, p. 185. The *Report* of the Saskatchewan Bureau of Health for 1914, p. 46, clearly states that such grants were already being paid and correspondence in the Premier Martin papers (p. 41130) seem to confirm this. There is, however, no listing for this expense under the Saskatchewan *Public Accounts* until 1918–19. Christine MacDonald, Legislative Library, Regina, to N. Sutherland, 30 October 1969; D.H. Bocking, Saskatchewan Archives, Saskatoon, to N. Sutherland, 12 December 1969

56 *Handbook*, pp. 186, 133, 154; see, for example, Brittain, 'Administration of the Toronto Department of Public Health,' Part II, PHJ, VI (August 1915), pp. 366–70; George Smith, 'The Results of Three Year's Work in the Department of Child Hygiene, Toronto,' *ibid.*, IX (July 1918), pp. 310–11.

57 Ontario Board of Health, *Report*, 1920, p. 38; see also *Handbook*, pp. 126–7.

58 *Handbook*, p. 29

59 See, for example, *ibid.*, p. 64; W.J. Bell, 'Maternal Mortality,' Ontario Board of Health, *Report*, 1921, pp. 184–91.

60 'Baby Clinics,' PHJ, IV (February 1913), p. 94; 'Human Sacrifice,' *ibid.*, pp. 95–6

61 Brittain, 'Administration of the Toronto Department of Public Health,' p. 368.

62 Enid M. Forsythe, 'Child Welfare Clinics,' *ibid.*, IX (April 1918), p. 170

63 Smith, 'Three Years' Work in the Department of Child Hygiene, Toronto,' *ibid.*, IX (July 1918), p. 310

64 *Handbook*, p. 130

65 Smith, 'Three Years Work in the Department of Child Hygiene,' PHJ, IX (July 1918), p. 313

66 PHJ, III (September 1912), p. 529; see also W.H. Atherton, 'Child Welfare and the City,' *ibid.*, II (October 1911), p. 465; NCW, *Yearbook*, 1913, p. vii.

67 NCW, *Yearbook*, 1914, p. 39
68 Baudouin, 'War Against Infant Mortality,' PHJ, V (May 1914), p. 306
69 Evans, 'Chairman's Address,' PHJ, XI (February 1920), pp. 70–8; *Handbook*, pp. 152–8
70 See, for example, 'Progress of Fort William's Campaign Against Infant Mortality,' PHJ, II (September 1911), p. 439; 'Infant Welfare Work in Regina,' *ibid.*, IV (June 1913), pp. 391–2; Vancouver Medical Health Officer, *Report*, 1916, pp. 15–16; *ibid.*, 1919, p. 21; Brown, 'Infant and Child Welfare Work,' PHJ, IX (April 1918), pp. 158–9; *Handbook, passim.*
71 A thirty-page pamphlet, *The Child* (n. pl.: Metropolitan Life Insurance Company, 1916), had at least one Canadian printing; see J.A. Amyot, 'The Place of Voluntary Effort in Federal Administration,' *Fourth Annual Canadian Conference on Child Welfare: Proceedings and Papers, Ottawa, 1923* (Ottawa: King's Printer, 1926), p. 57.
72 *Handbook*, p. 9
73 See, for example, the great increase in articles on infant care, and especially on breast feeding, in American popular magazines of the era. Many of these circulated widely in Canada. Clark E. Vincent, 'Trends in Infant Care Ideas,' *Child Development*, XXII (September 1951), p. 200.
74 *Handbook*, p. 70
75 *Ibid.*, p. 140; Ontario Board of Health, *Report*, 1920, p. 196; Vancouver Medical Health Officer, *Report*, 1916, p. 16; *ibid.*, 1921, p. 15
76 Evans, 'Chairman's Address,' PHJ, XI (February 1920), pp. 70–8.
77 'Birth Registration and Infant Welfare,' PHJ, IX (April 1918), p. 171
78 *Changing Size of the Family*, pp. 289–90
79 N.E. McKinnon, 'Mortality Reductions in Ontario, 1900–1942,' PHJ, XXXV (December 1944), pp. 481–4.
80 British Columbia, Registrar of Births, Deaths and Marriages, *Report*, 1889, p. 305; *ibid.*, 1894, p. 571; *ibid.*, 1899, p. 531; *ibid.*, 1904, p. 5; *ibid.*, 1909, p. 5; *ibid.*, 1914, p. L27; *ibid.*, 1918–19, p. B50. For the years noted up to 1909, the province recorded these deaths in two groups, those under 3 and those '3, and under 10.' For 1914 and for 1918–19, the categories were 'under 2' and '2 to 10 years.' Since ten-year-olds were thus not included in the figures used in the text for the years up to 1909 and were included after that date, the decline may have been slightly sharper than recorded.
81 For a convenient summary of much of the related data, see Canada, Dominion Bureau of Statistics, *Canadian Conference on Children 1965: Selected Statistics on Children* (Ottawa: Queen's Printer, 1965), pp. 41–61.
82 While it may be only roughly analogous to the Canadian experience, Hoffman's 1921 survey of changes in American mortality included the decline

in infant mortality as an important factor which had contributed to the general improvement of life expectancy in the United States, and especially in the previous fifteen years. Frederick L. Hoffman, 'American Mortality Progress During the Last Half Century,' in Ravenel, *A Half Century of Public Health*, pp. 94–117.

83 Urquhart and Buckley, *Historical Statistics of Canada*, pp. 14–15

CHAPTER 5

1 The quotation in the title of the chapter is from Mrs Adam Shortt, 'Some Social Aspects of Tuberculosis,' PHJ, III (June 1912), p. 307

2 See, for example, NCW, *Yearbook*, 1896, p. 455.

3 'Heredity,' *Canadian Methodist Magazine*, XIX (1884), pp. 257, 265–6

4 NCW, *Yearbook*, 1896, pp. 456–7

5 Canadian Conference of Charities and Correction, *Proceedings*, 1901, pp. 13–16

6 See, for example, Ontario, Provincial Secretary's Department, Feeble-Minded in Ontario, *Reports*, 1908, 1910, 1913–15; Helen MacMurchy, 'The Relation of Feeble-Mindedness to Other Social Problems,' National Conference of Charities and Correction, *Proceedings*, XLIII (1916), pp. 229–35; Helen MacMurchy, *The Almosts: A Study of the Feeble-Minded* (Boston: Houghton Mifflin, 1920).

7 NCW, *Yearbook*, 1918, p. 53

8 There were, however, some exceptions; see J.G. Adami, '"Unto the Third and Fourth Generation": A Study in Eugenics,' *Canadian Medical Association Journal*, II (November 1912), pp. 963–80.

9 Lucy M. Brooking, 'We Pay,' PHJ, V (April 1914), p. 216; C.K. Clarke, 'The Defective Immigrant,' *ibid.*, VII (November 1916), p. 465.

10 NCW, *Yearbook*, 1896, p. 456

11 'Heredity as a Cause of Mental Defectiveness,' PHJ, IV (March 1913), p. 126; see also, 'Editorial,' *ibid.*, III (June 1912), pp. 335–6, 'Editorial,' *ibid.*, III (September 1912), p. 511; A.P. Reid, 'Heredity and Public Health,' *ibid.*, IV (April 1913), pp. 225–8; Miss Mary A. Mackenzie, 'What Conservation of a Nation's Health Involves,' NCW, *Yearbook*, 1912, pp. 59–63

12 'Some Social Aspects of Tuberculosis,' PHJ, III (June 1912), p. 307

13 While there is no general history of the mental hygiene movement in Canada, some aspects of it are explained in Cyril Greenland, 'The Treatment of the Mentally Retarded in Ontario: an Historical Note,' *Canadian Psychiatric Association Journal*, VIII (October 1963), pp. 328–36; Cyril Greenland,

Charles Kirk Clarke: A Pioneer in Canadian Psychiatry (Toronto: The Clarke Institute of Psychiatry, 1966); The Canadian Mental Health Association, *Milestones in Mental Health: A Record of Achievements ... The Canadian Mental Health Association: 1918-1958* (Toronto: The Canadian Mental Health Association, 1958). For an account of the eugenics movement in the United States which also considers its European origins, see Mark H. Haller, *Eugenics: Hereditarian Attitudes in American Thought* (New Brunswick, N.J.: Rutgers University Press, 1963). Richard Hofstadter briefly outlined the movement in his *Social Darwinism in American Thought* (Rev. ed.; Boston: Beacon Hill, 1955), pp. 161-7. See also John Duffy, 'Mental Strain and "Overpressure" in the Schools: A Nineteenth-Century Viewpoint,' *Journal of the History of Medicine and Allied Sciences*, XXIII (January 1968), pp. 63-79.

14 See, for example, PHJ, III (December 1912), p. 727; 'Editorial,' *ibid.*, IV (March 1913), p. 161; Mrs M.K. Stead, 'The Nova Scotia League for the Care and Protection of the Feeble-Minded,' *ibid.*, V (April 1914), p. 219; 'Report of the Committee on the Care of the Mentally Deficient,' NCW, *Yearbook*, 1914, pp. 21-7; T.H. Wills, 'Hamilton Branch of the Provincial Association for the Care of the Feeble-Minded,' PHJ, IX (March 1918), pp. 112-15; M.K. Stead, 'Care of Mentally Deficient,' NCW, *Yearbook*, 1918, pp. 50-3. In 1916, while he was director of the short-lived Bureau of Social Research, J.S. Woodsworth conducted a survey of mental defectives in the prairie provinces. The results were published in newspapers in each of the provinces. Kenneth McNaught, *A Prophet in Politics: A Biography of J.S. Woodsworth* (Toronto: University of Toronto Press, 1959), pp. 73-4

15 Adami, 'Unto the Third and Fourth Generation,' p. 965. In expressing their concern about immigrants, the mental hygienists contributed a thread to the Anglo-Saxon racism which was popular amongst a number of English Canadians at this time. As the Church of England's Bishop of Huron put it, 'with the great immigration of foreign peoples into Canada there would be none of the old Anglo-Saxon stock left in 150 years, if race suicide prevails.' NCW, *Yearbook*, 1912, p. 69

16 'The Defective Immigrant,' PHJ, VII (November 1916), p. 462

17 'Mental Hygiene Survey – Province of Saskatchewan,' CJMH, III (January 1922), pp. 318-19

18 Marjorie Keys, 'The Problem of the Feeble-Minded,' PHJ, IX (March 1918), p. 99; Chas. G. Fraser, 'Feeble Minded and the Public Schools,' *ibid.*, VII (April 1916), pp. 237-8.

19 *A Statistical Review of Canadian Schools*, Canadian Council on Child Welfare Publication no. 6 (Ottawa: The Council, 1923), p. 25

20 'Survey of Intelligence Testing,' CJMH, III (April 1921), p. 40

21 'Mentally Deficient Children,' PHJ, IX (March 1918), p. 104
22 'The Gifted Child,' *ibid.*, III (April 1921), p. 267. See also Tait, 'The Exceptional Child,' PHJ, V (September 1914), p. 565.
23 PHJ, II (July 1911), p. 337; see also R.II. Cowley, 'Mentally Defective Pupils in the Public Schools of Toronto,' *ibid.*, V (April 1914), pp. 223–4.
24 'Nova Scotia Survey,' CJMH, III (April 1921), p. 45
25 See, for example, Canadian National Committee for Mental Hygiene, *Manitoba Survey (Confidential Report)*, (n. pl.: n. pub., 1918); 'Survey of the Province of Manitoba,' CJMH, I (April 1919), pp. 77–82; 'Mental Hygiene Survey of the Province of British Columbia,' *ibid.*, II (April 1920), especially pp. 14–28; E.K. Clarke, 'Survey of the Toronto Public Schools,' *ibid.*, II (July 1920), pp. 182–5; Morphy and Tait, 'Mental Hygiene Survey of Montreal's Protestant Schools,' *ibid.*, III (April 1921), pp. 49–95; E.J. Pratt, 'The Application of the Binet-Simon Tests (Stanford Revision) to a Toronto Public School,' CJMH, III (April 1921), pp. 95–116.
26 'Survey of Guelph Public Schools,' CJMH, I (January 1920), pp. 342–6; C.K. Clarke, 'Report of the Medical Director,' *ibid.*, II (October 1920), p. 252
27 'The Relation of the Juvenile Court to the Community,' *ibid.*, I (October 1919), p. 234. For the context of this discussion, see below, Part III.
28 'Mental Hygiene Survey of the Province of British Columbia,' *ibid.*, II (April 1920), pp. 28, 55; see also British Columbia, *Report of the Royal Commission on Mental Hygiene* (Victoria: King's Printer, 1927), pp. CC22–3
29 Child Welfare Association of British Columbia *Second Annual Convention* (Vancouver, B.C.: n. pub., n.d.), p. 15
30 'The Exceptional Child,' PHJ, V (September 1914), p. 568
31 Ontario, *Sessional Papers*, 1907, no. 62, p. 29; see also 'Editorial,' PHJ, IV (April 1913), p. 242; E.J. Conboy, 'Care of the Feeble-Minded,' *ibid.*, VII (December 1916), pp. 505–7.
32 Canadian Conference of Charities and Correction, *Proceedings*, 1905, pp. 11–25; Carrie M. Derick, 'Symposium on the Care of Defective Children,' NCW, *Yearbook*, 1905, pp. 72–7; Ottawa Local Council of Women, 'Minute Books, 1907–1912,' PAC MG28/I32 vol. 4, 5; Carrie M. Derick, 'The Montreal Local Council of Women and Mental Hygiene,' CJMH, I (July 1919), pp. 141–4
33 'Mental Hygiene Survey – Province of Saskatchewan,' CJMH, III (January 1922), p. 382; see also the recommendations of the Ontario Commissioner on the Care and Control of the Mentally Deficient, in F.E. Hodgins, 'The Mentally Deficient in Ontario,' PHJ, XI (March 1920), pp. 126–34
34 'The Exceptional Child,' p. 569.

35 See, for example, Alberta Mental Health Study, *Report*, 1968.
36 C.M. Hincks, 'The Scope and Aims of the Mental Hygiene Movement in Canada,' CJMH, I (April 1919), pp. 20–9; 'The First Year of the Canadian National Committee for Mental Hygiene,' *ibid*., pp. 70–6
37 Clarke and other workers constantly cited the clinic's findings in their talks and writings. See, for example, Helen MacMurchy, 'The Mentally Defective Child,' PHJ, VI (February 1915), pp. 85–6; Clarke, 'The Defective Immigrant,' *ibid*., VII (November 1916), pp. 462–5; C.K. Clarke, 'The Work of the Psychiatric Clinic at the Toronto General Hospital,' *ibid*., IX (March 1918), pp. 97–8; C.K. Clarke, 'A Study of 5,600 Cases Passing through the Psychiatric Clinic of the Toronto General Hospital. A Special Study of 188 Clinic Cases – also A Survey of 767 Cases of Illegitimacy,' CJMH, III (July 1921), pp. 11–24.
38 Clarke, 'Report of the Medical Director,' CJMH, II (October 1920), pp. 252–4. The standards set by the National Committee were summarized in *Fifth ... Canadian Conference on Child Welfare*, p. 59. In 1927, the British Columbia Royal Commission on Mental Hygiene concluded that the fault that then existed regarding immigration was 'in lack of facilities for examination rather than in the law.' *Report*, p. CC 30. The National Committee had also commissioned a major study of Canadian immigration. Greenland, *Clarke*, pp. 20–2; W.G. Smith, *A Study of Canadian Immigration* (Toronto: Ryerson, 1920).
39 See, for example, NCW, *Yearbook*, 1906, pp. iii–iv; 'Editorial Comment,' PHJ, V (May 1914), pp. 323–4; NCW, *Yearbook*, 1914, p. xi; Mrs M.H. Kerr, 'Defective Children,' PHJ, VI (December 1915), pp. 620–7; Mary E. Blackwell, 'Auxiliary Classes in the Public Schools,' *ibid*., pp. 622–7; Fraser, 'Feeble Minded and the Public Schools,' *ibid*., VII (April 1916), pp. 237–8; Peter Sandiford, 'The Attitude of the Educator Towards the Feeble-Minded,' *ibid*., VII (December 1916), pp. 496–7; Mrs W.E. Groves, 'Special Auxiliary Classes,' CJMH, I (July 1919), pp. 182–7; Child Welfare Association of British Columbia, *Second Annual Convention*, pp. 21–3; S.B. Sinclair, *Special Training for School-age Children in Need of Special Care: Ontario's Auxiliary Classes*, Canadian Council on Child Welfare, Publication no. 16 (Ottawa: The Council, 1928).
40 A. Josephine Dauphinee, 'Vancouver's Sub-Normal Problem,' CJMH, III (April 1921), pp. 117–24; 'Mental Hygiene Survey of the Province of British Columbia,' CJMH, II (April 1920), pp. 14–21. In 1924, the Putman-Weir study of education in British Columbia concluded that Vancouver had adopted an 'esoteric' philosophy of dealing with subnormal pupils. At a time when the annual cost per elementary pupil in the city was $65, for the School Board to employ twenty-five teachers to educate 208 subnormal at an annual

cost of $256 per pupil was, the commissioners decided, 'indefensible.'
British Columbia, *Survey of the School System* by J.H. Putman and G.M.
Weir (Victoria: King's Printer, 1925), pp. 391–4

41 *Fifth ... Canadian Conference on Child Welfare*, p. 56
42 Derick, 'The Montreal Local Council of Women and Mental Hygiene,'
CJMH, I (July 1919), pp. 141–5; 'Report of the Associate Medical Director,
Montreal, P.Q.,' *ibid.*, II (October 1920), pp. 255–6.
43 Child Welfare Association of British Columbia, *Report of the First Annual
Convention held in Vancouver, Dec. 12, 13 and 14, 1918* (Vancouver:
Grandview Printers, n.d.); *ibid.*, *Second Annual Convention* (Vancouver:
n. pub., n.d.)
44 'Report of the Nominating Committee,' CJMH, II (October 1920), p. 251
45 *Fifth ... Canadian Conference on Child Welfare*, p. 139
46 *Ibid.*, p. 56
47 British Columbia, *Report ... on Mental Hygiene*, pp. CC36–CC41
48 Canada, DBS, 'The Canadian Family,' p. 125; see also British Columbia,
'Final Report of the Royal Commission on Mental Hygiene,' *Sessional
Papers*, 1928.
49 British Columbia, *Report ... on Mental Hygiene*, pp. CC6, CC10
50 See, for example, *ibid.*, pp. CC36–7; MacLean *Statistical Review*, pp. 25–8,
36–40.

CHAPTER 6

1 The quotation in the title of the chapter is from Amyot, 'The Place of Voluntary Effort in Federal Administration,' *Fourth ... Canadian Conference on
Child Welfare*, p. 57
2 Saskatchewan, *A Survey of Education in the Province of Saskatchewan:
A Report by Harold W. Foght, Ph.D.* (Regina: King's Printer, 1918), pp.
52–62, 160–1
3 'Extending Health Services to the Rural Community,' *Fourth ... Canadian
Conference on Child Welfare*, p. 70; British Columbia, *Survey of the School
System*, p. 50
4 'Medical Inspection of Schools in Ontario,' PHJ, V (March 1914), p. 162;
'Medical Inspection of Schools,' *ibid.*, V (November 1914), p. 683
5 Ontario, Department of Education, *Report*, 1918, pp. 16–17
6 *Handbook*, pp. 101–21
7 Brown, 'Infant and Child Welfare Work,' PHJ, IX (April 1918), p. 160;
Ontario Board of Health, *Report*, 1920, pp. 39–40, 62, 156; *ibid.*, 1921,

pp. 175–80; J.W.S. McCullough, 'A Decade of Public Health Progress,' PHJ, XI (July 1920), p. 299; 'Child Welfare in Ontario,' *ibid.*, pp. 336–7

8 Saskatchewan Archives, Premier W.M. Martin Papers, 'Memorandum for Mr. Scott,' 19 July 1916

9 *Ibid.*, Martin to Browne, 22 February 1917

10 PHJ, XI (September 1920), p. 430

11 Jean E. Browne, 'Health Education in Rural Schools,' *ibid.*, XI (December 1920), p. 528; *Handbook*, pp. 171, 177, 179–80

12 Saskatchewan Bureau of Public Health, *Report*, 1917–18, pp. 27–8

13 NCW, *Yearbook*, 1918, pp. 154–5

14 Saskatchewan Bureau of Public Health, *Report*, 1917–18, pp. 27–8

15 *Ibid.*, 1919–20, pp. 9, 20–1; *Handbook*, pp. 185–6

16 NCW, *Yearbook*, 1918, pp. 117–18

17 Struthers, *The School Nurse*, p. 98

18 Ontario Board of Health, *Report*, 1920, p. 55

19 To sample the warm rhetoric of this debate, see 'The Ontario Health Officers Association,' PHJ, VI (June 1913), p. 375; 'Editorial,' *ibid.*, IV (August 1913), p. 469; 'Medical Inspection of Schools,' *ibid.*, IV (September 1913), pp. 516–17; 'Administration of Medical Inspection of Schools,' *ibid.*, V (March 1914), pp. 163–5; T.H. Whitelaw, 'Medical Inspection of Schools in Edmonton, Alberta,' *ibid.*, V (December 1914), pp. 714–7; Peter H. Bryce, 'The Work of Bureaus of Child Hygiene and of Medical Inspection in Schools,' *ibid.*, VII (February 1916), pp. 59–62; Toronto Bureau of Municipal Research, *Consolidation of Health Administration Under One Department* (Toronto: The Bureau, 1916); Toronto Bureau of Municipal Research, *Report*, 1917, p. 31; Struthers, *The School Nurse*, pp. 94–102; *Handbook*, pp. 121, 128.

20 Ontario Board of Health, *Report*, 1921, pp. 22–3, 167

21 See *Handbook*, pp. 48, 131.

22 NCW, *Yearbook*, 1920, p. 45; see also the report of the annual meeting of the Medical Health Officers of Nova Scotia in Liverpool on 4 July 1918, PHJ, IX (August 1918), pp. 369–72.

23 See, for example, Mrs Massey, 'What New Zealand Does to Promote the Health of Women and Children,' PHJ, IV (August 1913), pp. 462–4; 'The Health of Women and Children,' *ibid.*, IX (March 1918), pp. 137–9; Ontario Board of Health, *Report*, 1920, p. 38.

24 NCW, *Yearbook*, 1918, p. 131

25 *Handbook*, pp. 199–200; John Murray Gibbon, *The Victorian Order of Nurses for Canada: 50th Anniversary, 1897–1947* (Montreal: The Victorian Order, 1947), pp. 79–82; Canadian Red Cross, British Columbia Division, *Report*, 1920, pp. 8–9.

26 See, for example, the two special issues devoted to child health and welfare, *Public Health Journal*, IX (April and July), 1918.

27 The Red Cross had raised over $35,000,000 for its war work. Mackenzie Porter, *To All Men: The Story of the Canadian Red Cross* (Toronto: McClelland & Stewart, 1960), pp. 53-5.

28 Its work across Canada is summarized in Canadian Red Cross Society, *The Role of One Voluntary Organization in Canada's Health Services: A Brief Presented to the Royal Commission on Health Services on Behalf of the Central Council of the Canadian Red Cross Society* (Toronto: National Office, Canadian Red Cross Society, 1962), pp. 116-21, 125-7.

29 Canadian Red Cross, British Columbia Division, *Report*, 1920, pp. 8-9; Margaret M. Street, *Watch-fires on the Mountains: the Life and Writings of Ethel Johns* (Toronto: University of Toronto Press, 1973), chaps 13 and 14; see also Lillian G. Hiltz, 'History of Outpost Hospitals and Nursing Services in British Columbia' (Vancouver: British Columbia Division Canadian Red Cross Society, 1967), mimeographed.

30 Vera Wallace, 'The Ministering Angel, Plus a Little Knowledge,' PHJ, XV (March 1924), p. 121; Hiltz, 'History,' pp. 3-4

31 Jean Browne, 'The Programme of the Junior Red Cross,' *Fourth ... Canadian Conference on Child Welfare*, pp. 72-7. The early history of the Canadian Junior Red Cross is summarized in Canadian Red Cross, *The Role of One Voluntary Organization*, pp. 55-60.

32 Toronto *Globe*, 21 October 1920, p. 6; Canada, Department of Health, *Report*, 1921, pp. 22-3; Helen MacMurchy, 'Child Welfare in Canada,' *The Annals*, CV (January 1923), pp. 267-76

33 *Handbook*, p. 9

34 NCW, *Yearbook*, 1918, pp. 148, 154-5, 163-5

35 See, for example, *ibid.*, 1920, pp. 176-229; Mary Power, 'The Management of a Child Welfare Week in Small Cities and Towns with Results,' PHJ, IX (August 1918), 362-3; 'Saving Babies in Halifax,' *ibid.*, XI (February 1920), pp. 84-7; I.N. Cole, 'Mental Hygiene and the Baby Welfare Exhibit at Halifax,' CJMH, I (January 1920), pp. 347-9; Ontario Board of Health, *Report*, 1919, pp. 35-41; *Handbook*, pp. 18, 36, 53, 75, 84, 101, 150-1, 184.

36 Robert E. Wodehouse, 'Public Health Information Bearing on Pre-Natal Subjects,' PHJ, XI (May 1920), pp. 211-15

37 Ontario Board of Health, *Report*, 1919, 41-3; Miss Knox did the same job again in St Thomas. NCW, *Yearbook*, 1920, p. 211

38 See Ontario Board of Health, *Report*, 1920, pp. 171, 185-6; *ibid.*, 1921, pp. 181-2, 195, 202, 206, 210, 216, 222, 233, 238.

39 *Handbook*, p. 99; Canadian Red Cross, *The Role of One Voluntary Organization*, p. 126.

40 For a general historical survey of the development and extension of public health work in each province, see Defries, *The Development of Public Health in Canada, passim.*

41 A few years later, George M. Weir confirmed this judgment. Commenting on the Maritimes, Weir noted that 'these Provinces lag behind the rest of Canada in public health work.' *Survey of Nursing Education in Canada* (Toronto: University of Toronto Press, 1932), p. 142

42 See Rosen, *History of Public Health*, pp. 374-82; Lavinia L. Dock, 'The History of Public Health Nursing,' in Ravenel, *A Half Century of Public Health*, pp. 439-52

43 Elizabeth L. Smellie, 'The Responsibility of the Voluntary Agency With Regard to the Mother and Child,' *Fifth ... Canadian Conference on Child Welfare*, pp. 96-7

44 Macgillivrary S. Fraser, 'The Child Health Programme of a Community,' *Fourth ... Canadian Conference on Child Welfare*, p. 69

45 *Ibid.*

46 See Weir, *Survey of Nursing Education*, pp. 135-7; see also Canada, Royal Commission on Health Services, *Nursing Education in Canada*, by Helen K. Mussallem (Ottawa: Queen's Printer, 1965), chap 2; Mary Q. Innis, ed., *Nursing Education in a Changing Society* (Toronto: University of Toronto Press, 1970), chaps 4 and 9.

47 Weir, *Survey of Nursing Education*, p. 118

48 Amyot, 'The Place of Voluntary Effort in Federal Administration,' *Fourth ... Canadian Conference on Child Welfare*, p. 57

CHAPTER 7

1 The quotation in the title of Part III is from J.M. Gibson, 'The Children's Act,' *The Methodist Magazine*, XXXIX (1894), p. 39

2 Toronto *Globe*, 10 September 1887, p. 15; *ibid.*, 12 September 1887, p. 4; *Proceedings of the Annual Congress of the National Prison Association of the United States, held at Toronto, September 10-15, 1887* (Chicago: Knight Empress and Leonard, 1889), pp. 31-55, 48, 177, 250

3 'The Children's Act,' p. 38

4 J. Edward Starr, 'First Annual Report of the Juvenile Court,' PHJ, IV (April 1913), p. 199

5 Grace Aiton, 'The Selling of Paupers By Public Auction in Sussex Parish,' New Brunswick Historical Society, *Collections*, 16 (1961), pp. 93-110

6 Splane, *Social Welfare in Ontario*, pp. 215-54; Pinchbeck and Hewitt, *Children in English Society*, Vol. I, pp. 175-99, 223-59

7 Splane, *Social Welfare in Ontario*, pp. 148-51, 172-6

8 See J. Jerald Bellomo, 'Upper Canadian Attitudes Towards Crime and Punishment (1832-1851),' *Ontario History*, LXIV (March 1972), pp. 11-26; Susan E. Houston, 'Victorian Origins of Juvenile Delinquency: A Canadian Experience,' HEQ, XII (Fall 1972), pp. 254-80; Susan E. Houston, 'Politics, Schools, and Social Change in Upper Canada,' CHR (September 1972), pp. 249-71; P.B. Waite, 'Sir Oliver Mowat's Canada: Reflections on an Un-Victorian Society,' in *Oliver Mowat's Ontario*, ed. Donald Swainson (Toronto: Macmillan, 1972), pp. 12-32.

9 Narrowly focusing in on contemporary developments in the United States dealing with juvenile delinquency, American historian Anthony Platt describes this process as a 'legislative and popular drive to "criminalize."' He also explains that '"delinquency," aside from its psychological and subcultural motivation, is the product of social judgement and "procedural definition" by public officials.' As events described in these chapters clearly indicate, one can view Canadian child-savers in a less restrictive light. Anthony M. Platt, *The Child Savers: The Invention of Delinquency* (Chicago: University of Chicago Press, 1969), pp. 13, 180

10 George Johnson, *Crime in Canada: A Monograph* (Ottawa: Queen's Printer, 1893), pp. 15-16

11 Canada, Senate, *Debates*, 1907, pp. 822, 887-8

12 Ontario, *Sessional Papers*, 1895, no. 29, app., p. 49

13 C.S. Clark, *Of Toronto the Good: A Social Study: The Queen City of Canada As It Is* (Montreal: The Toronto Publishing Co., 1898), pp. 5-6, 84

14 Although the intellectual drift of these times apparently was towards a renewal of interest in the role of heredity in the creation of drunkards, paupers, and criminals, Canadian prison workers, reformers, and politicians were, like their British and American counterparts, overwhelmingly environmentalists. British agencies moving youngsters to Canada showed that they believed changing his setting would change the child. Only towards the end of the First World War did the mental hygienists inject for a time a very strong deterministic element into the discussions of reform-centred organizations. See above, chap. 5; Haller, *Eugenics*, chap. 3.

15 *Report ... into the Prison and Reformatory System*, p. 697

16 National Prison Association, *Proceedings*, 1887, p. 183

17 Provincial Archives of Ontario, Pamphlet Collection, 1903, Box 7, 'Reforming Delinquent Children: Address Delivered by J.J. Kelso, Toronto, at the Thirtieth National Conference of Charities and Correction, Atlanta, Ga. May

8, 1903,' p. 7; see also J.J. Kelso, 'Neglected and Friendless Children,' *The Canadian Magazine*, II (January 1894), p. 213

18 Ontario, *Sessional Papers*, 1895, no. 29, p. 17

19 Gibson, 'The Children's Act,' p. 39

20 See, for example, Ontario, *Statutes*, 1874 (1st sess.), c. 29; *ibid.*, 1888, c. 40.

21 *Ibid.*, 1893, c. 45; see also Manitoba, *Statutes*, 1898, c. 6, and British Columbia, *Statutes*, 1901, c. 9.

22 See Ontario, *Sessional Papers*, 1895, no. 29, app., p. 57; see Charles, *Changing Size of the Family*, p. 7.

23 Ontario, *Sessional Papers*, 1895, no. 29, app., p. 61

24 William Blackstone, *Commentaries on the Laws of England* (15th ed.; London: A. Strahan, 1809), 4 vols., IV, pp. 22–4

25 Houston, 'Victorian Origins of Juvenile Delinquency,' pp. 254–80; Splane, *Social Welfare in Ontario*, pp. 138–43, 148–51

26 Canada, *Statutes*, 1875, c. 43; see also *ibid.*, 1880, c. 39

27 Splane, *Social Welfare in Ontario*, pp. 168–76

28 Ontario, *Sessional Papers*, 1872–1873, no. 2, p. 72, quoted in Splane, *Social Welfare in Ontario*, p. 235

29 Canada, *Statutes*, 1870, c. 32; *ibid.*, 1884, c. 45

30 Ontario, *Statutes*, 1880, c. 34

31 *Ibid.*, 1888, c. 40. Canadians have never altogether resolved the problem raised by the sometimes artificial separation of the neglected and the delinquent. In some provinces, reported a federal government committee in 1965, a child coming from 'a certain home environment' would be 'charged and adjudged as a delinquent in proceedings before the juvenile court.' In another province 'coming from the same kind of home environment,' he would be dealt with 'as a so-called "protection" or "neglect" case,' against whom no charge would be laid. In the first, the child was likely to be 'scorned by the public as a young malefactor'; in the second, he might be 'the object of public sympathy and understanding.' Canada, Department of Justice, *Juvenile Delinquency in Canada: The Report of the Department of Justice Committee on Juvenile Delinquency* (Ottawa: King's Printer, 1965), p. 43

32 *Report ... into the Prison and Reformatory System*, p. 484

33 Ontario, *Sessional Papers*, 1895, no. 29, app., pp. 35–7; see also F. [S.] Card, 'The Ontario Reformatory for Boys,' *The Methodist Magazine*, XXXIX (1894), p. 310.

34 Canada, Senate, *Debates*, 1894, p. 349

35 Ontario, *Sessional Papers*, 1895, no. 29, p. 11

36 According to the Criminal Code, it was 'lawful for every parent, or person in the place of a parent, schoolmaster or master, to use force by way of correc-

tion towards any child, pupil or apprentice under his care, provided that
such force is reasonable under the circumstances.' Canada, *Revised Statutes*,
1906, c. 146

37 Ontario, *Sessional Papers*, 1895, no. 29, p. 25; see also, *ibid.*, 1902, no. 43,
p. 12; Canadian Conference of Charities and Correction, *Proceedings*, 1901,
pp. 19–20; NCW, *Yearbook*, 1904, pp. 84–5

38 Ontario, *Sessional Papers*, 1903, no. 43, p. 11; *ibid.*, 1904, no. 43, pp. 28–9

39 National Prison Association, *Proceedings*, 1887, p. 231

40 Toronto *News*, 15 April 1891, quoted in *Protection of Children: Early
History of the Humane and Children's Aid Movement in Ontario* (Toronto:
King's Printer, 1911), p. 68

41 *Report ... into the Prison and Reformatory System*, p. 268. Geoghegan
apparently did a great deal of boy's work in his parish. As an alternative to
the lock-up, he recommended that parents give such boys a 'good application of the switch.' If they had to be confined then Geoghegan would have
put them 'in a dark cell for a while and they would never forget it.' *Ibid.*

42 *Ibid.*, p. 277

43 *Ibid.*, pp. 689–90. Businessman, sometime mayor of the city, and 'devoted
and energetic head' of the Toronto Mission Union, which was 'the most extensive organization for mission work' in Toronto, having branches and departments spread almost all over the city, W.H. Howland had a broad and
very practical experience with its unfortunates. B.F. Bull, 'City Mission
Work,' *The Methodist Magazine*, XXXVII (1893), p. 583; see also Rutherford, 'Tomorrow's Metropolis,' CHA, *Historical Papers*, (1971), *passim.*

44 Canada, Senate, *Debates*, 1894, p. 302

45 Canada, *Sessional Papers*, 1889, no. 12, pp. 69–70; xxii

46 New Westminster *British Columbian*, 10 March 1891, p. 3

47 Kamloops *Sentinel*, 4 May 1894, p. 8

48 Vancouver *Daily World*, 4 June 1897, 7 June 1897, 8 June 1897; Victoria
Colonist, 5 June 1897, 8 June 1897

49 *Protection of Children*, p. 35

50 *Report ... into the Prison and Reformatory System*, p. 25

51 *Ibid.*, p. 724

52 *Ibid.*, pp. 729–30

53 Bull, 'City Mission Work,' *The Methodist Magazine*, XXXVII (1893), p. 580

54 *Of Toronto the Good*, p. 83

55 *Report ... into the Prison and Reformatory System*, p. 475

56 Ontario, *Sessional Papers*, 1888, no. 7, p. 253

57 *Ibid.*, 1903, no. 43, p. 59

58 *Report ... into the Prison and Reformatory System*, p. 90. Apparently most

were committed for theft; of the fifty-seven new inmates sentenced to the Reformatory in 1895, four were sent there for incorrigibility, three for sexual offences, three for vagrancy, and the rest for stealing of one kind or another. Ontario, *Sessional Papers*, 1896, no. 12, p. 107

59 *Report ... into the Prison and Reformatory System*, p. 96
60 *Ibid.*, p. 102
61 Ontario, *Sessional Papers*, 1896, no. 12, p. 5
62 Canada, *Sessional Papers*, 1890, no. 9, facing p. 114
63 Splane, *Social Welfare in Ontario*, p. 232; these and other relevant statistics are summarized in Table 3
64 *Report ... into the Prison and Reformatory System*, p. 277
65 *Ibid.*, p. 487
66 *Ibid.*, p. 788
67 See Houston, 'Victorian Origins of Juvenile Delinquency,' pp. 254–80. For the wider context of the early and mid-nineteenth-century view that an institution could assume many of the characteristics of a family, see James McLachlan, *American Boarding Schools: A Historical Study* (New York: Scribners, 1970), especially pp. 114–18; Alison Prentice, 'Education and the Metaphor of the Family: the Upper Canadian Example,' HEQ, XII (Fall 1972), pp. 281–303.
68 *Report ... into the Prison and Reformatory System*, pp. 88–90
69 See, for example, National Prison Association, *Proceedings*, 1887, pp. 177–8
70 Card, 'The Ontario Reformatory for Boys,' *The Methodist Magazine*, XXXIX (1894), p. 308. For less positive comments on this system, see 'The Prison System of Ontario,' *ibid.*, pp. 99–102.
71 See Michael Bliss, '"Pure Books on Avoided Subjects": Pre-Freudian Sexual Ideas in Canada,' CHA, *Report*, 1970, pp. 89–108; Bryan Strong, 'Ideas of the Early Sex Education Movement in America, 1890–1920,' HEQ, XII (Summer 1972), pp. 129–61.
72 *Report ... into the Prison and Reformatory System*, p. 475
73 *Ibid.*, p. 478; see also the comments of William W. Murray, the superintendent of the State Industrial School, Rochester, New York, *ibid.*, pp. 785–6.
74 The origin and nature of industrial schools in the nineteenth century is very well summarized in *ibid.*, especially pp. 55–62, 64–6, 229–30, 405–6, 776–86; see also Joseph M. Hawes, *Children in Urban Society: Juvenile Delinquency in Nineteenth-Century America* (New York: Oxford University Press, 1971), *passim*.
75 Ontario, *Statutes*, 1874 (1st sess.), c. 29; *ibid.*, 1884, c. 46
76 The officers are listed in Ontario, *Sessional Papers*, 1888, no. 7, pp. 254–5.

77 *Ibid.*, 1895, no. 29, app., pp. 26, 253; *Report ... into the Prison and Reformatory System*, pp. 98–103
78 Ontario, *Sessional Papers*, 1895, no. 29, app., p. 26

CHAPTER 8

1 The quotation in the title of the chapter is from *Protection of Children: Early History of the Humane and Children's Aid Movement in Ontario: 1886-1893* (Toronto: King's Printer, 1911), p. 66
2 Splane, *Social Welfare in Ontario*, pp. 251-2, 265-8; *Protection of Children, passim*
3 *Protection of Children*, p. 66
4 *Report ... into the Prison and Reformatory System, passim*
5 *Ibid.*, pp. 40, 100, 214–15
6 *Ibid.*, pp. 87–98, 216–18
7 Ontario, *Journals*, 1893, pp. 20, 75, 107, 117, 150, 199
8 Ontario, *Statutes*, 1893, c. 45
9 J.M. Gibson, 'The Children's Act,' pp. 40–1
10 *Ibid.*, pp. 41–3, 46
11 See, for example, Toronto *Globe*, 24 April 1893, p. 4; *ibid.*, 25 April, p. 4; *ibid.*, 10 May, p. 2; *ibid.*, 20 May, p. 13; NCW, *Yearbook*, 1894, p. 113
12 Ontario, *Sessional Papers*, 1893, no. 47, pp. 14–19. Although the Toronto Children's Aid Society was founded in July 1891, it devoted its early efforts to persuading the Ontario government to introduce the 'Children's Charter.' See *Protection of Children*, pp. 68–81.
13 For a thorough and engrossing account of the work of these early years, see Kelso's annual reports. The first appeared in Ontario, *Sessional Papers*, 1893, no. 47.
14 Manitoba, *Statutes*, 1898, c. 6; British Columbia, *Statutes*, 1901, c. 9; Bryce, *Historical Sketch ...*, pp. 29–30; Annie Margaret Angus, *Children's Aid Society of Vancouver, B.C.: 1901-1951* (n. pl.: n. pub., n.d.), pp. 5–6
15 For an account of Kelso's work in these years, see Ian Bain, 'The Role of J.J. Kelso in the Launching of the Child Welfare Movement in Ontario' (MSW thesis, University of Toronto, 1955).
16 *Protection of Children*, p. 13
17 *Ibid., passim*; Bain, 'The Role of J.J. Kelso,' chaps 4 and 5
18 Saywell, ed., *Journal of Lady Aberdeen*, p. 40
19 Ontario, *Sessional Papers*, 1907, no. 35, p. 46

20 *Protection of Children*, pp. 68–74
21 Toronto *Globe*, 28 October 1893, quoted in *Protection of Children*, pp. 79–81
22 Saywell, ed., *Journal of Lady Aberdeen*, p. 24; see also Kelso's comments in Ontario, *Sessional Papers*, 1894, no. 47, p. 19
23 See, for example, Vancouver Children's Aid Society, *Report*, 1905, p. 3
24 Ottawa Children's Aid Society, *Report*, 1906–7, p. 25
25 Ottawa Children's Aid Society, *Report*, 1904–5, pp. 12–13
26 Vancouver Children's Aid Society, *Report*, 1913; for a more general account of the institutional focus of these years, see Angus, *Children's Aid Society of Vancouver*, pp. 17–23.
27 Ontario, *Sessional Papers*, 1901, no. 43, p. 5; *ibid.*, 1905, no. 43, p. 15
28 *Ibid.*, 1910, no. 26, p. 51
29 *Ibid.*, 1911, no. 26, p. 59
30 Starr, 'First Annual Report of the Juvenile Court,' PHJ, IV (April 1913), p. 200
31 See table 3.
32 Saywell, ed., *Journal of Lady Aberdeen*, p. 25; see also Bain, 'J.J. Kelso,' pp. 106–10.
33 Ontario, *Sessional Papers*, 1895, no. 29, app., p. 60; *ibid.*, 1907, no. 35, pp. 8–11
34 *Ibid.*
35 Canada, *Statutes*, 1892, c. 29
36 Canada, Senate, *Debates*, 1894, p. 301
37 Canada, *Statutes*, 1894, c. 58
38 Ontario, *Sessional Papers*, 1895, no. 29, pp. 12–13; *ibid.*, 1896, no. 12, pp. 6, 106
39 Ontario, *Sessional Papers*, 1895, no. 29, p. 21; *ibid.*, 1905, no. 43, p. 50
40 *Ibid.*, 1901, no. 43, pp. 78–80; *ibid.*, 1905, no. 43, p. 7; *ibid.*, 1907, no. 35, p. 14
41 Ontario, *Statutes*, 1900, c. 56
42 Ontario, *Sessional Papers*, 1901, no. 43, pp. 79, 84–6; *ibid.*, 1903, p. 58
43 *Ibid.*, 1902, no. 43, pp. 10–16
44 Provincial Archives of Ontario, Pamphlet Collection, 1903, Box 7, Kelso, 'Reforming Delinquent Children,' p. 5
45 J.J. Kelso, *Helping Erring Children* (Toronto: Warwick, n.d.), pp. 5–6; see also Ontario, *Sessional Papers*, 1902, no. 43, p. 9.
46 Some confusion in names may result from the fact that in 1913 the name of the Central Prison for Ontario, an adult institution, was changed to the Reformatory for Ontario; see Margaret Kirkpatrick Strong, *Public Welfare*

Administration in Canada (Chicago: University of Chicago Press, 1930), pp. 161-3.

47 Ontario, *Sessional Papers*, 1901, no. 36, p. 71; *ibid.*, 1903, no. 39, pp. 47–53; *ibid.*, no. 43, pp. 57–8; *ibid.*, 1904, no. 43, pp. 83–120; Bain, 'J.J. Kelso,' pp. 156–60

48 Ontario, *Sessional Papers*, 1907, no. 35, pp. 12–13

49 *Ibid.*, 1905, no. 43, pp. 8–10; *ibid.*, 1907, no. 37, pp. 13–14

50 *Ibid.*, p. 13

51 National Prison Association, *Proceedings*, 1887, p. 49

52 Grace Abbott, *The Child and the State* (Chicago: University of Chicago Press, 1938), vol. II, pp. 330-3, 392–401; Robert H. Bremner, et al., *Children and Youth in America: A Documentary History* (Cambridge: Harvard University Press, 1971), vol. II, pp. 502–13; see also Platt, *The Child Savers*, pp. 101–36; Hawes, *Children in Urban Society*, pp. 158–90, 246. For a recent account which puts the founding of the Chicago Juvenile Court into the context of crime and criminal justice in that city, see Mark H. Haller, 'Urban Crime and Criminal Justice: The Chicago Case,' *Journal of American History*, LVII (December 1970), pp. 619–35.

53 See, for example, NCW, *Yearbook*, 1906, pp. 47–51; Ontario, *Sessional Papers*, 1907, no. 35, pp. 37–47; Canada, Senate, *Debates*, 1907, pp. 804–8, 820–30, 876–81, 887–902.

54 Bain, 'J.J. Kelso,' p. 85. It was on the basis of this relationship that Kelso later claimed that the children's court movement originated in Toronto. See his remarks in NCW, *Yearbook*, 1906, p. 51. For an analysis of American influence on Canadian child welfare at this time, see Tamara K. Hareven, 'An Ambiguous Alliance: Some Aspects of American Influences on Canadian Social Welfare,' *Histoire Sociale/Social History*, 3 (April 1969), especially pp. 86–90.

55 Hawes, *Children in Urban Society*, pp. 223–45; Peter Gregg Slater, 'Ben Lindsay and the Denver Court: A Progressive Looks at Human Nature,' *American Quarterly*, XX (Summer 1968), pp. 211–23; Canada, Senate, *Debates*, 1907, p. 805

56 Ottawa, Children's Aid Society, *Report*, 1905-6, p. 8

57 *Ibid.*, 1906-7, p. 7

58 *Ibid.*, pp. 21-2; *ibid.*, 1905–6, p. 24

59 *Ibid.*, p. 8

60 See, for example, Ontario, *Sessional Papers*, 1907, no. 35, p. 52

61 Canada, Senate, *Debates*, 1907, p. 805

62 Ottawa, Children's Aid Society, *Report*, 1906–7, p. 8; Canada, Senate, *Debates*, 1907, p. 902

63 See, for example, Canada, House of Commons, *Journals*, 1907–8, pp. 219, 477, 526, 544, 548, 568; *Canadian White Ribbon Tidings*, IV (February 1909), p. 1340; NCW, *Yearbook*, 1907, pp. 29–30; Ottawa, Children's Aid Society, *Report*, 1907–8, pp. 8–9.
64 Canada, Senate, *Debates*, 1907–8, pp. 971–82, 1037–9, 1042–6, 1149–65
65 Canada, House of Commons, *Debates*, 1907–8, pp. 12399–406
66 Canada, *Statutes*, 1908, c. 40; see also Canadian Welfare Council, *The Juvenile Court in Law* (Ottawa: The Council, 1952).
67 For a more thorough discussion of this matter, see Canada, Department of Justice, *Juvenile Delinquency in Canada*, pp. 29–34.
68 Hawes, *Children in Urban Society*, pp. 171–3
69 The Illinois Act was to be 'liberally construed' that the 'care, custody and discipline of a child shall approximate as nearly as may be that which should be given by its parents'...' Bremner, *Children and Youth in America*, vol. II, p. 511
70 Canada, Senate, *Debates*, 1907, pp. 804, 826
71 *Ibid.*, 1907–8, pp. 976–7, 981. In contrast to the virtual unanimity of those most directly concerned in 1907 and 1908 with erring young people, Bill C–192, a major revision of the Juvenile Delinquents Act of 1929 – successor to the 1908 Act – provoked sharp division and debate in the appropriate professional communities. See, for example, Canada, House of Commons, *Debates*, 1970–1, pp. 1893, 2272, 2407–16, 2423–36.
72 Canada, Senate, *Debates*, 1907–8, pp. 1043–4, 1153–64; Canada, House of Commons, *Debates*, 1907–8, pp. 12399–2406
73 NCW, *Yearbook*, 1908, p. 105

CHAPTER 9

1 The quotation in the title of the chapter is from Canadian Conference of Charities and Correction, *Proceedings*, 1912, p. 55
2 *Fifth ... Canadian Conference on Child Welfare*, p. 62
3 For the reasons for this decision, see W.L. Scott, 'The Canadian Juvenile Delinquent Act,' American Prison Association *Proceedings*, 1914, pp. 110–11
4 Manitoba *Free Press*, 6 February 1909, p. 9
5 International Congress of Women, *Report*, 1909, vol. 2, p. 402
6 Helen Gregory MacGill, *The Juvenile Court in Canada: Origin, Underlying Principles, Governing Legislation and Practice*, Canadian Council on Child Welfare Publication no. 17 (Ottawa: Canadian Council on Child Welfare, 1925), p. 32; Canadian Welfare Council, *Juvenile Courts in Canada*, Publica-

tion no. 121 (Ottawa: The Council, n.d.), pp. 46–51; Gordon S. Mundie, 'Juvenile Courts in Canada,' CJMH, III (October 1921), p. 275

7 *The Canada Gazette*, 26 September 1908, pp. 893–4

8 See, for example, Vancouver *Province*, 1 May 1908, p. 7; *ibid.*, 6 May 1908, p. 7; *ibid.*, 8 May 1908, pp. 7, 24; *ibid.*, 11 May 1908, p. 1; *ibid.*, 15 May 1908, p. 1; *ibid.*, 22 May 1908, p. 16; *ibid.*, 10 June 1908, p. 5; J.J. Kelso, 'Address on Social Service,' Canadian Club of Vancouver, *Addresses and Proceedings*, 1908–9 (n. pl.: n. pub., n.d.). Many of the problems of establishing the Vancouver juvenile court and successive efforts to provide it with a proper range of staff and services are informally related in Elsie Gregory MacGill, *My Mother the Judge: A Biography of Judge Helen Gregory MacGill* (Toronto: Ryerson, 1955), *passim*.

9 MacGill, *The Juvenile Court*, p. 33

10 Canadian Conference of Charities and Correction, *Proceedings*, 1912, p. 55

11 Starr, 'First Annual Report of the Juvenile Court,' PHJ, IV (April 1913), p. 196

12 Manitoba, Department of Education, *Report*, 1912–13, pp. 129–30

13 'Mental Hygiene Survey of British Columbia,' CJMH, II (April 1920), p. 32

14 *Ibid.*, pp. 32–3

15 Manitoba, Department of Education, *Report*, 1916–17, pp. 262–4; *ibid.*, 1917–18, p. 140; *ibid.*, 1918–19, p. 121; *ibid.*, 1919–20, pp. 123–4

16 *Handbook*, p. 102

17 *Ibid.*, p. 85

18 Starr, 'First Annual Report of the Juvenile Court,' p. 197

19 For an account of Lindsay's very personal methods of treating delinquents, see Hawes, *Children in Urban Society*, pp. 223–45; Bremner, *Children and Youth in America*, vol. 2, pp. 515–20.

20 In the opinion of a later Canadian Welfare Council report on juvenile courts, such a pattern was both inevitable and necessary. By their very nature, courts had to remain detached and impartial; they could not readily carry out extensive administrative responsibilities which properly belonged with other organizations in the community. Canadian Welfare Council, *Juvenile Courts*, p. 38

21 'Mental Hygiene Survey of British Columbia,' CJMH, II (April 1920), p. 32

22 MacGill, *The Juvenile Court*, p. 36

23 W.L. Scott, *An Explanation of the Need for the Dominion Act Dealing with Juvenile Delinquency* (Toronto: Superintendent of Neglected and Dependent Children of Ontario, 1908), pp. 11–12

24 See, for example, *Handbook*, pp. 105–6, 174–5

25 See, for example, Canadian Welfare Council, *Juvenile Courts*, pp. 41–3

26 See, for example, *Handbook*, p. 102
27 Canada, Department of Justice, *Juvenile Delinquency in Canada*, app. E, pp. 361–2
28 Canadian Conference of Charities and Correction, *Proceedings*, 1912, p. 54
29 *Fourth ... Canadian Conference on Child Welfare*, p. 39
30 *Ibid.*, pp. 156–9
31 *Ibid.*, p. 39
32 Canadian Welfare Council, *Juvenile Courts*, pp. 37, 46–52
33 Canada, *Statutes*, 1921, c. 37
34 Canada, *Proceedings of the Round Table Conference on Juvenile Delinquency* (Ottawa: King's Printer, 1928)
35 Canada, *Statutes*, 1929, c. 46; for an extensive comment on this new legislation see Canadian Welfare Council, *The Juvenile Court in Law* (4th ed.; Ottawa: Canadian Welfare Council, 1952).
36 MacGill, *The Juvenile Court*, pp. 28–9, 31
37 Canada, *Statutes*, 1918, c. 16
38 MacGill, *The Juvenile Court*, pp. 17–18; the long effort of child welfare workers to restrict a parent's extramarital sexual relationships by arguing that such activities endangered the child is related in Canadian Welfare Council, *The Juvenile Court in Law*, pp. 20–6.
39 *Fifth ... Canadian Conference on Child Welfare*, pp. 144–9; for a brief account of the origins of family casework, see Roy Lubove, *The Professional Altruist: The Emergence of Social Work as a Career, 1880-1930* (Cambridge: Harvard University Press, 1965), pp. 40–2.
40 *Fourth ... Canadian Conference on Child Welfare*, pp. 147–52, 165–7; D.B. Harkness, *Courts of Domestic Relations: Duties, Methods and Services of Such Courts: Are they Needed in Canada?* Canadian Council on Child Welfare Publication no. 11 (Ottawa: Canadian Council on Child Welfare, 1924)
41 Canadian Welfare Council, *Juvenile Courts*, pp. 38–9
42 See, for example, Helen Gregory MacGill, 'The Relation of the Juvenile Court to the Community,' CJMH, I (October 1919), pp. 232–6
43 *Handbook*, p. 171
44 *Fourth ... Canadian Conference on Child Welfare*, pp. 163–5
45 Manitoba, Department of Education, *Report*, 1915–16, p. 205
46 *Handbook*, p. 104
47 *Ibid.*, p. 175
48 MacGill, *The Juvenile Court*, p. 37
49 Manitoba, Department of Education, *Report*, 1919–20, p. 122
50 Urquhart and Buckley, *Historical Statistics of Canada*, pp. 638–9

51 Manitoba, Department of Education, *Report*, 1917–18, p. 140
52 Although McKerchar does not account for the other three, perhaps they were the group that had appeared between eight and fourteen times.
53 *Handbook*, p. 61
54 *Fourth ... Canadian Conference on Child Welfare*, p. 34
55 Urquhart and Buckley, *Historical Statistics of Canada*, p. 656
56 Scott, *An Explanation*, p. 8
57 Starr, 'First Annual Report of the Juvenile Court,' PHJ, IV (April 1913), p. 200
58 Manitoba, Department of Education, *Report*, 1916–17, p. 259; *ibid.*, 1919–20, p. 121
59 Saskatchewan Archives, Premier W.M. Martin Papers, F.J. Reynolds to Premier Martin, 24 November 1919
60 Manitoba, Department of Education, *Report*, 1917–18, p. 136
61 *Ibid.*, 1918–19, p. 121; see also *ibid.*, 1917–18, p. 138.
62 *Ibid.*, 1917–18, p. 137
63 *Ibid.*, 1916–17, p. 260; see also British Columbia, *Sessional Papers*, 1912, p. N27.
64 *Ibid.*, 1915, p. S14
65 'Mental Hygiene Survey of British Columbia,' CJMH, II (April 1920), p. 33
66 'Nova Scotia Survey,' CJMH, III (April 1921), p. 25
67 *Ibid.*, p. 21
68 British Columbia, *Sessional Papers*, 1912, p. N27
69 *B.C. Federationist*, 5 February 1912, p. 4; *ibid.*, 20 February 1912, p. 1; the charge was not reported in the Vancouver *World*, 4–12 February 1912.
70 British Columbia, *Sessional Papers*, 1915, p. 315
71 'Nova Scotia Survey,' CJMH, III (April 1921), p. 22; see also *Handbook*, p. 173.
72 British Columbia, *Sessional Papers*, 1919, pp. M47–8
73 'Mental Hygiene Survey of British Columbia,' CJMH, II (April 1920), p. 35
74 British Columbia, *Sessional Papers*, 1919, p. M47
75 'Mental Hygiene Survey of British Columbia,' CJMH, II (April 1920), pp. 34–5
76 British Columbia, *Sessional Papers*, 1912, p. N27; 'Nova Scotia Survey,' CJMH, III (April 1921), p. 22
77 Manitoba, Department of Education, *Report*, 1917–18, p. 137
78 *Handbook*, p. 86
79 'Nova Scotia Survey,' CJMH, III (April 1921), pp. 20, 22, 25

80 See, for example, Canada, Department of Justice, *Juvenile Delinquency in Canada*, pp. 11–18; James C. Hackler, 'A Developmental Theory of Juvenile Delinquency,' *The Canadian Review of Sociology and Anthropology/La Revue canadienne de Sociologie et d'Anthropologie,* VIII (May 1971), pp. 61–75; Herbert J. Walberg, 'Urban Schooling and Delinquency: Towards an Integrative Theory,' *American Education Research Journal,* IX (Spring 1972), pp. 285–300.

81 This sort of development is certainly at the root of much recent criticism of the operation of juvenile courts in the United States. See Platt, *The Child Savers,* pp. 159–63, and the many sources which he cites.

82 *The Child Savers,* p. 176. Platt conveniently summarized his ideas in 'The Rise of the Child-Saving Movement: A Study of Social Policy and Correctional Reform,' *The Annals,* CCCLXXXI (January 1969), pp. 21–38. For critical comment on Platt's position, see Haller, 'Urban Crime and Criminal Justice: the Chicago Case,' *Journal of American History,* LVII (December 1970), especially pp. 627–9.

83 Platt, *Child Savers,* pp. 176, 160–3

84 'Crime and Punishment in Canada: A Statistical Test of the "Conventional Wisdom,"' *La Revue canadienne de Sociologie et d'Anthropologie/The Canadian Review of Sociology and Anthropology,* VI (November 1969), p. 235; see also Vancouver *Sun,* 24 September 1969, p. 48.

85 Canada, Department of Justice, *Juvenile Delinquency in Canada,* especially chap. 5

86 Some of the very incomplete data on this topic are assembled in Table 3, below.

87 In 1899, as a result of a complaint made by the Winnipeg Labour Party, the Manitoba government ordered an enquiry into the handling by the Winnipeg Children's Aid Society of a particular case. In finding himself 'unable to visit the Society with any blame and to find that any real ground of complaint' existed, Judge James E.P. Prendergast provided external confirmation of the real seriousness of at least one such case. Provincial Archives of Manitoba, Children's Aid Society of Winnipeg, 1899

88 Splane, *Social Welfare in Ontario,* p. 232

89 Urquhart and Buckley, *Historical Statistics of Canada,* pp. 14, 644

90 Ontario, *Sessional Papers,* 1921, no. 25, p. 131

91 *Handbook,* p. 145; Urquhart and Buckley, *Historical Statistics of Canada,* pp. 14, 644

92 Vancouver Children's Aid Society, *Report,* 1905, p. 10; *ibid.,* 1910, p. 7; *ibid.,* 1913, p. 6. This last year was one of considerable economic depression in British Columbia.

93 Vancouver Children's Aid Society, *Report*, 1914, p. 7; *ibid.*, 1915, p. 6; *ibid.*, 1916, p. 8; *ibid.*, 1917, p. 7; *ibid.*, 1918, p. 8
94 *Handbook*, p. 62
95 *Fifth ... Canadian Conference on Child Welfare*, pp. 147–8
96 See Urquhart and Buckley, *Historical Statistics of Canada*, section Y
97 *Ibid.*, pp. 643, 651
98 To professionalize police work, Professor McDonald observes, perhaps reduces the proportion of cases – especially those involving juveniles – disposed of informally by the constable on the beat and increases the proportion who are formally charged with an offence. McDonald, 'Crime and Punishment in Canada,' p. 234; see also Canada, Department of Justice, *Juvenile Delinquency in Canada*, pp. 5–9.
99 *Fourth ... Canadian Conference on Child Welfare*, pp. 33–4
100 Canada, Department of Justice, *Juvenile Delinquency in Canada*, p. 45
101 Ontario, Department of Public Welfare, Children's Aid Branch, *Report*, 1931, p. 17; Urquhart and Buckley, *Historical Statistics of Canada*, p. 651
102 See Canada, Department of Justice, *Juvenile Delinquency in Canada*, pp. 44–5, 142–75
103 Ontario, *Sessional Papers*, 1904, no. 43, p. 89

CHAPTER 10

1 The quotation in the title of Part IV is from Adelaide Hoodless, 'The Social Influence of the Home,' typescript of an address given in November 1902. Hoodless material, University of Guelph Library. An earlier version of some of Part IV appeared in *The Journal of Education*, 19 (Spring 1973), pp. 63–73.
2 Saint John *Daily Sun*, 25 June 1889, p. 1
3 For warm recollections of the 'little red building,' see Edmund H. Oliver, *The Country School in Non-English Speaking Communities in Saskatchewan* (n.pl.: Saskatchewan Public Education League, n.d.), pp. 3–5
4 J.M.S. Careless, 'Aspects of Metropolitanism in Atlantic Canada,' ed. Mason Wade, *Regionalism in the Canadian Community, 1867–1967* (Toronto: University of Toronto Press, 1969), pp. 117–29
5 Katherine F.C. MacNaughton, *The Development of the Theory and Practice of Education in New Brunswick, 1784–1900* (Fredericton: University of New Brunswick, 1946), p. 239
6 New Brunswick, *Journals*, 1889, p. A 141

7 MacNaughton, *Education in New Brunswick*, pp. 216–21; see also George F.G. Stanley, 'The Caraquet Riots of 1875,' *Acadiensis*, II (Autumn 1972), pp. 21–38.

8 New Brunswick, *Journals*, 1889, pp. A148–51; see also F. Henry Johnson, *A Brief History of Canadian Education* (Toronto: McGraw-Hill, 1968), pp. 130–2.

9 New Brunswick, *Journals*, 1889, p. A15

10 *Ibid.*, pp. A145–7

11 *Ibid.*, 1890, pp. A111, A115

12 *Ibid.*, 1889, p. A144

13 MacNaughton, *Education in New Brunswick*, p. 237

14 New Brunswick, *Journals*, 1889, p. A144

15 Saint John *Daily Sun*, 1 November 1890, p. 1

16 *Ibid.*, 20 September 1889

17 Canada, Department of Labour, *The Employment of Children and Young Persons in Canada* (Ottawa: King's Printer, 1930), p. 98

18 New Brunswick, *Journals*, 1890, p. A122

19 For Bailey's academic career, see Richard A. Jarrell, 'Science Education at the University of New Brunswick in the Nineteenth Century,' *Acadiensis*, II (Spring 1973), pp. 65–72.

20 The introduction of Pestalozzi's ideas into Canadian education are described in Charles E. Phillips, *The Development of Education in Canada* (Toronto: W.J. Gage, 1957), pp. 411–17 and in Albert Herman Miller, 'The Theory and Practice of Education in Ontario in the 1860's' DED dissertation, University of British Columbia, 1968), pp. 326–31. Ryerson's museum is described in F. Henry Johnson, 'A Colonial Canadian in Search of a Museum,' *Queen's Quarterly*, LXXVII (Summer 1970), pp. 217–30, and 'The Fate of Canada's First Art Museum,' *ibid.*, LXXVIII (Summer 1971), pp. 241–9. Cubberley's account still remains one of the best explications of the Oswego Movement in the United States. Elwood P. Cubberley, *Public Education in the United States: A Study and Interpretation of American Educational History* (rev. ed., Boston: Houghton Mifflin, 1947), pp. 384–99.

21 Saint John *Daily Sun*, 20 September 1889

22 Saint John *Daily Sun*, 22 September 1890, p. 1; *ibid.*, 26 September 1890, p. 1; *ibid.*, 30 September 1890, p. 2; *ibid.*, 4 October 1890, p. 6

23 New Brunswick, *Journals*, 1890, p. A128

24 New Brunswick, *Journals*, 1889, p. A193

25 *Ibid.*, 1890, pp. A175–80

26 See, for example, The Ontario Readers, *First Reader*, Part I (Toronto: W.J. Gage, 1884), p. 28; Part II, pp. 4–5. From his classes on the teaching

of reading at the Normal School in Winnipeg in 1888, William P. Argue learned that the subject could be taught by the 'Alphabetic ... Word ... Sentence ... Phonic ... Phonetic ... [and] Eclectic' methods. The latter, he wrote, began 'with the word method and after about 50 words' were taught, became 'the method of slow pronunciation.' The fourteen pages of Argue's notebook concerned with teaching reading emphasized the techniques of teaching oral reading. Argue outlined what must have been a very common way of introducing a reading story for the children at this time. 'The child may glance over lesson and tell what words are unknown to him. The teacher tells these words and asks children to write them. Teacher writes sentences having these words in them. Ring on the changes. Question so that you may be sure that the children have the thought. Then take the book.' A photocopy of the notebook, now the possession of Margaret Musselman, is in the Special Collections of the University of British Columbia Library.

27 The Ontario Readers, *Second Reader* (Toronto: W.J. Gage, 1884), p. 5
28 New Brunswick, *Journals*, 1889, p. A196
29 *Ibid.*, 1890, p. A65
30 *The Reporter and Fredericton Advertiser*, June 1889, p. 5; New Brunswick, *Journals*, 1889, pp. A71–4
31 New Brunswick, *Journals*, 1889, pp. A96–7, A153
32 MacNaughton, *Education in New Brunswick*, pp. 240–3
33 New Brunswick, *Journals*, 1889, pp. xxxvi–xxxvii, A96–7
34 *Ibid.*, 1890, pp. A96–7
35 *Ibid.*, 1889, p. A157
36 For an examination of how Canadians put together their systems of education, see the introduction and appropriate chapters of Michael B. Katz and Paul H. Mattingley, eds., *Education and Social Change: Themes from Ontario's Past* (New York: New York University Press, 1975).
37 For a brief survey of the general trend over the nineteenth and first half of the twentieth century of such changes as increasing enrolment, lengthening schooling, improving and compelling attendance, and the like on Canadian education, see Phillips, *Development of Canadian Education*, pp. 179–90. The legislative effort to compel attendance in British Columbia is summarized in F. Henry Johnson, *A History of Public Education in British Columbia* (Vancouver: University of British Columbia Press, 1964), pp. 55–6.
38 Urquhart and Buckley, *Historical Statistics of Canada*, pp. 587–9, 594
39 M.P. Toombs, 'A Saskatchewan Experiment in Teacher Education,' *Saskatchewan History*, XVII (Winter 1964), p. 2
40 Honora M. Cochrane, ed., *Centennial Story: The Board of Education for the City of Toronto* (Toronto: Thomas Nelson & Sons, 1950), p. 278

41 Vancouver School Board, *Report*, 1903, p. 8; *ibid.*, 1921, pp. 11–12
42 Manitoba, Department of Education, *Report*, 1899, p. 24; *ibid.*, 1920–1, p. 100
43 Urquhart and Buckley, *Historical Statistics of Canada*, pp. 590–1
44 Provincial and federal legislation regarding the employment and education of young persons is summarized in Canada, Department of Labour, *The Employment of Children and Young Persons in Canada*, pp. 91–134. The way in which some such legislation was administered is explained in J.P. Cowles, *The Juvenile Employment System of Ontario*, Canadian Council on Child Welfare Publication no. 5 (Ottawa: Canadian Council on Child Welfare, 1923).
45 Canada, Department of Labour, *Employment of Children and Young Persons*, p. 16. While the Department of Labour expressed in this monograph some doubts about the accuracy of the exact figures noted for agricultural employment, it accepted the general trend which they indicate. See *ibid.*, pp. 14–25. One should also note that by comparing 1921 figures only with those for 1891 and not the census reports and other data for the years in between one ignores many shorter term fluctuations in juvenile employment. These are fully discussed in the above monograph.
46 See, for example, F. Musgrove, 'Population Changes and the Status of the Young Since the Eighteenth Century,' *Sociological Review*, II (March 1963), especially pp. 79–82.
47 Canada, Dominion Bureau of Statistics, *Illiteracy and School Attendance in Canada: A Study of the Census of 1921 with Supplementary Data* (Ottawa: King's Printer, 1926), p. 9. Unfortunately, the census data collected for these years is not complete enough to allow one to make simple and direct comparisons between the census of 1891 with that of 1921 or either of the two between. In 1921, for example, the enumerators asked only three questions under the heading of education: '(1) Can you read? (2) Can you write? and (3) Months at School since September 1, 1920.' *Ibid.*, p. 5
48 *Ibid.*, pp. 84–6
49 *Ibid.*, pp. 56, 84–6, 90–2
50 The Dominion Bureau of Statistics suggested that its information was more accurate than that collected by the school systems. Unlike public school records, the census was uniform across the nation, it included all pupils and not just those in publicly controlled schools, and it did not include duplicate registrations for children who moved from place to place over the school year. See *ibid.*, pp. 87–9
51 Compiled from data contained in Urquhart and Buckley, *Historical Statistics of Canada*, pp. 587–9. Although Ontario records are incomplete, the over-all

trend was the same in that province. Percentage average daily attendance rose there from 52.2 in 1891 to 76.0 in 1923. *Ibid.*, pp. 588–9

52 Manitoba, Department of Education, *Report*, 1899, p. 24; *ibid.*, 1920–1, p. 100

53 This is a complex matter in which the accumulated effects of small differences are considerable. See Canada, DBS, *Illiteracy and School Attendance*, p. 86.

54 *A Statistical Review of Canadian Schools*, Canadian Council on Child Welfare Publication no. 6. (Ottawa: Canadian Council on Child Welfare, 1923), p. 12

55 Canada, DBS, *Illiteracy and School Attendance*, p. 85

56 While there have been a number of descriptive studies of Canadian teachers and particularly of Canadian teachers' organizations, historians and other social scientists have not yet applied to the changing profession of teaching the sort of analysis they have given to doctors and engineers. The one serious venture in this area is Jerry Bruce Roald, 'Pursuit of Status: Professionalism, Unionism, and Militancy in the Evolution of Canadian Teachers' Organizations' (DED dissertation, University of British Columbia, 1970). Roald's bibliography lists nearly all the descriptive studies.

57 Urquhart and Buckley, *Historical Statistics of Canada*, p. 595

58 *Ibid.*, p. 594

59 Canada, Dominion Bureau of Statistics, *Historical Statistical Survey of Education in Canada* (Ottawa: King's Printer, 1921), p. 63

60 See Roald, 'Pursuit of Status,' chaps 1 and 2.

61 Canada, DBS, *Illiteracy and School Attendance*, pp. 9, 71–6, 84; and the discussion in MacLean, *A Statistical Review*, pp. 5–8

62 Saskatchewan, Department of Education, *Report*, 1909, p. 16

63 Using Massachusetts as a case study Michael Katz brilliantly demonstrates that one of the major and probably inevitable consequences of educational developments in the United States in the nineteenth century was that, by the 1870s, 'American urban education had become bureaucratic: schools were hierarchical, differentiated, rule-bound organizations run by specialists.' Michael B. Katz, ed., *School Reform: Past and Present* (Boston: Little, Brown, 1971), p. 219. See also his *Class, Bureaucracy and Schools. The Illusion of Educational Change in America* (New York: Praeger, 1971).

64 Peter Sandiford, ed., *Comparative Education: Studies of the Educational Systems of Six Modern Nations* (Toronto: Dent, 1918), pp. 434–5

65 Urquhart and Buckley, *Historical Statistics of Canada*, p. 594; Ontario Department of Education, *Report*, 1890, pp. 156–8, 386; *ibid.*, 1920, pp. 299–303, 386

66 *Rural Schools in Canada: Their Organization, Administration and Supervision* (New York: Teachers College, 1913), pp. 151–3

67 In 1903, for an enrolment of 4334 pupils the Vancouver School Board employed a city superintendent to supervise its ninety-two classroom and three manual training teachers. In 1923, for an enrolment of 19,649 pupils, the board employed two municipal inspectors, supervisors of primary, drawing, manual training, special classes, sewing and domestic science, a social service worker, a psychologist, a director of night schools, and a medical health officer to supervise and assist its staff of 546 classroom teachers, 20 manual training, 16 domestic science, 2 music and 3 physical drill instructors, 4 dentists, 10 nurses, and 3 attendance officers. Vancouver School Board, *Report*, 1903, p. 30; *ibid.*, 1923, p. 102

68 Miller, *Rural Schools in Canada*, p. 65. Miller also outlined practical difficulties which faced inspectors, such as low salaries, inadequate experience, a very wide range of duties, enormous districts, little training. See *ibid.*, pp. 143–90

69 See Vancouver School Board, *Reports*, 1903–14.

70 Manitoba, Department of Education, *Report*, 1914–15, p. 15

CHAPTER 11

1 The quotation in the title of the chapter is from NCW, *Yearbook*, 1896, p. 383

2 *Ibid.*

3 30 May 1895, p. 1

4 CAR, 1902, p. 472

5 University of Guelph Library, Hoodless Papers, Adelaide Hoodless, 'The Social Influence of the Home,' typescript of an address given in November 1902

6 NCW, *Report*, 1895, p. 86; see also Margaret Ross, 'The New Conception of Education,' *The British Columbia Monthly*, XIII (August 1918), p. 17.

7 'Parent and Teacher,' *The Canadian Magazine*, V (October 1900), p. 538

8 Of his extensive writing on the kindergarten, James L. Hughes' most important contribution to the literature was his *Froebel's Educational Laws for All Teachers* (New York: Appleton, 1899).

9 The early history of the kindergarten in Ontario is outlined in Barbara E. Corbett, 'The Public School Kindergarten in Ontario, 1883–1967: A Study of the Froebelian Origins, History, and Educational Theory and Practice of the Kindergarten in Ontario' (DED dissertation, University of Toronto, 1968), pp. 95–118. See also Bruce N. Carter, 'James L. Hughes and the Gospel of Education: A Study of the Work and Thought of a Nineteenth

Century Canadian Educator' (DED dissertation, University of Toronto, 1966), pp. 106–10.

10 Nova Scotia, *Journals*, 1890, app. 5, pp. 128–9; for another Halifax opinion see 'The Kindergarten: Froebel's Claims to Consideration on the part of Educationists,' *The Educational Review*, Saint John, N.B., December 1887, pp. 136–7.

11 'The Triumph of the Kindergarten Philosophy,' *Methodist Magazine and Review*, LV (1905), p. 122

12 Mrs George Bryce, *Historical Sketch of the Charitable Institutions of Winnipeg*, The Historical and Scientific Society of Manitoba. Transaction no. 54 (Winnipeg: The Manitoba Free Press, 1899), p. 24; see also '1st Annual Report of the Winnipeg Free Kindergarten Association,' reprinted in *Kindergarten Settlement Association of Winnipeg For the Years 1892–1942* (Winnipeg: n. pub., n.d.), pp. 2–3.

13 James L. Hughes, 'The School of the Twentieth Century,' *Methodist Magazine and Review*, XLV (1897), p. 239

14 Hughes, *Froebel's Educational Laws*, p. ix

15 For an account of the American experience, see Timothy L. Smith, 'Progressivism in American Education 1880–1900,' *Harvard Educational Review*, XXXI (Spring 1961), especially pp. 178–81; Marvin Lazerson, *Origins of the Urban School: Public Education in Massachusetts, 1870–1915* (Cambridge: Harvard University Press, 1971), chap. 2.

16 *The Christian Guardian*, 12 March 1902, p. 161, quoted in Magney, 'The Methodist Church and the National Gospel, 1884–1914,' Committee on Archives of the United Church of Canada, *Bulletin*, no. 20 (1968), p. 58

17 WCTU Archives, Toronto, Richmond Hill, WCTU 'Minute Book,' 14 May 1884; they did not actually succeed in organizing a Band until March 1886.

18 New Westminster *British Columbian*, 7 April 1893; 8 April 1893

19 NCW, *Yearbook*, 1897, p. 214

20 WCTU Archives, Ontario WCTU, 'Minute Book,' 14 October 1886; see also New Westminster *British Columbian*, 22 November 1892, p. 1; Victoria *Colonist*, 1 December 1893, p. 6.

21 See Ruth E. Spence, *Prohibition in Canada: A Memorial to Francis Stephens Spence* (Toronto: The Ontario Branch of the Dominion Alliance, 1919) for an account of how the temperance movement conducted its political campaign.

22 How to conduct such campaigns was carefully explained in *Woman's Journal*, XV (February 1901), p. 2.

23 New Brunswick, *Journals*, 1892, p. x

24 Nova Scotia, *Journals*, 1890, app. 5, p. 125

25 Vancouver *News Advertiser*, 4 January 1892, p. 1; New Westminster
    British Columbian, 5 January 1892, p. 4; *ibid.*, 6 January 1892, pp. 1, 5
26 Kamloops *Sentinel*, 30 March 1894, p. 4; Victoria *Colonist*, 30 November
    1893; *ibid.*, 24 January 1896; *ibid.*, 14 May 1897; New Westminster *British
    Columbian*, 9 April 1892; *ibid.*, 11 March 1893
27 NCW, *Yearbook*, 1897, pp. 216-17
28 Victoria *Colonist*, 30 November 1893
29 NCW, *Yearbook*, 1897, p. 216
30 *The Acts and Proceedings of the General Assembly of the Presbyterian
    Church in Canada*, 1892, p. 39, quoted in Edward A. Christie, 'The Official
    Attitudes and Opinions of the Presbyterian Church in Canada with Respect
    to Public Affairs and Social Problems, 1875-1925' (MA thesis, University of
    Toronto, 1955), pp. 296-7
31 British Columbia, *Public Schools Report*, 1893, p. 524; see also Ontario,
    Sessional Papers, 1904, no. 12, pp. xxvii-xxviii.
32 *Woman's Journal*, XV (September 1900), p. 8
33 Viola Elizabeth Parvin, *Authorization of Textbooks for the Schools of
    Ontario*, 1846-1950 (Toronto: University of Toronto Press, 1965), pp.
    142-3, lists such school texts in the general area of temperance education
    which were authorized in Ontario between 1875-1939. In addition to those
    listed, the University of British Columbia's collection of Canadian school
    textbooks includes *New Brunswick Health Reader No. 1, With Special
    Reference to the Effects of Alcohol, Tobacco, etc. Upon the Human System*
    (Saint John, N.B.: J. & A. McMillan Limited, 1893).
34 New Brunswick, *Statutes*, 1893, c. 19; see also New Brunswick, *Synoptic
    Report of the Proceedings of the House of Assembly*, 1893, pp. 118-19.
35 Nova Scotia, *Statutes*, 1895, c. 1
36 John Millar, *School Management and the Principles and Practices of
    Teaching* (Toronto: William Briggs, 1897), pp. 270-93; see also the similar
    course in Saskatchewan, Department of Education, *Report*, 1906, pp. 70-1
37 Spence, *Prohibition in Canada*, p. 55; to sample the range of one year's
    political activities see CAR, 1904, pp. 569-74.
38 Quoted in Phillips, *Development of Canadian Education*, p. 452
39 Canada, Royal Commission on the Relation of Labor and Capital, *Report*,
    p. 119
40 Orville E. White, 'The History of the Practical Education Courses in Cana-
    dian Secondary Schools' (MA thesis, McGill University, 1951), summarizes
    pioneering efforts at practical education; see also Ontario, *Sessional Papers*,
    1894, no. 44, Part VI; Phillips, *Development of Canadian Education*, pp.
    441-4, 451-3; J. Donald Wilson, Robert M. Stamp, Louis Phillippe Audet,

Canadian Education: A History (Scarborough: Prentice-Hall, 1970), pp. 294–7.

41 Canada, *Sessional Papers*, 1886, no. 10, pp. 209–10

42 Quoted in White, 'Practical Education,' pp. 333–4

43 Royal Commission on the Relations of Labor and Capital, *Report*, p. 120

44 Quoted in J. Castell Hopkins, ed., *Canada: An Encyclopedia of the Country* (Toronto: Linscott Publishing, 1898), vol. 3, p. 220

45 See Robert Leslie Jones, *History of Agriculture in Ontario, 1613–1880* (Toronto: University of Toronto Press, 1946), chaps 14–19; J. Spelt, *The Urban Development in South-Central Ontario* (Assen, The Netherlands: Van Gorcum, 1965), pp. 139–43.

46 A.J. Madill, *History of Agricultural Education in Ontario* (Toronto: University of Toronto Press, 1930), chap. 9

47 Canada, *Sessional Papers*, 1891, no. 6D, p. 108; see also the unpublished mss in the Robertson Papers, Special Collections, University of British Columbia Library, Ishbel Robertson Currier, 'Brief Biography of James Wilson Robertson'; Edwin John Pavey, 'James Wilson Robertson: Public Servant and Educator' (MED thesis, University of British Columbia, 1971).

48 Canada, *Sessional Papers*, 1891, no. 6D, p. 141

49 Over these years Robertson gave a full account of his educational and other activities in his annual reports and in his appearances before the Commons' Select Committee on Agriculture and Colonization. See Canada, *Sessional Papers*, 1894, no. 8D; *ibid.*, 1898, no. 8C, pp. 5–10; *ibid.*, 1901, no. 15; Canada, *Journals*, 1894, app. 4. For an account of his work in one part of Canada, see G.C. Church, 'Dominion Government Aid to the Dairy Industry in Western Canada,' *Saskatchewan History*, XIV (Spring 1963), pp. 41–58.

50 Saywell, ed., *Canadian Journal of Lady Aberdeen*, p. 284

51 Herbert Francis Sherwood, 'Children of the Land: The Story of the Macdonald Movement in Canada,' *The Outlook* (23 April 1910), pp. 897–8

52 H.B. MacLean, interview with the writer, 23 February 1966; CAR, 1902, p. 475

53 Canada, *Journals*, 1908, app. 2, p. 90

54 James W. Robertson, *The Macdonald Sloyd School Fund: Manual Training in Public Schools* (Ottawa: E.J. Reynolds, 1899), p. 5

55 James W. Robertson, 'Professor Cappon's Article in Queen's Quarterly, January, 1905,' *Queen's Quarterly*, XII (April 1905), pp. 420–4

56 CAR, 1902, p. 403

57 University of British Columbia Library, Special Collections, Robertson Papers, 'Education for the Improvement of Rural Conditions,' 20 July 1907

CHAPTER 12

1 The quotation in the title of the chapter is from J.W. Robertson, 'The Macdonald Fund,' National Education Association, *Report*, 1909, reprinted in Canada, Royal Commission on Industrial Training and Technical Education, *Report of the Commissioners* (Ottawa: King's Printer, 1913) [hereafter RCITTE, *Report*] , vol. 2, pp. 157–8

2 *Ibid.*, p. 154

3 For an account of the life of Macdonald, see J.F. Snell, *Macdonald College of McGill University: A History from 1904–1955* (Montreal: McGill University Press for Macdonald College, 1963), part 1, and Maurry H. Epstein, 'Sir William Macdonald: A Biographical Sketch,' *McGill Journal of Education*, V (Spring 1971), pp. 53–61. For a different and much less sympathetic view of him, see Canada, *Report of the Royal Commission on the Relations of Labor and Capital in Canada: Evidence – Quebec*, pp. 529–33.

4 While neither the seed-growing contest nor the manual training scheme appear to have been the product of any over-all plan, Robertson drew up the rest of the program with the help of a committee of the Dominion Educational Association. Dominion Educational Association, *Proceedings*, 1901, pp. 23, 84–93; *ibid.*, 1917, pp. 12–14

5 J.W. Robertson, *The Macdonald Sloyd School Fund*, p. 7; RCITTE, *Report*, vol. 2, p. 153

6 RCITTE, *Report*, vol. 2, p. 153

7 Robertson, *The Macdonald Sloyd School Fund*, p. 27; for the Menominie story see Lawrence E. Cremin, *Transformation of the School: Progressivism in American Education, 1876–1957* (New York: Alfred A. Knopf, 1962), pp. 142–7.

8 Late in his life, one of their number warmly recalled his recruitment and early experiences as a Macdonald-Robertson exemplar of manual training. A.H. Leake, 'Looking Backward,' Industrial Arts Teachers of Ontario, *Bulletin* (March 1950).

9 White, 'Practical Education,' p. 599

10 Ontario, Department of Education, *Report*, 1907, pp. 638–874

11 Ontario, Department of Education, *Education for Industrial Purposes*, A Report by John Seath, Superintendent of Education for Ontario (Toronto: King's Printer, 1911), p. 269

12 RCITTE, *Report*, vol. 2, p. 154

13 White, 'Practical Education,' pp. 97, 176, 319, 474, 610

14 The best Canadian discussion of the whole range of practical education in the period is Albert H. Leake, *Industrial Education: Its Problems, Methods*

and Dangers (Boston: Houghton Mifflin, 1913). See also Albert H. Leake, *The Vocational Education of Girls and Women* (New York: Macmillan, 1918). For an excellent account of how contemporary Americans and Englishmen wrestled with what they meant by manual training, see Marvin Lazerson, *Origins of the Urban School*, especially chaps 4–5, and R.J.W. Selleck, *The New Education, 1870–1914* (London: Pitman, 1968), especially chap. 4.

15 See, for example, Manitoba, Department of Education, *Report*, 1909, p. 28.

16 RCITTE, *Report*, vol. 1, p. 10

17 Leake, *Industrial Education*, chap. 3

18 Hughes, 'The School of the Twentieth Century,' *Methodist Magazine and Review*, XLV (1897), p. 349

19 See, for example, British Columbia, Department of Education, *Courses of Study for the Public, High and Normal Schools of British Columbia* (Victoria: King's Printer, 1920), pp. 1–2, 13

20 See, for example, *ibid.*, pp. 28–31. For a critical examination of this sort of curriculum, see Leake, *Industrial Education*, chap. 4.

21 See, for example, Dominion Educational Association, *Proceedings*, 1913, pp. 73–86

22 NCW, *Yearbook*, 1902, p. 114

23 Toronto *Globe*, 2 January 1910, p. 12; *B.C. Federationist*, 7 February 1913, pp. 1, 4; see also John Keith Foster, 'Education and Work in a Changing Society: British Columbia, 1870–1930' (MA thesis, University of British Columbia, 1970), pp. 72–83; and H.A. Logan, *Trade Unions in Canada: Their Development and Functioning* (Toronto: Macmillan, 1948), pp. 65–7.

24 Robertson, *The Macdonald Sloyd School Fund*, pp. 22–3

25 'Practical Education,' pp. 616–17; see also Foster, 'Education and Work in a Changing Society,' pp. 17–18.

26 Leake, *Industrial Education*, especially chaps 4 and 9. See also his annual report for 1917–18 in Ontario, Department of Education, *Report*, 1917–18, p. 65.

27 British Columbia, *Survey of the School System*, p. 96

28 For an example of the initial interest, see the report of the Nova Scotia Legislature Committee on Education in 1902. CAR, 1902, p. 458

29 Ontario, Department of Education, *Education for Industrial Purposes*, p. 3

30 'Essentials in a System of Vocational Education,' *Vocational Education*, 2 (May 1922), p. 4

31 This campaign is outlined in Robert M. Stamp, 'Technical Education, the National Policy, and Federal-Provincial Relations in Canadian Education, 1899–1919,' CHR, LII (December 1971), pp. 404–23.

32 Canada, Department of Labour, Director of Technical Education, *Proceedings of the First National Conference on Technical Education* (Ottawa: King's Printer, 1921); White, 'Practical Education'; Foster, 'Education and Work in a Changing Society'; Stamp, 'Technical Education, the National Policy, and Federal-Provincial Relations in Canadian Education, 1899–1919,' CHR, LII (December 1971)

33 In arguing that the movement did not originate the school garden James Collins Miller noted that some Nova Scotia schools apparently had school gardens as early as 1886. Robertson may have learned of the idea during his travels as commissioner of agriculture. Miller, *Rural Schools in Canada*, p. 78

34 R.H. Cowley, 'The Macdonald School Gardens,' *Queen's Quarterly*, XII (April 1905), pp. 416–18

35 See, for example, H.B. Spotton, *The Elements of Structural Botany with Special Reference to the Study of Canadian Plants* (Toronto: W.J. Gage, 1886), p. 1.

36 Manitoba, Department of Education, *Report*, 1905, p. 3

37 Belle C. Gibson, *Teacher-Builder* (Victoria: Morriss Printing Company, 1961), pp. 39–45

38 RCITTE, *Report*, vol. 2, p. 155

39 Madill, *History of Agricultural Education in Ontario*, pp. 104, 226; see also S.B. McCready, 'Adventures of a Schoolmaster,' *Western Ontario Historical Notes*, IX (December 1951), pp. 130–45

40 Ontario, Department of Agriculture, *The Macdonald Institute in Relation to Nature Study in Our Public Schools: A Letter to the Schools* (Toronto: King's Printer, 1904)

41 RCITTE, *Report*, vol. 1, pp. 308–10

42 *Ibid.*, vol. 4, p. 2196

43 James W. Robertson, *Conservation of Life in Rural Districts* (New York: Association Press, 1911), pp. 11–12

44 To sample this growing interest, see the report of the New Brunswick Agricultural Commission of 1908, summarized in CAR, 1909, pp. 448–9; Canada, House of Commons, *Journals*, 1908, app. 2; John MacDougall, *Rural Life in Canada: Its Trend and Tasks* (Toronto: The Westminster Company, 1913); John MacDougall, 'The Rural Problem,' *Social Service Congress, Ottawa, 1914: Report of Addresses and Proceedings*, pp. 147–57; Hugh Dobson, 'The School and the Rural Problem,' *ibid.*, pp. 173–6; Canada, Commission of Conservation, *Report*, 1914, pp. 134–8; *ibid.*, 1916, pp. 24–31; Christie, 'The Presbyterian Church in Canada,' pp. 39–42.

45 Canada, *Statutes*, 1912, c. 3

46 *Ibid.*, 1912–13, c. 5

47 Canada, Commission of Conservation, *Report*, 1917, pp. 215-25

48 White, 'Practical Education,' pp. 497-8. The summer school attracted 260 teachers in 1913 and 371 in 1914.

49 Provincial Archives of British Columbia, Department of Education Records; Gibson, *Teacher-Builder*, pp. 65-85

50 Madill, *Agricultural Education in Ontario*, p. 103

51 Canada, Commission of Conservation, *Report*, 1917, p. 13

52 Saskatchewan, *A Survey of Education*, pp. 59-64; British Columbia, Department of Education, *Report*, 1917-18, pp. D52-64

53 Quoted in Chalmers, *Schools of the Foothills Province*, p. 51

54 Miller, *Rural Schools in Canada*, p. 80

55 *Public Education in Nova Scotia: A History and Commentary* (Kingston: The Jackson Press, 1919), p. 102

56 Charles G.D. Roberts and Arthur L. Turnell, ed., *A Standard Dictionary of Canadian Biography: The Canadian Who Was Who* (Toronto: Trans-Canada Press, 1934), pp. 275-6; Ruth Howes, 'Adelaide Hunter Hoodless,' in Mary Quayle Innis, ed., *The Clear Spirit: Twenty Canadian Women and Their Times* (Toronto: For the Canadian Federation of University Women by the University of Toronto Press, 1966), pp. 103-19

57 NCW, *Yearbook*, 1902, p. 120

58 Toronto *Globe*, 30 April 1900, p. 6

59 See, for example, NCW, *Yearbook*, 1896, pp. 388-92; *ibid.*, 1898, p. 271; RCITTE, *Report*, vol. 4, pp. 49-50

60 NCW, *Yearbook*, 1901, pp. 117-18

61 RCITTE, *Report*, vol. 1, pp. 53-4

62 See Leake, *Vocational Education of Girls and Women*, chaps 2 and 3

63 Manitoba Archives, Dora Dibney Papers

64 *Public School Domestic Science* (Toronto: Copp Clark, 1898)

65 British Columbia, Department of Education, *Courses of Study*, 1920, pp. 31-3, 56-9; White, 'Practical Education,' p. 97. The figures are for 1918-19.

66 To examine the changes in home economics made over the 1920s, see the special issue of *Vocational Education*, 18 (January 1927), pp. 1-41.

67 Innis, *Clear Spirit*, pp. 11-30

68 *Report of Mrs. Hoodless on Domestic Science: Including a Recent Visit to the Schools of Philadelphia and Washington* (Toronto: Warwick Bros. and Rutter & Rutter, 1899), p. 7

69 I am indebted to my former students Nan Cart, Kathy Read, Bill McNulty, and Steve Erickson for their help with this topic.

70 *Manual of Drill and Calisthenics* (Toronto: W.J. Gage, 1879), pp. 4-5

71 Patricia Anne Vertinsky, 'Education for Sexual Morality: Moral Reform and

the Regulation of American Morality in the Nineteenth Century' (DED dissertation, University of British Columbia, 1975); Michael Bliss, '"Pure Books on Avoided Subjects": Pre-Freudian Sexual Ideas in Canada,' CHA, *Report*, 1970, pp. 89–108; Innis, *Unfold the Years*, pp. 50–2; Murray G. Ross, *The Y.M.C.A. in Canada: The Chronical of a Century* (Toronto: Ryerson, 1951), pp. 186–93; Mary Eleanor Keyes, 'John Howard Crocker, L.L.D., 1870–1959,' *Western Ontario Historical Nuggets*, XXXII (March 1966); Philip Snowden, 'The Physical Education of British Children,' PHJ, II (May 1911), pp. 215–17

72 Canadian Conference of Charities and Correction, *Proceedings*, 1912, p. 23

73 See Carl Berger, *The Sense of Power: Studies in the Ideas of Canadian Imperialism, 1867–1914* (Toronto: University of Toronto Press, 1970), especially chap. 10.

74 Saskatchewan Archives, Premier Walter Scott Papers, Borden to Scott, 29 January 1909

75 Hughes, *Manual of Drill and Calisthenics*; Millar, *School Management*, pp. 18–32

76 The annual reports of Miss Mabel Peters, Westfield, N.B., convener of its Committee on Vacation Schools and Supervised Playgrounds to the National Council of Women provides a convenient summary of the early growth of the playground movement in Canada. See, for example, NCW, *Yearbook*, 1905, pp. 99–100; *ibid.*, 1911, pp. 55–8. See MacLean, *A Statistical Review*, pp. 31–5, for a nation-wide survey of public playground activities in Canadian urban centres by 1921–2.

77 CAR, 1907, p. 618

78 Strathcona's imperial sentiments were expressed earlier in the gesture when he raised, equipped, and transported 600 mounted men to serve, at his own expense, as the Strathcona Horse in the Boer War. See Beckles Willson, *Lord Strathcona: The Story of His Life* (London: Methuen, 1902), pp. 243–5. Neither this nor the other two biographies of Strathcona mention the Strathcona Trust nor the earlier assistance to Mrs Hoodless, mentioned below, p. 575. W.T.R. Preston, *The Life and Times of Lord Strathcona* (London: Everleigh Nash, 1914) and John Macnaughton, *Lord Strathcona* (New York: Oxford, 1926)

79 Quoted in British Columbia, Department of Education, *Report*, 1910, p. A60

80 Saskatchewan Archives, Premier Walter Scott Papers, J. Duff to commissioner of Education, 12 January 1910

81 *B.C. Federationist*, 21 February 1913, p. 3; *ibid.*, 7 February 1913, p. 4. Canadian labour's attitude to the peace movement of the time is briefly discussed in Charles Lipton, *The Trade Union Movement of Canada, 1827–1959* (Montreal: Canadian Social Publications, 1966), pp. 156–61

82 Archie Bell, *Sunset Canada* (Boston: The Page Company, 1918), p. 235

83 Saskatchewan, *A Survey of Education*, p. 125; see also British Columbia, *Survey of the School System*, p. 96.

84 Miss Cartwright, 'Physical Education and its Place in the School; the Function of the Strathcona Trust; and the Training of Teachers,' Dominion Educational Association, *Proceedings*, 1913, pp. 109–20

85 Strathcona Trust, *Syllabus of Physical Exercises for Schools* (Toronto: Executive Council, Strathcona Trust, 1911), n.p.

86 Hughes, *Manual of Drill*, p. 7

87 Strathcona Trust, *Syllabus*, pp. 22–3

88 Vancouver School Board, *Report*, 1910, p. 31

89 Manitoba, Department of Education, *Report*, 1913–14, pp. 64–5; British Columbia, Department of Education, *Courses of Study*, 1920, p. 9; Bingay, *Public Education in Nova Scotia*, pp. 123–4.

90 *School and Teachers' Bulletin*, quoted in RCITTE, *Report*, vol. 2, pp. 310–13

91 Morgan and Burpee, *Canadian Life in Town and Country*, p. 173.

92 *Plan re Rural Schools*, 6 January 1902, cited in Pavey, 'James Wilson Robertson,' p. 64

93 RCITTE, *Report*, vol. 2, p. 156–8; see also CAR, 1902, pp. 405–7.

94 H.B. MacLean, interview with the writer, 23 February 1966

95 See, for example, CAR, 1906, p. 413

96 University of British Columbia Library, Special Collections, Robertson Papers, Macdonald Consolidated School, Hillsborough, PEI, 'Record Book.'

97 *Ibid*; RCITTE, *Report*, vol. 4, pp. 1760–2

98 University of British Columbia Library, Special Collections, Robertson Papers, Jones to Robertson, 13 January 1906; CAR, 1906, p. 413; compilations in Miller, *Rural Schools in Canada*, p. 107

99 RCITTE, *Report*, vol. 4, p. 1762

100 Leake, *Agricultural Education*, pp. 92–8

101 RCITTE, *Report*, vol. 4, pp. 1759–62; see also the tax records of the school in Miller, *Rural Schools in Canada*, pp. 106, 108.

102 CAR, 1909, p. 477

103 *School and Teachers Bulletin*, quoted in RCITTE, *Report*, vol. 2, p. 310

104 RCITTE, *Report*, vol. 2, pp. 312–13; CAR, 1908, pp. 420–3; *ibid*., 1909, pp. 448–9

105 Canada, DBS, *Historical Statistical Survey*, p. 93

106 Ontario, Department of Education, *Report*, 1904, pp. xxiv–xxvii; McCutcheon, *Public Education in Ontario*, pp. 111–13

107 Manitoba, *Sessional Papers*, 1910, p. 393; *ibid*., 1911, pp. 562–8; see also the tables in Miller, *Rural Schools in Canada*, pp. 111–12.

108 Manitoba, *Sessional Papers*, 1911, p. 569

109 Manitoba, Department of Education, *Report*, 1914–15, p. 71

110 *Ibid.*, 1920–1, pp. 8–9; Canada, DBS, *Historical Statistical Survey*, pp. 94–5

111 Saskatchewan, *A Survey of Education*, chap. 8

112 Saskatchewan, Department of Education, *Report*, 1921, pp. 18–19

113 Canada, DBS, *Historical Statistical Survey*, p. 95

114 *Ibid.*, pp. 96–7; Chalmers, *Schools of the Foothills Province*, pp. 46–7

115 Canada, DBS, *Historical Statistical Survey*, p. 97; for an account of the province's characteristic device for consolidation, the rural municipal school district, see Johnson, *History of Public Education in B.C.*, pp. 94–6.

116 The early history of the Macdonald Institute is outlined in Edith Child Rowles, *Home Economics in Canada: The Early History of Six College Programmes: Prologue to Change* (Saskatoon: University of Saskatchewan, n.d.), pp. 36–49; that of Macdonald College is summarized in Snell, *Macdonald College*; see also Pavey, 'James Wilson Robertson,' chap. 3.

117 RCITTE, *Report*, vol. 2, p. 158

118 Toronto *Globe*, 5 April 1900, p. 5

119 University of Guelph Library, Hoodless Papers, James Mills, president, Ontario Agricultural College to Mrs Hoodless, 9 March 1900; *ibid.*, Mrs Hoodless to Hon. Richard Harcourt, minister of education, 23 October 1901; *ibid.*, Mills to Robertson, 31 October 1901; *ibid.*, Robertson to Mills, 16 December 1901

120 *The Farmer's Advocate*, 22 December 1904, p. 1778; CAR, 1904, p. 532

121 NCW, *Yearbook*, 1908, p. 83

122 Sherwood, 'Children of the Land: the Story of the Macdonald Movement in Canada,' *The Outlook* (23 April 1910), p. 901

123 RCITTE, *Report*, vol. 2, pp. 157–8

124 CAR, 1906, pp. 380–1

125 John Calam, 'McGill Trains Teachers: 1857–1964,' *The Teacher's Magazine*, XLV (September 1965), pp. 24–5

126 Snell, *Macdonald College*, pp. 56–9, 169–71

127 Ontario Agricultural College, *Programme of Closing Exercises at Macdonald Institute Nature Study Department*, 1905

128 Vancouver School Board, *Report*, 1905, p. 6

129 Rowles, *Home Economics in Canada*, p. 82

130 Interview with the writer, 23 February 1966

131 RCITTE, *Report*, vol. 4, pp. 2093–2101, 2105–8

132 CAR, 1902, pp. 458–9

133 *Ibid.*, p. 455; John Adams, *The Protestant School System of the Province of Quebec* (Montreal: Longmans and E.N. Renouf, 1902)

134 RCITTE, *Report*, vol. 4, pp. 2084–90
135 Ontario, Department of Education, *Education and Industrial Efficiency: Report of Albert H. Leake, to the Minister of Education on Recent Developments in the Schools of the Eastern States* (Toronto: King's Printer, 1906)
136 NCW, *Yearbook*, 1907, pp. 54–7; *ibid.*, 1908, pp. 93–6
137 RCITTE, *Report*, vol. 4, pp. 1753–4
138 Alberta, Department of Education, *Report*, 1912, p. 81
139 Victoria *Colonist*, 14 July 1909, pp. 1–2; *ibid.*, 15 July, pp. 1–2; *ibid.*, 16 July, pp. 1–2
140 Manitoba, *Sessional Papers*, 1912, no. 3, pp. 281–356
141 Ontario, Department of Education, *Education for Industrial Purposes*
142 Saskatchewan appointed a Commission on Agricultural and Industrial Education in 1912 which reported in 1913. CAR, 1913, p. 618
143 RCITTE, *Report*, vol. 1, p. v
144 Stamp, 'Technical Education, the National Policy, and Federal-Provincial Relations in Canadian Education, 1899–1919,' CHR, LII (December 1971), pp. 404–15; for an account of King's interest in industrial and labour affairs, see R. MacGregor Dawson, *William Lyon Mackenzie King: A Political Biography, 1874–1923*, vol. 1 (Toronto: University of Toronto Press, 1958), especially chaps 4–7.
145 RCITTE, *Report*, vol. 1, pp. vi–xii
146 Vancouver *World*, 3 June 1910, p. 20; Toronto *Globe*, 3 June 1910, pp. 1, 6–7
147 RCITTE, *Report*, vol. 1, pp. 58–61
148 See Pavey, 'James Wilson Robertson,' chap. 5.
149 RCITTE, *Report*, vol. 1, pp. 8–11
150 *Ibid.*, pp. 15–39
151 Stamp, 'Technical Education, the National Policy, and Federal-Provincial Relations in Canadian Education, 1899–1919,' pp. 417–22; see Rhys D. Fairbaine, 'Work of the Ontario Association for the Promotion of Technical Education,' in Canada, Commission of Conservation, *Report*, 1915, pp. 27–33, for an account of work it stimulated in Ontario.
152 Canada, *Statutes*, 1919, c. 19
153 *Vocational Education*, 28 (August 1928), pp. 8–20
154 Vancouver *Province*, 28 November 1910, pp. 5, 7, 19, 22; *ibid.*, 29 November, pp. 6, 8, 16, 21; *ibid.*, 30 November, p. 8; *ibid.*, 1 December, p. 6; for detailed accounts of two other visits, see 'Inquiry at St. Hycinthe: A Typical Town,' and 'Inquiry at Berlin: A Typical City in Ontario,' RCITTE, *Report*, vol. 4, pp. 1912–27; 2122–42
155 Vancouver School Board, *Report*, 1910, p. 10

CHAPTER 13

1 Edmund H. Oliver, *The Country School in Non-English Speaking Communities in Saskatchewan* (n. pl.: n. pub., n.d.)
2 Saskatchewan, Department of Education, *Report*, 1916, pp. 16–17; the whole campaign is summarized in Morley P. Toombs, 'The Control and Support of Public Education in Rupert's Land and the North-West Territories to 1905 and in Saskatchewan to 1960' (PHD dissertation, University of Minnesota, 1962), pp. 558–73; see also assorted files in Saskatchewan Archives, Premier Walter Scott Papers, 1915–16.
3 Black had helped Scott assemble some of the ideas expressed in the address which opened the campaign. See Saskatchewan Archives, Premier Walter Scott Papers, Black to Scott, 3 May 1915, and Scott to Black, 30 June 1915.
4 CAR, 1916, pp. 712–13
5 Toombs, 'Control and Support of Public Education,' pp. 565–8
6 CAR, 1916, pp. 711–12
7 Urquhart and Buckley, *Historical Statistics of Canada*, p. 19
8 Canada, DBS, *Census of Canada*, 1921, vol. 2, pp. xii–xiii
9 *Ibid.*, vol. 1, pp. 542–3; see also Warren E. Kalbach, *The Impact of Immigration on Canada's Population* (Ottawa: DBS, 1970), pp. 71–4, 87–93.
10 See Manoly R. Lupul, 'Educational Crises in the New Dominion to 1917,' chap. 13, in Wilson, Stamp, and Audet, *Canadian Education*, for a convenient summary and bibliography of this extremely contentious issue in Canadian history. The wider context is outlined in Brown and Cook, *Canada 1896–1921*, chaps 4, 13.
11 'Immigrant Social Aspirations and American Education, 1880-1930,' *American Quarterly*, XXI (Fall 1969), pp. 523–43
12 To explicate the matter of the creation of new ethnic identities in Canada is beyond the scope of this study. Of interest, however, is Elizabeth Wangenheim's discussion of the situation as it worked out in the case of the Ukrainians. In her view, the process which brought them to a sense of ethnic oneness which was both Ukrainian and Canadian was intimately related to the troubled course of Ukrainian nationalism in the homeland. Indeed, veterans of the European battles who later emigrated or fled to Canada took the lead in creating 'in a large majority' of Ukrainians in Canada 'a sense of their common Ukrainian identity.' Elizabeth Wangenheim, 'The Ukrainians: A Case Study of the "Third Force,"' in Peter Russell, ed., *Nationalism in Canada* (Toronto: McGraw-Hill, 1966), p. 80. Strife beyond the seas, however, was apparently not an essential element in the process. In his paper on the Scandinavians in western Canada, Jorgen Dahlie notes that the new environment

'might even have contributed to the intensification of the immigrant's desire to be a part of the Norwegian, Danish or Swedish mosaic.' Jorgen Dahlie, 'Learning on the Frontier: Scandinavian Immigrants and Education in Western Canada,' *Canadian and International Education/Education Canadienne et Internationale*, I (December 1972), p. 66

13 Canada, *Sessional Papers*, 1887, no. 12, pp. 78, 237–41

14 *Ibid.*, 1890, no. 6, p. 158

15 Minutes of New Finland School District No. 435, quoted by Gilbert Johnson, 'The New Finland Colony,' *Saskatchewan History*, XV (Spring 1962), p. 70

16 Vladimir J. Kaye, *Early Ukrainian Settlement in Canada, 1895-1900: Dr. Josef Oleskow's Role in the Settlement of the Canadian Northwest* (Toronto: University of Toronto Press for the Ukrainian Canadian Research Foundation, 1964), p. 215. Kaye reports that Winnipeg Presbyterians helped with the early expenses of this school. *Ibid.*, p. 221

17 J. Donald Wilson and Jorgen Dahlie, 'Negroes, Finns, Sikhs: Education and Community Experience in British Columbia,' *Canadian Uutiset* (March–April 1972), no paging

18 George Quinn, 'Impact of European Immigration upon the Elementary Schools of Central Toronto, 1815-1915' (MA thesis, University of Toronto, 1968), pp. 85–6

19 J. Skwarok, OSBM, *The Ukrainian Settlers in Canada and Their Schools* (Edmonton: Basilian Press, 1959), pp. 25–6

20 Manitoba, Department of Education, *Report*, 1907, p. 21

21 *Ibid.*, 1913–14, p. 64

22 Kaye, *Early Ukrainian Settlements in Canada*, p. 165

23 26 August 1914, quoted in Ol'ha Woycenko, *The Ukrainians in Canada* (Ottawa, Winnipeg: n. pub., 1967), p. 93

24 Paul Yuzyk discusses this aspect of the Ukrainians in Manitoba in his *The Ukrainians in Manitoba: A Social History* (Toronto: University of Toronto Press, 1953), especially chap. 4.

25 For a brief, uncritical survey and bibliography of ethnic advancement, see Canada, Department of the Secretary of State, Canadian Citizenship Branch, *The Canadian Family Tree* (Ottawa: Queen's Printer, 1967).

26 C.B. Sissons, 'Illiteracy in the West,' *The University Magazine*, XII (October 1913), p. 450

27 28 June 1916, quoted in Woycenko, *The Ukrainians in Canada*, p. 21

28 H. Keith Hutchison, 'Dimensions of Ethnic Education: The Japanese in British Columbia, 1880-1940' (MA thesis, University of British Columbia, 1972), pp. 27, 57–60

29 Ole Hjelt, 'Nybyggerliv i Kanada,' *Nordmanns-Forbundent*, XIV (1921), quoted in Jorgen Dahlie, 'Learning on the Frontier: Scandinavian Immigrants and Education in Western Canada,' *Canadian and International Education*, I (December 1972), p. 60

30 Cornelius J. Jaenen, 'Ruthenian Schools in Western Canada, 1897–1919,' *Paedegogica Historica*, X (1970), pp. 517–41

31 See W.L. Morton, 'Manitoba Schools and Canadian Nationality, 1890–1923,' CHA, *Report*, 1951, pp. 53–5.

32 See Keith A. McLeod, 'Politics, Schools and the French Language, 1881–1931,' in Norman Ward and Duff Spafford, eds., *Politics in Saskatchewan* (Don Mills: Longmans, 1968), pp. 130–1.

33 Toombs, 'A Saskatchewan Experiment in Teacher Education'

34 Manitoba Department of Education, *Report*, 1914–15, pp. 145–6

35 Skwarok, *Ukrainian Settlers*, p. 53

36 Toombs, 'A Saskatchewan Experiment in Teacher Education,' pp. 10–11

37 CAR, 1913, p. 655

38 Skwarok, *Ukrainian Settlers*, pp. 94–101; Jaenen, 'Ruthenian Schools in Western Canada, 1897–1919,' pp. 534–40

39 CAR, 1913, p. 654

40 See, for example, Woycenko, *Ukrainians in Canada*, pp. 96–105

41 Canada, *Journals*, 1899, app. 3, pp. 279–80

42 XIV (March 1900), p. 478

43 Manitoba, Department of Education, *Report*, 1913–14, p. 20

44 See, for example, the coverage of each in CAR, 1906, pp. 443–7, 457, 477–80; *ibid.*, 1913, pp. 559–68, 617–20, 652–5.

45 CAR, 1913, p. 566

46 Sissons began the systematic study of bilingual schooling in the West in a series of articles for the Toronto *Globe*. He later summarized his conclusions in 'Illiteracy in the West,' *The University Magazine*, XII (October 1913), pp. 440–51.

47 CAR, 1916, p. 672

48 22 January 1916, p. 15

49 Saskatchewan, Department of Education, *Survey of Education*, chap. 16

50 Manitoba, Department of Education, *Report*, 1913–14, p. 62

51 J.T.M. Anderson, *The Education of the New-Canadian: A Treatise on Canada's Greatest Educational Problem* (London and Toronto: Dent, 1918)

52 Sissons noted, however, that to some extent illiteracy in Manitoba was the result of 'unwillingness to pay the price.' 'Illiteracy in the West,' p. 447.

53 Anderson, *Education of the New Canadian*, pp. 122–3. The book was Anderson's DPAED dissertation for the University of Toronto.

54 The matter was discussed in Norman F. Black's DPAED dissertation for the
   University of Toronto, *English for the Non-English* (Regina: Regina Book
   Shop, n.d. [1913]); J.W. Eaton, 'The Direct Method in the Teaching of
   Modern Languages,' *Queen's Quarterly*, XX (April 1913), pp. 447–60;
   C.B. Sissons, *Bi-lingual Schools in Canada* (Toronto: Dent, 1917), pp. 199–207.

55 *Men in Sheepskin Coats: A Study in Assimilation* (Toronto: Ryerson,
   1947), p. 59

56 For the political background to this support see W.L. Morton, *Manitoba:
   A History* (Toronto: University of Toronto Press, 1957), chaps 13–14.

57 Quoted in CAR, 1913, p. 618

58 'Ruthenian Schools in Western Canada, 1897–1919,' pp. 519–20, 541

59 Sissons, *Bi-lingual Schools in Canada*, p. 215

60 CAR, 1915, p. 701; see also W.G. Smith, *Building the Nation: A Study of
   Some Problems Concerning the Churches Relations to the Immigrants*
   (Toronto: Canadian Council of the Missionary Education Movement,
   1922), p. 174.

61 Allan Smith argues that Canada's basic character as a heterogeneous
   society made it impossible for Canadians to articulate 'a national Canadian
   type in which all elements of Canadian society could see something of themselves.' 'Metaphor and Nationality in North America,' CHR, LI (September
   1970), p. 258

62 George Fisher Chipman, 'The Refining Process,' *The Canadian Magazine*,
   XXXIII (October 1909), p. 548

63 Oliver, *The Country School*, p. 7

64 Milton Gordon, *Assimilation in American Life: The Role of Race, Religion,
   and National Origins* (New York: Oxford, 1964), p. 85. Gordon explains
   that he took the term from Stewart G. Cole and Mildred Wiese Cole,
   Minorities and the American Promise (New York: Harper, 1954),
   chap. 6.

65 'Winnipeg: The Melting Pot,' *The Canadian Magazine*, XXXIII (September
   1909), p. 410. Although Gordon distinguishes between Anglo-conformity
   and the 'melting pot' – the idea which 'envisaged a biological merger of
   the Anglo-Saxon peoples with other immigrant groups and a blending of
   their respective cultures into a new indigenous American type' – many
   Canadians of this time obviously meant the former when they used the
   latter. Gordon, *Assimilation*, p. 85

66 H.H. Stevens, 'Immigration From the Orient,' *Social Service Congress*,
   pp. 249–53

67 Quoted in Morton, *Manitoba: A History*, pp. 352–3

68 Charles W. Peterson, *Wake up, Canada!: Reflections on Vital National
   Issues* (Toronto: Macmillan, 1919), p. 21

69 R.L. Brydges, 'Socialization of the Public School,' *Social Service Congress*, p. 137

70 Canadian Conference of Charities and Correction, *Proceedings*, 1912, p. 40

71 Sissons, *Bi-lingual Schools*, p. 4; Woodsworth was Sissons' cousin and college friend.

72 Sissons, *Bi-lingual Schools*, p. 212

73 CAR, 1916, pp. 671–7; Morton, 'Manitoba Schools and Canadian Nationality 1890–1916,' CHA, *Report* (1951), pp. 56–9

74 See, for example, CAR, 1916, pp. 392–9; *ibid.*, 1917, pp. 435–9; *ibid.*, 1918, pp. 579–81. Ramsay Cook explains the complex connections between wartime national politics and schooling in Manitoba in 'Dafoe, Laurier, and the Formation of the Union Government,' CHR, XLII (September 1961), especially pp. 189–93.

75 CAR, 1916, pp. 712–16; *ibid.*, 1917, pp. 763–9, 782; *ibid.*, 1918, pp. 686–90; see also Keith A. McLeod, 'Politics, Schools and the French Language, 1881–1931,' in Norman Ward and Duff Spafford, eds., *Politics in Saskatchewan* (Toronto: Longmans, 1968), pp. 135–41.

76 CAR, 1918, pp. 688–9

77 *Ibid.*, 1919, pp. 550–1; Robert M. Stamp, 'Empire Day in the Schools of Ontario: the Training of Young Imperialists,' *Journal of Canadian Studies*, VII (August 1973), pp. 32–42, puts the 'patriotic' element of this program into its wider context.

78 For accounts of how the policy was worked out in practice, see Robert England, *The Central European Immigrant in Canada* (Toronto: Macmillan, 1929); Charles H. Young, *The Ukrainian Canadians: A Study in Assimilation* (Toronto: Nelson, 1931), especially chap. 8; C.A. Dawson and Eva R. Younge, *Pioneering in the Prairie Provinces: The Social Side of the Settlement Process* (Toronto: Macmillan, 1940), especially pp. 170–2.

79 Manitoba, Department of Education, *Report*, 1920, pp. 143–6

80 Saskatchewan, Department of Education, *Report*, 1921, pp. 73–4

81 Anderson, *Education of the New Canadian*, pp. 159–60

82 Manitoba, Department of Education, *Report*, 1918–19, p. 9

83 'The Immigrant Settler,' *The Annals*, CVII (May 1923), p. 42–3

84 Canada, DBS, *Illiteracy and School Attendance*, p. 8; enumerators were instructed to record positive responses to the reading and writing questions not merely for English or French but for any language. Canada, DBS, *Census of Canada, 1921*, vol. 2, pp. xviii–xix

85 In this regard, Jaenen accepts M.R. Lupul's explanation that Ukrainians rapidly passed through three stages of development – Ukrainian, Ukrainian-Canadians to become finally Canadians of Ukrainian descent. 'Ruthenian Schools in Western Canada, 1897–1919,' p. 540. Less simplistic and more

suggestive of what appears to have actually transpired was a process in which, as Canada became an ethnically plural society, a 'constellation of ethnic groups' became 'more like each other in some ways' and 'less like each other in other ways.' See Frank G. Vallee, Mildred Schwartz, and Frank Darknell, 'Ethnic Assimilation and Differentiation in Canada,' *Canadian Journal of Economics and Political Science*, XXIII (November 1957), p. 549.

86 In the summer of 1909, about 400 delegates had attended the seventh convention in Victoria. Vancouver *Daily News Advertiser*, 18 July 1909.
87 Dominion Educational Association, *Proceedings*, 1917, passim
88 *Ibid.*, pp. 12–14
89 Manitoba, Department of Education, *Report*, 1913–14, pp. 8, 15, 72
90 *Ibid.*, pp. 107–8
91 *Ibid.*, 1912–13, pp. 45–8
92 *Ibid.*, 1913–14, pp. 6–7, 64
93 *Ibid.*, 1912–13, p. 46
94 *Ibid.*, pp. 8, 30
95 *Ibid.*, 1914–15, pp. 9–11, 154–8
96 *Ibid.*, 1913–14, p. 51
97 Dominion Education Association, *Proceedings*, 1917, pp. 80–4
98 CAR, 1919, pp. 544–5
99 Bingay, *Public Education in Nova Scotia*, pp. 115–16
100 British Columbia, Department of Education, *Courses of Study*, 1920
101 George Hindle, *The Educational System of British Columbia: An Appreciative and Critical Estimate of the Educational System of the Mountain Province* (Trail: Trail Printing and Publishing, 1918), pp. 52–6, 104–7; British Columbia, Department of Education, *Survey of the School System*, p. 20
102 British Columbia, Department of Education, *Survey of the School System*, p. 200
103 *Ibid.*, p. 119, 132, 158; see also the discussion pp. 157–63, 405–7.
104 *Ibid.*, p. 158
105 Saskatchewan, Department of Education, *Survey of Education*, p. 85
106 Corbett, 'The Public School Kindergarten in Ontario,' pp. 152–6
107 Ontario, Department of Education, *Report*, 1923, p. 85
108 Richardson's survey found kindergarten supervisors in London and Toronto and primary supervisors in Regina, Vancouver, and Winnipeg. William Leeds Richardson, *The Administration of Schools in the Cities of the Dominion of Canada* (Toronto: Dent, 1922), p. 298
109 'Looking Backward,' Industrial Art Teachers of Ontario, *Bulletin* (March 1950), no paging
110 NCW, *Yearbook*, 1904, p. 120

111 CAR, 1904, p. 580
112 'Sir William Macdonald and Agricultural Education,' *Queen's Quarterly*, XII (January 1905), pp. 315–522
113 International Congress of Women, *Report*, 1909, vol. 1, p. 357; see also Vincent Massey, 'Primary Education in Ontario,' *The University Magazine*, X (October 1911), p. 496.
114 Dominion Education Association, *Proceedings*, 1913, p. 82
115 'Blot Out Toronto's School Board,' 20 March 1920, p. 1
116 Saskatchewan, Department of Education, *Report*, 1909, p. 46
117 Manitoba, Department of Education, *Report*, 1913–14, p. 77
118 *Ibid.*, 1918–19, p. 18
119 Quoted in Toombs, 'The Control and Support of Public Education,' p. 568
120 See, for example, Toronto Bureau of Municipal Research, *Report*, 1916, pp. 14–18; *ibid.*, 1921, p. 7
121 British Columbia, Department of Education, *Survey of the School System*, pp. 367–435
122 *Ibid.*, p. 44
123 Joel Spring, 'Education and Progressivism,' *History of Education Quarterly*, X (Spring 1970), p. 53. The 'new' education in England also 'contained within itself ambiguities and contradictions.' Selleck, *The New Education*, p. 335

CHAPTER 14

1 Canada, Commission of Conservation, *Civic Improvement* (Ottawa: n. pub., 1916), p. 31
2 'Child Welfare in Canada,' *The Annals*, CV (January 1923), p. 275; much of this article is taken from the Introduction to the *Handbook*, pp. 5–15.
3 Child Welfare Association of British Columbia, *Report of the First Annual Convention held in Vancouver, Dec. 12, 13 and 14, 1918* (Vancouver: Grandview Printers, n.d.), pp. 7–8
4 Richard Allen, *The Social Passion: Religion and Social Reform in Canada, 1914–1928* (Toronto: University of Toronto Press, 1971), pp. 12–13
5 *Social Service Congress, Ottawa, 1914: Report of Addresses and Proceedings*, pp. 89–115, 127–36
6 See, for example, Canada, Commission of Conservation, *Urban and Rural Development in Canada: Report of Conference held in Winnipeg, May 28–30, 1917* (Ottawa: n. pub., 1917), pp. 91–8; and J.M. Bliss, 'The Methodist Church and World War I,' CHR, XLIX (September 1968), especially pp. 229–33; and Brown and Cook, *Canada 1896–1921*, chap. 15.

7 Child Welfare,' PHJ, IX (June 1920), pp. 291–2

8 *Ibid.*, 1921, pp. 22–3; Toronto *Globe*, 21 October 1920

9 Charlotte Whitton, 'The Canadian Council on Child Welfare, 1920,' *Canadian Welfare*, XXXII (May 1956), pp. 3–7

10 *Handbook*, pp. 9–10, 12–13

11 *Fourth ... Canadian Conference on Child Welfare*, p. 17

12 For an account of the growth of the Council and Charlotte Whitton's central role in it, see Tamara K. Hareven, 'An Ambiguous Alliance: Some Aspects of American Influences on Canadian Social Welfare,' *Histoire Sociale/Social History*, 3 (April 1969), especially pp. 90–4.

13 Ontario, *Sessional Papers*, 1895, no. 29, app., pp. 1–4; *Fifth ... Canadian Conference on Child Welfare*, pp. 7–9. In each case, these estimates are slightly on the conservative side. Twenty-nine of the 1894 and fifty-five of the 1925 delegates were clearly identified as being employed in some child or family welfare position.

14 *Ibid.*, p. 10

15 Hilda Neatby, *So Little for the Mind: An Indictment of Canadian Education* (Toronto: Clarke, Irwin, 1953), especially chaps 2–3

16 Peter H. Bryce, 'History of Public Health,' *Canadian Therapeutist and Sanitary Engineer*, I (June 1910), p. 291

17 How this notion applied to events in the United States at this time is surveyed in Wiebe, *The Search for Order*, pp. 111–32

18 While research into 'transnational' networks in health, education, and social welfare is not very far advanced, three recent essays sketch in the context in which they might be investigated. See James A. Field, Jr, 'Transnationalism and the New Tribe,' in *Transnational Relations and World Politics*, ed. Robert O. Keohane and Joseph S. Nye, Jr (Cambridge: Harvard University Press, 1972), pp. 3–22; Kjell Skjelsbaek, 'The Growth of International Nongovernmental Organization in the Twentieth Century,' *ibid.*, pp. 70–92; Diana Crane, 'Transnational Networks in Basic Science,' *ibid.*, pp. 235–51.

19 PHJ, I (October 1910), p. 518; *ibid.*, II (November 1911), pp. 503–4; *ibid.*, VIII (December 1917), p. 342; Mazÿck P. Ravenel, 'The American Public Health Association, Past, Present, Future,' in Mazÿck P. Ravenel, ed., *A Half Century of Public Health: Jubilee Historical Volume of the American Public Health Association* (New York: American Public Health Association, 1921), p. 23

20 PHJ, I (September 1910), p. 472

21 Hastings H. Hart, 'Twenty-five Years of Child Welfare Work in Canada,' *The Survey*, XL (May 1918), p. 171

22 Carter, 'James L. Hughes and the Gospel of Education,' especially chap. 5

23 Corbett, 'The Public School Kindergarten in Ontario,' pp. 24–5, 102–3
24 Pavey, 'James Wilson Robertson,' pp. 11–13, 78–9, 104, 117–18
25 Leake, *Industrial Education*; Leake, *The Means and Methods of Agricultural Education*; Leake, *The Vocational Education of Girls and Women*. The first two won Hart, Schaffner, and Marx prizes.
26 Bain, 'The Role of J.J. Kelso,' passim
27 Hareven, 'An Ambiguous Alliance: Some Aspects of American Influences on Canadian Social Welfare,' *Histoire Sociale/Social History*, 3 (April 1969), p. 98
28 Ontario, *Sessional Papers*, 1881, no. 8, p. 15, quoted in Splane, *Social Welfare in Ontario*, p. 49
29 PHJ, XI (February 1920), pp. 70–8
30 Allen, *The Social Passion*, p. 3
31 *Canadian White Ribbon Tidings*, III (15 February 1907), p. 815; *ibid.*, IV (15 February 1908), pp. 1120–1; *ibid.* (February 1909), pp. 1340–2, 1352
32 Nearly 300 women also served on these committees. Ontario, *Sessional Papers*, 1896, no. 17, pp. 35–66
33 NCW, *Yearbook*, 1896, pp. 3–26
34 McNaught, *A Prophet in Politics*, chap. 4
35 Allen, *The Social Passion*, pp. 24–5
36 'Mothers' Allowances,' PHJ, IX (December 1918), pp. 545–6;
37 *Handbook*, pp. 109–12
38 Ontario Teachers' Manuals, *History of Education* (Toronto: The Minister of Education for Ontario, 1915), pp. 4, 177–81
39 'Human Sacrifice,' PHJ, IV (February 1913), p. 96
40 A.D. Blackader, '... Causes Underlying Heavy Infantile Death ...,' PHJ, III (July 1912), p. 368
41 Mme Jules Tessier, 'The Value of Milk Depots,' *ibid.*, VIII (March 1917), p. 66
42 Ella Cory Benson, 'The Women of Today,' *Western Women's Weekly*, II (6 December 1918), p. 15
43 See Canada, Dominion Bureau of Statistics, Demography Branch, *Children in Gainful Occupations* (Ottawa: King's Printer, 1929) and Canada, Department of Labour, *The Employment of Children and Young Persons in Canada* (Ottawa: King's Printer, 1930)
44 Since the uncertain state of Canadian vital statistics before 1921 makes suspect any figures taken from these years, I have drawn on three sets of evidence to infer rather than to prove this conclusion. First, the vital statistics of British Columbia showed that the proportion of those between 40 and 60 in the total number of deaths for the year shifted from 47 per cent in

1874 to 32 per cent in 1884 to 19 per cent in 1894, to 20 per cent in 1904 to 23 per cent in 1914. British Columbia, Registrar of Births, Deaths and Marriages, *Report*, 1874, p. 4; *ibid.*, 1884, p. 295; *ibid.*, 1894, p. 571; *ibid.*, 1904, p. 5; *ibid.*, 1914, p. L27. Second, I supposed that what happened after 1921 continued a trend which began before that date. Because the average age at death between 1921 and 1952 rose from 39.0 to 55.8 years for males and from 41.1 to 58.2 for females, I assumed that improvements in health – particularly in sanitation – had also produced a rise in the average age of death in Canada between the 1880s and the 1920s. *Canada Year Book*, 1955, p. 200. Third, where long-term data is available, as in Sweden, they show that the principal beneficiaries of nineteenth century health improvements were in the young-adult and adult age groups. I therefore surmised that the Canadian experience may well have been roughly the same. See Odin W. Anderson, 'Age-Specific Mortality Differentials Historically and Currently: Observations and Implications,' *Bulletin of the History of Medicine*, XXVII (November-December 1953), pp. 521–9.

45 *Fifth ... Canadian Conference on Child Welfare*, p. 217
46 Urquhart and Buckley, *Historical Statistics of Canada*, pp. 252–3, 53, 108
47 See Charlotte Whitton's detailed survey of this legislation in *Fifth ... Canadian Conference on Child Welfare*, pp. 63–6.
48 Ontario, *Statutes*, 1921, c. 53
49 New Brunswick, *Statutes*, 1917, c. 23
50 See, for example, British Columbia, *Statutes*, 1920, c. 2
51 *Fifth ... Canadian Conference on Child Welfare*, p. 147
52 *The Canadian Mother's Book*, chap. 8
53 F. Henry Johnson, 'Changing Conceptions of Discipline and Pupil-Teacher Relations in Canadian Schools' (DPAED dissertation, University of Toronto, 1952), chap. 3

Bibliographic Note

English Canadians expressed their growing concern for their youngsters through an astonishingly rich literature. Fortunately, they eased the historian's task by frequently repeating themselves. In surveying these extensive sources, I tried to keep in mind three rough rules of thumb. First, I wanted to examine both official and unofficial material on each topic at the local, provincial, and national levels. Second, I tried to draw on all parts of the country for examples. Third, I searched for accounts of children whose lives exemplified the many aspects of the study. Since the notes show the degree of my success with the first, and the text with the second and third, I will not repeat the details here.

An array of public records reveals the national concerns of Canadians of the late nineteenth and early twentieth centuries. Debates in the House of Commons, in the Senate, and in Parliamentary Committees indicate that a matter had reached a point of decision or crisis and lay bare how the central issue appeared to some Canadians. For the historian of childhood, however, *Sessional Papers* – that annual collection of reports of departments, commissions, surveys, boards, and institutions – are more generally useful. The published annual reports on immigration in Canada, Department of Agriculture, *Reports*, 1870–92, in Canada, Department of the Interior, *Reports*, 1893–1917, and Canada, Department of Immigration and Colonization, *Reports*, 1918–25, provide much valuable information on both English immigrant children and on many aspects of life in immigrant communities. Some pre-1900 records in the Department of Manpower, and Public Archives of Canada MG 29/B 43, the Charlotte A. Alexander Papers, usefully supplement the published records.

Annual and special reports of the Departments of Labour and Health are also useful. *The Labour Gazette* (September, 1900–), gives a running account of the development of practical education in Canada and of the changing place of children in the work force. Canada, Department of Health, *Handbook of Child Welfare Work in Canada*, edited by Helen MacMurchy (Ottawa: King's Printer, 1923), summarizes the child health and welfare work of this department. It also surveys what provincial health, welfare, and education officials were doing and, to a much less thorough extent, the activities of their municipal counterparts as well.

Federal, provincial, and municipal governments have collected an enormous amount of useful information in statistical form. M.C. Urquhart and K.A.H. Buckley, eds., *Historical Statistics of Canada* (Toronto: Macmillan, 1965), conveniently assembles much of this data and in its extensive notes provides an invaluable guide to other sources. A number of census monographs, most notably Canada, Dominion Bureau of Statistics, *Illiteracy and School Attendance in Canada: A Study of the Census of 1921 With Supplementary Data* (Ottawa: King's Printer, 1926); Canada, DBS, 'The Canadian Family,' by A.J. Pelletier, F.D. Thompson, and A. Rochan, *Seventh Census of Canada, 1931: Monographs*, vol. 12 (Ottawa: King's Printer, 1942); and Canada, DBS, Eighth Census of Canada, *The Changing Size of the Family in Canada*, by Enid Charles (Ottawa: King's Printer, 1948), show many changes in the lives of Canadian children.

The affairs of national organizations are excellent guides to changes in Canadian concerns about their youngsters. From *Women Workers in Canada: Being a Report of the Proceedings of the First Annual Meeting and Conference of the National Council of Women of Canada* (Ottawa: The Council, 1894), through to *The Year Book of the National Council of Women of Canada, 1920* (n. pl.: n. pub., n.d.), accounts of the National Council's addresses, discussions, resolutions, and reports of its branches and committees provide an invaluable guide to the steps through which Canadians transformed a generalized concern for children and families into a series of increasingly specific proposals and programs. The extensive holdings of the Public Archives, MG 28/I25, National Council of Women Papers, supplement the published reports. The wide-ranging concerns of the council are complemented by the deliberations of such more specialized organizations as Canadian Conference of Charities and Correction, *Proceedings*, 1900, 1901, 1905, 1911, and 1912; Dominion Educational Association, *Proceedings*, 1901, 1909, 1913, and 1917; and Canadian Conference on Child Welfare, *Proceedings*, 1921, 1923, and 1925.

J. Castell Hopkins, *The Canadian Annual Review of Public Affairs* (Toronto: The Annual Review Publishing Company, 1902–), lays out a convenient and often thorough survey of national and provincial issues. It also assists one to select those times when newspapers will contain stories, editorials, and letters to the editor on regional and national topics. To examine national opinion before the CAR began publication, I systematically surveyed *The Canadian Methodist Magazine*, I (1875) to LXIII (1906), *The Dominion Churchman* (later *The Canadian Churchman*), III (1876) to XXXI (1904), and *The Canadian Magazine*, I (1893) to XV (1900). Although the Woman's Christian Temperance Union Archives in Toronto has some issues of its official publication, *The Woman's Journal*, beginning with XIII (13 August 1898), what was probably a more useful source than any of the above three does not appear to have survived. Its successor, however, *The Canadian White Ribbon Tidings*, I (January, 1904–) also reflects the WCTU's broad interest in all phases of child and family welfare. What began as *The Canadian Therapeutist and Sanitary Engineer*, I (1910), and soon became *The Public Health Journal of Canada*, displays between I (1910) and XI (1920), a continually widening interest in child and family health and welfare. In contrast, the early volumes of *The Canadian Journal of Mental Hygiene*, I (1919–20) to III (1921–2), reflects mostly the narrow point of view of its founders.

Although their quality varies, provincial *Sessional Papers* are an even more useful source of information on children than their federal counterparts. For reasons apparent in the study, I made greatest use of Ontario records. When I did consult those of other provinces, however, I found that they often provided the same wealth of detail and example. Ontario, Provincial Board of Health, *Reports*, 1882–1921, clearly reveal the interconnections amongst scientific, organizational, and professional concerns that accompanied the improvement of the public health. In addition to confirming that Ontario's problems were not unique, Saskatchewan, Bureau of Public Health, *Reports*, 1910–22, provide a more thorough view of the difficulty of transforming urban practices into a form suitable to rural areas. From his initial report in Ontario, *Sessional Papers*, 1894, no. 47, up to the First World War, J.J. Kelso annually put together the most useful single source of information on Canadian child welfare. He provides case histories, great detail on the work of his office, on each Children's Aid Society in the province, on some societies elsewhere, and on the industrial schools in the province. In addition, he alerts one to changes in ideas and refinements of practices through his habit of reprinting speeches, articles, and reports that interested him.

The annual reports of the departments of education in New Brunswick, Ontario, Manitoba, and other provinces give two perspectives on educational change. The comments of provincial and urban officials indicate how they gradually added the ideas of the new education to their continuing concerns for upgrading the teaching of traditional subjects, for extending the system to meet the needs of a growing population, and for improving rates of attendance and retention.

Inspectors' reports show how wide the gap was between theory and practice and how arduous a task it was to close it. In addition to these published reports, in the Saskatchewan Archives I sampled files of the provincial Department of Education and those on education in the papers of Premiers Walter Scott and W.M. Martin. Premiers' papers are particularly useful in identifying educational matters which were of real concern to politicians and their constituents.

Reflecting the way that reform moved slowly from the local to the provincial setting, until the closing years of this study there are comparatively few really useful records of provincial voluntary organizations. Since there were a number of provincial plebiscites on prohibition, temperance organizations provide the main exception to this condition. I sampled the minute books of the Ontario WCTU and the printed reports of its British Columbia counterpart. The Canadian Red Cross, British Columbia Division, *Reports*, 1920–5, illustrate how one organization tried to extend health services to rural Canada.

Especially in their early years, printed reports and other records of local organizations lay bare much about both the assumptions they held and the practices under which they operated. The child and family centred minutes of the Stoney Creek Women's Institute, Public Archives MG 28/I47, 1897–1904, were the only local rural records I was able to examine. The privately financed Toronto Bureau of Municipal Research, *Reports*, I (1915) to IX (1923), which directed themselves to improving the efficiency of educational and other municipal agencies, provide a sharp contrast to the concerns of the Women's Institutes.

Although in John T. Saywell, ed., *The Canadian Journal of Lady Aberdeen, 1893–1898* (Toronto: Champlain Society, 1960), pp. 194–5, Lady Aberdeen argued that Ottawa was not in any way typical of Canada, records of its local organizations are readily available. In MG 28/I37, the Public Archives possesses the very revealing printed annual reports of the Protestant Orphan's Home in Ottawa from 1864 to 1924, and the minute books from 1863 to 1896. The minutes of the executive and other meetings of the Ottawa Local Council of Women from 1894 to 1939 are stored in Public Archives MG 28/I32. I examined them for the fifteen-year period from January 1894 to February 1909. In addition, I read the reports of the local Children's Aid Society over the critical twelfth to fifteenth years of its operation in Ottawa, Children's Aid Society, *Reports*, 1904–5 to 1907–8.

The records and reports of Vancouver organizations are well represented in the city's Public Library and the University of British Columbia Library. I was thus able to examine the reports of the Vancouver School Board from 1903 to the 1920s, the Vancouver Children's Aid Society from 1905 to 1918, the Vancouver Medical Health Officer from 1911 to 1921, and the Vancouver Local Council of Women from its founding in 1894 up to the 1920s. Although I only glanced through them, the records of the Vancouver Parks Board are also available for most of the period.

Although newspapers are undoubtedly one of the finest sources through which to examine both local and national events, they are also enormously time-consuming to use. With the generous help of many of my students, however, I was able to sample the Vancouver and Victoria papers of the 1890s with some thoroughness. For other provinces, and for the years after the CAR began to publish, I used Vancouver, Winnipeg, Toronto, Saint John, and other newspapers only when some other source suggested that it would be profitable to do so.

Five special reports – two federal and three provincial – are extremely useful for understanding aspects of childhood in this period. Both the evidence presented to the commission and Canada, *Report of the Royal Commission on the Relations of Labor and Capital in Canada* (Ottawa: King's Printer, 1889), give a vivid picture of urban youngsters at work in the late nineteenth century. This generally dismal portrait is supported and extended in Ontario, *Report of the Commissioners Appointed to Enquire into the Prison and Reformatory System of Ontario, 1891* (Toronto: Warwick, 1891). One cannot understand either the 'new' education nor its context without examining Canada, Royal Commission on Industrial Training and Technical Education, *Report* (4 vols.; Ottawa: King's Printer, 1913–14); Saskatchewan, *A Survey of Education in the Province of Saskatchewan: A Report by Harold W. Foght, Ph.D.* (Regina: King's Printer, 1918); and British Columbia, *Survey of the School System* by J.H. Putman and G.M. Weir (Victoria: King's Printer, 1925).

In addition to the Scott and Martin papers, one can also look through the records of two other important persons in the reform movement. The Special Collections Division of the library of the University of British Columbia holds the James Wilson Robertson Papers. The library of the University of Guelph has much material on Adelaide Hoodless which, when supplemented by a file of her correspondence to the Ontario Minister of Education in the Public Archives of Ontario, indicates the broad scope of her work.

Although, as the notes reveal, children appear fleetingly in much Canadian historical writing, few secondary works deal with them directly. By far the largest literature exists in the history of Canadian education and J. Donald Wilson, Robert M. Stamp, and Louis-Philippe Audet, *Canadian Education: A History* (Scarborough: Prentice-Hall, 1970), thoroughly survey it in their 'Suggestions for Further Reading.' Michael B. Katz and Paul M. Mattingley, eds., *Education and Social Change: Themes from Ontario's Past* (New York: New York University Press, 1975), presents some interesting recent research in the field. In the introductory essay, 'Towards a History of English-Canadian Youngsters,' I survey the historiography of Canadian childhood, family life, and education in its 'transnational' contexts.

Richard Allen, *The Social Passion: Religion and Social Reform in Canada, 1914-1928* (Toronto: University of Toronto Press, 1971), makes a persuasive case for interpreting the social activities of this era in terms of the social gospel. While it appeared too late to influence this study, Robert Craig Brown and Ramsay Cook, *Canada 1896-1921: A Nation Transformed* (Toronto: McClelland and Stewart, 1974) vividly portrays the context, as it were, in which the new consensus on childhood was framed.

Richard B. Splane, *Social Welfare in Ontario, 1791-1893: A Study of Public Welfare Administration* (Toronto: University of Toronto Press, 1965) is an indispensible guide to the organization and administration of nineteenth century social welfare – including the public health – in Canada. Tamara K. Hareven, 'An Ambiguous Alliance: Some Aspects of American Influences on Canadian Social Welfare,' *Histoire Sociale/Social History*, 3 (April 1969), pp. 82-98, carries some parts of the story forward to the 1930s. R.D. Defries, ed., *The Development of Public Health in Canada* (Toronto: Canadian Public Health Association, 1940), chronicles the growth of public health services in Canada and in each of the provinces. Canadian Red Cross Society, *The Role of One Voluntary Organization in Canada's Health Services: A Brief Presented to the Royal Commission on Health Services on Behalf of the Central Council of the Canadian Red Cross Society* (Toronto: National Office, The Canadian Red Cross Society, 1962) provides the best single account of the work of a voluntary organization in Canadian health or welfare. Canada, Department of Justice, *Juvenile Delinquency in Canada: The Report of the Department of Justice Committee on Juvenile Delinquency* (Ottawa: Queen's Printer, 1965), briefly surveys the historical dimension of preventing and curing juvenile crime. Lynn McDonald, 'Crime and Punishment in Canada: A Statistical Test of the "Conventional Wisdom,"' *La Revue canadienne de Sociologie et d'Anthropologie/The Canadian Review of Sociology and Anthropology*, VI (November, 1969), pp. 212-36, uses recent data to question the major assumptions of the reformers.

As the text makes clear, I arrived at many of my notions of what happened to children in Canada by relating my data with the ideas of foreign historians. In arguing that the child was a central theme in humanitarian progressivism, Robert H. Wiebe, *The Search for Order, 1877-1920* (New York: Hill and Wang, 1967), helped confirm my growing conviction that Canadian events led along the same lines. His discussion of the public health movement also helped me to organize my own account of the matter. Although it contains a useful bibliography, the greatest merit of Robert Bremner et al., *Children and Youth in America: A Documentary History*, vol. II, *1866-1932* (Cambridge: Harvard University Press, 1971), is that it introduces its readers to a great many American youngsters. In contrast to Bremner's harsh realities, Bernard Wishy, *The Child and the Republic:*

The Dawn of American Child Nurture (Philadelphia: University of Pennsylvania Press, 1968), describes the changes he sees taking place in middle-class notions about child rearing over the nineteenth century. Since the publication of Philippe Ariès, *Centuries of Childhood: A Social History of Family Life*, trans. R. Baldick (New York: Knopf, 1962), historians have begun to look at this old institution in a new way. John N. Edwards, ed., *The Family and Change* (New York: Knopf, 1969), provides a convenient summary of research on the family in the social sciences, and Theodore K. Rabb and Robert I. Rotberg, eds., *The Family in History: Interdisciplinary Essays* (New York: Harper, 1973) does so for history.

Although I have come to considerably different conclusions from any of them, I have been greatly influenced by four historians of American education. Lawrence E. Cremin, *The Transformation of the School: Progressivism in American Education, 1876-1957* (New York: Knopf, 1961), first aroused my interest in what became my topic and his *American Education: The Colonial Experience, 1607-1783* (New York: Harper and Row, 1970), strengthened my belief that educational historians can fruitfully examine the intellectual and social context in which teaching and learning take place. In both 'Progressivism in American Education, 1880-1900,' *Harvard Educational Review*, XXXI (Spring 1961), pp. 168–93, and 'Immigrant Social Aspirations and American Education,' *American Quarterly*, XXI (Fall 1969), pp. 523–43, Timothy L. Smith provided me with hypotheses to test in the Canadian environment and assisted me to keep my examination as 'child-centred' as possible. In all his writings, but especially in the essays in *Class, Bureaucracy, and Schools: The Illusion of Educational Change in America* (2nd ed., New York: Praeger, 1975), Michael Katz has forced me to take cognizance of my customary Whig outlook and to examine thoroughly some of the negative results of change. Since I reviewed it just before tackling the final draft of my chapters on education, I gave most careful attention to the ideas in Marvin Lazerson, *Origins of the Urban School: Public Education in Massachusetts, 1870-1915* (Cambridge: Harvard University Press, 1971).

Despite its annoying lack of documentation, Kathleen Heasman, *Evangelicals in Action: An Appraisal of their Social Work in the Victorian Era* (London: Bles, 1962), showed me more clearly than any other work how widespread 'child saving' was in the nineteenth century and how ideas about how to tackle children's problems flowed through the emerging 'transnational' networks. While I came to differ sharply with both of them, I found Anthony M. Platt, *The Child Savers: The Invention of Delinquency* (Chicago and London: University and Chicago Press, 1969), and Joseph M. Hawes, *Children in Urban Society: Juvenile Delinquency in Nineteenth Century America* (New York: Oxford University Press, 1971), helped me to reach my own position on the changing treatment of youthful offenders. Although both were published too late to help shape this study, two books will make invaluable guides to those who continue in the field. Ivy Pinchbeck and Margaret Hewitt, *Children in English Society*, vol. II, *From the Eighteenth Century to the Children Act 1948* (Toronto: University of Toronto Press, 1973) is a very thorough if generally uncritical survey of the work with children in England. Robert M. Mennel, *Thorns and Thistles: Juvenile Delinquents in the United States, 1825–1940* (Hanover, N.H.: The University Press of New England, 1973) is easily the best historical study on this topic. Its bibliographic essay provides an excellent guide to the literature on juvenile delinquency.

Index